D0455624

The Neuroscience
of
Human Relationships

Attachment
and the
Developing
Social Brain

Also by Louis Cozolino

The Neuroscience of Psychotherapy:
Building and Rebuilding the Human Brain

The Making of a Therapist:
A Practical Guide for the Inner Journey

The Neuroscience
of
Human Relationships

Attachment
and the
Developing
Social Brain

Louis Cozolino

W. W. Norton & Company
New York · London

For information about permission to reproduce selections from
this book, write to Permissions, W. W. Norton & Company, Inc.,
500 Fifth Avenue, New York, NY 10110

Manufacturing by Quebecor World-Fairfield Graphics
Book design by Charlotte Staub
Production Manager: Leeann Graham

Library of Congress Cataloging-in-Publication Data

Cozolino, Louis J.
  The neuroscience of human relationships : attachment and
the developing social brain / by Louis Cozolino.
      p. cm.
  Includes bibliographical references and index.
  ISBN-13: 978-0-393-70454-9
  ISBN-10: 0-393-70454-8

  1. Neuropsychology. 2. Interpersonal relations.
3. Attachment behavior. 4. Developmental psychology. I. Title.
QP360.C69 2006
612.8—dc22   2006040010

ISBN 13: 978-0-393-70454-9
ISBN 10: 0-393-70454-8

W. W. Norton & Company, Inc.,
500 Fifth Avenue, New York, N.Y. 10110
    www.wwnorton.com
W. W. Norton & Company Ltd.,
Castle House, 75/76 Wells St., London W1T 3QT

0 9 8 7 6 5 4 3 2

To my wife,

Susan,

with love
and
gratitude

Contents

Acknowledgments

It takes a village to write a book, an odd and dispersed sort of village, but a village nonetheless. First I would like to thank the village chief, my editor Deborah Malmud, and her tribe at W. W. Norton Professional Books for their help, guidance, and patience through the birthing processes. I would especially like to thank Andrea Costella, who, with forbearance and a kind heart, was always available to offer advice and good counsel.

Many people at Pepperdine University, friends and colleagues, provided support and encouragement for this project. My thanks go to Robin Aulger, John Baker, Bob deMayo, Monica Nichelson, Ed Shafranske, Tylor Vu, and Margaret Weber, day by day, year in and year out, for their countless contributions to my work. I gratefully acknowledge the help of my research assistants Melissa Flannigan, Olivia Hannon, Sharon Hirose, and Susan Sprokay for their diligence, dedication, and hard work on projects interesting, taxing, inspiring, and downright boring. This manuscript also benefited greatly from the editorial artistry of three of Pepperdine's finest, Bruce Singer, Shannon Calde, and Rebekka Helford.

Many thanks to Linda Hudson and Christopher Warner of the Otis School of Design for their help in thinking through the drawings used in this book, and to their students, artists Nathan Frizzell (nate909@hotmail.com) and Mototo Kamada (mkamada1965 @ yahoo.com), who did excellent work in taking our ideas, mixing in their own, and bringing the drawings to fruition. I would also like to thank Carole Urmy for the use of her short story and Drs. Hiromi Kobayashi and Paul Whalen for images derived from their studies on eye morphology and amygdala activation.

My respect and appreciation to my teachers, colleagues, and friends—Alex Caldwell, Lennart Heimer, Francine Inbinder, Brendan Maher, Michael McGuire, David Meltzer, Hans Miller, Joe Palombo, Arnold Scheibel, Allan Schore, John Schumann, Renee Schwartz, Sandy Shapiro, John Watkins, and Jeff Weinberg—for contributing knowledge, inspiration, and wisdom in all combinations. Many thanks to my friend Daniel Siegel, whose tireless dedication to me, the field of interpersonal neurobiology, and to living life serves as a constant source of encouragement and inspiration in my own life. In the same spirit, I would like to thank my friend John Wynn, whose love, intelligence, and limitless enthusiasm for learning have become a central part of my own inner world. Both Dan and John dedicated considerable time to this manuscript, providing valuable editorial and conceptual feedback during the entire creative process.

Special thanks go to Michelle Walker for her diligence and dedication to this project over the last 2 years. There is no way to measure the value of working with someone who is able to tolerate the complexities of my obsessive neurosis and the general absurdities of daily life with enthusiasm, good humor, and human caring. It's a *mitzvah*.

The Neuroscience
of
Human Relationships

Attachment
and the
Developing
Social Brain

Part I

The Emergence of Social Neuroscience

Introduction

I–Me–Mine

The miracle is that the universe created a part of itself to study the rest of it, and that this part, in studying itself, finds the rest of the universe in its own inner realities. —John Lilly, 1972, p. 219

When it comes to human consciousness, we experience ourselves as individuals. Although we think of ourselves as "having" a variety of relationships, the operative term remains *I. I* have these relationships, *I* make plans with friends, *I* keep in touch with family. Our experience of the world is constructed around the notion of the isolated self, and it is from this perspective that Western science has explored the brain. Yet, even though we cherish the idea of individuality, we live with the paradox that we constantly regulate each others' internal biological states (DeVries et al., 2003; Hofer, 1984, 1987). While most obvious in childhood and during intense states of love and bereavement, our interdependence is a constant reality of our existence. As a species, we are just waking up to the complexity of our own brains, to say nothing of how brains are linked together. We are just beginning to understand that we have evolved as social creatures and that all of our biologies are interwoven.

Half a century ago, these insights led systems theorists to shift the focus of psychotherapy from the individual patient to the family unit. The symptoms of the identified patient were reinterpreted as a by-product of the family's struggle for homeostasis. But is the family the best frame of reference from which to understand human experience? Should we zoom even further out, or zoom back in to the individual, to get the best picture? If we use Mother Nature as a guide, we see that when she likes an idea, she tends to stick with it, and she does so by conserving structures and strategies through increasing layers of complexity. Assuming this is true (which I do), we stand to learn a great deal from zooming in *and* out, from "neurons to neighborhoods," while resisting the urge to become attached to any particular frame of reference. In this way, we may gain a deeper understanding of the interwoven tapestry of biological, psychological, and social processes that comprise human life.

Unveiling the Social Synapse

Look closely at the body and you will discover layer upon layer of highly complex, interlocking systems. As you examine each layer, you will discover countless individual cells (neurons in the nervous system) that differentiate and migrate to specific locations throughout the body. These cells, in turn, grow into an infinite variety of forms, organize into functional systems, integrate with other systems, and, ultimately, create an individual. This process we accept easily; but what about the notion that nature used this same strategy to connect individual animals (humans) into a larger biological organism called a species?

Individual neurons are separated by small gaps called *synapses*. These synapses are not empty spaces by any means; rather, they are filled by a variety of chemical substances engaging in complex interactions that result in *synaptic transmission*. It is this synaptic transmission that stimulates each neuron to survive, grow, and be sculpted by experience. In fact, the activity within synapses is just as important as what takes place within the neurons themselves. Over vast expanses of evolutionary time, neural or synaptic transmission has grown ever more intricate to meet the needs of an increasingly complex brain.

We know that neurons communicate via these chemical signals that activate and influence one another through the transmission of multiple biochemical messengers. When it comes right down to it, doesn't communication between people, as complex as it is, consist of the same basic building blocks? When we smile, wave, and say hello, these behaviors are sent through the space between us via sight and sound. These electrical and mechanical messages are received by our senses, converted into elec-trochemical signals within our nervous systems, and sent to our brains. The electrochemical signals generate chemical changes, electrical activa-tion, and new behaviors, which, in turn, transmit messages back across the social synapse.

The *social synapse* is the space between us. It is also the medium through which we are linked together into larger organisms such as fam-ilies, tribes, societies, and the human species as a whole. Because our lives are lived at the border of this synapse and because so much com-munication is automatic and below conscious awareness, most of what goes on is invisible to us and taken for granted. Much of this book fo-cuses on unveiling the social synapse and exploring some of its many mechanisms. Through this exploration we will examine how people, like neurons, excite, interconnect, and link together to create relationships.

If you can accept the possibility of the existence of a social synapse, perhaps you might consider a second theoretical leap. Neurons have three sequential levels of information exchange that are called first, sec-ond, and third messenger systems. They are (1) the communication across the synapse that (2) changes the internal biochemistry of the cell, which, in turn, (3) activates mRNA (*messenger ribonucleic acid,* the material that translates protein into new brain structure) and pro-tein synthesis to change cellular structure. It is through these processes that the brain changes in response to experience. Zooming out to the level of individual people embedded in a matrix of relationships, could it be possible that these three levels of information exchange are also taking place there? In other words, when we interact, could we also be impacting each other's internal biological state and influencing the long-term construction of each other's brains? This, in essence, is what I believe is occurring, and another focus of what is explored in this book. It has been a fascinating journey of discovery for me, and I hope that you will enjoy coming with me as I share my findings with you.

The Discovery of the Brain

Honestly, when was the last time you thought about your brain? Except for the occasional headache, which feels like it is in the head, we don't even remember we have brains. In essence, a well-functioning brain is invisible, which may account for why, at this point in our history, we know more about the movement of the planets than the workings of our brains. In fact, a century ago, anatomists and physicians thought that the seat of consciousness resided in the heart with the brain serving as the body's air conditioner, cooling the blood as it passed through.

Studying the brain is like exploring a vast and ancient country with diverse landscapes, cultures, and customs. Our brains defy reduction to simple cause-and-effect relationships and anatomical boundaries; like complex cultures, many of the interactions are subtle to the point of invisibility. To understand a culture, you need to be immersed in it, to stay alert for small clues that may carry deep significance. Even a subtle diversion of gaze in the town square can tell the story of two people or two nations. The brain's deeper significance is infinitely more complex than anything scientists have ever encountered. To add to this complexity is the fact that each of our brains is unique, a mixture of our long and circuitous evolutionary history and the millions of personal experiences that shape it throughout our lives.

Like every living system—from single neurons to complex ecosystems—the brain depends on interactions with others for its survival. Each brain is dependent on the scaffolding of caretakers and loved ones for its survival, growth, and well-being. So we begin with what we know: *The brain is an organ of adaptation* that builds its structures through interactions with others. So maybe it is better that we forget we have brains. Because to write the story of this journey, we must begin our guidebook with the thought: *There are no single brains.*

Our brains are built in the enigmatic interface between experience and genetics, where nurture and nature become one (Crabbe & Phillips, 2003; LeDoux, 2003). At first, genes serve as a template to organize the brain and trigger critical and sensitive periods; later, they orchestrate the ongoing transcription of experience into genetic material. Through the biochemical alchemy of template and transcription genetics, experience becomes flesh, love takes material form, and culture is passed through a group and carried forward through time.

The fact that the brain is such a highly specialized organ of adaptation is both good news and bad news. The good news is that if unexpected challenges emerge, our brains have a greater chance to adapt and survive. When good-enough parenting combines with good-enough genetic programming, our brains are shaped in ways that benefit us throughout life. And the bad news? We are just as capable of adapting to *unhealthy* environments and *pathological* caretakers. The resulting adaptations may help us to survive a traumatic childhood but impede healthy development later in life. Our parents are the primary environment to which our young brains adapt, and their unconscious minds are our first reality. Because the first few years of life are a period of exuberant brain development, early experience has a disproportionate impact on the development of neural systems. In this way, early negative interpersonal experiences become a primary source of the symptoms for which people seek relief in psychotherapy.

Interpersonal Neurobiology

Interpersonal neurobiology assumes that the brain is a social organ that is built through experience. Through interdisciplinary exploration it seeks to discover the workings of experience-dependent plasticity, or the ways in which the brain is constructed by experience. At the core of interpersonal neurobiology is a focus on the neural systems that shape attachment. And, in turn, interpersonal neurobiology considers how these systems are shaped by relationships. The bidirectional causality between neural structure and experience requires a continual shift in focus from the brain to social behavior and back again to the brain.

The social construction of the brain and the role of attachment relationships are particularly important in interpersonal neurobiology, as is the application of scientific data to parenting, psychotherapy, and education (Siegel & Hartzel, 2003). In addition to data from neuroscience and psychology, interpersonal neurobiology utilizes research from psychoanalysis, ethology, comparative anatomy, genetics, and evolution. In examining the social synapse we can look at narratives and storytelling, eye contact, touch, attachment patterns, and body language.

Thus far, those of us interested in interpersonal neurobiology are primarily psychotherapists and educators attempting to utilize neuroscientific data to inform and improve our work (Cozolino, 2002; Schore, 1994; Siegel, 1999). Like curious toddlers, we are full of questions, such as:

- Which networks comprise the social brain?
- How is the brain built and rebuilt by relationships?
- How do brains regulate one another during moment-to-moment interactions?
- How do parents, therapists, and educators activate and guide neuro-plastic processes?
- What are the effects of isolation, stress, and trauma on the social brain?
- What are the processes through which relationships both create and cure mental illness?

Caregiver nurturance sets us on a course of physical and psychological health—or, when it is lacking, disease and mental illness. Because of the link between interpersonal experiences and biological growth, we are particularly interested in the impact of these early caretaking relationships when the neural infrastructure of the social brain is forming. We also know that the brain is capable of change at any time and that social interactions are a primary source of brain regulation, growth, and health. Those of us who study interpersonal neurobiology believe that friendships, marriage, psychotherapy—in fact, any meaningful relationship—can reactivate neuroplastic processes and actually change the structure of the brain.

In thinking about these processes a multitude of questions arise: How does therapy work? What are the best ways for parents to help build their baby's brain? Why do some people seem to have no conscience whereas others are crippled with shame and guilt? Why do some find cues to abandonment in almost every human interaction? How does the brain stay healthy and how can we regain mental health after we fall ill? Interpersonal neurobiology, along with social neuroscience (Adolphs, 2003), affective neuroscience (Panksepp, 1998), and sociophysiology (Adler, 2002; Gardner, 1997), are among the emerging fields of study attempting to bridge the gap between the biological and social sciences. They all share the goal of understanding individuals within the context of the relationships into which they are born, develop, and live their lives.

Parents, educators, and therapists—those of us who should be most concerned with shaping minds—usually pay little attention to the brain. I have heard therapists say that psychotherapy is an art and that the brain is irrelevant to their work. I would respond, as with any art, that a thorough knowledge of our materials and methods can only enhance our skills and capabilities. The brain is a treasure trove of information about where we have come from, what we are capable of, and why we act as we do. It holds many secrets about how we can know ourselves better and improve the way we do psychotherapy, teach, and parent our children.

As a therapist, I am especially interested in how relationships reshape the brain throughout life. The tens of thousands of hours of interacting with clients have provided me with an intuitive sense of how and why therapy works. I have watched as my focused attention, consistency, and caring have been taken in like water at a desert oasis. I have experienced the gradual building of confidence and strength as my presence has been integrated and used as a source of security, guidance, and emotional safety. I have also experienced how working with my clients has changed me, inspired me, and helped me to grow. *It is the power of being with others that shapes our brains.*

Chapter **|**

The Social Brain

. . . the history of the evolution of mammals is the
history of the evolution of the family.
—Paul MacLean, 1990, p. 247

A fundamental characteristic of Western science and philosophy is the conception of the thinker as alone rather than embedded within a human community. It is a philosophy that leads us to look for answers that are technical and abstract instead of looking within lived experiences and human interactions. Researchers in neurobiology and neuroscience have studied the brain through scanners and on the dissection table, but, in doing so, they have often neglected the fundamental context of social interaction in which the brain was meant to flourish. The struggle between paradigms is nowhere more apparent than in psychiatry with its dual histories in psychoanalysis and neurology. Reiss expressed this ongoing tension when he said, "Psychiatry has been forced into the chronically uncomfortable position of straddling biomedicine and the social sciences and seems always to hunger for relief" (1991, p. 290). Although relief is usually gained by choosing sides between the brain and the mind, research repeatedly points to the inadequacy of either perspective alone.

One of the challenges of combining the social and biological sciences is the disparity of perspectives and personalities between the two groups. Scientists are, admittedly, not particularly social people, and few think of physicians as paragons of empathy. A tragic example of this disparity comes from the recent history of the treatment of children in orphanages. In response to the spreading of infectious diseases and the resulting high number of orphanage deaths, physicians attempted to keep the children safe by separating them from one another and ordering that their handling be kept to a minimum. Yet they still died at such alarming rates that admission forms and death certificates were signed at intake for the sake of efficiency. It was not until the children were held, rocked, and allowed to interact with one another that their survival rate improved (Blum, 2002).

Scientists have had to expand their thinking to grasp this idea: *The individual neuron or a single human brain does not exist in nature.* Without mutually stimulating interactions, people and neurons wither and die. In neurons this process is called *apoptosis;* in humans it is called depression, grief, and suicide. From birth until death, each of us needs others who seek us out, show interest in discovering who we are, and help us feel safe. Thus, understanding the brain requires knowledge of the healthy, living brain embedded within a community of other brains: Relationships are our natural habitat. Because therapists, teachers, and parents intuitively grasp this profound reality, just as laboratory scientists often do not, we decidedly "nonscience" types who choose to teach preschool, do psychotherapy, or study group behavior have a great deal to offer neuroscience. We are in a position to help research scientists know where to look as they explore how the brain grows, learns, and thrives throughout life.

The notion of the brain as a social organ emerged in neuroscience in the 1970s. Since then, researchers have been mapping the neural circuitry of social behavior. The theory that primates possess neural networks dedicated to social cognition was initially proposed by Kling and Stecklis (1976). In the process of observing monkey colonies in captivity, they would lesion the brains of certain monkeys and monitor their social behavior. They found that damage to certain brain structures resulted in aberrations of social behavior and a decline in group status. There is, however, no one module in the brain dedicated to social behavior; rather, there are multiple sensory, motor, cognitive, and emotional processing streams that contribute to the emergence of social intelligence (Karmiloff-Smith et al., 1995).

Why Relationships?

Think about meeting a man at a party: Your brain is simultaneously processing his tone of voice, direction of gaze, body language, hand gestures, eye movements, as well as the content of what he says. You are having physical and emotional reactions to him based on gender, appearance, odor, and who he reminds you of both consciously and unconsciously. Based on these quick observations, you decide what to say, how to act, and whether to approach him or move to the opposite end of the room. All of this is but a small fraction of the information your brain and body are processing during even the most superficial interactions. When the other is significant for us, either as a source of affection or danger, countless additional evaluative processes become activated. Neural networks dedicated to the evaluation of others have a long evolutionary history. Those of us who can better predict the intentions and actions of others have an obvious advantage in terms of safety, competition, and mating.

But why do we have relationships, maternal instincts, friendships, family, and society? Why not be like a reptile that digs a hole, lays some eggs, and moves on? The newborns of some species even have to flee from their parents to avoid being eaten! Wouldn't life be easier without gossip, grudges, and in-laws? Perhaps not. Using evolution as an organizing principle, we begin with the assumption that our social brains have been shaped by natural selection because being social enhances survival. Our best guess is that larger and more complex brains allow for a greater variety of responses in challenging situations and across diverse environments. Our brains allow us to fashion clothing, build houses with heating systems, and create space stations with artificial environments that let us expand our habitats and sources of food. But does this explain the salient role of relationships in the evolution of the human brain?

We know that the expansion of the cortex in primates corresponds with increasingly larger social groups. There is not only safety in numbers but the ability for task specialization such as hunting, gathering, and caretaking. So, whereas many animals need to be born immediately prepared to take on the challenges of survival, human infants have the luxury of years of total dependency during which their brains can grow, adapt, and be shaped by very specific experiences. As the size of primate groups expanded, the grooming, grunts, and hand gestures adequate in small groups were gradually shaped into spoken language. As social groups grew even larger, more cortical geography was needed to process increasingly complicated social information. This coevolution of language *and* brain allowed for the development of higher levels of symbolic and abstract functioning. In other words, relationships are a fundamental and necessary building block in the evolution of the contemporary human brain.

Survival of the Nurtured

Our first months of life are dedicated to getting to know our mother: her smell, taste, feel, and the look of her face. We gradually experience her ability to attune to us and soothe our distress as her presence becomes synonymous with safety. Our mothers and fathers shape our brains from the inside out in a dance of interacting instincts. For human babies, survival doesn't depend on how fast they can run, whether they can climb a tree, or if they can tell the difference between edible and poisonous mushrooms. Rather, *they survive based on the abilities of their caretakers to detect the needs and intentions of those around them.* For humans, other people are our primary environment. If we are successful in relationships, we will have food, shelter, protection, and children of our own. We will get what we need.

When I think of Darwin's survival of the fittest, I picture body-builders, alpha male gorillas, or lions stalking their ultimately doomed prey. But what does it mean to be the "fittest" in our modern society? Certainly it is not the romantic notion of the noble savage. The instincts to run fast, fight others, and catch our own food have been channeled into hobbies and sports. Remember, survival of the fittest is entirely dependent on the environment to which the organism is trying to adapt. In the first decade of the 21st century we are adapting to information overload, spiraling expectations, and being stuck in traffic. The freeway is our savanna; the

Internet superhighway is our Galapagos. Could the fittest in our society actually be the average citizen, going about his daily routine with a solid sense of self, able to successfully navigate relationships and regulate the stress of sitting through business meetings?

In contemporary society the real challenges are multitasking, balancing the demands of work and family, information management, and coping with stress. We need to maintain perspective, pick our battles carefully, and remain mindful of ourselves in the midst of countless competing demands. What prepares us best for these demands? In some ways, it is the same thing that prepared our ancient ancestors to survive in their world: early nurturance, which plays a vital role in the development and integration of the diverse systems within our brains. Optimal sculpting of the prefrontal cortex through healthy early relationships allows us to think well of ourselves, trust others, regulate our emotions, maintain positive expectations, and utilize our intellectual and emotional intelligence in moment-to-moment problem solving. We can now add a corollary to Darwin's survival of the fittest: *Those who are nurtured best, survive best.*

Maternal and paternal instincts—in fact, all caretaking behaviors—are acts of nurturance that trump personal survival. Achieving such an altruistic state depends upon the successful inhibition of selfish, competitive, and aggressive impulses. Too often, however, that inhibition is incomplete. The fact that much of psychotherapy is dedicated to coming to terms with negative or conflicting messages from parents strongly suggests that our evolution as caretakers is still a work in progress.

When a parent abuses, neglects, or abandons a child, the parent is communicating to the child that he is less fit. Consequently, the child's brain may become shaped in ways that do not support his long-term survival. Unloving behavior signals to the child that the world is a dangerous place and tells him Do not explore, do not discover, and do not take chances. When children are traumatized, abused, or neglected, they are being given the message that they are not among the chosen. As they grow, they have thoughts, states of mind, emotions, and immunological functioning that are inconsistent with well-being, successful procreation, and long-term survival. With all due respect to the old adage, we could also say that what doesn't kill us makes us *weaker.*

Dylan—Learning to Say Goodbye

A few years ago Shelly called me about Dylan, her 3-year-old son. His preschool teacher had reported that Dylan had become violent toward her and some of the other children. Dylan's father Chet had been diagnosed with cancer a year earlier and was now close to death. Shelly had watched with sorrow as her husband grew sicker and pushed Dylan away. At first she had thought Chet's declining physical condition had something to do with his harsh dismissal of Dylan, but she now suspected it was Chet's way of dealing with leaving his family behind. "Actually," Shelly said to me, "Chet told me so himself. I asked him why he was being so hard on Dylan, and he looked at me and said, 'It will be easier for Dylan if he learns not to love me.'" Shelly was silent for a while before quietly adding, "That just broke my heart." She went on to tell me that over the last few months Dylan seemed to be regressing. He was having toileting accidents, frequent nightmares, and bouts of inconsolable crying. "We haven't told him what's happening to his dad," she continued, "but he seems to know that something is really wrong." We ended our first conversation by making an appointment for the following week.

At the time of our appointment, I entered the playroom to find Dylan crouching behind a chair. I observed him as he watched his mother fill out forms with my cotherapist. From time to time, he would pop up from his hiding place, shoot at his mother with an imaginary gun, and dip down again behind the chair. After introducing myself to Shelly and talking with her for a few minutes, I sat on the floor next to two chests of toys. Thinking of Dylan and what toys he might like to play with, I began rummaging through the chests. As the women left for the observation room, Dylan stared at me intently from behind his chair. If he caught me looking back at him, he would huddle down, hiding his eyes.

After a few unsuccessful attempts to engage him by asking questions or inviting him to play, I decided to play on my own. I wondered if, perhaps, he was showing me how it felt to be rejected and have to play alone. I tried to remember all those times in my life when I had felt rejected. If I could get into that state of mind, it might help me to connect with Dylan. He watched closely as I pulled out a toy, played with it for a while, and replaced it with another. I finally came upon a wooden train set. Putting together a few pieces of track, I began to slowly push the train on the track while doing my best steam engine sound: "Choo, Choo, Choo, Choo." Instead of getting the next piece out of the toy chest as I approached the end of the track, I said, "Choo, Choo, Choo. Oh no, I'm running out of track! What am I going to do? Choo, Choo, Choo."

Dylan darted from his hiding place, startling me as he ran to the toy chest, picked out a piece of track, attached it to the existing track, and shot back behind his chair. "Whooo, that was a close one!" I said as I continued to slowly move the train forward. "Choo, Choo, Choo. . . ." Halfway through the new length of track, I repeated, "Oh no!" Dylan popped out of his hiding place to repeat his train-saving heroics. This time, he smacked me on the back as he ran by.

We repeated this scenario a few more times. Dylan's smack gradually evolved into longer and longer touches as he passed. He no longer retreated behind the chair but would stand near the train waiting for his turn. Then, as if maintaining "electricity" with home base in a game of tag, he kept one hand on my shoulder as he reached out with the other to grab new track. Finally, he planted himself in my lap and added track from there. He slowly became less serious and began to giggle and squeal with delight. We spent the last half of the session like that, Dylan sitting in my lap, looking at the tracks he had set up, telling me stories of the other kids at preschool, talking about his favorite toys—and, to my surprise, explaining to me what was happening at home.

Because working with young children involves symbolic play and the imagination of both therapist and child, you can never be certain of exactly what may happen in therapy. Dylan seemed angry at his mother for what I imagine was her failure to protect him from the pain and confusion he was experiencing. Through his initial actions with me, Dylan posed many questions: "Am I important to you? Am I needed? Am I wanted? Am I safe? Will I survive?" For a child his age, all of these questions are one and the same.

By playing by myself, I gave Dylan an opportunity to evaluate me in this strange situation. Allowing him to save the train gave Dylan the chance to demonstrate his competence and value. He found he could smack me without retaliation and then move closer, testing my safety and acceptance of him. His play became a dance of intimacy, bonding, and attachment. When he finally felt safe, he wanted sustained physical and verbal contact. He showed me what he had lost and what he needed from his father. Dylan, despite his regressive behaviors—or maybe because of them—had become very receptive to messages sent across the social synapse. Because of this receptivity, his channels of communication were relatively easy to reactivate.

However, Dylan was only one element of the communication break-down in his family. Besides connecting with Dylan, I wanted to help Chet say goodbye to his wife and son. I also suspected that Dylan and Shelly would need some help adjusting to their new life after Chet's death. Shelly was encouraged by the connection I was able to forge with Dylan and was eager to have me talk with Chet. This would be a chal-lenge. Not only was Chet unable to leave his bed, but he wanted no part of sympathetic relatives, well-meaning rabbis, or, most especially, a ther-apist. Still, Shelly and I set up a time for me to visit with Chet, knowing only too well that he would probably refuse to speak with me at all.

As I walked into his room, Chet's skeletal form did everything but pull the covers up over his face to avoid me. He shot a glare or two in my direction and remained silent. I felt like I was once again with Dylan in the playroom, only this time there were no trains to help us bond. Certain that Chet had already heard all the clichés, platitudes, and com-forting remarks from others, I was careful to avoid my impulse to say them. After sitting quietly for a few minutes, I began telling him about my sessions with Dylan and how fond I had become of him. I also told him what I thought was going on in his son's heart and what Dylan needed from him.

Chet began crying softly, but his sadness quickly changed to anger. He was angry at dying, at his friends, his wife, his doctors, and at God. He was even angry at Dylan for the many years ahead of him. He stared at the paper cup in his hand, slowly crushing it, the water run-ning out through his fingers and onto the blanket. "I know it's no one's fault, just bad luck, I'm just so pissed off!" Inexplicably, I reacted to his anger with sadness. I felt my eyes grow moist. Seeing my tears, Chet, too, began to cry again. We cried together for a while and, then, as we sat in the growing darkness, Chet began to speak. He told me about meeting his wife, their courtship and marriage, and his experience of Dylan's birth.

In the few sessions I had with Chet before his death, I discovered that it was his anger that kept him silent. I gave him opportunities to be angry, but soon we both realized that he needed to say goodbye to his family, his friends, and to Dylan. From that point forward, he would muster up some of his failing energy each day—to play with Dylan, to reminisce with his wife, and to talk about their future without him. If a tragic, young death can be considered good, such was Chet's.

My social brain was in overdrive while working with Dylan and Chet. I watched their movements, facial expressions, and gaze, and listened to the tones and cadences of their voices. I was the wooden body of the cello and they were the strings as I resonated with their feelings and emotions, both expressed and held within. I imagined how I would feel in each of their situations in order to help myself establish an empathic attunement with them. With both of them, I blended observations and ideas to try to discern what was in their hearts. Memories of my own childhood emerged, allowing me to interact with Dylan at his level of development and understanding. My paternal instincts also led me to want to comfort and soothe Dylan's distress—I felt my body relax as he felt increasingly safe with me. In an entirely different way, being with Chet required me to face our shared mortality and the cruelty of fate. We shared that all too human experience of inhabiting a universe that neither of us can understand.

Interwoven Hearts

I felt connected to Dylan from the moment I first saw him crouching behind his chair in the clinic. In addition to all the instinctual appeal of an adorable 3-year-old, I could see the pain and fear in Dylan's face. Seeing his discomfort only added to my urge to approach, engage, and soothe him. My unconscious memories of being a frightened and confused child may have resonated in a way that made my desire to take care of him a means of soothing myself. By communicating through actions, gestures, touch, sounds, and words, we gradually bridged the social synapse, soothing and perhaps healing some of the emotional pain within each of us. A similar process occurred with Chet, as we supported each other in facing our fears of death, while keeping in mind what had to be done before we ran out of time.

This complex, magical, and sometimes scary phenomenon we call human relationships is all around us. How the connections occur, what impact they have on us, and how relationships change the architecture and functioning of the brain are the essential questions of interpersonal neurobiology. Far from detaching ourselves from felt experience, as is routinely accepted as the operative mode of science, our work *requires* the inclusion of our experience. Our personal experiences are no less important than the empirical evidence found in the laboratory.

Thinking of Dylan's experience with his parents, the quality and nature of their attachments, and what will happen after his father's death, we naturally wonder how all of these experiences will shape Dylan's brain. How will biochemical changes affect his ability to handle stress and the functioning of his immune system? How will his implicit memories affect his ability to bond with, and attach to, others as he grows into adulthood? What kind of friend, husband, and father will he become? The temporal development and integration of Dylan's brain and psyche, in the context of his relationships with others, are a core concern of interpersonal neurobiology.

Will Dylan come to therapy years from now with symptoms and coping strategies that cause him problems? Will he panic at any sign of rejection? Will he spend his life searching for a father figure in a coach, teacher, or boss through whom he may hope to symbolically reconnect with Chet? What if, years from now, Dylan comes to you for therapy? How will you bridge the social synapse, how will *you* establish trust, and what will you do to activate the neuroplastic processes in Dylan's brain to help him alter patterns of implicit memory, behavior, and feelings? What will happen in your own psychotherapy to help you know yourself well enough to help Dylan? This is the stuff of interpersonal neurobiology: from the inside out, from the laboratory to the consulting room, from neurons to neighborhoods, from one human being to another.

Interpersonal neurobiology is the study of how we attach and grow and interconnect throughout life. It is our story: yours, mine, Chet's, and Dylan's. It is the story of how we become dysregulated and unhealthy, and how we regain our emotional balance and mental health. It is also the story of how genes and environments interact to create who we are and how we create each other through relationships, cultures, the stories we tell, and the imaginary worlds we create, inhabit, and explore. The transformative power of intimacy has its roots in the evolution and development of the brain through parenting, friendship, and love. This same power is used in psychotherapy, education, and ministry.

In the chapters to come I will interweave science and experience in an effort to expand our understanding of human relationships. Just as biochemists study the flow of chemicals between neurons, we will look at the flow of information between individuals across the social synapse. We will also look at how relationships impact the functioning and growth of the brain's neural circuitry. In exploring the evolution, development, and functioning of the brain, we may achieve a deeper appreciation of the complexity and importance of our interactions with one another, especially those closest to us.

Chapter 2

The Evolving Brain

*To have a child is to discover a piece of your heart
in another's body.*

—An anonymous poet

The size of our brains, and those of our primate cousins, correlates with both the length of our juvenile period and the complexity of our social structure. In other words, long childhoods and complex societies make for larger brains and visa versa. Given our dependence on groups for our very survival, primates have evolved elaborate neural networks for interacting with others as well as reading their minds and predicting their intentions (Cheney, Seyfarth, & Smuts, 1986). These systems of attaching, predicting, and communicating are all functions of the social brain. Being a member of a complex society requires a brain that is born ready to learn a vast amount of social information that takes many years to master. At the same time, the social brain is born relatively immature and necessitates a long period of dependency. Humans, having the most complex brains and intricate society, have the most prolonged period of abject dependency of any species (Cacioppo & Berntson, 2002).

Compared to other primates, human babies are born quite early relative to the maturity of their brains. If we followed the pattern typical for other primates, we would gestate inside of our mothers for up to 24 months (Gould, 1977). Our prematurity may be partly the result of needing to get through a narrow birth canal before our heads grow too large. Continuing gestation outside of our mother's body may also be a strategy to increase the effects of social relationships on the developing brain. Our early emergence into the world and our total dependency on caretakers may maximize the shaping of the brain as a social organ. In order to accomplish this extrauterine gestation, human mothers have evolved to be very adept caretakers.

Based on these evolutionary and developmental factors, the brain is shaped as a reflection of an interlocking system of children, caretakers, and the community at large. Relationships have become the environment of the social brain in much the same way as a field behind a barn might be the environment of a mouse. As the location of food sources change, so does the mouse's brain, developing new neurons and new neural connections in areas involved with foraging, retrieval, and spatial mapping. Similarly, the social group is the human environment, with the brain adapting to an ever-changing stream of interpersonal information and constellations of relationships.

To facilitate the continued growth of the brain, the cranial sutures don't close for many months after birth and the skull continues to grow into puberty. This extended developmental period allows for the growth of neurons and the expansion of dendritic connections especially in the neocortex, the area most involved with social cognition and inhibitory control. We not only need to process and utilize social information, but also inhibit self-serving, aggressive, and sexual impulses in order to participate in social groups. Inhibition also aids attention, concentration, and learning while maximizing plasticity in networks that are capable of higher cognition, contemplation, and empathy. Powerful inhibitory abilities are necessary for parents to deal with the unrestrained impulses and needs of children. As parents, we learn to defer personal gratification (and sleep) in order to become competent caretakers.

How much of this presentation is based on conjecture and how much is based on scientific evidence? There are a number of clues pointing to evolution's selection of a social course for the human brain. One clue comes from the sclera or "whites" of our eyes. In most other primates, iris and sclera are virtually identical in color, an evolutionary selection that disguises the direction of eye gaze from conspecifics and predators.

A white sclera allows others to see the direction of our eye movement—as we shall see, a bit of natural selection with social benefits. Furthermore, humans also have the greatest horizontal exposure of the sclera relative to the size of the iris, another variable maximizing the "readability of human eyes" (Kobayashi & Kohshima, 1997). Whereas in other primates the sclera is dark to hide gaze direction, in humans, camouflage gave way to revealing the direction of our attention and possible intentions (see Figure 2.1).

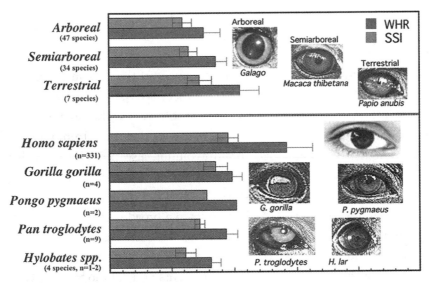

Figure 2.1. By emphasizing the contrast between sclera and pupil and elongating the visible horizontal portion of the eye, evolution is in the process of maximizing the communication value of the human eye. Compare the information available from the human eye with that from the primitive primates at the top of the chart and the gorilla and chimpanzee *(Pan troglodytes)* below. Image courtesy of Dr. Hiromi Kobayashi.

In addition to the direction of our gaze, blushing and pupil dilation also let others know of our interest, distress, or embarrassment and provide important and often unconscious clues to our willingness to engage in a relationship. Blushing is an "interpersonal vascular signal" that adds a subjective track to communication (Lynch, 1985). Pupil dilation provides additional information (about which we ourselves may be unaware) to others about our internal state. Structural changes to the human eye, pupil dilation, and blushing greatly enhance our ability to communicate with one another. It appears that social communication has been chosen by natural selection to be of greater survival value than disguising our intentions and feelings, so much so that we even have ways of unintentionally "outing" ourselves to others. These and many more developments during evolution highlight a shift from survival of the fittest *individuals* to the survival of the *group* as a whole.

The Triune Brain

To understand the structure and development of the human brain, it is useful to examine what is known (or theorized) about its evolution. Many primitive structures have been conserved within the modern human brain for new applications in networks dedicated to more complex functions (Taylor, 1999). Brain evolution also provides us with a window to our own functioning and dysfunctioning, including some of the conflicts we experience in society and within ourselves.

The neuroscientist Paul MacLean offered a broad theory of brain evolution he called the *triune brain*. His model has been extremely useful for therapists and educators because it is in line with the theories of both Darwin and Freud. The triune brain presents an evolutionary explanation that may account for some of the contradictions, discontinuities, and pathologies of human consciousness and behavior (MacLean, 1990). MacLean described the human brain as a three-part phylogenetic system reflecting our evolutionary connection to both reptiles and lower mammals. He called the evolutionary layers the reptilian, paleomammalian, and neomammalian brains, which parallel the structures of the brainstem, limbic system, and cortex (MacLean, 1985). Think of it as a brain within a brain within a brain, each successive layer devoting itself to increasingly complex functions and abilities.

The model of the triune brain serves the valuable function of providing a connective metaphor that encompasses the artifacts of evolution, the contemporary nervous system, and some of the inherent difficulties related to the organization and disorganization of human experience. MacLean suggests that the "linkup" between the three brains is problematic because of their differing "mentalities" and the fact that only the neomammalian brain is capable of consciousness and verbal communication. MacLean's description of the nonverbal reptilian and paleomammalian brains as influencing processing in the neomammalian brain at an unconscious level parallels Freud's conception of the conscious and the unconscious minds. As we will see in our discussion of memory, the early lessons learned by these "implicit" (unconscious) reptilian and paleomammalian networks can exert a lifelong influence on conscious behavior and experience (MacLean, 1990).

Although MacLean's model is a helpful place to begin, it soon becomes inadequate in explaining many of the brain's complexities. In reality, MacLean's reptilian and paleomammalian brains have continued to evolve along with the neomammalian brain. Newer systems, emerging to address the changing requirements of survival, have conserved, modified, and expanded components of preexisting systems. Another problem with MacLean's model is that there are no clear delineations between layers, with regions such as the insula and cingulate cortex possessing legitimate "dual citizenship" of both the paleo- and neomammalian cortices. Furthermore, all three layers are linked together in complex vertical neural networks, thereby allowing the whole brain to coordinate everything from simple motor movements to complex abstract functions.

Hemispheric Specialization

The primate brain has right and left cerebral hemispheres that have grown increasingly dissimilar during the course of our evolution (Geschwind & Galaburda, 1985a; Rilling & Insel, 1999). The differentiation between the hemispheres has replaced redundant side-to-side networks with specialized processing systems that allow for more diverse functions and higher-level processing. For example, cortical specialization has resulted in the formation of a conscious linguistic self that is biased toward the left and a physical emotional self biased toward the right. Language functions (both spoken and written) are biased toward the left hemisphere in most adults, and the left hemisphere is more involved in conscious coping and problem solving than the right, most likely because of its language abilities (Corina, Vaid, & Bellugi, 1992). The left hemisphere functions best within the middle range of affect and is biased toward positive and prosocial emotions (Silberman & Weingartner, 1986).

The right hemisphere, on the other hand, is generally responsible for appraising the safety and danger of others and organizing the sense of corporeal and emotional self (Devinsky, 2000). Appraisal—our positive or negative associations to a stimulus—results in an approach or avoidance response, and emotion is the conscious manifestation of this mostly unconscious process of evaluation (Fischer, Shaver, & Carnochan, 1990; Fox, 1991). This is why the right hemisphere is generally associated with the unconscious mind.

Evolving Social Communication

The ratio of the size of the cortex to the entire brain seems to have expanded in parallel with primate group size (Dunbar, 1992). "Mob mentality" notwithstanding, larger and more complex social groups require more brainpower from their members. Given that larger groups increase the probability of success in warfare and competition for resources, it is likely that the brain, language sophistication, and group size evolved in tandem.

There is relatively little genetic difference between humans and other primates. The ratio of the size of our frontal lobes to the rest of our cortex is also similar to our primate cousins, and many of their subcortical structures are conserved within the human brain (Semendeferi et al., 1997, 2002). Nevertheless, the human brain is unique in the animal kingdom for the complexity of cortical structures and the symbolic processes those structures mediate (see Figure 2.2). You and I possess a complex set of letter symbols that reflect a vast amount of shared understandings that allow me to record my thoughts on paper, and you to understand them. As far as we know, no other animal is capable of this level of information storage, utilization, and sharing. Of course, when we think about how much we suffer from information overload, perhaps we have experienced too much evolution for our own good!

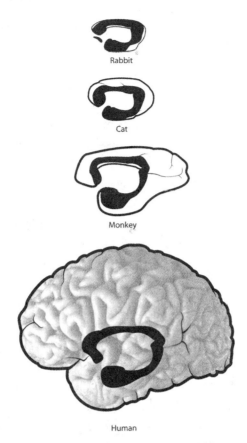

Figure 2.2. **A rough representation of the expansion of the cerebral cortex relative to limbic structures in four mammalian brains. Image based on the work of Paul MacLean.**

Grooming, or the manual inspection of another animal's fur for insects and other possible problems, is one way in which primate groups maintain coherence, cooperation, and bonding. Because time spent in social grooming increases with group size, its use as a means of group cohesion most likely became unmanageable as groups grew in number. The emergence of facial and hand gestures, sign language, and the use of words may have been driven by the need for more efficient means of social bonding and information exchange (Dunbar, 1992, 1993). Because most of our language production involves gossip and nonessential personal information, its continued role in social coherence cannot be doubted

(Dunbar, 1996). Our powerful impulse to share information with each other led Benjamin Franklin to observe, "Three can keep a secret, if two of them are dead."

What is the source of human language? It may have begun as a combination of the sounds and gestures we still see in other primates. This possibility may explain why handedness and language functions are linked in the brain. Most of us are right-handed, which is controlled by the left brain, and language is lateralized in the left hemisphere. During evolution, brain areas controlling gestures may have been gradually adapted during the creation of language. As semantic abilities expanded, language became more descriptive and useful, gradually replacing gestures in importance. Our present use of hand gestures to augment spoken language probably reflects these evolutionary origins. Coordinated use of words, emotions, and bodily gestures requires the simultaneous participation of both hemispheres.

Conservation, Response Speed, and Flexibility

The fundamental behavioral tendency of all organisms is to approach what is life sustaining and avoid that which is dangerous. The success of rapid and accurate approach/avoidance decisions determines whether an organism lives long enough to reproduce and carry its genes forward to the next generation or is fated to go not so gently into that good night. The most primitive subcortical fight-or-flight circuitry—shared with our reptilian ancestors—is interwoven with the most highly evolved association areas of the cerebral cortex used to consciously analyze threat. Thus, although conscious input is possible during stressful situations, under conditions of extreme threat, later evolving emotional and cognitive processes are directed by ancient, rapid-acting neural networks that are fundamental to survival.

The modern human brain reflects millions of years of evolutionary adaptation that embody compromises between response speed and the flexibility made possible by a larger but slower cortex (Mesulam, 1998). Each neural network reflects elements of this compromise and, like most design compromises, results in functional shortcomings. Evolution is driven and directed by the physical survival of the species, not by the happiness of individuals. Thus, much of the brain's functioning is based upon primitive fight-or-flight mechanisms as opposed to conscious and compassionate decision making. Because of this reality, the conscious and unconscious management of fear and anxiety are core components of our attachment relationships and character.

How does evolution make its "choices"? An important example can be seen in the conservation of the primitive deer-in-the-headlights startle response. Think about a time when you were startled: Did you come to an abrupt stop, freeze all of your movements, and hold your breath as you scanned the environment for a threat? All of these responses maximize our ability to avoid detection, locate the source of possible danger, and prepare to fight or flee. As sophisticated as language has become, it is still the creation of *sound*; the freeze response results in the inhibition of language in highly stressful and traumatic situations. Evolution has granted us language but maintained the freeze rule. When the threat passes, we begin to relax and find our voices again, perhaps even to laugh at our own reactions. But what if we can never relax? What if our early experience shapes our brain to be in a constant state of fear? When this evolutionary compromise interferes with the proper development and integration of neural networks, psychopathology may result.

What hard evidence do we have that supports this theory of language inhibition during stress? It turns out that the speechless terror often reported by victims of trauma appears to have a neurobiological substrate. In fact, decreased activation in Broca's area (located in the left frontal cortex) has been found in individuals in high states of arousal (Rauch et al., 1996). This inhibitory effect on Broca's area impairs not only language production but also the encoding of conscious memory for traumatic events. It may then interfere with the development of coherent narratives that serve to process the experience and lead to neural network integration and psychological healing. The dissociation we see in trauma survivors may well be an artifact of the loss of the cognitive flexibility provided by conscious awareness and language.

Another of evolution's "decisions" involves the vital importance it has placed on interpersonal experiences during the first years of life. Early memories, lost to our consciousness, nevertheless continue to shape our experience of those around us throughout our lives. The persistence of past learning into a present where it is irrelevant or even destructive is extremely problematic. The impact of these and other design compromises is certainly responsible for most of the difficulties people bring to psychotherapy. Warren was one such person.

Warren—The Summer Wind

Warren was afraid he was going crazy. He was having nightmares, panic attacks, and an almost impossible time getting any sleep, admitting to me, "I'm having a hard time concentrating and remembering what I'm supposed to do. I've also been snapping at my wife and son for no reason." Warren worked as an insurance salesman, had been married for 2 years, and had a 1-year-old son and another child on the way. He told me during our first interview that everything had been fine until 6 months ago, when he and his wife moved from Kentucky to Southern California.

"My wife thinks I'm under too much stress," he said. "She worries about me. She says it's because I'm missing Kentucky, or it's all the extra driving I have to do now. . . ." His voice trailed off, and then he added, "But we had to move here. I got a good promotion, and we need the extra money, so what else could I do?" He had already gone to his family doctor and a cardiologist to make sure he was not having problems with his heart. He also backed off a bit on his work schedule and began to spend more time with his family. Even so, his symptoms persisted.

During our first few sessions, I learned about Warren's life and was especially interested in finding out whether he had had any traumatic experiences. He described his life as "pretty normal," with a good childhood and a loving family. While searching his memory for any possibly relevant experience, he casually said, "Oh, yeah, I did get my leg blown off." I sat there, managing my surprise, as he pulled his pant leg up to reveal a prosthetic leg and foot. "Well, that may have been traumatic," I said. "Let's talk about that."

Warren was an 18-year-old, just graduating from boot camp when Iraq invaded Kuwait. In the space of 8 months, he went from his high school prom in rural Kentucky to driving a supply truck on the push toward Baghdad. He did his best to describe the exhilaration and terror he and his buddies experienced during this drive. They moved mostly at night, depending on global positioning satellites (GPS) and night vision goggles, routinely getting lost in the dark, alien terrain. Their caravan of trucks, tanks, and personnel carriers engaged the enemy in occasional gunfire but was under orders to proceed as quickly as possible to maintain the supply chain to their forward troops. As they drove deeper into Iraq, resistance increased and the caravan encountered regular gunfire and rocket attacks. Trucks were hit, troops were killed, and Warren's fear steadily increased as they pressed forward through the night.

Although Warren doesn't recall a great deal about the night he was hit, he does remember that they had gone off course and found themselves driving in circles near a desert town. They had just started to suspect that they were at risk of an ambush when the firing began. The next thing Warren remembered was waking up in a hospital room in Kuwait and being transferred to a hospital in Germany. Later, he learned that his truck had been hit by a rocket. The explosion had severed Warren's left foot and lower leg and knocked him unconscious. He came home a month later, was fitted for a prosthetic, and began physical therapy. He was young and strong and in good shape; he took well to using his new leg and foot. Warren didn't recall any psychological effects of his experiences and was told by army doctors that because he was knocked unconscious, he didn't have to worry about PTSD. As he finished telling me this story, his eyes widened in surprise. "Could this be PTSD," he asked, "after all these years?"

As we explored the events surrounding his recent symptoms, he remembered the day of his first anxiety attack. He was driving from Los Angeles to Palm Springs for a business meeting. As he drove deeper into the desert, he missed the exit and had to circle around in a big arc to get to his destination. It was an important meeting, he was running late, and he grew increasingly anxious as he searched for the right streets. It was at this point that he found himself breathing heavily and feeling dizzy. He pulled over to the side of the road to calm down, making a note to himself to see a doctor and have a stress test. "I remembered the smell, that desert smell, the dry air and the dryness of my skin—that feeling was what I remember about driving through Iraq." During his tour of duty, he had wondered how people survived the heat in the Middle East and remembered having that same thought as he drove through the California desert.

Despite the fact that for more than a decade Warren was without symptoms from his combat experiences, he was having them now. His anxiety, sleep disturbances, and panic strongly suggested that the primitive circuits of his brain did remember his earlier traumatic experiences, and his sensory experiences were triggering his subcortical fear circuitry. Although Warren had a hard time believing that his symptoms were connected to events from long ago, they gradually subsided during treatment focused on consciously processing his combat experiences. The recent stress of moving, his new job, and the increasing demands on his time may have made him more vulnerable to the intrusion of these memories, which were triggered by his return to the desert.

We need to have the participation of our entire brains to fully process experience. When we are overwhelmed by traumatic experiences, our brains lose the ability to maintain neural integration across the various networks dedicated to behavior, emotion, sensation, and conscious awareness. When memories are stored in sensory and emotional networks but are dissociated from those that organize cognition, knowledge, and perspective, we become vulnerable to intrusions of past experiences that are triggered by environmental and internal cues. In the process of psychotherapy, we attempt to reintegrate these dissociated networks by consciously processing traumatic memories. This reintegration, in turn, allows the networks of conscious cortical processing to develop the ability to inhibit and control past traumatic memories.

The reactivation of trauma by seemingly random experiences or sensory cues from the external environment—even if we have protected ourselves with dissociation or amnesia—reflects the vulnerability of our brains to discontinuities of experience. All of the obvious associations between Warren's past experiences and what he was experiencing in the present were lost on him prior to being guided to reflect on them. Through our therapeutic interactions, I was able to serve as an external neural circuit or auxiliary executive system that helped Warren to put the pieces of his experiences into a coherent and meaningful narrative. Once the narrative was in place and he could accept it, he no longer feared he was crazy. Rather, he was impressed with his brain's ability to store implicit emotional information and make it experientially accessible so many years later. The process of therapy brought continuity and integration back into Warren's life. Together we had overcome, at least to some extent, one or two of the compromises between speed and response flexibility bequeathed to Warren by his evolutionary history.

Part II

The Social Brain: Structures and Functions

Chapter 3

The Developing Brain

> . . . the brain is structured with an innate capacity
> to transcend the boundaries of . . . its own body in
> integrating itself with . . . the world of other brains.
> —Daniel Siegel

When we think about the billions of neurons with their trillions of connections that constitute the brain, we also need to remember that the brain is a living system designed by evolution for learning and memory. The brain—in fact, the entire nervous system—is constantly pulsing with chemical and electrical activity, expanding, contracting, and expanding again. Neuroscientists refer to the constantly changing brain as "plastic." The shaping of the nervous system begins early in gestation with the organization of the neural tube and continues to modify its structure throughout life (Thatcher, 1980). Whereas brainstem reflexes and limbic activity organize much of the infant's experiences, the developing cortex gradually takes on more control as it establishes increasingly efficient neural circuitry and synchronous patterns of firing.

From the start, our brains require a large amount of energy. Patterns of increasing energy consumption in different regions of the brain during the first year of life proceed in "phylogenic order," meaning that the development of more primitive brain structures precedes later-evolving ones. Networks dedicated to individual senses develop before the association areas that connect them and the executive systems, to which they will one day supply information (Chugani et al., 1987, 1998; Chugani & Phelps, 1991). The growth and coordination of the different senses parallel such behavioral changes as hand–eye coordination, and the ability to inhibit incorrect movement gradually increases with the maturation of the frontal lobes (Bell & Fox, 1992; Fischer, 1987).

Periods of exuberant neural growth are referred to as critical or *sensitive periods*. Because there is so much neural growth and organization during sensitive periods, early interpersonal experiences are very influential on our long-term development and well-being. The right hemisphere appears to have a relatively higher rate of growth during the first 18 months of life, paralleling the rapid development of sensory and motor capabilities (Chiron et al., 1997; Thatcher, Walker, & Guidice, 1987). At the same time, right-hemispheric networks led by the medial areas of the frontal lobes are establishing the basic structures of attachment and emotional regulation (Schore, 1994). During this period, the development of the left hemisphere is slowed, with some areas reserved for later-developing language functions (Gould, 1977). Perhaps the primacy of nonverbal learning in infancy mirrors our earlier evolutionary history, whereas the development of language reflects the unveiling of a uniquely human path.

During the second year of life, a growth spurt occurs in the left hemisphere. We learn to crawl and then to walk as we become acquainted with the world. An explosion in language skills and increased locomotion propel us into an extended exploration of the social and physical worlds. Within the frontal lobes there is a shift in development from the orbital medial to the dorsal lateral areas, which link with other cortical regions that sculpt the language network (Tucker, 1992). In this way the movements of hands and eyes become connected to visual stimuli and words. The corpus callosum, a large bundle of neural fibers that connects the hemispheres, begins to develop toward the end of the first year. The maturation of the corpus callosum allows for the integration of left-hemisphere semantic capabilities with the emotional and somatic networks centered in the right hemisphere.

Neurons

Neurons, the basic unit of the nervous system, are cells that transmit signals to one another via chemical messengers. There are billions of neurons in the nervous system, with anywhere from 10 to 100,000 synaptic connections each. The diverse capabilities of the nervous system emerge from the infinitely complex patterns of neuronal excitation that arise from such numbers (Post & Weiss, 1997). Each cell is an active ecosystem, taking in nutrients, generating energy, and adapting to environmental changes. Cells are comprised of various proteins that, in turn, are made up of amino acids. Gleaned from the foods we eat, amino acids are assembled into proteins based on the instructions contained within each cell's DNA. These new proteins are then transported throughout the cell. This process of protein synthesis begins at conception and continues for days after we die.

Remember, the brain is a living system. Neurons are, by their nature, social; they shun isolation and depend on their neighbors for survival. If they aren't sending and receiving messages from other neurons on a constant basis, they literally shrink and die. Most neurons have fibers, called *axons,* that become covered with myelin, which serves as an insulator that enhances axons' firing efficiency. One way of measuring the maturity of a neural network is to measure its degree of myelination (van der Knapp et al., 1991). Many neurons develop elaborate branches, called *dendrites,* that interconnect with the dendrites stemming from other neurons. Thus, a second measure of neural development is the size and degree of dendritic branching in individual neurons. Neurons that fail to communicate with other neurons die off through a process called *apoptosis.* Paradoxically, a third way to measure brain development is by the decrease in the overall number of neurons, as survivors take over and form increasingly efficient networks (Edelman, 1987; Huttenlocher, 1994; Purves & Lichtman, 1980). It turns out that the pruning of neurons that have not established positive connections is a vital component of the growth and development of the brain.

Half the volume of the brain is made up of *glial cells* that play a role in the construction, organization, and maintenance of neural systems. Although our knowledge of glial cells is limited, researchers suspect they are also involved in neural growth and communication (Pfrieger & Barres, 1996; Sontheimer, 1995; Vernadakis, 1996). Glial cells appear to participate in neural communication both by modulating synaptic transmission and carrying their own messages.

Genes

Soon after conception, the genetic code contained in our DNA guides the growth and organization of the cells that will become the nervous system. The rapid construction of the basic structures of the nervous system is programmed by genes contained within our DNA, which provide a template for the construction of the uniform structures of the nervous system. Although the unfolding of the *genetic template* of the nervous system is relatively unaffected by experience, this type of genetic organization is only half the story.

A second level of genetic involvement in building the brain is called *genetic transcription* (Kandel, 1998). Transcription genes control the experience-dependent aspects of the brain's organization and development by allowing the brain to be shaped and reshaped by learning. The transcription of protein into neural structure via RNA accounts for approximately 70% of the brain's structure that is added after birth (Schore, 1994). It is through gene transcription that environmental stimulation allows for ongoing learning and adaptation (Black, 1998). Thus, nature and nurture contribute to the building of the brain via the template and transcription functions of our genes.

Nervous System

How does the brain reach out to, and connect with, the rest of the body? The nervous system is divided into the central (CNS) and the peripheral (PNS) nervous systems. The CNS includes the brain and spinal cord, and the PNS is comprised of the autonomic and somatic nervous systems. The autonomic and somatic systems are involved in the communication with sense organs, glands, and, thus, the whole body. The autonomic nervous system has two branches: the sympathetic and parasympathetic systems. The sympathetic system controls the activation of the nervous system in response to a threat or other forms of motivation. The parasympathetic system supports the conservation of bodily energy, immunological functions, and the repair of damaged systems.

The brain itself consists of three general regions: the brainstem, limbic system, and cerebral cortex. The brainstem—the inner core of the

brain—oversees the internal milieu of the body by regulating temperature, heart rate, and basic reflexes. The limbic system is involved with
emotion, learning, memory, and the mediation of primitive approach-
avoidance responses (Patterson & Schmidt, 2003). The cerebral cortex
organizes sensory, motor, and conscious experiences, as well as our
learned interactions with the world. The growth of the cortex is largely
experience-dependent, whereas the organization of the brainstem relies
largely on a genetic template.

Let us take a moment to examine the cortex more closely. It consists
of six important areas: the frontal, insula, cingulate, temporal, parietal,
and occipital cortices. Each is represented on both sides of the brain and
specializes in certain functions:

- The occipital lobe comprises the areas for visual processing.
- The temporal lobe is involved with auditory processing, receptive
  language, and memory functions.
- The parietal lobe links the senses with motor abilities and creates
  the experience of a sense of our body in space.
- The insula and cingulate cortices integrate limbic processing and
  link it to cortical networks.
- The frontal lobes regulate motor behavior, language, executive functioning, abstract reasoning, and directed attention.

The left and right sides of the limbic system and cerebral cortex have
gradually differentiated during primate evolution, allowing for the kind
of skill specialization of which language is the best-understood example.
The two cerebral hemispheres communicate with each other primarily
via the corpus callosum, whose long neural fibers connect the corresponding areas of the left and right cerebral hemispheres. Most tasks we
perform rely on complex patterns of activation in different cortical and
limbic regions on both sides of the brain.

Neural Networks

And now, back to our highly social neurons. Millions of individual neurons link up to form neural networks that perform the many functions
of the nervous system. In turn, neural networks can interconnect,

allowing for the evolution and development of increasingly complex skills, abilities, and abstract functions. The specific combination of activated neurons involved in a particular function is known as its *enstantiation*. Enstantiations encode all of our abilities, emotions, and memories and are sculpted and modified by experience. Once neural patterns are established, new learning relies on the modification of established enstantiation patterns.

How does learning occur within these neural networks? Cells connect through changes in synaptic strength among neurons in response to an inner or outer stimulus. In a process called long-term potentiation (LTP), excitation between cells is prolonged, allowing them to become synchronized in their firing patterns and organized into neural networks (Hebb, 1949). Excitation also stimulates the transcription of RNA, resulting in the protein synthesis required for neuronal growth (Malenka & Siegelbaum, 2001). In addition to the modification of existing neurons, new neurons continue to appear in regions involved with ongoing learning, contributing to the continual growth and shaping of neural networks (Eriksson et al., 1998; Gould, Reeves, Graziano, & Gross, 1999; Gould, Tanapat, Hastigs, & Shors, 1999; Gross, 2000; Kempermann et al., 2004).

For our present purposes, think of learning as the modification of neural networks, the result of countless interactions between the organization provided by genetic templates and trial-and-error learning. Well before birth, the fetus engages in spontaneous activity that stimulates the mother to think about her new child. Newborns continually move all parts of their bodies, allowing them to discover their hands and feet as they attract attention. Although these movements seem random, they may actually be the brain's *best guess* at which intentional movements will eventually be needed for more mature motor skills (Katz & Shatz, 1996; Shatz, 1990).

As the infant matures, neural circuits gradually become less dependent on spontaneous activity and guided more by the environment. As sensory systems develop, they provide increasingly precise input to shape neural network formation and increasingly complex patterns of behavior. As positive and negative values are connected with certain perceptions and movements—such as the appearance of the mother and reaching out to her—emotional networks are integrated with sensory and motor systems.

Integration of neural networks involves the flow of information through efficient interconnections and a balance of influences from participating systems (Pribram, 1991). Directions of integration include top-down (cortical to subcortical and back again) and left-right (across the two hemispheres of the brain). Top-down integration includes the ability of the cortex to process, inhibit, and organize the reflexes, impulses, and emotions generated by the brainstem and limbic system (Alexander et al., 1986; Cummings, 1993). Left-right integration allows us to put feelings into words, consider feelings in conscious awareness, and integrate the positive and negative affective biases of the left and right hemispheres (Silberman & Weingarter, 1986).

Early relationships play a central role in the building of the brain. A simple game of peek-a-boo activates a baby's sympathetic nervous system and leads to a cascade of biological processes: noradrenalin and endorphins are released in the brain, enhancing the child's energy and sense of elation (Schore, 1997). In this way, relationships not only add to the development and expansion of neurons but provide the added energy for their growth and survival. The effect of good parenting is to provide an optimal metabolic environment for growth through biochemical stimulation and the enhancement of neuroplastic processes. And all this does not just help the baby—the adult brain is affected in similar ways. The same game of peek-a-boo will deepen the child–parent bond through the activation and growth of both of their brains. The child's wide eyes, smiles, and giggles make the parent happy, increase the child's sense of well-being, and raise the child's serotonin and dopamine levels. And you thought you were only having fun playing peek-a-boo!

The Teenage Brain

Based mostly on dogma about the "fixity" of the brain later in life, most research in brain development has focused on early childhood. In fact, nothing could be further from the truth! Although parents of teenagers sometimes wonder if aliens have taken over their children's brains, the truth is that their behavior is more likely a result of a sensitive neuroplastic period. Not surprisingly, when teenage brains were closely examined with modern techniques, a great deal of neural plasticity was found. It turns out that the teenage brain undergoes disorganization and reorganization from the onset of puberty into the early 20s. The discovery of the reorganization of the adolescent brain supports the notion that natural developmental milestones and life challenges coincide with sensitive periods of neural development and enhanced plasticity (Nelson et al., 2005). All in all, neuroplasticity offers a slightly more reasonable explanation than extraterrestrials.

The kinds of changes discovered in the adolescent brain (roughly 12–18 years of age) show a loss of the overall number of neurons (gray matter) with an increase in the number of myelinated fibers (white matter) connecting functional neural networks. It is logical to assume that these changes represent a process of selection and reorganization of neural networks with a goal of faster and more efficient information processing. Enhanced efficiency and speed of communication among cortical areas and between cortical and subcortical structures ultimately leads to increased integration of brain functions located in diverse regions of the central nervous system. Table 3.1 summarizes some of these findings.

Table 3.1. **Structural Changes in the Brain During Adolescence**

Increases in white matter:	Result in enhanced:
Cerebral cortex	Cognitive processing[1]
Corpus callosum	Hemispheric communication,[2] cognitive and emotional integration,[3] memory storage and retrieval[4]
Frontal–hippocampal circuits	Planning, foresight, and self-regulation[5]
Broca's–Wernicke's circuits	Language capacity[6]
Decreases in gray matter:	**Reflect:**
Cerebral cortex	Selection of neurons[7]
	Organization of neural networks,[8] shaping of neural systems,[9] and enhanced processing efficiency[10]

[1] Giedd, 2004; Sowell et al., 2002; Pfefferbaum et al., 1994; [2] Giedd et al., 1996; [3] Thompson et al., 2000; [4] Rajapakse et al., 1996; [5] Benes et al., 1994; [6] Paus et al., 1999; [7] Giedd, 2004; [8] Gogtay et al., 2004; [9] Sowell et al., 2002; [10] Thompson et al., 2000; Jernigan et al., 1991; Spear, 2000.

What underlies this disorganization and reorganization of the social brain during adolescence and early adulthood? On the surface, there appear to be three social transitions taking place: (1) moving away from the family of origin, (2) establishing an identity and connection with a peer group, and (3) the creation of a new family. Eventually, as adults, we are able to integrate all three into a complex set of attachment relationships. The brain, in fact, *needs* to be plastic to develop new relationships, a new self-image, and to learn of new roles in society. The tasks in front of the adolescent require breaking with the values and structures of the original family in order to become as desirable as possible to peers and potential mates. This shifting among social contexts requires ongoing plasticity in networks of the social brain.

The changes in the brain's reward circuitry required for new attachments during adolescence can also lead to confusion, disorientation, and depression. These biological and behavioral shifts are no doubt connected to the many impending life transitions that lay ahead. Unfortunately, these shifts are fraught with dangers related to an increased vulnerability to risky behaviors and addiction coupled with poor judgment and lack of adequate impulse control (Chambers et al., 2003; Rosenberg, 1995; Spear, 2000; Teicher et al., 1995).

The transition from the first to the second year of life sees a shift from affection to control in parents as toddlers' increased mobility and lack of judgment puts them in constant danger. A similar process occurs during adolescence. It goes without saying that parenting an adolescent is no easy task. It requires a balance of supportive affection and discipline as we simultaneously try to encourage their enthusiasm while reigning in their impulsive brains. Driven by hormonal surges, peer pressure, and, for many, an overpowering desire to obtain their driver's license, teenagers head into life at full speed with a lead foot, bad judgment, and inadequate inhibition (Canetti et al., 1997; Dahl, 2004). The toddler heads toward the stairs, drunk with the glee of being able to run through space. The adolescent heads toward sex and drugs, intoxicated with his or her newfound independence, unconcerned by any potential dangers.

The Adult Brain

It may be hard to teach old dogs new tricks, but it is also true that for some of us, the passage of time results in the attainment of wisdom. Wisdom is a different kind of trick, one that involves the integration of thoughts and feelings, perspective, compassion, and understanding. In these areas, it is *adults* who excel. The reason that wisdom often comes with age is likely due to the ongoing neural plasticity of the brain. As Mohammad Ali once said, "The man who views the world at 50 the same way he did at 20 has wasted 30 years of his life."

When we examine the changes in the physical structure of the adult brain, we see a general decrease in the number of cortical neurons (gray matter), with subcortical structures far less affected by the passage of time. The connectivity between neurons (white matter) increases into midlife and then begins to decline. Although the loss of structural mass over time is almost always interpreted as reflecting declining function, remember that apoptosis is a normal aspect of brain maturation earlier in development and correlates with increased functioning (Mesulam, 1987; Petrella et al., 2005). Is it possible that, for some aging brains, there is a new kind of programmed loss and reorganization of neural processing that correlates with increased wisdom?

Wisdom may be related to the simultaneous utilization of both hemispheres in processing information about the self and the world. In terms of cognitive processing, older adults are somewhat slower and show a bilateral pattern of brain activation (Beason-Held et al., 2005; Cabeza et al., 1997; Maguire & Frith, 2003). But is taking longer to process information necessarily a bad thing? Might neural reorganization that uses both sides of the brain give us more time to think and more information on which to base our actions? Whereas the stories of young adults are organized around their immediate personal experiences, stories from older individuals often integrate both inner and outer realities into an understanding of the world that is a central component of what we think of as wisdom. Hemispheric *integration* later in life may be an evolutionary selection, just as hemispheric *specialization* may support specific skill building more relevant to early life. Table 3.2 summarizes the changes that occur in the adult brain.

Table 3.2. **Structural Changes in the Brain During Adulthood**

Gray matter changes:	Result in/reflect:
Decreases in the density and volume of cortical gray matter (i.e., fewer neurons)	Neural systems become more focused, specific, and efficient later in life[1]
Posterior temporal lobe increases until age 30, then decreases	The initial increase and subsequent slow decrease in the brain's focus on processing and remembering external events[2]
Subcortical volume loss is much less pronounced during aging	Subcortical structures are less dependent on environmental factors and show less variability[3]
White matter changes	**Result in/reflect:**
Increases in volume until midlife and decreases thereafter	Continuing organization and connection of neural systems until 40–50 years of age, then a pruning down of systems[4]
Cerebral spinal fluid changes	**Result in/reflect:**
Volume increases throughout life	Decreases in brain size[5]

[1] Sowell et al., 2003; Bartzokis et al., 2001; Good et al., 2001; Jernigan et al., 2001; Pfefferbaum et al., 1994; [2] Sowell et al., 2003; Sowell et al., 2002; [3] Good et al., 2001; Grieve et al., 2005; [4] Bartzokis et al., 2001; Sowell et al., 2003; Ge et al., 2002; Grieve et al., 2005; Resnick et al., 2000; Guttmann et al., 1998; Pfefferbaum et al., 1994; [5] Good et al., 2001; Resnick et al., 2003; Sowell et al., 2003.

Adults whom we think of as "wise elders" are those who had higher abilities early in life, continued to grow and learn throughout life, and are evolutionarily "selected" to be the containers of cultural wisdom in their later years. Keep in mind that written language is just a few thousand years old. Before writing, cultural wisdom was transmitted orally from the old to the young. Not surprisingly, adult brains tend toward storytelling, which may reflect our obligation to transmit cultural wisdom to the next generation. Perhaps adults are at a disadvantage in many memory and IQ tests originally designed to assess the academic progress of students during childhood and adolescence. An understanding of the adult brain informs us that their ability may lie not in learning but in teaching, a task more in line with the life cycle of their brains and its evolutionary role in the maintenance and continuity of cultural knowledge.

Barbara—Wisdom 101

Barbara was a woman in her mid 50s who sought therapy for what she referred to as "empty nest syndrome." Her children had both gone off to college a few years earlier, leaving her with a less-than-satisfying marriage and a desire to pursue a graduate degree in primary education. As Barbara progressed through the first semester of her program, she had many struggles and crises of confidence. Although she remembered doing fine in college and graduating with honors, she feared that she was showing the early signs of dementia. "I'm old enough to be my classmates' mother," she told me. "They're all just out of college, used to studying and memorizing information. I just can't keep up with them. I think I'm going to flunk out!"

Although her grades were fine and she got good reviews from her professors, she said she had to study day and night just to keep up. It didn't help that her husband was critical of both her intelligence and her decision to go to school. Despite her struggles, it turns out that she was ranked near the top of her class and was being groomed for one of the better placements after completing her academic requirements. Her fellow students had come to rely on her not only for the study groups she held in her home, but for her advice on personal matters. She was told by a couple of students that her openness about her struggles and the way she applied what they were studying to her personal experiences helped them to make sense of what they were learning. Barbara also found that her young peers weren't even reading most of the materials she thought they were memorizing without effort. All of the information she gathered contradicted her fears and supported her strengths. At the end of one of these sessions, I smilingly told her, "Your self-image is in need of an overhaul."

Whereas it might be true that Barbara couldn't memorize new information as well as the 20-somethings around her, she was actually learning in a different way: not as a student but as a wise elder. For her, memorizing had been replaced by an embodiment of the information and a desire to share her learning with others. Although she dismissed the role she took in organizing study groups and cooking for her classmates as "just my mothering reflex," it was actually part of the way she simultaneously attached, learned, and taught. She integrated her new learning, her past experiences, and her relationships with those around her into her educational experience. In fact, she was told by one of her professors that he felt guilty charging her tuition because she had become like one of the faculty.

Her husband Ben was another type of elder. Uninterested in new experiences, he spent most of his time alone, watching television. He had few friends and seldom varied his routine. He found Barbara's interest and new friends threatening to his security and worried that she might outgrow him when she no longer needed a father for her children. As Barbara became more secure and confident in her new life, the focus of therapy shifted to couples work and her husband's underlying depression.

Barbara's experiences support the notion that the brain is built of millions of neurons with trillions of connections that come together to create what we call an individual. But it doesn't stop there! Nature then continues to interweave individuals in ways that expand collaboration in the service of survival. Neurons that fire together, wire together. People who are able to attend to one another, touch, talk, and connect also fire together, wire together, and survive together. Our ability to connect depends on complex and wide-ranging neural networks throughout our brains that have been shaped through millions of years of neurobiological evolution. It is to these systems and their abilities that we now turn our attention.

Chapter 4

The Social Brain:
A Thumbnail Sketch

We have the common goal of turning as much philosophy as possible into science.
—E.O. Wilson, 1998, p. 12

The human brain is a social organ criss-crossed with neural networks dedicated to receiving, processing, and communicating messages across the social synapse. If you have already studied the brain from a more traditional perspective, either as a neurologist or neuropsychologist, exploring the social brain requires some shifts in perspective. For one, the most important cortical areas are no longer those on the surface of the brain but those hidden from view. This is where the primitive structures central to our experience of self and our connection with others reside.

As part of this understanding, the cingulate and insula cortices could, and perhaps should, be considered as the fifth and sixth cortical lobes. Another shift in perspective involves cerebral dominance: For social and emotional functioning, the right side of the brain, and not the left, is the dominant hemisphere. Finally, and perhaps most important, is that we think of the brain not as a fully formed structure but as a dynamic process undergoing constant development and reconstruction across the lifespan. Keeping these three conceptual shifts in mind, let's take a look at some of the key structures and systems of the social brain.

From primitive brainstem reflexes that orient us toward our mother's voice to the participation of the broad circuitry required for acts of altruism, the entire brain participates in social behavior. The complexity of the brain makes any exploration simultaneously detail-rich and miserably incomplete. So don't worry about remembering and understanding everything we discuss the first time around. Instead, think of this chapter as an overview of the structures and systems we will explore throughout the book. Many of the upcoming chapters contain separate sections focusing on specific neural networks of the social brain. Table 4.1 outlines the neural structures, networks, and systems we will cover here and throughout the book.

Table 4.1. **Structures and Systems of the Social Brain**

Cortical and subcortical structures:

Orbital medial prefrontal; somatosensory, cingulate and insula cortices; amygdala, hippocampus, and hypothalamus

Sensory, motor, and affective systems:

Face recognition and facial expression systems; mirror and resonance systems

Regulatory systems:

Stress regulation (the HPA system of hormonal regulation)
Fear regulation (orbital medial prefrontal cortex–amygdala balance)
Social engagement (the vagal system of autonomic regulation)
Social motivation (reward representation and reinforcement)

Cortical and Subcortical Structures

Three structures—the orbital medial prefrontal, insula, and cingulate cortices—are the most evolutionarily primitive areas of the cortex. Buried beneath and within the folds of the cortex like ancient stones covered by moss, they are surrounded by later developing cortical structures. In fact, the actual neural structures of the insula and cingulate cortices are a mixture of an earlier evolving three-layer organization typical of limbic structures and a later evolving six-layer organization seen throughout most of the rest of the cortex. In one of the parallels between ontogeny (development of the individual) and phylogeny (evolution of the species), the more primitive cortical regions develop earlier than the rest of the cerebral cortex.

Whereas most of the cortex, especially the somatosensory cortex, is involved with the processing of external sensory information, motor movements, and decision making, these structures are involved with our emotions and internal experience and maintain a deep and intimate connection with primitive limbic structures. Because of their hidden location and minimal involvement in readily observable behaviors (such as walking and talking), they have not played a prominent role in the history of neurology. However, when we shift our focus to caretaking, relationships, and emotional experience, these cortices are more important than many of the structures that cover them. One of the primary jobs of five of the six cortical lobes (cingulate, insula, parietal, temporal, occipital) is to process internal and external information, combine it with past experience, and feed this information forward to the prefrontal lobe (the sixth cortical lobe) for analysis and decision making (see Figure 4.1).

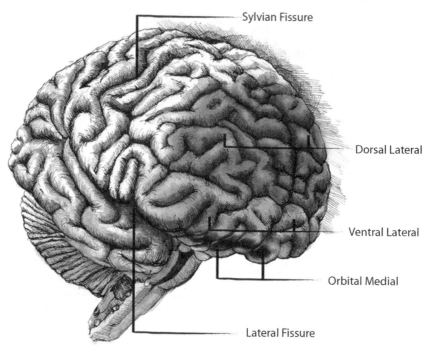

Figure 4.1. **A frontal view of the brain showing the three major regions of the prefrontal cortex and the fissures that border the frontal lobes.**

The subcortical structures that are central for processing social information include the amygdala, hippocampus, and hypothalamus (Adolphs, 2003). The amygdala is a key component in neural networks associated with experiences of fear, attachment, early memory, and emotion across the lifespan. The hippocampus organizes explicit memory and conscious learning in collaboration with the amygdala, the cerebral cortex, and other structures. The hypothalamus translates many of our social interactions into bodily processes via the hypothalamus–pituitary–adrenal (HPA) axis (see Figure 4.2).

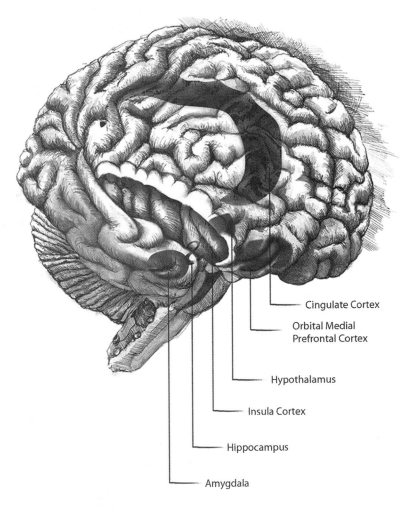

Cingulate Cortex

Orbital Medial
Prefrontal Cortex

Hypothalamus

Insula Cortex

Hippocampus

Amygdala

Figure 4.2. **These structures are hidden beneath the surface of the brain.**

Besides the orbital and medial regions, the prefrontal cortex includes the most recently evolved structures and is considered the highest-order executive region of the brain. Although the prefrontal lobes are not involved in any of the brain's basic sensory or motor processing, they do receive highly processed information from all other brain regions. The prefrontal lobes organize and coordinate the constant stream of incoming information and utilize it to perform tasks such as affect regulation, planning, coordinating actions with intended goals, and abstract reasoning (Barbas et al., 2003; Dias, Robbins, & Roberts, 1996; Gray, Braver, & Raichle, 2002; Ingvar, 1985; Mega et al., 1997; Öngür & Price, 2000). Together, all the regions of the prefrontal cortex work to coordinate attention, cognition, and affective functioning (Bechara, Damasio, & Damasio, 2000; Gehring & Willoughby, 2002).

Orbital Medial Prefrontal Cortex

The orbital medial prefrontal cortex (OMPFC) sits at the apex of the neural networks of the social brain. In structure, function, and connectivity, it is as much an extension of the limbic system as it is a full citizen of the cerebral cortex (Fuster, 1997; Mesulam & Mufson, 1982). It serves as a convergence zone (association area) for polysensory and emotional information; its direct connections with the hypothalamus allow it to integrate information from the external and internal worlds with the emotion, motivation, and reward systems. Its inhibitory role in autonomic functioning, via the amygdala and other subcortical structures, allows it to participate in vital functions of affect regulation (Fuster, 1985; Schore, 1994). These interconnections allow social information to be gathered from, and transmitted back to, all of the sensory systems in order to be immediately employed to guide perceptions, actions, and interactions.

Somatosensory Cortex

The somatosensory cortex, located at the front-most portion of the parietal lobes, processes information about bodily experiences. It lies just behind the central gyrus and wraps deep within the sylvian fissure that divides the parietal from the frontal lobes. Along with the insula and anterior cingulate cortices, it contains multiple representations of the body that process and organize our experience of touch, temperature, pain, joint position, and our visceral state. All in all, these different processing streams combine to create our experience of our somatic selves. The somatosensory cortex also participates in what we call intuition or "gut feelings" by activating implicit memories related to our experiences and helping us to make decisions with conviction (Damasio, 1994). Why do we include the somatosensory cortex and this larger system as part of the social brain? First, it is experience-dependent and forms in the context of early relationships. Second, the experience of our own bodies becomes the model for our connection, understanding, and empathy in relationship with others (Damasio et al., 2000).

Cingulate Cortex

The cingulate cortex is a primitive association area of visceral, motor, tactile, autonomic, and emotional information that begins to participate in brain activity during the second month of life (Kennard, 1955). It first appeared during evolution in animals exhibiting maternal behavior, play, nursing, and when making sounds became involved with communication between predator and prey, potential mates, and mother and child (MacLean, 1985). Amphibians, reptiles, and more ancient animals lack a cingulate cortex as well as long-term social and emotional bonds. The caretaking and resonance behaviors made possible by the cingulate also provide an important component of the neural infrastructure for social cooperation and empathy (Rilling et al., 2002).

The integration of some aspects of cognitive and emotional processes is regulated by the cingulate, as well as the activation, modulation, and coordination of frontal and motor circuitry (Bush, Luu, & Posner, 2000; Paus et al., 1993; Sutherland et al., 1988). Destruction of the anterior cingulate in mammals results in mutism, a loss of maternal responses, infant death due to neglect, and emotional and autonomic instability (Bush, Luu, & Posner, 2000; Bush et al., 2002; Joseph, 1996; Jürgens & von Cramon, 1982).

Insula Cortex

The insula begins life on the lateral surfaces of the brain, only to become hidden by the rapid expansion of the frontal and temporal lobes. We find it by exploring the depths of the lateral fissure or by cutting away the lateral portion of the frontal lobes. The location of the insula—and the fact that its functions are related to internal experience—has made our understanding of it relatively sketchy. Based on our present understanding, the insula is described as the "limbic integration cortex" because of its massive connections to all limbic structures and its feed-forward links with the frontal, parietal, and temporal lobes (Augustine, 1996).

Like the sensory and motor cortices, the insula is organized somatotopically (i.e., like a map of the body). It appears to provide a means to connect primitive bodily states with the experience and expression of bodily awareness, emotion, and behavior (Carr et al., 2003; Phan et al., 2002). In tandem with the anterior cingulate, the insula allows us to be aware of what is happening inside our bodies and reflect on our emotional experiences (Bechara & Naqvi, 2004; Critchley et al., 2004; Gundel et al., 2004). Facial expressions, changes in the direction of eye gaze, and the awareness of untrustworthy others all activate the insula (Kawashima et al., 1999; Morris, Friston, et al., 1998). Damage to the right insula can result in anosognosia, a condition wherein a patient seems unaware of, and unfazed by, severe paralysis on the left side of the body (Garavan, Ross, & Stein, 1999). Recent research suggests that the insula is involved with mediating the entire range of emotions from disgust to love (Bartels & Zeki, 2000; Calder, 2003).

Amygdala

What we call the amygdala is actually a set of interconnected nuclei (or large clusters of neurons) centrally involved in attention, learning, and emotion. The amygdala specializes in the appraisal of danger and mediates many aspects of the fight-flight response and emotional memory (Davis, 1997; Ono, Nishijo, & Uwano, 1995; Phelps & Anderson, 1997). Combined with the anterior cingulate and OMPFC, the amygdala guides decision making and adaptive responses based on past learning (Baxter et al, 2000). The central (middle) and basal (bottom) portions of the amygdala are more primitive structures involved with rapid, automatic reactions to environmental dangers, signaling the sympathetic nervous system to activate the fight-flight response. The direct connection of the amygdala with the autonomic nervous system serves to translate its appraisals into immediate survival reactions. Amazingly, the amygdala achieves a high degree of maturity by the eighth month of gestation, allowing it to associate a fear response to a stimulus *prior* to birth (LaBar et al., 1995; Ulfig, Setzer, & Bohl, 2003).

Hippocampus

The hippocampus is situated at the junction between the cortex and limbic system on both sides of the brain. In lower mammals such as the rat, the hippocampus is a specialized spatial map of foraging territory. In humans the parietal lobes evolved from the hippocampus and assist it in complex visual–spatial processing. The human hippocampus and its adjacent structures have become specialized in the organization of spatial, sequential, and emotional learning and memory (Edelman, 1989; Mc-Gaugh et al., 1993; Sherry et al., 1992; Zola-Morgan & Squire, 1990). In contrast to the amygdala, the hippocampus is a late bloomer, continuing to develop into early adulthood (Benes, 1989). Our lack of conscious memory for early childhood, known as childhood amnesia, is likely due to the slow developmental course of the hippocampus (Fuster, 1996; Jacobs et al., 2000; McCarthy, 1995).

Hypothalamus

The hypothalamus is a small and ancient structure that sits at the center of the brain, below the thalamus and halfway between the cortex and the brainstem. It has extensive connections with the structures of the social brain within the frontal lobes, limbic system, and brainstem. I include the hypothalamus as part of the social brain because it is centrally involved with the translation of conscious experience into bodily processes and thus the transduction of early experience into the building of the brain and body. Its various nuclei organize many bodily functions, such as temperature regulation, hunger, thirst, and activity level.

The hypothalamus is also involved in the regulation of sexual behavior and aggression. As the head of the HPA (hypothalamic–pituitary–adrenal) axis, it translates brain processes into hormonal secretions from the anterior pituitary. Among the hormones produced by the pituitary, FSH (follicle-stimulating hormone) and prolactin are involved in reproduction and nursing. ACTH (adrenocorticotropic hormone), which is sent to the adrenal glands via the bloodstream, stimulates the production of cortisol, our primary stress hormone.

Sensory, Motor, and Affective Systems

It is in the temporal lobes that our senses are integrated, organized, and combined with deep primitive drives of emotional significance in a "vertical" linkup of all three levels of the triune brain (Adams et al., 1997). This convergence of information allows us to make rapid survival-related decisions in response to complex social input such as eye gaze, facial expressions, and body postures. Cells involved both in reading and identifying facial expressions are located in adjacent areas of the temporal lobes (Desimone, 1991; Hasselmo et al., 1989). Neurons in the temporal lobes have also been shown to detect identity, eye contact, and an open mouth—all vital information for primate survival (Brothers & Ring, 1993).

Face Recognition and Facial Expression Systems

When we see faces, the areas of the brain that become activated lie in a processing stream dedicated to the identification of visual stimuli. This ventral "what" tract of visual processing starts at the back of the brain in the occipital lobe and then crosses through the parietal lobe and the temporal lobe on its way to the frontal lobe (Lu et al., 1991). The association region of the occipital lobe dedicated to the identification of faces is the fusiform face area (FFA)(Gauthier et al. 2000; Halgren et al., 1999). Within this tract, highly processed visual information from the rest of the occipital lobe is combined and interconnected with other clusters of cells that are responsible for eye gaze, body posture, and facial expression as the brain constructs complex perceptions from basic visual building blocks (Jellema et al., 2000). As tasks change, so do the brain regions recruited for analysis. If a face we look at contains emotion, the amygdala becomes activated in the right hemisphere; when we are asked to put a name to a face, the hippocampus becomes activated on the left side of the brain.

Regions in the anterior (front) portions of the superior temporal sulcus (STS; a *sulcus* is an infolding on the surface of the cortex) integrate information about various aspects of the same person (form, location, and motion), allowing us to identify others from different angles, in various places, and while they are in motion (Jellema, Maassen, & Perrett, 2004; Pelphrey, Mitchell, et al., 2003; Vaina et al., 2001). The invariant aspects of faces are represented in the FFA; the changeable ones are processed in the STS. Both familiar and unfamiliar faces cause activation

in the FFA, but the left amygdala only appears to be activated by unknown faces that may need to be evaluated for their positive or negative
(safe or unsafe?) value (Dubois et al., 1999).

Mirror and Resonance Systems

The STS also contains what have come to be called "mirror neurons." These
neurons are activated either when we witness others engaging in functional
behaviors (such as using a tool or picking up an object) or when we ourselves engage in these actions. By bridging neural networks dedicated to
perception and movement, mirror neurons connect the observed and the
observer by linking visual and motor experience. Mirror systems are suspected to be involved with many social functions, including learning, the
evolution of gestural and verbal language, and empathic attunement.

Have you ever found yourself reflexively looking up because you saw
other people doing it? How about yawning soon after another person
yawns? Or maybe, while at the movies, you find yourself imitating the
expressions of one of your favorite movie stars during a particularly sus-
penseful scene. These are what are known as *resonance behaviors*. These
behaviors (based on mirror systems) are the reflexive imitation responses
we make when interacting with others. Whereas mechanisms for resonance may have originally evolved to synchronize group behaviors such
as hunting, gathering, and migration, connections with visceral and
emotional circuitry now allow the same systems to support emotional
resonance, attunement, and empathy (Rizzolatti & Arbib, 1998; Rizzolatti et al., 1999). It is hypothesized that mirror systems and resonance
behaviors evolved into our ability to attune to the emotional states of
others. They provide us with a visceral–emotional experience of what the
other is experiencing, allowing us to know others from the inside out.

Regulatory Systems

The body's regulatory systems are involved in the maintenance of internal homeostatic processes, balancing approach and avoidance, excitation
and inhibition, and fight and flight responses. They also control metabolism, arousal, and our immunological functioning. It is through these
systems that we regulate our own and each other's biological and
emotional states.

Stress Regulation (HPA) System

The hypothalamic–pituitary–adrenal axis (HPA) regulates the secretion of hormones involved with the body's response to stress and threat. Immediate reaction to stress is vital for short-term survival, whereas rapid return to normalization after the threat has passed is essential for long-term survival. Prolonged stress, such as the type that occurs with attachment disturbances, parental deprivation, or prolonged traumatic stress, results in system damage and breakdown. The long-term effects of such trauma are mediated via the HPA system.

Fear Regulation System

What is our experience of fear? We turn to the amygdala again, because it alerts a variety of brain centers that a fight-flight response is required. In turn, the activation of the sympathetic branch of the autonomic nervous system results in symptoms of anxiety, agitation, and panic. The prime directive of the amygdala is to pair stimuli with a fear response to protect us. The amygdala works so fast that it can pair stimuli and a fear response far ahead of conscious awareness.

On the other side of the fear regulatory system is the orbital medial prefrontal cortex (OMPFC), which has a reciprocal relationship with the amygdala in that the OMPFC can inhibit the amygdala based on conscious awareness (Beer et al., 2003) (see Figure 4.3). By the same token, when we are very frightened (i.e., have high levels of amygdala activation), the OMPFC becomes inhibited, and we have a difficult time being rational, logical, and in control of our thoughts. Since the networks connecting the OMPFC and the amygdala are shaped by experience, our learning history of what is safe and dangerous, including our attachment schema, are thought to be encoded within this system.

Social Engagement System

The tenth cranial nerve, also called the vagus, is actually not a single nerve but a complex communication system between the brain and body. The vagus system extends from the brainstem to multiple points within the body, including the heart, lungs, throat, and digestive system. Its afferent (sensory) and efferent (motor) fibers allow for rapid continuous feedback between

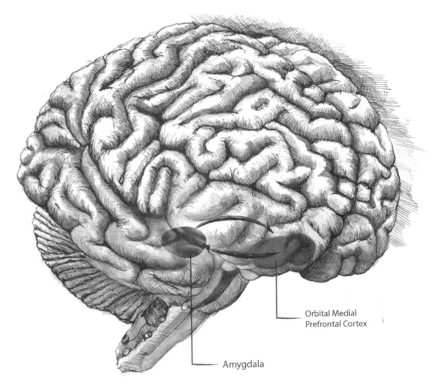

Orbital Medial
Prefrontal Cortex

Amygdala

Figure 4.3. **The networks connecting the orbital medial prefrontal cortex and the amygdala are hypothesized to be involved with fear conditioning, emotional regulation, and attachment schema.**

brain and body to promote homeostatic regulation and the optimal maintenance of physical health and emotional well-being (Porges, Doussard-Roosevelt, & Maiti, 1994). The vagus system is a central component of the autonomic nervous system. In the absence of external challenge, the vagus works to enhance digestion, growth, and social communication. When a challenge does arise, a decrease in vagal activation facilitates sympathetic arousal, high energy output, and the fight-flight response. The vagus allows us to maintain continued social engagement by modulating and fine-tuning sympathetic arousal during emotional interpersonal exchanges.

Social Motivation System

Nelson and Panksepp (1998) postulate the existence of a "social motivation" system modulated by oxytocin, vasopressin, endogenous endorphins, and other neurochemicals related to reward, decreased physical pain, and feelings of well-being. Although conserved from more primitive approach-avoidance and pain regulation circuitry, the social motivation system extends into the amygdala, anterior cingulate, and orbital medial prefrontal cortex. These circuits and neurochemicals are thought to regulate attachment, pair bonding, empathy, and altruistic behavior. Put in a slightly different way, Fisher (1998) suggests that the social motivation system can be divided into three categories: those involved in (1) bonding and attachment (regulated by peptides, vasopressin, and oxytocin), (2) attraction (regulated by dopamine and other catecholamines), and (3) sex drive (regulated by androgens and estrogens).

In addition, the dopamine reward system of a subcortical area known as the ventral striatum is involved with more complex analysis of social motivation. The ventral striatum becomes activated with an expectation of a social reward, such as when we anticipate positive attention (Kampe et al., 2001; Pagnoni, Zink, Montague, & Berns, 2002; Schultz et al., 1992). For example, once the cortex has determined that we find someone attractive, the ventral striatum becomes activated when he or she looks our way, giving the signal that the possibility for being rewarded with a desirable outcome has increased (Elliott, Friston, et al., 2000; Schultz et al., 1997; Schultz, 1998). The activation of the ventral striatum translates the anticipation of reward into a physical impulse to approach. In this way, those whom we find attractive exert what feels like a gravitational pull on us.

Linda—"My Husband Makes Me Sick"

A few years ago I received the following voice-mail message at work: "Uh, hello there, my name's Linda, and I got your name from a friend who recommended that I call you. I'm a nervous wreck, I'm burnt out at work, and my husband makes me sick. Please call me when you get the chance." Not such an unusual message to leave for a therapist. My first thought was that Linda was suffering from anxiety, possibly depression, and that she might be having some marital difficulties. Without giving it very much thought, I assumed that saying her husband makes her sick was a euphemism to express her annoyance with him. At the time, it never occurred to me to take this statement literally.

Later that week, Linda came in for her first session. True to her word, she was anxious and worn out. She and her husband Richard had been married for almost 2 years and had a 10-month-old baby named Lucy. After introducing herself, Linda's expression lightened and her voice became higher as she spoke about her job as an account executive and how much she enjoyed raising Lucy. But when she began speaking of Richard, she lowered the tone of her voice and her face grew serious, almost somber. "Richard," she said unsmiling, "is always anxious. He's an overachiever. At first I found that to be totally attractive, but now it's like everything is a competition, a race, a referendum on his quality as a person. The only way he can relax is to drink wine or smoke marijuana. Otherwise, he just sits there fidgeting until he darts off to the next thing."

Before the baby came, Linda and Richard seemed to get along pretty well, and they would both drink and smoke together to relax. The trouble began when Linda became pregnant, straight, and sober. For her part, she found being pregnant relaxing, and it seemed to put her job into perspective. However, it was a different story for Richard. "Over the last year and a half," Linda told me, "Richard has made me more and more crazy. I've always been a pretty calm person, but being around him makes me a nervous wreck. It's just like he became completely stressed out as soon as I got pregnant, and he's still a nervous wreck now. It's as if his nervousness and agitation are contagious. Even when we're in separate rooms, I can feel his anxiety through the walls, and I get tense. The only time I feel good is when he's at work, but even then I worry about him calling me in a crisis about something and getting me all worked up. His anxiety is wearing me out. I keep getting colds, aches and pains, and I don't have any energy. I feel like it's crazy, letting him affect me like this. He says everything's fine and I'm the one who's crazy. Maybe I *am* crazy? What do you think?"

After assuring her that she seemed anxious and exhausted, but very sane, we discussed her family history for the rest of that session and most of the next. Linda had grown up in an emotionally chaotic family where being attuned to the feelings and moods of others was vital for day-to-day survival. She retained her sensitivity to the feelings and needs of others into adolescence and adulthood, which made her so successful working with her "high-strung" celebrity clients. To help Linda feel a bit saner, I took a few minutes to discuss the networks of the social brain.

I explained that evolution had shaped many neural networks to read the behaviors, intentions, and inner emotions of others and that a childhood such as she had experienced would fine-tune these circuits and make them supersensitive to those around her. Thus, what allowed her to survive childhood and be successful at work also made her more vulnerable to her husband's anxiety.

I described to Linda how the networks that receive and send social communication are interwoven with others that regulate our own emotions, moods, energy level, psychological health, and our ability to fight off illnesses. Anxiety *is* contagious, I told her, and, transmitted via mirror and resonance systems, it alerts our muscles to respond; it activates our fear and alarm circuitry through the amygdala down through the HPA axis and spreads throughout the body. Because of all of the networks of the social brain, interacting with her husband could make her sick. Not only that, it could reduce her energy, increase her difficulty in learning new information, and increase the difficulty of solving problems that, in the past, she could have handled with ease.

Networks of the Social Brain

What were the pragmatic solutions to Linda's problems? Richard had to learn how to relax and/or Linda had to develop ways of desensitizing her resonance systems and develop better boundaries. Because Richard wasn't aware of a problem, it would be up to Linda to learn to create better boundaries for herself. Becoming aware of a lack of boundaries can often allow people to begin experimenting with creating them. Moment-by-moment she had to become aware of her own internal state and differentiate it from her husband's. Slowly she had to learn to replace other peoples' feelings with feelings of her own. This process is an excellent example of how conscious consideration of an internal state, via the orbital medial prefrontal, insula, and anterior cingulate cortices and other areas of the social brain, allows us to modulate our emotions and alter our state of mind. It is via these circuits that psychotherapy is able to change the brain. Over the months to come, Linda and I worked on creating boundaries and making her resonance systems a bit less sensitive.

Based on our present level of understanding, the structures, networks, and systems described in this chapter comprise the core components of the social brain. Separating them from the rest of the brain, although absurd in reality, is a way for us to gain an understanding of how brains link together with one another. Because of these brain systems you are able to feel soothed by your husband's voice or become enraged by his infidelity. They allow us to tell a story in a gesture or a glance. They translate good relationships into a sense of well-being and robust physical health. They can also take early abuse and neglect and turn them into a lifetime of anxiety, fear, and illness.

Throughout the chapters that follow, I refer to these systems as we examine different aspects of brain development, parenting, psychopathology, and everyday social functioning. We also revisit them in more depth as we explore the terrain of relationships, attachment, interpersonal communication, and a myriad of other ways in which humans connect and reconnect through the life of the social brain.

Chapter 5

Social and Emotional Laterality

If a story doesn't work emotionally, it does not work at all.

—Yann Martel, 1993, p. viii

More than a century ago, the left cortex was dubbed the "dominant" hemisphere because of its leading role in language. Damage to an area in the left frontal lobe (called Broca's area) resulted in a consistent disturbance in language. It was this initial brain–behavior connection upon which the fledgling field of neurology staked its claim. It was also the first solid piece of evidence that specific functions might exist in distinct areas, lending support to what was called the "localizationist" theory of brain functioning. In time, more relationships were discovered between specific functions and areas of the cortex (see Figures 5.1 and 5.2).

We have learned a great deal about the brain over the last 100 years, and our ideas about the roles of each hemisphere and their working relationship with one another have become increasingly sophisticated. Although it remains true that the left hemisphere usually takes the lead in semantic and conscious processing, social and emotional dominance leans toward the right.

As the story of the brain has expanded, we have discovered that mammals are characterized by a right-hemispheric bias in the control of emotion, bodily experience, and autonomic processes. This asymmetry is found not just in the cerebral cortex but in subcortical and brainstem structures as well. The right cortex is also far more densely connected with subcortical regions than the left (Shapiro, Jamner, & Spence, 1997;

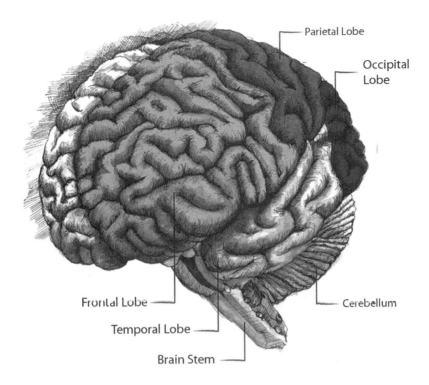

Figure 5.1. **The major topographical regions of the cerebral cortex: the four cortical lobes on the surface of the cortex, the cerebellum, and the brainstem.**

Stuss & Alexander, 1999). For example, the social engagement system utilizes a network of autonomic and emotional control in the right cortex, the right central nucleus of the amygdala, and the right-sided nuclei of the hypothalamus (Porges et al., 1994). Because the right brain is grounded in bodily and emotional experience, it serves as the infrastructure of many primitive components of social brain functioning. The experience of a personal emotional self, as opposed to the social self, also appears to be primarily organized in the right hemisphere (Keenan et al., 2000).

Right-brain functions are similar to Freud's notion of the unconscious. They develop earlier, are guided by emotional and bodily reactions, and their nonlinear mode of processing allows for multiple overlapping realities. These and other characteristics make right-brain functioning similar to Freud's conception of the primary process thinking of early

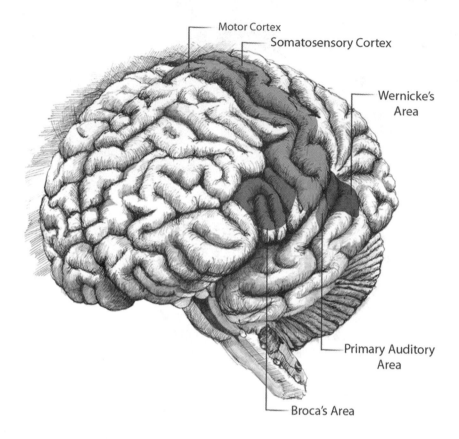

Figure 5.2. **Regions of interest to the field of neurology in the exploration of brain–behavior relationships: Wernicke's area (receptive language), Broca's area (expressive speech), motor cortex (motor behavior), somatosensory cortex (sensory experience), primary auditory area (audition).**

childhood and the apparent illogic of dreams in adult life. Perhaps most significantly, the right brain responds to negative emotional stimuli prior to conscious awareness. Thus unconscious emotional processing based on past experiences invisibly guides our moment-to-moment thoughts, feelings, and behaviors (Kimura et al., 2004). The phenomena of projection and transference—central to Freud's case for the existence and influence of the unconscious—are generated through these networks. Because the right brain develops first, it organizes and stores many early social and emotional experiences that can emerge in later relationships, especially when we are under stress.

The bias against left-handedness across many cultures reflects an intuitive understanding of the relationship of the left hand (right brain) to the more primitive, uncivilized, and dark aspects of our nature. Some of these biases date back to prehistory, when the left hemisphere may have exerted less control over the right, leading humans to be less "polite" and more dangerous. By offering the right hand in greeting, early humans may have been more likely to speak and behave in a "civil" manner, and less likely to act out their primitive and dangerous impulses. Five-thousand-year-old cave drawings depicting right-handed hunters suggest that the bias toward right-handedness existed even then (Coren & Porac, 1977).

Although we can only speculate about the reasons for the evolution of hemispheric specialization, it obviously provides increased neural "real estate" for the development of new skills and abilities, instead of having redundant hemispheres performing identical functions. The dominance of the right hemisphere for bodily and emotional functioning and its ability to process this information reflexively and unconsciously have freed the left cortex to attend more to the environment and to engage in logical and abstract reasoning. Meanwhile, the increasing ability of the left hemisphere to filter and inhibit input from the right has enhanced the dissociation between the cognitive and emotional processing of the left and right sides of the brain (Porges, 1994). And although this increasing inhibitory ability has led the left hemisphere to greater cognitive heights as it developed the capacity to separate itself from the body and emotions, it can also result in too great a separation between mind and body. Experiencing the world from high atop the left hemisphere led Descartes to equate human existence with thinking, much to the detriment of philosophy and neurology. Thus we have found that with specialization and increasingly complex interrelationships, the brain also became vulnerable to the types of dissociation we see in psychological disturbances. Table 5.1 summarizes hemispheric biases of the social brain.

Development

Through primate evolution, not only have the hemispheres grown increasingly different in their functional specialization, but their developmental

Table 5.1. Hemispheric Biases of the Social Brain

Left Hemisphere	Right Hemisphere
General Hemsipheric Biases	
Cognition	Emotion[1]
Semantics	Prosody/gestures[2]
Abstract abilities	Somatic regulation[3]
Detail analysis	Global analysis[4]
Humor/mania	Sadness/depression[5]
Moderate arousal	High levels of arousal[6]
Hemsipheric Biases of the Social Brain	
Approach	Bonding/affiliation[7]
	Avoidance[8]
Other awareness	Self awareness[9]
Social emotions	Personal emotions[10]
Positive affect	Negative affect[11]
	Reading facial expressions[12]
	Reading gaze directions[13]
	Facial recognition[14]
	Intonation[15]

Note: References in superscript apply to both left and right columns. *Note:* Table content drawn from the following sources: [1] Stuss & Alexander, 1999; Voeller et al., 1988; [2] Borod, 1993; Bowers et al., 1993; Lattner et al., 2005; Cutting, 1992; Goldberg & Costa, 1981; [3] Spence et al., 1996; Shapiro et al., 1997; Anderson & Phelps, 2000; [4] Nebes, 1971; Galin, 1974; Rossion et al., 2000; Semmes, 1968; [5] Pascual-Leone Ribio et al., 1996; Pascal-Leone, Wasserman, et al., 1996; Klein et al., 1999; Grisaru et al., 1998; Hénriques & Davidson, 1991; [6] Lane & Jennings, 1995; Schiffer et al., 1995; [7] Henry et al., 1984; Shapiro et al., 1997; [8] Sutton & Davidson, 1997; [9] Keenan et al., 2000; Platek et al., 2004; [10] Best & Queen, 1989; Ross et al., 1994; Van Lancker, 1991; [11] Borod et al., 1986; [12] Ahern et al., 1991; Borod et al., 1986; Dimberg & Petterson, 2000; Dopson et al., 1984; Hugdahl et al., 1989; Johnsen & Hugdahl, 1991; Mandal & Ambady, 2004; Moscovitch & Olds, 1982; [13] Ricciardelli et al., 2002; Watanabe et al., 2002; [14] Haxby et al., 1999; Katanoda et al., 2000; Platek et al., 2004; [15] Nicholson et al., 2003.

timelines have taken divergent paths. The right hemisphere experiences a growth spurt during the first 18 months of life, whereas areas of the left are held back for later-developing abilities (Gould, 1977; Chiron et al., 1997). During these critical 18 months, the child learns hand–eye coordination, crawling, and walking—all while becoming acquainted with his or her world. Countless early interactions shape right-brain circuitry to recognize and react to the people around us, shaping our subsequent responses to others, our sense of safety and danger, and our ability to regulate our emotions. Although the social brain is capable of learning throughout life, stable attachment patterns are apparent by the end of the first year (Ainsworth, Blehar, Waters, & Wall, 1978) (see Figure 5.3).

The orbital medial prefrontal cortex (OMPFC) is the first region of the frontal lobe to develop and is larger in the right hemisphere. Richly connected with subcortical networks of learning, memory, and emotion, the right-biased OMPFC connects more directly with the body, modulating vagal tone and HPA functioning (Barbas, 1995; Price, 1999; Porges, 2003b; Sullivan & Gratton, 2002). These connections reflect the role of the OMPFC as the executive center of the right-hemispheric networks of attachment, social relationships, affect

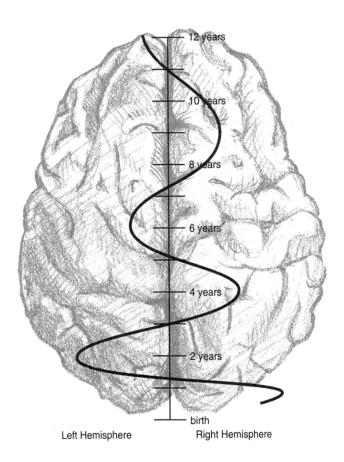

Left Hemisphere   Right Hemisphere

Figure 5.3. **Alternating growth spurts of the right and left cerebral hemispheres during childhood. Image adapted from Thatcher et al., 1987.**

regulation, and higher-level input into bodily homeostasis. These systems are built during childhood in an experience-dependent manner through the attunement and connections of the right hemispheres of parent and child.

The linking up of right hemispheres is accomplished through eye contact, facial expressions, soothing vocalizations, caresses, and exciting exchanges. Sensitive caretakers learn to regulate their interactions with their child, respond to the child's responses, and allow for synchronized engagement and disengagement. As children and caretakers move in and out of attunement, the cycle of joining, separating, and reuniting becomes the central aspects of developing psychobiological regulation. Caretakers intuitively slacken their scaffolding as their childrens' self-regulatory capacities increase. Through these separations and reunions, their children learn that they can survive on their own, that caretakers return, and that they (children) have some ability to regulate their bodily and emotional states on their own.

Damage to the right hemisphere compromises our ability to interpret the significance of facial expressions, hand gestures, and tone of voice (Blonder, Bowers, & Heilman, 1991; Searleman, 1977). Right OMPFC lesions result in difficulties not only in reading emotional facial expressions, but limit the impact of others' facial expressions on our behavior (Zald & Kim, 2001). Deprivation of visual input to the right hemisphere during infancy results in deficits in the ability to identify faces, whereas the same lack of input to the left hemisphere results in no such deficit (Le Grand, Mondloch, Maurer, & Brent, 2003).

Integration

As the brain grows over the first years of life, so does the experience of self. Soon after birth, the insula and cingulate cortices begin to organize the early sense of the body and the ability to differentiate self from others. As the parietal lobes develop, an integrated sense of the self as a whole within the environment gradually takes shape. All the while, the networks of the OMPFC, amygdala, and related structures are building networks of attachment and affect regulation. Later, autobiographical memory will rely on these somatic, emotional, and physical sensations to construct the stories of the self that will further shape our identities.

As the fibers of the connecting corpus callosum mature, they facilitate increased communication and integration between the two sides of the brain. The right and left hemispheres gradually come to cooperate in an analysis of both global (right) and specific (left) aspects of our surroundings (Fink, Halligan, et al., 1996; Rossion et al., 2000). Thus, our emerging experience of self results from the coordination and synchrony of circuits in the right and left hemispheres. Although some circuits organize aspects of conscious awareness, most serve as the background "glue" of our experience, an interwoven network of sensory, motor, and affective circuitry. When conditions are right, all of these networks integrate to provide us with the experience of a safe, coherent, and livable inner world.

Our physical experience provides us with patterns of bodily movements, relationships between objects, and a sense of ourselves in space—a kind of sensory, motor, visceral grid—that serve as the infrastructure of our developing thought (Johnson, 1987). As children, we might repeatedly put blocks into a pail and then dump them back out. We may experience the acts of eating and drinking as putting something into our body, only to have it come back out, and when we go to sleep, we may see it as disappearing into bed each night and then reappearing each morning. These repeated patterns of physical containment are used to organize and understand more abstract notions, such as when we "come out" of hiding during a game of hide and seek, when we manage to "get out" of trouble, or when we "fall in" love. Our experience and understanding of these concepts are embedded in our physical sense of moving in and out of containment (Johnson, 1987). Abstract notions are tied to our bodies through metaphor, thus connecting our minds to the world through the experience of our bodies.

Countless learning experiences are organized and stored in right-hemisphere networks; these stored experiences give rise to what we call "gut feelings." Patients with OMPFC or somatosensory cortex damage have difficulty drawing upon past experiences when making decisions. They may be able to understand the points for or against a choice but lack a "feel" for the right choice that would allow them to "pull the trigger" and make a decision. It can be assumed that this final step (more emotional than cognitive) requires a "sense" of certainty that comes more from the body than from thought. This perspective has led to the idea of "somatic markers" as a kind of visceral–emotional shorthand providing unconscious input into our conscious choices (Damasio, 1994). In this sense we see that emotions derive ultimately from the physical self, we learn to access our bodily grid to locate ourselves within the world, and we ground the idea of our unique self within it.

Emotions

Whereas more primitive organisms use heat or smell to make approach/ avoidance decisions, we use reflexive bodily activation and our emotions to discern whether something is positive or negative (Damasio et al., 2000; Schulkin, Thompson, & Rosen, 2003). Positive emotions orient us to stay on course and explore the environment, whereas negative emotions lead us to make adjustments to our situation (Cacioppo & Gardner, 1999). Emotions are our conscious experiences and interpretations of our bodily states, involving many of the brain's neural networks (Calder, Lawrence, & Young, 2001). Because our thoughts and emotions are so interconnected, it is difficult to know if they are distinct from one another or really different aspects of the same neural processes (Damasio, 1995; Panksepp, 2003).

Still, hemispheric bias does exist with regard to emotions: The left hemisphere appears biased toward positive (approach) emotions, whereas the right seems biased toward negative (withdrawal) emotions (Canli et al., 1998; Davidson, 1992; Davidson et al., 1990; Paradiso et al., 1999). A history of depression or current depressed affect correlates with decreased left frontal activation (Henriques & Davidson, 1990; 1991). States of stress, anxiety, fear, trauma, and pain all result in heightened activation in right-sided structures (Baker & Kim, 2004; Hari et al., 1997; Rauch et al., 1996; Spivak et al., 1998; Wittling, 1997).

In response to playing a competitive game, the right amygdala is activated by losing whereas the left is activated by winning (Zalla et al., 2000). Even when we watch movies, greater left frontal activation is correlated with more intense positive affect during the film and a better review afterward (Wheeler et al., 1993). Infants who tend to cry in response to maternal separation show higher right frontal EEG activation when compared to infants who do not cry (Davidson & Fox, 1989). This same pattern of activation occurs in children of depressed mothers during the expression of negative (but not positive) emotions (Dawson, Panagiotides, Klinger, & Spieker, 1997).

What we experience as negative emotions—those that lead us to fight, flee, or distance ourselves from something or someone—are evolutionarily more primitive than positive emotions. Positive feelings related to humor, social affiliation, and aesthetic responses have arisen as a function of an expanded neocortex and the specializations of the hemispheres (Paradiso et al., 1999; Wild et al., 2003). An unfortunate artifact of the evolution of laterality may be that the right hemisphere, biased toward negative emotions and pessimism, develops first and serves as the core of self-awareness and self-identity (Keenan et al., 1999). To be human may be to have vulnerability toward shame, guilt, and depression. So although both sides of the brain are involved in emotion, the dominant role of the right hemisphere in defensive and negative emotions gives it executive "veto power" over the left. Just as the left can block emotional and visceral input from the right, the right can override conscious processing and emotional well-being in reaction to threat.

Pedro—Something Is Just Not Right

Pedro and I met while we were both working at a veterans' hospital. He was an engineer responsible for keeping the buildings functioning, whereas my job was to tame the chaos within. We would often chat on a shaded bench about sports, politics, or our favorite topic: the illogic of the VA system. Once, after Pedro had been absent for a few days, I heard that he had been in a car accident. I was told that it was nothing too serious—he was just taking some time off and would be back in a week or 2. When Pedro returned, we met at our usual spot. He told me that his car had been hit broadside while going through an intersection and his head had bounced off the side glass. He was still a bit black and blue, and I noticed that the left side of his face looked stiff and still, refusing to participate in the normal flux of expressions displayed on the right. "Some nerve that goes to my face is pinched or damaged," he told me. "I can't feel the left side of my face." The doctors told him it would probably clear up when the inflamed nerve settled down.

As the months went by, the left side of Pedro's face remained still. He slowly learned to adapt to chewing on the right side and wearing a cap that covered part of his face. He was a private man and wasn't comfortable sharing his struggles about his new disability. I used my interest in neurology as a way to coax him into giving me details of his experience. He appeared willing to talk as long as it was for "medical purposes." Many months after the accident, he said, "You know, there is something about my accident that I thought you would be interested in. Ever since it happened, being sad feels different. When I feel sad or cry, or when I look at my baby and get that strong feeling of love for her, it doesn't feel the same. It's like, without my face moving, my feelings can't come all the way out, all the way to the surface."

I wondered if a lack of facial expressions on the left side of his face kept Pedro's right hemisphere from getting the feedback from facial muscles, leaving him with a sense of an incomplete experience of his emotions. Put in a slightly different way, Pedro's right brain and the left side of his face comprised a functional system for the experience and expression of emotion. With his current handicap, this system became less active and emotionally less satisfying. Fortunately, the doctors were right, and the feeling on the left side of his face gradually returned. He described it as similar to the feeling you get a few hours after having dental work done, when the anesthesia begins to wear off. With the return of physical sensations came a fuller experience of his emotions. But what is it like for people who *never* have these feelings?

Alexithymia as Hemispheric Disconnection

Alexithymia, the inability to consciously experience and process emotional information, is characterized by deficits in functions usually identified with the right hemisphere. Clients who suffer from alexithymia often recognize that others have feelings but report that they are unable to find them within themselves. This occurs despite evidence of strong physiological responses to emotionally negative stimuli that can be measured in the laboratory (Stone & Nielson, 2001). It is as if their feelings have been excluded from awareness, even in their dreams (Parker et al., 2000). Interestingly, higher levels of alexithymia are correlated with a history of repeated trauma (Kosten et al., 1992; Krystal, 1988; Zeitlin et al., 1993).

Alexithymia may reflect a lack of integration of right-hemisphere emotional and somatic information with the linguistic and cognitive systems of the left (Habib et al., 2003; Papciak et al., 1985; Taylor, 2000). This lack of integration would leave the conscious self of the left hemisphere with little input from the emotional, intuitive, somatic, and imaginative processing of the right. Indeed, patients with alexithymia are described as having a concrete or stimulus-bound cognitive style and restricted imagination (Bagby & Taylor, 1997; Silberman & Weingarten, 1986). The theory of such an "interhemispheric transfer deficit" was supported by findings with patients who suffered from PTSD with, and without, alexthymia. Those with alexithymia were found to have deficits in transferring sensory–motor information between hemispheres, whereas those without alexithymia had no such deficits (Zeitlin et al., 1989). Could this sensory–motor dissociation be another aspect of the ability of the left hemisphere to inhibit input from the right?

People with alexithymia have other difficulties related to right-hemispheric functioning, such as impaired reading of facial expressions and processing of verbal and nonverbal emotional information (Jessimer & Markham, 1997; Lane et al., 1996; McDonald & Prkachin, 1990). They have been shown to process faces more in the left than in the right hemisphere and show less activation in the anterior cingulate (Kano et al., 2003). Recall that the anterior cingulate is centrally involved with emotional and somatic experience. The size of the right anterior cingulate has been demonstrated to correlate with the degree of alexithymia in men (Gundel et al., 2004). "Alexithymic-like" difficulties in identifying and describing feelings are more common in victims with right-sided versus left-sided strokes (Spalletta et al., 2001).

As you can see, lateral dominance is no straightforward dichotomy. It is a complex set of interacting neural networks that has been shaped by evolution and reshaped by experience-dependent plasticity. The emerging picture is one of right-hemisphere dominance in the processing and analysis of social and emotional information. Our ability to form and sustain relationships relies on the participation and integration of right-hemispheric networks with those biased toward the left. Optimal parenting appears to result in maximal integration of right and left systems as well as a smooth balance between cortical and subcortical systems on both sides. Although our exploration of the social brain leads us to discuss many systems that are biased toward the right hemisphere, it is essential to remember that they can function to their full potential only in dynamic balance with all other systems.

Part III

Bridging the
Social Synapse

Chapter 6

Experience-Dependent Plasticity

When the child successfully accomplishes communi-
cation with others . . . normal development occurs.
—Tronick & Weinberg, 1997

Back in my undergraduate days, it was popular to debate whether something was the result of nature *or* nurture. Musical talent, intelligence, and speed swimming had avid proponents on both sides of the argument. Later, during my graduate studies in psychology, it was important that we learn whether a psychiatric illness was organic *or* functional: in other words, a product of the brain or the mind. Organic illnesses were those with known biological causes such as Alzheimer's and Korsakoff's, whereas functional disorders were ones thought to be caused by emotional conflict. At the time, depression, anxiety, and obsessive–compulsive disorders were thought to fall in the functional category. By sorting disorders into dichotomous categories, we were comforted by the illusion that we were moving closer to an understanding of the human condition. Fortunately, we have come a long way in the last few decades.

We now know that nature and nurture work together to shape our brains, abilities, and disabilities. We also know that the mind arises from the brain, and that all psychiatric illnesses involve organic processes. Nature and nurture become one during development, and the line between organic and functional has dissolved into what is now called *experience-dependent plasticity.* This term means that our brains are structured and restructured by interactions with our social and natural environments.

Although we know far more about human behavior than we do about brain plasticity, research is beginning to elucidate some of the components of brain building stimulated by mother–child interactions. And although most of what we know about plasticity has been discovered in other species, the evolutionary conservation of structures and strategies allows us to learn a great deal about our own brain from our more primitive cousins. Although it may be rash to draw any definitive conclusions about humans through the study of other animals, we can develop hypotheses to test with humans as our technology improves (Hofer, 1987).

We do know that the connection between mother and child is a potent determinant of brain development and adaptation. In an optimal situation, each is transfixed by the sights, sounds, and movements of the other, hungry to learn the language that would bridge the gap between them. The mother's impact on her child's brain is widespread and profound; early interactions build neural networks and establish biological set points that can last a lifetime. The centrality of the mother–child relationship is reflected in the Jewish proverb that states, "God could not be everywhere and therefore he made mothers." In the other direction, a new mother's brain is stimulated to change and grow upon the birth of her child. Her brain is reshaped through a combination of pregnancy-related hormones and the intense sensory and emotional stimulation provided by her newborn.

Maternal Plasticity

We know that rats raised in enriched environments have larger, more complex brains than those raised without stimulation and challenge. Specifically, they have more neurons, synaptic connections, blood capillaries, and mitochondrial activity (Diamond et al., 1964; Kempermann et al., 1997a & 1998; Kolb & Whishaw, 1998; Sirevaag & Greenough, 1988). These findings suggest that a more stimulated brain is also a more complex, active, and resilient brain. On the other hand, rats raised in impoverished environments who have offspring develop brains similar to those rats raised in enriched environments (Diamond et al., 1971). This finding strongly suggests that having children enriches, stimulates, and challenges the brain to grow.

Evidence of brain growth has been found in the hypothalamus of both new mother and virgin rats that have been given pups to nurture. While performing maternal behaviors, the forebrain and limbic system of mother rats show increased activation of fos, a protein involved in gene transcription (Lonstein et al., 1997). The presence of fos indicates that, during interactions with her pups, the brain of the mother is being stimulated to grow and learn via activation of the genetic transcription that orchestrates the experience-dependent structural changes of her neurons (Fleming & Korsmit, 1996; Fleming, Suh, Korsmit, & Rusak, 1994; Stafisso-Sandoz et al., 1998). What these data clearly mean is that brain growth is stimulated by *interaction with pups* and not only by *pregnancy-related hormones*.

The receptive sensory field of the rat's brain also changes in response to childbearing, with the skin around the nipples represented by 50% more neurons than those in nonlactating mothers (Xerri et al., 1994). It has also been discovered that motherhood improves rat learning and memory by stimulating growth within hippocampal neurons (Kinsley et al., 1999). Hippocampal size increases during breeding season and is also correlated with the size of the area where the mothers forage for food. This finding suggests that the hippocampus can expand on an "as needed" basis to support her memory for the locations of a greater number of food sources and thereby enhance the survival of her pups (Jacobs et al., 1990).

What are the implications for humans? Although we can't yet examine neural changes in human mothers without removing their brains for analysis, we can infer that mothers and children stimulate each other's brains to grow (Fleming, O'Day, & Kraemer, 1999; Hatton et al., 1987; Modney et al., 1994; Salm et al., 1988; Theodosis & Poulain, 1984). We do know that most mothers experience a period of heightened arousal and responsiveness after childbirth, when their newborn takes on "special salience" (Fleming & Corter, 1988). Parents and nonparents have been shown to demonstrate different patterns of brain activation in response to the crying and laughing of infants, reflecting experience-dependent brain changes resulting from parenting experiences (Seifritz et al., 2003). Is it possible that the emotional lability we see in many new mothers is an expression of a heightened sensitivity to interpersonal cues required for optimal attunement and learning?

Plasticity in the Newborn

Like its mother, a newborn comes with a brain primed to attend, absorb, and learn from human contact. The growth spurt of the right hemisphere during the first 18 months shapes the neural substrate for early social and emotional learning. This experience-dependent neural sculpting is accomplished through attunement with the right hemisphere of the parent (Schore, 2000). Mothers tend to hold their babies in their left arms, affording the babies an enhanced ability to hear their mother's heartbeat (Sieratzki & Woll, 1996). This position also affords the visual information from the baby direct access to the mother's right hemisphere. The social and emotional learning gleaned through countless hours of primal resonant interactions serves as the foundation for the gradual development of affect regulation, attachment schema, and self-identity.

We are only now beginning to understand a number of vital mechanisms involved in the transposition of maternal behavior into biological structure. One is the construction of networks within centers of the social brain, such as the orbital medial prefrontal cortex (OMPFC), anterior cingulate, insula, and amygdala (Schore, 1994). The second is the organization of regulatory networks related to arousal, such as the networks that connect the OMPFC and amygdala and shape the "smart" networks of the vagus that help to regulate our interpersonal emotions (Porges, 2003a). Yet another is the stimulation of growth of glucocorticoid receptors in the amygdala, hippocampus, and components of the HPA axis; these receptors diminish both the experience of stress and its negative impact upon the body (Meaney et al., 1989). These components of brain building impact core aspects of ANS regulation, immunological functioning, and affect regulation throughout life. In turn, these become interwoven with our attachment schema, ability to establish and maintain relationships, and vulnerability to physical and mental illness.

Building the Brain

What impact does the sight of a mother's face have on her baby's social brain? For one, it triggers high levels of endogenous opiates, which are responsible for the pleasurable aspects of social interactions and act directly on the subcortical reward centers. Positive and exciting stimulation by the mother also triggers the production of corticotrophin-releasing factor (CRF) in the infant's hypothalamus, thereby activating the sympathetic nervous system. CRF, which controls endorphin and ACTH production in the anterior pituitary, also stimulates the production of dopamine.

In a nutshell, biological changes correlate with heightened states of excitement and elation in the infant during interactions with its mother. These same neurochemicals are centrally involved in the regulation of brain metabolic energy levels and the maturation of the cortex and limbic system (Cirulli et al., 2003; Schore, 1997). The biochemical cascade activated by infant–mother interaction also triggers the birth of new neurons, protein synthesis, and neural growth. Thus, caretakers do more than regulate the present psychobiological state of an infant; *they activate the growth of the brain through emotional availability and reciprocal interactions* (Emde, 1988). The deficits in abstract abilities often seen in isolated and institutionalized children reflect the lack of early contact required for the development and integration of the brain, in general, and more specifically in many experience-dependent neural circuits of the frontal lobes (Goldfarb, 1945).

During early critical periods, serotonin and dopamine also play an important role in the responsiveness of the cortex to environmental stimulation. These neuromodulators influence the ontogeny (development) of cortical circuitry and have long-lasting effects on the development of neural networks. Monoamine activation of both glycogenolysis (i.e., a cascade of biochemical reactions that triggers the release of glucose in conditions of intense activity) and the pentose phosphate pathways that mediate brain-building processes underscores the preeminent role of monoamines in the generation of the high quantities of energy required for the developing brain (Schore, 1997).

The networks of the social brain are especially experience-dependent— which makes sense, given that we have to attach and reattach to different individuals and groups and play a variety of social roles throughout our lives. Our ability to form attachments and successfully navigate the social world depends on our ability to regulate our impulses and emotions. Thus, along with building neural networks of social communication, we are also shaping networks that regulate our emotions and behaviors.

Regulating Affect

From the submolecular to the geopolitical, our existence depends on a constant interaction with, and balancing of, the multiple forces that contribute to life. Within the CNS this process is witnessed in the excitation and inhibition that occur among neurons, brain structures, and neural networks. What we call *affect regulation* is the outward expression of just one level of this infinitely complex homeostatic process. Our ability to enjoy being inside of ourselves, successfully engaging with others, and managing life's day-to-day stressors depends on the attainment of affect regulation. A child maintaining concentration in school, an accountant sticking with a long day of tedious calculations, and a wife going home to her husband despite being attracted to another man—all rely on the inhibition of impulses and emotions while maintaining a memory for future consequences. In addition, these actions require that we keep long-term goals in mind, flexibly solve problems, and consider the perspectives and needs of others.

In order to assure the gradual development of neural systems involved in affect regulation, a child needs to be protected from intense, prolonged, and overwhelming affective states. In one sense, a child "borrows" the prefrontal cortex of the parent while modeling the development of its own nascent brain on what is borrowed. Emotionally stimulating interactions generate brain growth, whereas dysregulated affect and prolonged stress result in neuron loss throughout cortical–limbic circuits. Prefrontal growth includes the maturation of axons down to the areas of the vagal nerve, the hypothalamus, and the medulla, which are all involved with autonomic regulation (Nauta, 1964; Yasui et al., 1991). This circuit is a core component of cortical–limbic networks that modulate arousal, inhibition, and habituation.

The presence of good-enough caretakers greatly contributes to the development of circuits that are vital to affect regulation and the social brain. Abuse, neglect, understimulation, and prolonged shame reduce levels of endorphins, CRF, and dopamine and increase stress hormones and noradrenalin. This biochemical environment inhibits plasticity and creates a vulnerability to psychopathology. Also, as you might imagine, abused and neglected children show less adaptive affective regulation than others whom we consider "well-balanced" (Gaensbauer, 1982; Schore, 1994).

The prefrontal lobes, especially the orbital medial frontal regions in the right hemisphere, regulate the balance between the parasympathetic-dominated shame states (lateral tegmental) and states of positive emotion, activity, and exploration dominated by sympathetic arousal (ventral tegmental). The neural networks involved in these two functions need to be fully developed and integrated for optimal affective regulation. The development of these circuits enables the child to tolerate increasing levels of emotion while maintaining self-regulation and keeping levels of stress hormones at optimal levels (Schore, 1994). These increasing abilities, in turn, enhance the brain's ability to grow, connect, and integrate.

Repeated experiences of moving from regulation to dysregulation and back to a regulated state are stored in networks of sensory, motor, and emotional memory. The participation of caretakers in this process and their repeated assistance in moving an infant back to regulated states build and reinforce these circuits. The experience, memory, and control of transition states become encoded as implicit memories of positive state transitions. From a psychoanalytic perspective, these implicit memories are our autoregulatory "good inner objects" that bias us toward restoring regulation when we are challenged. Thus, positive parent–child interactions establish an environment within the brain that maximizes positive emotional rebound as well as neural growth and affect regulation.

Focus on the Social Engagement System

Although we may take the existence of relationships for granted, sustained social engagement represents a complex evolutionary accomplishment. Whereas basic approach-avoidance defensive strategies suffice for nonsocial animals, caretaking, cooperation, and group coherence require subtle and continuous self-regulation. Mammals not only have to know *whom* to approach but also *when, how,* and *for what purposes.* Sometimes humans also have to stay in proximity to those whom we don't fully trust or toward whom we need to be deferential. The infinite subtleties of social interactions require a system of bodily and emotional regulation that is finely calibrated for such a complex task. This is where the all-or-nothing nature of the fight/flight mechanisms of the autonomic nervous system just won't do.

In an attempt to explain the evolution of affective regulation that allowed for the development of complex social relationships, Stephen Porges proposed the *polyvagal theory* of social engagement (Porges, 1998, 2001, 2003b). At the core of Porges's theory is the sequential evolution of three separate autonomic subsystems, all of which have been conserved in mammals. The first system, the "vegetative" vagus, controls bodily shutdown and immobilization and depends on parasympathetic processes. We share this ancient unmyelinated system with most other vertebrates. The second is the mobilization or fight/flight system, which depends on the sympathetic branch of the autonomic nervous system (ANS). The third system, which we focus on here, is the *social engagement system*. Also called the "smart" vagus, the social engagement system is a myelinated branch of the vagal system that exerts an inhibitory, modulatory, or calming influence on sympathetic arousal. It is the evolution and development of this system, according to Porges, that allows us to modulate autonomic arousal in a prosocial manner and controls the muscles of our eyes, faces, mouths, and inner ears in the service of social communication.

Porges suggests that the vagal system evolved as a refinement of the more primitive ANS. Its purpose is to provide subtler regulation of visceral and autonomic activity, allowing for the dance of engagement and disengagement with others without activating fight/flight responses. The social engagement system modulates our visceral, emotional, and behavioral states in a manner that supports sustained social contact. In order to understand the social engagement system, it is first necessary to take a look at the vagal system.

Vagus means "to wander," and wander it does. It begins in the brainstem and projects independently of the spinal cord to organs throughout the body. Although the vagus is referred to as the 10th cranial nerve, this is a bit of a misnomer. It is not a single nerve but rather a complex, bidirectional, neural feedback system. Because it has both sensory *and* motor fibers, it provides the brain with monitoring and control functions over many bodily systems in support of homeostatic regulation. Motor fibers of the vagus originate in the nucleus ambiguous and the dorsal motor nucleus. The nucleus ambiguous, with projections to the heart, palate, larynx, and bronchi, is involved with the "smart vagus" in processing emotion, motion, and interpersonal communication. The dorsal motor nucleus, with projections to the trachea, lungs, and gastrointestinal tract, is the source of the vegetative vagus and helps to regulate respiration and digestion (see Figure 6.1) (Porges et al., 1994).

In the absence of challenges and environmental demands, the ANS and the vegetative vagus serve the restorative and growth needs of the body. In response to adverse challenges, growth and homeostatic requirements are quickly put on a back burner. In these situations, the sympathetic branch takes over and the standard fight/flight response becomes engaged. The addition of the smart vagus allows us to become excited and to stay engaged with others without requiring sympathetic arousal or adrenal activation. This makes positive and exciting engagement possible without defensiveness or attack; caretaking, affiliation, and cooperation thus become possible.

The experience-dependent "vagal brake" mediates rapid and conscious control of heart rate, creating alternative sources of soothing. In conjunction with oxytocin and vasopressin and based on experiences of safety and trust, the vagal brake allows for modulation of the fight/flight response, thereby making possible the evolution of courting and sustained pair-bonding behaviors (Porges, 1998). This system is necessary for the inhibition of defensive aggression in response to distress cues; such inhibition allows for ongoing relationships and cooperation in large groups, despite transient disagreements and conflict (Blair, 1995).

The development of this engagement system and the fine-tuning of the vagal brake to regulate affect appear to depend on the quality of attachment relationships in early childhood. The shaping and tuning of the smart vagus is one way that early experience shapes our brains. During the first years of life, the vagal system develops and integrates with other cortical and limbic structures to regulate our experience and behavior. It allows us to engage in relationships, use them to regulate affect, and internalize them to aid in self-regulation. In a sense, this vagal system allows us to translate what we learn from experience with caretakers into moment-to-moment bodily experience. Control of the primary facial, mouth, and throat muscles involved in communication and the

THE VAGAL SYSTEM

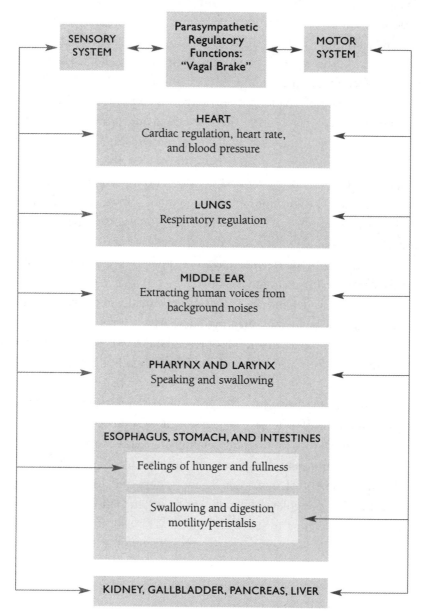

Figure 6.1. Adapted from Porges (2003a & b).

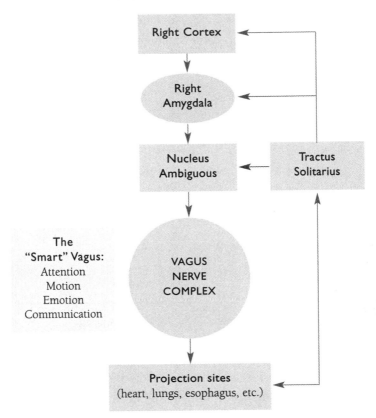

Figure 6.2. **Proposed vagal system for emotional regulation.** Adapted from Porges, Doussard-Roosevelt, & Maiti (1994) and Porges (2003a & b).

linking of them with an awareness and control of internal states allow this system to coordinate the cognitive and emotional processing necessary for relational communications (see Figure 6.2).

The "tone" of the vagus refers to the vagal system's ability to regulate the heart and other target organs (Porges et al., 1996). The development of vagal tone is likely due to an interaction between innate temperament and experience-dependent influence during childhood. Inadequate development of vagal tone can impact all levels of psychosocial and cognitive development (Porges, Doussard-Roosevelt, & Maiti, 1994). Children with poor vagal tone have difficulty in suppressing emotions in situations that demand their attention, making it difficult for them to engage with their parents, sustain a shared focus with playmates, and maintain attention on important material in the classroom (see Table 6.1). Perhaps some of the children that receive a diagnosis of attention-deficit hyperactivity disorder (ADHD) may suffer from insufficient vagal tone.

Table 6.1. Correlates of Vagal Tone

Higher vagal tone correlates with:	Lower vagal tone correlates with:
Ability to self-regulate	Irritability
Self-soothing capacity by 3 months of age	Behavioral problems at 3 years of age
Range and control of emotional states	Emotional dysregulation
More reliable autonomic responses	Distractibility
Suppression of heart rate variability	Hyper-reactivity to environmental and
Enhanced attentional capacity and ability	visceral stimuli
to take in information	
Positive social engagement	Withdrawal
Increased behavioral organization	Impulsivity/acting out
Consistent caretaking/secure attachment	Insecure attachment

We all have the experience of disagreements and arguments with partners, parents, and children. We may even become so angry that we go for a walk or put ourselves in "time-out." In most instances we are able to experience our feelings and maintain adequate control over our emotions in order to continue communicating and working through a problem. As adults, good vagal regulation allows us to become upset, anxious, or angry with a loved one without withdrawing or becoming physically aggressive. We can hypothesize that many who engage in domestic violence, child abuse, and other forms of aggressive behavior may not have had the kinds of early attachment relationships required to build an adequate vagal system. Thus, good parenting not only teaches appropriate responses in challenging interpersonal situations, but it also builds the vagal circuitry required to successfully carry out those responses.

The social engagement system emphasizes that evolution is not just a matter of developing new and more complex brain regions, but that systems need to be modified and combined to perform increasingly complex functions. Social behavior and emotional regulation derive from our ability to regulate each other's ANS with facial gestures, actions, expressions, and vocal communication—and all this within an ongoing stream of reciprocal and contingent behaviors. Positive parenting contributes to the building of positive vagal tone, which, in turn, supports ego strength, physical health, and the ability to engage in sustained and mutually regulating social interactions.

Charlie—Born to Be Wild

A few years ago I received a call from a young man named Charlie, requesting an appointment for therapy. He was on tour with his band so he couldn't come in right away, but he wanted to make an appointment for as soon as possible when he was back in town. All he could tell me was that he had a "pretty bad temper" and thought he needed anger management training. When the time of the appointment rolled around, I found not one but *five* young men in my waiting room. To my eyes they looked like quintuplets: black clothes, spiked hair, pierced faces, tattooed arms, and snarling expressions. Flashing back to my long-haired snarling self from the 1960s, I liked them immediately. When I appeared, Charlie stood up and the other four began to chant, "Go get shrunk, go get shrunk, go get shrunk." I soon learned that these guys were Charlie's bandmates, his closest friends, support group, and adopted family. It was one of them who had found my name on the Internet and stood over Charlie as he called to make the appointment.

Charlie's story was not unusual. He grew up with a violent father and an alcoholic mother. Because he didn't have a supportive family life, in junior high Charlie became extremely attached to his school music teacher, who became his surrogate father and spent time with him, buying him dinner and teaching him to play the drums. "Mr. Sorrento saved my life," Charlie said with reverence. "There were so many times when I made better choices because I knew he cared about me and I didn't want to disappoint him." Charlie ran away from home at 17, coming to Los Angeles and living wherever he could find a vacant sofa. He spent his days meeting musicians, trying to put a band together, playing gigs, and dreaming of making it big. After about 4 years, his current group began to gel. They got a recording contract and began to gain some notoriety in the music industry. According to Charlie, his bandmates had stories similar to his own.

The reason he wanted to come to therapy was his temper. As a child, he always told himself that he never wanted to grow up to be like his parents. His parents primarily communicated with him by hitting, yelling, and throwing things at him. As a teenager and young man living hand-to-mouth in a big city, the violence they had taught him was adaptive. He had to fight for survival, and he knew how to fight. Charlie described situations where he would be threatened by someone and would warn him to back off. He knew that once he "let go," he wouldn't and couldn't stop. "Past a certain point, it's as if whoever is challenging me becomes my parents, and they not only get what they deserve but everything my fucked-up parents deserve. The problem is, when I have a disagreement with my bandmates, the same feelings come up and I have to just run away so I won't hurt them." Charlie smiled, "I used to destroy hotel rooms because I thought that was what musicians were supposed to do—but that shit got expensive."

I began by complimenting Charlie: on his choice of coming to therapy, on his decision to run away from those he cared for instead of becoming violent, and, most of all, for finding a group of guys for whom he cared and who cared for him. Nodding his head slowly, Charlie said, "They're my family. For the first time in my life I have a real home and I want to be domesticated." His self-awareness, ability to articulate his feelings, and emotional sensitivity stood in stark contrast to his gothic porcupine exterior. In the sessions to come, I focused on developing the kind of supportive and caring relationship he had formed with Mr. Sorrento 10 years earlier. My role as a teacher would be to help Charlie understand how his brain had been shaped by his early experiences—and how it could be reshaped in the present.

We discussed how his parents had shaped his hair-trigger ANS to be combat ready. As Charlie told me stories of the neglect and abuse he had survived, I shared his pain and anger and then explained how these experiences had determined his present reactions. I taught him about the growth of the vagal system and the types of nurturing interactions it requires for adequate development, and he could clearly see that he had had few of those types of experiences with his parents. "My mother just wasn't the mothering type," he would say. "God knows why she had me. I must have been an accident." Charlie was, however, quick to see how the kind of caring and patience he received from Mr. Sorrento and his bandmates could help him to change his brain.

Charlie and I worked on a variety of relaxation and cognitive techniques to keep him calmer when in proximity to others when he became upset. We discussed ways of avoiding either fleeing or fighting while keeping in mind how much he cares for the people with whom he becomes upset. Group hugs, back massages, arm wrestling, and telling stories of good times were all used to help Charlie relax and reconnect when his fight/flight systems became activated. When his bandmates saw Charlie getting upset about something, they would start shouting, "Share the love, share the love," and flock around him joking, smiling, and wrestling him to the ground. On a number of occasions they made me promise that everything I knew about them had to stay confidential because their fans wouldn't understand this side of their personalities. After all, they were supposed to be indifferent to everything and everyone except music and anarchy.

Therapy with Charlie was a long process with a lot of emergency calls from hotel rooms and tour buses, but it slowly had a very positive impact. Charlie taught the other guys the techniques we talked about, and they often invoked my name to remind him "Remember to breathe" and "Remember, we love you." Because each of the guys had emotional challenges of his own, they said they were *all* in therapy with me and that I was the sixth member of the group. I'm convinced that the success of the therapy was due to the fact that they were all in it together and actively helped Charlie to practice what we had discussed. Having Charlie's "family" so involved in treatment maximized the leverage of the cognitive techniques, his education about how the brain develops and functions, and the human connection I was able to make with him. In essence, we were teaching Charlie's brain how to join the group mind—how to reshape the brain that was trained to have a hair-trigger autonomic nervous system into one with a vagal tone that could sustain proximity and intimate relationships. As for me, I adapted to the roles of surrogate father, bandmate, and therapist, finding them all satisfying and enriching.

As we have seen, a child's brain links up to his or her mother's brain to slowly learn self-regulatory capacities. This early linkup between mother and child changes both of their brains, leading them to become inner objects for one another. With good-enough parenting, a child is provided with a brain that allows him or her to be part of the group mind through social awareness and appropriate affect regulation. For people such as Charlie, the networks of their social brain are not optimized for sustained positive connection, making them vulnerable to chaotic relationships, substance abuse, and mental illness. Because these networks continue to be plastic, an enriched environment established later in life can allow for the development of skills and abilities that were not part of its original shaping. Together with his bandmates, I was able to create an enriched social environment for Charlie that allowed him to find his way to the love and connection not present during his early life. Just as St. Exupery's Little Prince tamed the fox, now Charlie had to become tamed (or domesticated, as Charlie put it) in order to care for others in the gentle, consistent way he had needed to be cared for as a child.

Chapter 7

Reflexes and Instincts: Jumpstarting Attachment

All the soarings of my mind begin in my blood.
—Rainer Maria Rilke, 1921

Newborns were once thought of as passive recipients of external stimulation. But ask any mother of a healthy baby, and she will tell you there's no such thing as a passive newborn. In fact, infants are now regarded as competent participants in relationships. When we look more carefully at infants, we begin to realize just how well infants communicate their needs and get them met. In fact, newborns influence and socialize the behaviors of their caretakers as much as they are socialized (Bateson, 1972; Rheingold, 1969). Mother and infant continually adjust to each other's sounds, gestures, movements, and emotions in a lyrical duet (Trevarthen, 1993). As they bond, both of their brains are shaped and reshaped in response to one another (Hofer, 1984).

Early in gestation, spontaneous neural firing causes movements of our arms, legs, and trunk. These reflexive movements activate and enhance neural development and eventually become shaped into complex, voluntary, and purposeful movements. By the third month of gestation, we are grasping, orienting, and making avoidance-like movements. By the fourth month, the sucking reflex becomes prominent. The fifth month sees the emergence of the walking reflexes and at 6 months the familiar knee jerk and other tendon reflexes are in place. We begin to cry by the seventh month and, by month 8 all our reflexes are in place and we are now ready to enter the social world.

Nature also equips newborns with an array of reflexes that trigger maternal instincts, increase eye contact, and prolong physical contact. Infant rooting and sucking reflexes help obtain nurturance, while the automatic hand grasp (palmar grasp) and the reaching out of the arms (Moro reflex) help newborns hold onto their mothers (Eliot, 1999). Reflexive orienting toward the mother, smiling, and imitating her facial gestures all trigger positive emotions in the mother. Even the simple act of breastfeeding helps mothers feel calmer and makes them more receptive to relationships (Uvnäs-Moberg et al., 1996). By making the mother feel good, the infant keeps her close despite stress, sleep deprivation, and life's distractions. Mothers' brains are activated by the smells, sights, and sounds of their newborns, creating a preoccupation with attuning to their needs. This preoccupation focuses a mother's attention as her brain adapts and attaches to her child.

Beginning with the last months of pregnancy, most mothers appear to enter a state of preoccupation with their infants that lasts well into the first year of the infant's life (Winnicott, 1963). This maternal preoccupation involves an increased attunement to visceral and emotional communication that may coincide with a shift to greater right-hemisphere bias. Evolution may have designed this shift as a purposeful maternal regression to more primitive modes of communication, allowing for a better linkup with her newborn (Maestripieri, 1999).

Smells and Pheromones

How quickly we bond to our newborns—and they to us—is really quite amazing. New mothers can recognize the smell of their newborns after an hour of contact, and babies soon learn to distinguish the smell of their mother's body and breast milk (Kaitz et al, 1987; Porter et al., 1983; Porter & Winberg, 1999; Russell, 1976). The smell of the nipple increases a baby's level of arousal and activity, helping it to find the breast and trigger brain growth (Porter & Winberg, 1999). In fact, the earliest evolving form of social communication most likely took place between chemical substances known as pheromones. Pheromonal communication across the social synapse has been discovered in all life forms from single-celled organisms to insects, reptiles, mammals, primates, and even humans.

Have you ever noticed how wonderful a baby's head smells? A baby's brain consumes a lot of energy and becomes pretty hot, yet his or her perspiration is pleasing to us. Secreted by specialized scent glands and contained in saliva, sweat, urine, feces, and other bodily secretions, pheromones carry information about territory, dominance, sexual availability, congregation, and behaviors involved in caretaking (Duvall, 1986). In nonhuman species, they also stimulate grooming, nest building, regurgitive feeding, emigration, and disposal of the dead (Joseph, 1990). Studies of the pheromonal communication in vertebrates have discovered a vomeronasal system specialized in the detection of chemical messages, separate from the olfactory system. Although the vomeronasal system evolutionarily predates the olfactory system, they share a common function of detecting chemicals in the air and transmitting their presence to brain structures that analyze their meaning. The vomeronasal system is specialized to detect "social smells" and consists of the vomeronasal organ (also known as Jacobsen's Organ after its discoverer), the vomeronasal nerve, and the accessory olfactory bulb.

Although many question the importance of pheromonal communication in humans, there is little doubt of its importance for most mammals. Introducing the scent of an unfamiliar male to a mouse who is pregnant by another male results in a loss of embryonic implantation and a return to estrus (heat) (Bruce, 1959; Halpern & Martinez-Marcos, 2003). Anestrus rats return to estrus when exposed to male pheromones, whereas ewes will only allow strange lambs to suckle from them if their vomeronasal system has been damaged (Booth & Katz, 2000; Moncho-Bogani et al., 2005; Mora & Cabrera, 1997; Whitten, 1956). Female pigs express lordosis (an arching of the back in preparation for intercourse) when exposed to male pheromones, and female elephants use pheromones to signal to males when they are ready to mate (Dorries et al., 1997; Lazar et al., 2004; Wysocki & Preti, 2004). Vomeronasal systems have been discovered in cats, horses, cattle, armadillos, and chimpanzees (one of our closest primate cousins). Anyone who has a dog has witnessed many instances of the importance of social smell.

It has been generally accepted that Jacobsen's Organ is present in humans during gestation but degenerates into a vestigial structure early in life. This suggests that it may play an important role in early bonding but decrease in significance in later relationships. And although recent studies have discovered anatomical parts of the vomeronasal system in two-thirds of the normal human adult population, it is still unclear whether it continues to be functional (Halpern & Martinez-Marcos, 2003; Keverne, 2004; Martinez-Marcos et al., 1999; Moncho-Bogani et al., 2005; Monti-Bloch et al., 1994; Takami, 2002). Despite these controversies, it is safe to assume that, just like other mammals, some form of pheromonal communication does occur across the human social synapse. The success of the perfume and deodorant industries speak to the continued importance of social odors and our attempt to control them.

The enlargement of the primate neocortex has enabled us to simultaneously process multiple channels of sensory information and appears to have rendered pheromonal communication increasingly less important. Still, evidence does exist that humans can identify their young, influence each other's moods, and synchronize the timing of menstrual cycles via pheromones (Grosser et al., 2000; Wysocki & Preti, 2004). If pheromones have an influence in human social relationships, then mother–infant bonding would be one of the primary relationships in which we would expect to see them playing a significant role. Perhaps if we looked more closely, many more pheromonal processes would be discovered.

Sounds and Sights

While specific words are no doubt meaningless to an infant, the tone and prosody of the mother's voice rapidly become recognizable. Meanwhile, human mothers come to recognize their own baby's cry during the first day of life (Formby, 1967). By orienting their heads to the sound of their mothers' voices, newborns increase the possibility of eye contact, whereas their instinct to seek circles and complex figures directs the eyes toward the mother's face (Johnson et al., 1991a). Newborns can, in fact, recognize familiar faces within hours after birth (Bushnell, Sai, & Mullin, 1989; Field et al., 1984; Walton, Bower, & Bower, 1992). Reflexive smiling evokes smiling from caretakers, further stimulating and engaging the infant in the attachment and brain-building process.

Within hours of birth, newborns orient to direct eye contact from others (Farroni et al., 2002). They are able to open their mouths and stick out their tongues in imitation of adults and can discriminate between happy, sad, and surprised facial expressions (Field et al., 1982; Meltzoff & Moore, 1983, 1992). Happy faces cause newborns to widen their lips, sad faces cause pouting, and surprised looks elicit wide open mouths. These reflexes continue into adulthood in the conscious and unconscious activation of facial muscles in imitation of those with whom we interact (Dimberg et al., 2000; Myowa-Yamakoshi et al., 2004). Mothers instinctively respond to distress cries with nurturing behaviors and respond to nondistress vocalizations by imitating them. This reflexive imitation begins to teach the newborn the relationship between facial expression, social interactions, and, eventually, internal emotional states.

Vision, in general, and the emotionally expressive face, in particular, have come to play central roles in human bonding and attachment (Schore, 1994). The infant and mother gaze into each other's eyes, linking their hearts, brains, and minds. Endorphin and dopamine levels in both mother and child rise and fall as they grow close, separate, and come close again. This dance of proximity and distance provides them with alternating rushes of well-being and distress, teaching them that to be close feels good and that to be separated causes pain. The sounds, feel, and sight of the mother's expressive face elevate dopamine and endorphin levels, making the mother the infant's primary source of enjoyment and well-being. The resultant increase in sympathetic arousal (if not too prolonged) is associated with heightened activity, excitement, and elation. Mothers usually sense when their infant is becoming overaroused and break off activity to allow for reregulation.

Obligatory attention to eyes and faces, a brainstem reflex, locks in the infant's gaze to the mother's (Baker & Berthoz, 1977; Stechler & Latz, 1966). Motor reflexes, tracking faces, orientation to sound, and imitation all decline in the months following birth (Field et al., 1986; Johnson, 1990; Maratos, 1982; Muir, Clifton, & Clarkson, 1989; Vinter, 1986). This decline suggests that once early reflexes have done their job in linking mother and child, they are slowly inhibited by the developing cortex and replaced by increasing amounts of voluntary control of social engagement. In fact, when adults show reflexive orientation and imitation, it is usually a sign of cortical damage such as occurs in dementia (Lhermitte, Pillon, & Serdaru, 1986).

Touch

Fortunately for me, my grandmother was tireless in her physical affection. As a little boy, I could spend hours lying across her lap as she rubbed, scratched, and tickled my back; there was no place I would rather be. Her open jar of hand lotion was always within reach, and I came to associate its smell with a sense of calm and safety. When she would stop, a slight twitch or whine from me would set her hand back in motion. She was proud of how smooth her hands were, and I, of course, couldn't have been more delighted. I remember feeling like I had hit the jackpot when she came home from a doctor's visit with the bad news that she was experiencing some early signs of arthritis. The doctor suggested that she use her hands as much as possible, and I was sure this meant rubbing me even more. She smiled and let me believe that she was now under "doctor's orders" to rub my back every day.

The skin is our largest sense organ. For most of us, being scratched, massaged, and caressed not only feels good but is an important component of intimacy. Children hang onto their parents, lovers become entangled, and after decades of marriage, it still feels good to hold hands. The touch of someone we love calms, soothes, and decreases stress. When someone is in physical or emotional pain, we move toward them with physical expressions of warmth and comfort. Clearly, touch is an important channel of communication and a vital mechanism of human bonding.

When a mother embraces her newborn, she instinctually maximizes the area of skin contact and heat exchange—which, it turns out, helps the infant's hypothalamus establish and regulate body temperature. In the first 9 minutes after birth a mother spends 80% of the time touching, rubbing, stroking, and massaging her newborn (Klaus et al., 1970). Within several days after birth, mothers and fathers are able to blindly identify their newborn by touching their cheek or the back of their hand (Kaitz et al., 1992, 1993, 1994). At the same time, infants soon come to recognize the shape, texture, and size of their mother's nipples (Rochat, 1983; Rochat & Hespos, 1997). Human milk is relatively low in fat, thus requiring prolonged nursing and skin-to-skin contact time in order to connect mother and child and establish the lifelong relationship between food and emotional nurturance (Jelliffe & Jelliffe, 1978). Unlike mothers of some other species, human mothers tend to find ways to maintain contact with their infants, carrying them while engaged in other tasks. Prompt physical contact in response to a child's cry is an instinctive response that is most effective in soothing an infant in distress (Bell & Ainsworth, 1972).

I was fascinated to discover that skin contains two different types of sensory receptors: some transmit information to the somatosensory cortex for identification and manipulation of objects, whereas others activate the insula, anterior cingulate, and orbital medial cortex (Francis, S. et al., 1999; Olausson et al., 2002; Rolls et al., 2003). This second touch system, connected to the core of the social brain, is dedicated to communicative emotional touch. It is this system that modulates skin-to-skin contact, soothing emotions, hormonal activation, and sexual responses to physical proximity and affectionate caress. Light touch and comfortable warmth lead to increases in oxytocin and endorphins that enhance social bonds through an association with a feeling of well-being. Touch also leads to mild sedation, decreases in blood pressure, and aids in autonomic regulation and cardiovascular health (Knox & Üvnas-Moberg, 1998; Weller & Feldman, 2003).

The life-changing impact of touch underlines the importance of physical contact for physiological regulation and attachment, especially to those who are the most vulnerable. Preterm infants either held against the skin of their parents in pouches or massaged regularly, cry less, develop faster, gain more weight, sleep better, and are discharged earlier from the hospital than those with less contact (Anderson, 1991; Bergman et al., 2004; Field et al., 1986; Ottenbacher et al., 1987). Massage has been shown to enhance the development of both ill and healthy infants and to decrease levels of stress hormones in children and adults (Acolet et al., 1993; Dieter et al., 2003; Schanberg & Field, 1987; Weiss et al., 2001). Even depressed and aggressive adolescents show decreases in their negative symptoms after massage (Diego et al., 2001, 2002; Field, 2002b; Jones & Field, 1999).

Maternal depression is a challenge for children because it usually coincides with less touch and physical interaction (Field, 1997, 2000). In turn, children of depressed mothers become more difficult to soothe, adding to the difficulties of caretaking for the depressed mother. In one study, teaching depressed mothers to massage their infants both increased the amount of touch and decreased levels of stress hormones in their infants. In time, the infants showed increased alertness, emotionality, sociability, and soothe-ability (Field et al., 1996). Touching their children not only activated smiles and positive expressions in infants but also made the mothers feel better (Onozawa et al., 2001). Depressed mothers receiving massage also showed decreases in anxiety, depression, and cortisol levels, similar to their newborns. Patients with cancer and other medical disorders who receive therapeutic massage benefit from increased levels of dopamine, serotonin, oxytocin, and endorphins, as well as higher levels of natural killer cells (Goodfellow, 2003; Hernandez-Reif et al., 2004; Lund et al., 2002).

Ever wonder why scratching our own back doesn't feel as good as having someone else do it for us? Beside the fact that some spots are impossible to reach, reward feels best when it is unpredictable (Berns et al., 2001; Fiorillo et al., 2003; Mirenowicz & Schultz, 1994). Thus familiarity of touch can lead to a decreased sense of reward—which may be responsible for the 7-year itch. On the other hand, the benefits of touch are not restricted to human relationships. All of the rubbing, purring, scratching, and petting that goes on between humans and their cats point to their value as emotional regulators for us. Petting a cat and having it rub against us activates the same affiliative centers in the brain (Allman & Brothers, 1994; Machne & Segundo, 1956). I have certainly known quite a few people who, despite their ambivalence about people, are completely committed to their cats and dogs. Clients with problematic relationships often experience symptomatic relief after getting a pet, and many therapists now use dogs in the consulting room to help relax their clients.

Focus on the Cingulate Cortex

The cingulate cortex is a vital structure of the social brain that coordinates maternal behavior, nursing, and play (see Figure 7.1; MacLean, 1985). It evolved around the time sound became an aspect of social communication and certain scent glands were modified into mammary glands for nursing (Duvall, 1986; Kennard, 1955; Robinson, 1967). The emergence of the cingulate cortex provided the basic circuitry for

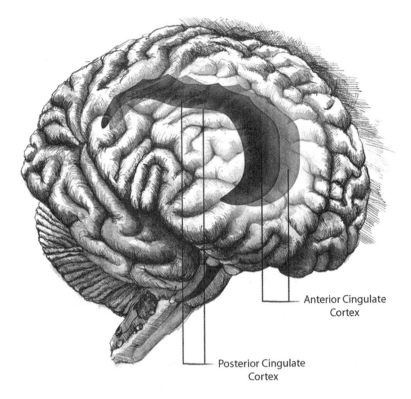

Anterior Cingulate
Cortex

Posterior Cingulate
Cortex

Figure 7.1. The anterior and posterior portions of the cingulate extend front to back on both sides of the cerebral cortex. Because of their location on the medial surfaces of each hemisphere, they, like the insula cortices, are not visible when the brain is examined from the surface.

the evolution of communication, cooperation, and empathy (Rilling et al., 2002). Emotional and attentional processing streams appear to be integrated in the cingulate cortex, which makes sense when we realize that the emergence of caretaking relationships requires that our attention be diverted from the environment to significant others based on their needs as opposed to our own (Yamasaki et al., 2002).

The cingulate appears to be involved in simultaneously monitoring personal, environmental, and interpersonal information and allocating attention to whatever is most salient. We see this multiple functioning clearly in mothers of securely attached children, who are able to shift fluidly from housework or conversation with other adults to monitoring and attending to the needs of their children. Related to this function is the role of the anterior cingulate in the detection of errors, the adjustment of responses according to new information, and engagement in deception (Carter et al., 1998; Carter et al., 2000; Kerns et al., 2004; Kozel et al., 2004; Langleben et al., 2002).

At this point in human evolution, the cingulate cortex is involved in cognitive, emotional, sensory, and motor processing, integrating input from the entire cortex with subcortical structures (Bush, Luu, & Posner, 2000; Devinsky, Morrell, & Vogt, 1995; Gehring & Knight, 2000; Maguire et al., 1998; Paus et al., 1993; Shima & Tanji, 1998). This view of the cingulate was first suggested by James Papez (1937) when he described it as "the seat of dynamic vigilance by which environmental experiences are endowed with an emotional consciousness" (p. 737). Various portions of the cingulate cortex become active when we are asked to recall emotional memories, remember familiar people, or perform tasks requiring both emotion and cognition (Maddock, 1999; Maddock et al., 2001; Phan et al., 2002; Shah et al., 2001).

Cingulate Sounds

The cingulate can trigger a variety of emotional sounds that are not necessarily mood congruent, suggesting the intentional use of sound for deception. For example, the cingulate is capable of triggering whimpering sounds in a healthy animal. These sounds fool a predator into thinking the healthy animal would be an easy catch, luring it away from those who truly are injured (Joseph, 1996). Mutism is a common symptom of cingulate damage, and electrical stimulation of the anterior cingulate will trigger sounds similar to infant distress calls. Distress calls from an infant correlate with activation of the anterior cingulate, and hearing her infant's cry activates the same brain areas in the mother (Braun & Poeggel, 2001; Lorberbaum et al., 1999).

Emotional, Self-, and Other Awareness

Individual differences in the ability to detect emotional signals both from others and from within correlate with activation in the anterior cingulate (Critchley et al., 2004; Lane et al., 1998). The cingulate also becomes activated when we, or those we love, experience physical pain or social stress, such as when we are playing a game of catch and the other players exclude us from the game (Botvinick et al., 2005; Davis et al., 1997; Eisenberger et al., 2003; Eisenberger & Lieberman, 2004; Jackson et al., 2005; Koyama et al., 1998; Lenz et al., 1998; Panksepp, 2003; Singer et al., 2004). Interestingly, when physical pain is relieved either by analgesics or thorough a placebo effect, the same regions of the anterior cingulate become active (Petrovic et al., 2002). The common neurobiology of physical pain and social rejection may provide a clue as to why healthy, intimate relationships consistently correlate with better cardiovascular health, immunological functioning, and resistance to stress (Robles & Kiecolt-Glaser, 2003).

Subjects with alexithymia (the inability to experience or describe feelings) have smaller right anterior cingulate cortices, whereas individuals with larger anterior cingulates report more worry and fearfulness (Gundel et al., 2004; Pujol et al., 2002). The anterior cingulate becomes activated when we see others with angry facial expressions or when we are asked to be self-reflective or make judgments about ourselves (Eisenberger & Lieberman, 2004; Hutchinson et al., 1999; Johnson et al., 2002; Kelley et al., 2002; Ohira et al., 2001; Singer et al., 2004). The posterior cingulate gyrus appears to play a role in emotional processing and autobiographical memory (Critchley et al., 2003; Maddock, Garrett, & Buonocore, 2001, 2003). See Table 7.1 below for some of the consequences of damage to the anterior cingulate cortex.

Table 7.1. **Consequences of Damage to the Anterior Cingulate Cortex**

Decreased maternal behavior	Brothers, 1996; Hadland et al., 2003
Decreased empathy	Brothers, 1996
Emotional instability	Brothers, 1996; Bush et al., 2000
Disruption of HPA and ANS functioning	Diorio et al., 1993; Jürgens et al., 1982
Increased response to stress	Diorio, Viau, & Meaney, 1993
Decreased expressiveness	Damasio & Van Hoesen, 1983
Less motivation to communicate	Damasio & Van Hoesen, 1983; Hadland et al., 2003
Mutism	Bush, Luu, & Posner, 2000
Inappropriate social behavior	Hadland et al., 2003; Price et al., 1990
Impulsiveness and increased motor activity	Price et al., 1990

Spindle Cells/Von Economo Neurons

The anterior cingulate contains spindle-shaped neurons that appear to have evolved in humans and great apes to connect and regulate divergent streams of information (Nimchinsky et al., 1995, 1999). These cells may provide the neural connectivity necessary both for the development of self-control and the ability to engage in sustained attention to difficult problems (Allman et al., 2001, 2005). From the perspective of interpersonal neurobiology, these spindle cells are especially fascinating because they emerge after birth and are experience-dependent. Early neglect, stress, and trauma may negatively impact the development and organization of spindle cells, resulting in deficits in the abilities organized by the anterior cingulate. It also suggests that part of the impact of early experience on lifelong cognitive and emotional functioning may be based on the construction and health of these structures.

When we consider the putative roles of the cingulate cortex, we find considerable parallel and overlap with the functions of the prefrontal cortex. Possible explanations for this similarity include that (1) they are redundant, (2) they are interactive and synergistic, or (3) the prefrontal cortex is an evolutionary expansion and improvement of the anterior cingulate (Cohen, Botvinick, & Carter, 2000). All three of these possibilities may, in fact, be true. The anterior cingulate may be an earlier evolving, more primitive version of the prefrontal cortex that organizes social, emotional, and cognitive functions earlier in development. The later developing prefrontal cortex may be an evolutionary expansion and improvement of the cingulate that is more capable of conscious input and continued plasticity throughout life.

Allman and colleagues (2001) suggest that we view the anterior cingulate as a specialization of the neocortex that supports behavioral flexibility in contexts of changing situations, emotions, and complex problem-solving. The cingulate may have the capacity to integrate diverse functional input at a deeper level than can occur between areas of the prefrontal cortex. It may also have an earlier sensitive period and less plasticity later in life. As we learn more about the cingulate cortex, we will almost certainly unlock new secrets of the social brain.

The fact that so much of the social brain develops during the first few years of life can create a number of problems. As adults we may find ourselves having thoughts, feelings, and emotions that are often out of line with current realities. During those first months and years of life, when our worlds are centered on the emotional and unconscious worlds of our parents, the infrastructure of our social brains is unconsciously shaped. Joaquin's story demonstrates how, as adults, we can discover facets of our histories, things we have always known but never consciously thought.

Joaquin—"What Am I So Afraid of?"

Joaquin came to therapy feeling anxious and exhausted. He was 35 years old, with a successful import business that kept him very busy. He talked to me as if he were leading a meeting of his shareholders—visionary and expansive, he gave me an intensive sales pitch. He had had a series of relationships that invariably started strong but faded when he became restless or dissatisfied. Despite his bravado and apparent mastery of business, Joaquin was quite fearful. He feared falling into poverty, having to return home a failure, and was very afraid of taking risks. He hoarded his money, kept his home orderly and neat, and had difficulty dealing with strong emotions, both his own and other peoples'. He labeled all of his past girlfriends as "hysterical" because they expressed feelings that were "out of control."

As we got to know each other, I reflected to Joaquin the paradox between his big personality and his fearfulness. "Who, me?" was his first response, but over time he discovered, with amazement, that he was fearful. Not only was he afraid in a number of business situations, but despite his social sophistication, he had anxiety about interacting with other people. "How did this happen to me?" Joaquin boomed. "That's a good question!" I responded. I suggested that an answer may come from his early life and encouraged him to tell me what he remembered about his childhood.

Joaquin recalled a good childhood; his family had emigrated from Eastern Europe before he was born and he had grown up with his parents, grandparents, and a number of aunts and uncles. No one in his family talked much about their experiences before coming to America, but they lived a comfortable life and he remembers always being surrounded by family and friends. There was no deprivation, trauma, or abandonment that he could recall, and, despite occasional arguments between members of his family, relationships were maintained and disagreements eventually resolved. "What am I so afraid of?" Joaquin wondered. I suggested to him that his fears may not be based in his own experiences but be something he may have learned from his family. "But they've never talked about anything frightening," he replied. "Well," I answered, "maybe you should spend some time with them and get them to talk about what their lives were like before you were born."

At our next session, Joaquin burst through the door carrying a pile of notes. He sat down at the edge of his chair and leaned toward me, eager to share his discoveries. "You're not going to believe this," he said. Joaquin had found out that there had been political oppression, brutal secret police, and torture in his family's past. His mother's younger brother had been shot and killed while they were walking down the street one quiet afternoon and her father had been ripped out of bed in the night, never to be seen again. For years, the family had tried to find him without success. They knew that if they stayed in their country, they would eventually all be killed, so they made a family decision to escape and seek refuge elsewhere.

Selling everything they owned, they were smuggled out of their country and made their way to the United States, where relatives helped to set them up in business. Joaquin was born a year later. For all of his life, Joaquin's family kept an unspoken agreement not to share their suffering with him. They wanted to protect him from their pain, and, perhaps, renew their own lives through his innocence. Although at first family members were hesitant to talk with him about their history, once they started talking the stories began to roll out in a stream of gestures, shouts, and tears. Their discussion went late into the night, ending with exhausted hugs and everyone lying awake in their beds, replaying the words and images they had exhumed after so many years.

In the months to come, Joaquin and I gradually made connections between his family's history and his own life. While these stories had never been shared in words while he was growing up, he had learned about his family's history through gestures, eye contact, and facial expressions. He recalled how his mother held him close when they walked down the street and the frightened look in her eyes when he strayed too far from her side. His family spent as little money as possible and hoarded what they had as if always preparing to take flight. They avoided making new friends and lived as an island unto themselves, immunizing themselves from the risk of betrayal. Although Joaquin never understood any of these actions in the context in which they occurred, he experienced the emotions within the context of his life. As he looked into his mother's eyes to determine whether the world was safe or dangerous, her expression told him to be afraid—despite the fact that they may have been at an amusement park or on their way to school.

Joaquin's experience reflects the strength of unconscious communication transfer across the social synapse and the early building of the right hemisphere through the emotional attunement with the members of his family. His family brought their past into Joaquin's present and painted their new life with their emotional history. Despite their silence and desire to protect him from their pain, he received it via the multichannel linkups between their brains, integrating their fear of the world, other people, and the expectation that something bad would surely happen again. His participation in these early relationships built Joaquin's anterior cingulate cortex and the other structures of his social brain, shaping his attachment patterns, his emotional experiences, and his ability to regulate his affect.

As an adult, Joaquin's life revolved around preparing for the attacks and violations he had never directly experienced or even heard about but had lived through via the unconscious connection with the minds and brains of his family. If we could examine Joaquin's brain, we would probably find higher levels of stress hormones and lower levels of receptors for these chemicals. We would probably also find lower levels of communication between neural networks dedicated to thinking and emotion. If we had videotapes of his early interactions with his mother, we would likely see her fearful facial expressions when he ventured too far away; we would also find a higher level of emotional arousal in her, which was transferred to Joaquin.

With this information, we now had a model that connected Joaquin's development with his adult experiences. The fact that he had come to therapy certainly didn't mean that he had left his mistrust at home. Our first order of business, despite the positive connection we had established, was to dig deep to explore any anxiety and distrust that might exist between us. Our relationship was to become the primary tool of brain change, and he had to trust me as much as possible before I would be able to help him. As I became important in Joaquin's life, I also became an alternative source of information about other people, the world, and the future.

In the months that followed we examined his thoughts, attitudes, and behaviors to see how well they fit the trajectory of his family's history and whether or not they were appropriate to the realities of his present life. Some of the questions that emerged were: Do I have to work as hard as I do? Do I need as much money as I'm making? Is the world really as dangerous as I experience it to be? Do I have to hold people away to protect myself from betrayal or loss? An awareness of the incongruity of his past experiences and the present situation took all bets off the table and opened up discussion about other possible options. Connecting his present life with his family history provided us with a narrative that allowed conscious examination of experience and the possibility of change. Whether or not the story we co-created was accurate, I don't know, but we liked it, came to a tentative belief in its veracity, and were most impressed by its usefulness. We agreed that it not only made sense but provided us with a valuable tool for our work.

There are many lessons in Joaquin's story. First and foremost is that we greatly underestimate the degree of information we are communicating to those around us, especially to the children for whom we care (Yehuda et al., 2005). We also underestimate how much our unconscious processes, while invisible to us, are often apparent to others. The receiver need not be conscious of the messages they are receiving and what they are learning. Parents who have unresolved trauma or conflicts will communicate their inner emotional world to their children. This early learning shapes the brain in a manner that can determine personality, behavior, thoughts, and even belief systems without our awareness. Once Joaquin gained access to the truth about his early experiences, we used our understanding of brain development to explain aspects of his life that were incongruent with the realities of his present life, and help him to become free from his family's emotional history.

Chapter 8

Addicted to Love

Lucy was having that great love affair [with heroin]
she had always dreamed of. It was dangerous and
rocky, violently depleting, but in the few minutes
that it was sweet, it made her feel the all-
encompassing heat of love.

—Ann Patchett, 2004, p. 235

The experience of being in love has been likened to an illness, an addiction, and even insanity. If you've ever fallen "madly" in love or been "insanely" jealous, you have a good idea why. Certainly people can become as obsessed with other people as an addict does with drugs. Love and addiction share a loss of reason, an absence of self-control, and an obsessive longing that *must* be satisfied. Paul MacLean (1990) suggested that substance abuse might be an attempt to compensate for a lack of the satisfying biochemicals stimulated by positive relationships. Put another way, drug addicts may satisfy their need for intimacy by manipulating the biochemistry of bonding and attachment (Gawin, 2001; Kilts et al., 2001). Think of how drug-addicted individuals often become indifferent to other people.

The attachment that addicts have to the paraphernalia, behaviors, and lifestyle of drug addiction may be due, in part, to the activation of reward circuits during exposure to these objects and experiences. The anguish caused by separation from mother or abandonment by a lover has also been likened to the experience of drug withdrawal (Herman & Panksepp, 1978). Cocaine craving results in robust activation of the anterior cingulate and decreased activation in the frontal lobes (Leon & Shadlen, 1999; Wexler et al., 2001). Remember that the anterior cingulate evolved to allow for maternal behavior, nurturance, and bonding, whereas the frontal lobes control foresight and inhibition. This combination drives the addict toward a drug as it drives others to a lover, with little inhibitory control or consideration for future consequences. Thus, although both drug addiction and social relationships are complex, there is considerable evidence to support the validity of MacLean's insight regarding a possible link between the two (Panksepp et al., 1978; Insel, 2003).

Internalized Mother

Should we think of our mothers as our first true loves? We are touched, held, kissed, fed, cared for, and rocked to sleep by our mothers. We gaze into their eyes and learn the joy of connection and the pain of separation. Early in life, we learn the smells, sights, touch, and sounds of our mother's presence, unconsciously associating these experiences with our bodily and emotional states. We all have what is called an *internalized mother,* a network of visceral, somatic, and emotional memories of our earliest interactions with our mothers. These unconscious memories serve as the core of self-esteem, our ability to self-soothe, and the nature and quality of our adult relationships. This foundational relationship establishes the biological, behavioral, and psychological structure of our expectations about the world and hope for the future.

To develop healthy affect-regulation and self-esteem, a baby needs to internalize experiences with its mother, such as:

- Soothing touch
- Being held softly and securely
- Comforting warmth
- The experience of homeostatic balance in regard to sleep, hunger, stimulation, etc.
- Repeated experiences of emotional transitions from states of distress to states of calm
- A sustained positive emotional state

Depending on the quality of our attachment experiences, all of these stimuli come to activate positive or negative states of mind. Although we don't consciously remember these experiences, they shape our neural infrastructure and exert a lifelong influence on us. This internalization process of early relationships is a central aspect of the consolidation of the self and our ability to cope with challenge, stress, and trauma.

Relationships as Regulators

Early bonding and attachment experiences result in a cascade of biochemical processes that stimulate and enhance the growth and connectivity of neural networks throughout the brain (Schore, 1994). On the other hand, withdrawal from those on whom the baby depends for biological stimulation and growth causes distress, pain, and anxiety (Hofer, 1984, 1987). Face-to-face interactions activate the child's sympathetic nervous system and increase oxygen consumption, energy metabolism, and gene expression. These higher levels of activation correlate with increased production of oxytocin, prolactin, endorphins, and dopamine; some of the same biochemical pathways involved in addiction.

The regulatory capacity of relationships is especially evident during infancy. When immature brains depend completely on caretakers for emotional and physical survival, even a brief separation results in measurable hypothalamic–pituitary–adrenal (HPA) responses (Hennessy, 1997). Early successful attachments set the stage for the social regulation of biological processes throughout life. It has also been found that the maturation of heart rate regulation correlates with attachment patterns: the more secure the mother–child attachment rating, the more regular (and regulated) the heart rate (Izard, Porges, et al., 1991). This correlation reflects the experience-dependent nature of development of both the HPA axis and the smart vagus. The dysregulation of the HPA axis and other homeostatic processes during early development is a likely contributor to the later development of mental illness (Verebey, Volavka, & Clouet, 1978).

Neurochemical Modulators

Relationships and addictive drugs both modulate the levels of neurochemicals in our brains, making us feel everything from misery to ecstasy. Warm and happy feelings, the desire to hold, touch, and nurture, the pain of separation and the joy of reunion have neurochemical correlates driving these powerful emotions. The dopaminergic systems activate foraging behavior involved in nesting and baby retrieval, whereas oxytocin, vasopressin, and endorphins mediate systems of intimate "close-up" caretaking, such as nursing, fondling, and cooing (Panksepp, 1998).

Neuropeptides (endorphins, oxytocin, and vasopressin) modulate pleasure, pain, attachment, and sexuality (Kovács et al., 1998; Pitman et al., 1990). The monoamines (dopamine, norepinephrine, and serotonin) regulate our energy, activity level, and sense of well-being; dopamine is a key neurotransmitter in human reward systems; norepinephrine modulates arousal and fight/flight reactions; and serotonin mediates mood, emotion, and aggression. Together these neurochemicals regulate our sense of safety, danger, despair, and joy. Their production and availability determine our background affect, our desire to form relationships, and our ability to cope with day-to-day stress.

Endorphins

The secretion of endogenous opioids, such as endorphins, reduces pain and creates a feeling of well-being and elation. Endorphins are strongly reinforcing and shape our preferences from early life (Kehoe & Blass, 1989). The central nucleus of the amygdala, a key component of fear circuitry, has a high density of opioid receptors (Goodman et al., 1980; Kalin, Shelton, & Snowdon, 1993). Thus, part of the emotional impact of endorphins is the inhibition of amygdala activation, making us feel calm, safe, and less vigilant. Cocaine also causes decreased activation of the core components of the social brain (amygdala, anterior temporal lobe, and OMPFC), suggesting that part of its intoxicating effect involves turning off the machinery of social evaluation, interpersonal vigilance, and the experience of shame. No wonder cocaine and heroin are experienced as an emotional revelation to those with histories of abuse, low self-esteem, and sensitivity to criticism.

Opioids shape early bonding experiences by promoting a core sense of safety and contributing to the positive emotional aspects of our internalized mothers. Opioid systems in animals have been found to modulate distress calls, play, grooming, affiliation behavior, and sexual arousal

(Vanderschuren et al., 1995, 1997). Research with primates suggests that the activation of the opioid systems of mother and child propels and regulates the attachment process. When primates come together for contact, grooming, or play, endorphin levels increase in both parent and child (Keverne, Martens, & Tuite, 1989). Human mothers often report feeling distress, anxiety, and sadness when separated from their newborns. In large part, this response is caused by the precipitous declines in endorphin levels that are triggered by separation. Simultaneously, separation from the mother results in declining levels of endorphins and the experience of distress in an infant.

When administered methadone (a compound similar to morphine), mother rats show a disruption of their maternal activity and diminished signs of affiliation during reunion with their pups (Grimm & Bridges, 1983). The attachment behavior of infant rats is similarly reduced by morphine, a finding that supports the reciprocal role of opioid systems in the regulation of attachment behavior (Kalin, Shelton, & Lynn, 1995). When baby guinea pigs are separated from their mothers, they cry or give distress calls that cease upon the administration of morphine (Herman & Panksepp, 1978). Morphine even gets a puppy's tail to wag in the same way as it does when its mother approaches (Knowles, Conner, & Panksepp, 1989). In the opposite direction, when guinea pigs and primates are given naltrexone (a drug that blocks the effects of endogenous opioids), separation cries, clinging behavior, and distress calls increase (Kalin, Shelton, & Barksdale, 1988; Kalin et al., 1995; Panksepp, Nelson, & Siviy, 1994).

These data all suggest that proximity of the mother is translated into the biochemical language of opiates. Higher levels make us feel safe, relaxed, and happy, whereas low levels make us feel anxious and stimulate behavior designed to increase proximity, caretaking, and a sense of safety. The soothing effects of opioids tell us that we are in the right place with the right person, just as heroin tells the addict that all is right with the world and that seeking attachment is not necessary.

Self-harm may also be regulated by endorphins. Adults who engage in repeated self-harm almost always describe childhoods that included abuse, neglect, or deep and sustained shame. Self-injurious behaviors in humans, most often in borderline clients, occur in response to real or imagined abandonment. Research has shown that self-harm decreases or ceases altogether in these individuals when they are given naltrexone (Pitman et al., 1990; van der Kolk, 1988). This finding would suggest that abandonment distress is reversed via the release of endorphins caused by the self-inflicted injury. The analgesic effects of these endogenous opioids may account for the sense of calm and relief reported after cutting, burning, or other self-injurious behaviors. As with heroin, the endogenous endorphins secreted as a result of self-harm become addictive and reinforce the continued use of self-inflicted injuries as a means of emotional regulation.

Oxytocin and Vasopressin

The molecules that control sexual behavior and egg-laying in reptiles evolved into oxytocin and vasopressin in humans. Found only in mammals, these chemicals are produced in the hypothalamus sent down into the pituitary and up into the limbic system and cortex. They are released into the circulation of a woman's bloodstream during labor, suckling, vaginal stimulation, and copulation (Panksepp, 1998). Oxytocin activates maternal behavior, inhibits irritability, aggressiveness, and infanticide, and drives the affiliative aspects of mothering (Bartels & Zeki, 2004; Insel, 1992, 2003; Üvnas-Moberg & Eriksson, 1996). When an infant suckles at its mother's breast, the nipple sends signals to the hypothalamus that trigger the release of oxytocin into the bloodstream. Oxytocin then causes contractions of the muscles within the breasts, which force milk to the nipples. This response becomes conditioned to the sights and sounds of her child, so that a mother may find that she expresses milk when she hears her baby cry.

Vasopressin facilitates pair bonding, attachment, and the maintenance of monogamy in a number of mammalian species (Young, Lim, Gingrich, & Insel, 2001). Its reciprocal relationship with testosterone contributes to its ability to decrease aggression in males in intimate and caretaking relationships (Delville et al., 1996). The large number of oxytocin and vasopressin binding sites in many areas of the amygdala plays a role in conditioned fear, autonomic regulation, HPA activation, and reproductive behavior (Carter, 1998, 2003; Veinante & Freund-Mercier, 1997). The amount of maternal behavior shown to pups correlates with the amount mothers received during infancy and with the number of oxytocin receptors in regions of their brains (medial preoptic area, septum, amygdala) controlling maternal behavior (Champagne et al., 2001). Here we find another experience-dependent biochemical set point: the number of oxytocin receptors in structures of the social brain.

In both male and female rats, the touch, pressure, and warmth of another led to increased levels of oxytocin, decreases in blood pressure, and mild sedation. This reaction to positive touch may explain why intimate relationships and extensive social networks correlate with physical and emotional health and well-being (Uvnäs-Moberg, 1997). Oxytocin and vasopressin appear to play a role in the protein synthesis necessary for neuroplastic processes involved in pair bonding and the learning of many social behaviors (Insel, 1997; Ostrowski, 1998). Oxytocin release can become conditioned to all kinds of social interactions, psychological states, and mental imagery. This potential for generalization may explain part of the benefit of transference in the psychotherapeutic relationship and the ongoing ability of relationships to change the social brain. Affiliation with a therapist, teacher, or any caring other may trigger brain processes that facilitate flexibility and openness to change (Uvnäs-Moberg, 1998).

The dual activation of endorphins and oxytocin allows the mother to be gratified by contact with her infant. Oxytocin interacts with dopamine receptors to block habituation, allowing us to find those we love continually (if not consistently) rewarding. Because of this process, mothers habituate to other peoples' children but not their own. Thus, evolution has used multiple reward systems to keep us focused on staying close and taking care of one another, especially our children.

Dopamine

The dopamine reward system has evolved into an important motivator of social interactions, bonding, and attachment (Insel, 2003). The pathway of this reward circuitry is a dopaminergic loop that begins in the ventral tegmental area in the brainstem (where dopamine is produced), projects to the amygdala, and then on to the thalamus. Projections from the thalamus ascend into the anterior cingulate and the OMPFC, which, in turn, send projections back down to the ventral tegmental region to modulate dopamine production. The OMPFC, sitting at the apex of this hierarchical network, is thought to be central to the organization and reinforcement of both attachment and addiction (London et al., 2000; Volkow & Fowler, 2000).

Dopamine neurons are activated as we learn what is rewarding, when reward values change, and when we link a series of events with an eventual reward (Hollerman & Schultz, 1998; Montague et al., 1996; Schultz, 1998). In this way, dopamine circuits are involved with the ongoing neural plasticity of learning about changes in the value, timing, and strength of rewards (Tremblay, Hollerman, & Schultz, 1998). In rat pups, repeated separation from the mother decreases dopamine activity and increases behavioral reactivity to stress. As adults, they show decreased exploratory and affiliative behavior and increased sensitivity to cocaine, suggesting that early separation or stress may make them less able to benefit from relationships and more vulnerable to drug abuse (Meaney, Brake, & Gratton, 2002). When people find others to be "unrewarding," they may become more likely to seek out alternative rewards. Money, status, objects, cats and dogs, or even the exquisite suffering involved in self-harm can be conditioned to activate pleasure centers. The problem is, when you depend on a substitute for love, you can never get enough.

Focus on the Social Motivation System

The idea of being addicted to love may be more than a metaphor. The biochemical systems regulated by relationships are the same as those impacted by cocaine and heroin, and the experiences of craving, dependency, and withdrawal are similar in both romance and addiction. Social behavior is as varied and complex as the biochemicals and neural networks underlying it. Primitive structures and neurochemical systems driving reproduction, foraging, pair bonding, and mothering were likely conserved and combined with later evolving emotional and cognitive reward systems to create our current relationship styles. Whereas neural hormones such as oxytocin and vasopressin have been widely studied for their role in maternal behavior, central reward circuitry modulated by dopamine and norepinephrine is a key component of human relationships. These once separate systems are now interwoven and mutually reinforcing. One example of this crossover is how oxytocin stimulates dopamine production to promote maternal behavior and other emotional aspects of caretaking (Panksepp, 1994). Table 8.1 lists some of the primary neurochemicals involved in social relationships and their specific contributions to social relationships.

The neural networks involved in the regulation and release of motivational biochemicals are triggered from multiple brain regions involved in everything from primitive reproductive processes (thalamus), to fear and anxiety regulation (amygdala), to moral and aesthetic judgments (prefrontal cortex). Whereas processes of bonding, attachment, and caretaking are initially regulated by the biology of reward, *relationships* come to regulate us as these biochemical processes become entrained with social interactions.

In examining the way our brains analyze rewards, Schultz stated, "The brain not only detects and analyzes past events, it also constructs and dynamically modifies predictions about future events on the basis of previous

Table 8.1. **Biochemistry of Social Motivation**

Androgen and estrogen	Sex drive
Testosterone	Monogamy and paternal behavior
Dopamine	Attraction
Norepinephrine and serotonin	Well-being, reward prediction, behavioral preparedness, foraging for food
Oxytocin and vasopressin	Attachment, nest building, pup retrieval, nursing, anxiety reduction
Endorphins/opioids	Grooming, affiliation, maternal behavior, sexual arousal, social reward, play behavior, down-regulates anxiety

Booth & Dabbs, 1993; Berg & Wynne-Edwards, 2001.

experience" (2000, p. 205). Although this statement was made concerning the expectation of food reward in a laboratory animal, the same principle operates in attachment schema. Interactions with caretakers are analyzed based on their emotional reward value, then unconsciously applied to future situations. These implicit predictions allow us to benefit from past learning by having them available in situations the brain deems relevant (Schultz & Dickenson, 2000). Of course, the brain isn't always right and often misapplies past experience to present situations, resulting in prejudice, transference, and all sorts of interpersonal distortions.

As we have already seen, the neural networks of the brain connect from side to side, up and down, back to front, and among many clusters of nuclei. One set of up-and-down circuits connects the frontal regions and the thalamus via structures called the basal ganglia (*ganglia* means, bundle of neurons). The general purpose of these circuits appears to be connecting sensory experiences (thalamus), executive decision making (frontal lobes), and motivational information with motor movements (basal ganglia). The motivational component organizes the needs of the body and our memories of what has been rewarding in the past. The basal ganglia's central involvement in motor behavior allows for the immediate translation of motivation into action. See Figure 8.1 for a visual representation of these circuits.

The ventral striatum (VS) consists of two major components of the basal ganglia: the putamen and the caudate nucleus. Neurons within these structures become activated in response to salient novel stimuli, to basic rewards (such as food), and to the expectation of rewards that have been experienced in the past (Apicella et al., 1992; Delgado et al., 2000; Ljungberg et al., 1992). These functions suggest that the ventral striatum receives and stores information about past events and triggers a state of motivational and behavioral preparedness to be rewarded (Everitt et al., 1989). The VS receives afferents (information) from the amygdala and the frontal and temporal lobes, as well as the dopamine centers of the substantia nigra and the ventral tegmentum (Schultz, 2000).

The circuits from the cortex provide the VS with information about predictable environmental events. The amygdala brings a store of past reward value, and the substantia nigra and ventral tegmental areas provide

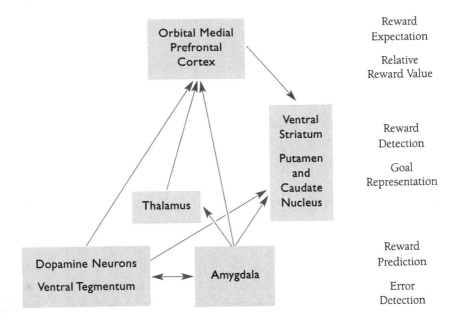

Figure 8.1. **Social motivation and the dopaminergic reward system.**
Adapted from Schultz (2000).

the biochemical trigger that motivates us to act (Schultz et al., 1992). Activation in the ventral striatum is based on expectation, even before the reward is presented, allowing for immediate action. After all, in evolutionary terms, "he (or she) who hesitates is lost." The more general role of the basal ganglia in motor movement and control makes it a logical location for a system of reward anticipation and immediate action. Through this rapid, automatic prediction, the past not only serves the present but in many ways determines it. That is, predictions become self-fulfilling prophesies by triggering patterns of behavior and cognition that shape our reactions to present situations. Although rapid changes of prediction can occur in laboratory situations, early social learning is resistant to change, requiring motivation, time, and discipline to accomplish.

Stan—"I've Got You under My Skin"

I was greeted by Stan's message when I arrived at work on a lazy summer afternoon. "Doc, I think I'm going crazy, you've got to help me. Please call ASAP!" I called Stan back and we made an "emergency" appointment for later that evening. Suddenly, the day didn't seem to be so lazy. My first thought when I saw him was that he looked terrible. We hadn't had a session for over a year, and I was surprised to see him looking so pale and anxious. At the time we terminated therapy, he was doing well in his career, making headway in communicating with his family, and searching for a significant other. At 38, everything seemed to be heading in the right direction. Looking at him now, his progress seemed to have vanished. He looked like a man whose life had gone terribly wrong.

About 15 months ago, shortly after we stopped working together, Stan began dating a woman. The relationship became very intense very quickly, and they were talking of marriage and family on their second date. "For the first 3 months," Stan said, "everything seemed just perfect. We were together all the time, traveled together, were physically compatible, and she was the sweetest, kindest woman I had ever met. Sometimes, lying in her arms, I felt this total sense of bliss: safe, comforted, and totally loved." He was describing what sounded like a child engulfed in his mother's love. "For those 3 months I thought I had found heaven on earth. I couldn't believe my luck. One day, it suddenly went away. She went from being kind, loving, and supportive to being upset with me almost all of the time. She would criticize and yell at me every day. I'd end up crying after hours of being berated, begging her to tell me what was going wrong."

Stan thought about breaking up with her on a daily basis but could never bring himself to do it. "The thought of losing her would send me into a state of panic, making me want to see her even more!" They argued and fought for hours, often through the night. According to Stan, she sometimes became physically violent, throwing things and hitting him. He had lost weight, was performing poorly at work, and described himself as physically exhausted. He had begun to feel so bad about himself that he withdrew from his friends, believing that they no longer liked him. "I think I have battered spouse syndrome! I think I have PTSD! Maybe I'm having a nervous breakdown!"

Stan was getting something from this relationship that he hadn't experienced since childhood: the addictive rush of attachment chemicals and the distress at their withdrawal. We set up daily meetings for a couple of weeks to reestablish our connection and to work intensely on changing his present situation. I hoped that increasing the salience and reward value of *our* relationship would provide some leverage against what seemed like a downwardly spiraling addiction. Although Stan had never been an addict, he had enough experience with addicted friends to recognize the symptoms. Once the connection between his relationship and drug addiction was made in his mind, we discussed the biochemical processes involved and how the addiction model seemed to fit his situation. "I keep going for the high and ignoring the fact that it's ruining everything in my life," Stan reflected. "There's no other way I can explain or justify this relationship. It's going to end badly, and prolonging it is only making it worse."

Still, it was hard. Stan said he felt like his heart was tugged in her direction, and he kept saying to himself, "Just one more night, just one more day." He would think, "She isn't really so bad, I can handle this." Then he would catch himself sounding like an addict in denial and try to get a grip on his feelings. As a part of our renewed work together, he agreed to attend support groups for drug addicts. Substituting his girlfriend's name for whatever substance was being discussed, he found the meetings helpful. When he finally did break off the relationship, he discovered that she had already started dating someone else a month earlier. He was devastated when he found out that she had been cheating on him, and it took him many months to get over the physical and emotional pain of both her betrayal and absence. Over months of "detoxification" he gradually felt his heart, mind, and body return to normal. He often described the relationship as an experience that almost killed him. Stan had been addicted to love.

As in most obsessive relationships, Stan had stopped seeing his friends and engaging in other activities that he once enjoyed. Renewing rewarding behaviors and reconnecting with friends whom he had neglected while in the throes of his relationship were an important part of his recovery. He had to reestablish the connections between his reward circuitry and healthy relationships. As he learned to lower his threshold for positive emotional stimulation, Stan also needed to relearn the value of nontraumatic intimacy that might now seem boring and uninteresting to him. Given the complex mixture of motivations and rewards in relationships, it is not surprising that they can be wonderful, difficult, and an endless source of fascination. Each relationship carries some combination of reinforcers that include love, lust, safety, status, danger, calm, and peril. Mediated by a variety of neural systems, each ranks differently in our personal hierarchies of needs, interests, and desires. But in the end, *we might as well face it, we're addicted to love.*

Chapter 9

Implicit Social Memory

*Everything that falls upon the eye is apparition, a
sheet dropped over the world's true workings.*
—Marilynn Robinson, 1980, p. 116

The everyday understanding of memory is the storage of images, emotions, and bits of information gleaned from day-to-day experience. Names, dates, historical events, and all kinds of trivia inhabit our memories, intermingled with the emotional experiences of our most intimate moments. Each of us relies on our memories as we struggle to remember where we left our keys, the name of an acquaintance, or how to solve a math problem. It turns out that the terrain of memory is far more complex than we ever imagined. Proust found memory so seductive that he took to his bed for years to write his masterpiece *Remembrance of Things Past*. He spent more than a decade in his darkened Paris apartment, exploring the vast kingdom contained within the few pounds of neurons behind his eyes.

Systems of Memory

There are two primary categories of remembrance: explicit and implicit memory. Each, in turn, contains a number of subtypes organized by different neural systems. Explicit memory includes sensory, semantic, episodic, narrative, and autobiographical memories. We depend on explicit memory to recognize and remember the faces of familiar others, the rules of etiquette, and the language and stories of our culture. Narrative memory, the basis of storytelling, has the added quality of being organized sequentially through time. This system of memory is especially important for the formation of emotional regulation and cultural identity. Autobiographical memory in which the narrator is at the center of the story, combines episodic, semantic, and emotional memories with self-awareness.

Categories of implicit memory include sensory, emotional, and procedural memories, as well as stimulus–response conditioning. Learning how to walk or serve a tennis ball are examples of procedural memories, as are many habitual emotional reactions to social situations, such as tensing up when a stern parent enters the room. Systems of implicit social memory include attachment schemas, instincts, inner objects, transference, and superego. It turns out that the vast majority of memory is implicit, and it is these memories that shape our emotional experiences, self-image, and relationships. Each form of memory has its own neural architecture and developmental timetable (Tulving, 1985). From a scientific perspective, we understand explicit systems better than implicit ones because they are more obvious and easier to test. Although we have begun to understand some of the structures involved in memory, just how memory is stored and retrieved is still pretty much a mystery.

The early sensory–motor and emotional memories of infants and toddlers are mediated via the amygdala, thalamus, cerebellum, and orbital medial prefrontal structures. This system organizes and retains primitive vestibular–sensory–emotional memories of early caretaking, rendering them of permanent psychological significance. These early implicit memories come to serve as the emotional background against which subsequent psychological development takes place. As the brain matures, the hippocampus, temporal lobes, and lateral prefrontal lobes begin to organize the systems of explicit memory. This is why implicit memory is often called "early memory" and explicit memory "late memory." In normally developing people, implicit and explicit memory systems are woven seamlessly together to create a unified conscious experience of the world. With severe trauma, memory systems can become "dissociated," resulting in disturbances of cognition, emotion, and the development of posttraumatic stress disorder (PTSD). Table 9.1 summarizes the functions of different memory systems.

Table 9.1. **Multiple Systems of Memory**

Implicit Memory	Explicit Memory
Early developing/subcortical bias	Later developing/cortical bias
Right-hemisphere bias	Left hemisphere bias
Amygdala centered/OMPFC	Hippocampal/dorsal lateral
Context free/no source attribution	Contextualized/known memory source
Implicit Social Memory	**Explicit Social Memory**
Attachment schema	Identity/social information
Transference	Narratives
Superego	Autobiographical descriptions
Background affect	Social rules, norms, expectations

Although most of our important social and emotional lessons occur during our early years, we have little to no conscious memory of learning them. This phenomenon, referred to as *infantile amnesia,* is due to the immaturity of hippocampal–cortical networks, whose functioning is required for the conscious recollection of the learning process (referred to as source attribution). Despite our lack of explicit memory for these experiences, they come to form the infrastructure of our lives. We experience these early lessons as the "givens" of life, rarely noticing their existence or questioning their veracity. We seldom realize that they are influencing and guiding our moment-to-moment experiences.

Early Social Memory

When does memory begin? The first forms of implicit social memory may develop as we float in the womb listening to the rhythms of our mother's heartbeat and the distinct tone of her voice. After coming into the world, we recognize the smell of her body and breast milk, the cadence of her voice, or her special touch (de Casper & Fifer, 1980; MacFarlane, 1975). Early implicit memory will later allow us to link the sight of our father with raising our arms, smiling, feeling lifted up, and a sense of safety and warm connection. Deep associations among intimacy, anxiety, love, and shame are forged in early implicit memory and become the core of our attachment schema and our ability to regulate our emotions (both of which we discuss further in the next chapter).

When implicit memory is unconscious, it cannot be thought about. It can, however, be demonstrated via attitudes, beliefs, and behaviors. Have you ever met a stranger and felt a strong and immediate emotional reaction? Such reactions to people, places, and objects may well be the residue of earlier memories. Think about "overreacting" to something; it implies that the difference between an appropriate reaction and how we actually react is attributable to an enhanced sensitivity based on prior learning. For example, children who suffer early abuse may enter their schoolage years agitated, aggressive, and destructive, engaging in fights, property damage, and even animal torture. In the absence of a memory of his or her trauma, the child's behavior is not experienced as a reaction to a negative event but as a natural part of the self, an indication of his or her essential "badness." This feeling is usually reinforced by an array of critical adults and feelings of shame that consolidate into a negative self-image.

As interpreters of implicit social memory, psychotherapists attempt to reconstruct a past that is simultaneously known and unremembered. What a client tells a therapist as a narrative may have little relation to what really happened. What a client knows or believes about his or her life is most often a tapestry of truths, distortion, fantasies, and family myths that may be quite different from the emotional realities of what the person experienced. Attempting to uncover implicit memory and integrating it into conscious experience is one of the central tenets of the therapeutic process. How, then, does early implicit memory intrude into adult consciousness in ways that are relevant to psychotherapy? Three forms of implicit memory that are addressed by therapists are lack of recall, superego, and transference.

Lack of Recall

Many people have only spotty memories of their childhoods; others say they have no memories at all before adolescence. This lack of explicit memory usually comes with an array of anxiety-based symptoms and the somewhat vague impression that their childhoods were either happy or unhappy. Ironically, this absence of memory is itself a form of memory. Lack of recall strongly suggests high levels of anxiety during childhood that mitigated against the consolidation of long-term memory. It also points to the possibility that dissociative defenses were employed to protect against the dysregulating impact of their earlier circumstances.

Although the lack of recall may be an implicit memory for a stressful childhood, no clear statement can be made about what exactly did happen. We can only speculate that as children, these individuals did not receive help in regulating their feelings or in understanding what was happening to them. Maybe they were not adequately protected from certain people in their lives who made them feel frightened, anxious, or ashamed. Perhaps they did not have the experience of people who listened to them or were able to help them articulate and share their feelings. All of these factors contribute to a lack of recall and need to be explored within a healing therapeutic relationship.

As we will soon see, a lack of recall is associated with attachment styles that are anxious, ambivalent, and dismissing. When children are unable to regulate their anxiety, they may turn away from those around them and attempt to self-regulate. These children may escape into hobbies, books, and fantasies or become immersed in activities outside of the home. Pushing away their disturbing reality, they will create an idea of their life, freeze it in their minds, and avoid an awareness of contradictory information. Despite this defensive approach, insecure and traumatized children have a difficult time self-regulating and suffer from anxiety, depression, and a variety of other symptoms. These symptoms are themselves forms of implicit memory; what the mind forgets, the body remembers in the form of fear, pain, or physical illness.

Starting with the hypothesis that childhood was experienced as a stressful and perhaps dangerous time, we begin to gather information. Fragments of memories, information from siblings and other relatives, and the trajectories of their lives can be used to construct a past that has some connection to the unknowable truth. This "constructed past" often fosters self-understanding, acceptance, and self-forgiveness by providing a model that places current experience in a historical context and works against a unilateral acceptance of blame.

Superego

Freud suggested that the superego is the internalization of the parents' values: the voice we hear inside our heads that serves as a moral compass and guides our behavior. At a deeper emotional level, the superego is our early implicit memory of our experience of how our parents experienced us. In other words, did our parents seem to cherish, love, and value us, or did they find us annoying, disgusting, or uninteresting? When we were with them, did we feel safe and protected or worthy of rejection and abandonment? Were we loved for who we were or for what we did that pleased them? When we gazed into their eyes, did they reflect back our love or did they appear irritated, indifferent, or unhappy? None of us is capable of accessing an explicit memory of these very early experiences. Our only access to these primitive experiences is what we see reflected in our self-esteem, the way we treat ourselves, and how we allow others to treat us.

Do we take care of ourselves, nurture ourselves, and feel we have value? Do we live under the scrutiny of an internal jury, second-guessing and criticizing our every thought and deed? How do we treat ourselves when we make a mistake? When we fail, can we face the disappointment, learn from the experience, and move on? If so, we probably had mature, healthy, and forgiving parents. Brutal self-criticism, overwhelming shame, and a merciless drive for perfection all reflect a harsh and punitive superego, suggesting that at the core of our experience, there is an anticipation of abandonment if we don't measure up to expectations. In this situation, we are usually completely conscious of how hard we are on ourselves but unaware that our feelings and behaviors are shaped by our implicit memories.

Before we start calling our parents unfeeling monsters, let's keep in mind that the superego is most often based on our parents' implicit memories of their own early experiences and unknowingly transferred by them to our own. I have worked with many adults who had loving parents who had some degree of obsessive–compulsive disorder (OCD). Individuals with OCD are usually made very uncomfortable by chaos, disorganization, or a fear of contamination. Thinking about all the mess, chaos, and disruption that go along with having a baby, it is easy to see how difficult it might be for an OCD parent to raise a child. Clients with OCD parents often have very harsh superegos; I imagine that they saw, in their parents' eyes, the reflected horrors of spilled juice, messy toys, and filled diapers. Their parents' anxiety and need for constant and total control serve as proof of the dangerousness of the world and the vital importance of "never slipping up." Combine these early experiences with a possible genetic bias toward anxiety and you have a potent combination for a harsh superego and a frightening experience of the world.

Transference

Our experience of others is created at the interface of our memories of people in our past and our experiences of people in our lives today. Thus we never experience a person as totally new but as some blend of our expectations, implicit schema, and who he or she really is. This mixture of the past and present in everyday life results from the fact that implicit memory processes are faster, automatic, and guide explicit memory and conscious experience. By the time we are consciously aware of someone, our experience already has been shaped by past experience. Reacting in a manner inappropriate to someone in a present situation is often the result of what is called transference, a distortion of the reality of the other based on our own past experience.

The speed of amygdala processing relative to the "slow" processing of explicit memory allows it to alert us to possible danger and generate a physiological reaction that occurs prior to what is being consciously processed. This background affect will then shape the perception of what we are consciously attending to (Nomura et al., 2003). Research has found that, although it takes our brain 400–500 milliseconds to bring sensations to conscious awareness, it takes only 14 milliseconds to implicitly react to, and categorize, visual information (Keysers et al., 2001). An example of this is amygdala activation in reaction to seeing faces presented too quickly for the viewer to be consciously aware of having seen them (Adolphs et al., 1994; Critchley, Daly, Phillips, et al., 2000; Morris et al., 1996; Morris Ohman et al., 1998; Whalen, 1998).

Transference is the activation of implicit social memories from the past—sensory and emotional memories of significant people in our lives that are acted out in contemporary relationships. One example of the power of transference is a female client who expects the therapist to become sexually involved with her based on past abusive experiences with caretakers and authority figures. Another might be a client who tries to manipulate a therapist into taking care of him and giving advice, attempting to discover his overprotective and controlling mother. These memories, evoked in any relationship, may be enhanced by the power differential and privacy of the therapeutic relationship and experienced as if they are being caused by the therapist. Transference is considered central to psychotherapy because it makes available the client's earliest struggles for love, safety, and survival that may not be available to explicit memory. One client who was showering me with critical comments had a flash of insight about the transference he was experiencing when he said, "You know it isn't personal—I just love to hurt people for not loving me enough."

Brian—"My Head Is Killing Me"

Sharon called to set up an appointment for her husband Brian. He had suffered from terrible headaches for the last few years and had become increasingly dependent upon pain medication to get through the day. Brian had seen many doctors, but none of them had found any sign of cancer, brain tumors, circulatory problems, or neurological damage. Still, the headaches continued. When his last doctor suggested seeing a therapist, Brian stormed out of the room while Sharon stayed behind and was given my number.

Brian sat in my waiting room, motionless, arms crossed, staring at the wall. He was a tall, muscular man of 30, with the moustache of a highway patrolman. I walked out to greet him and waited for him to look at me. His gaze remained locked on the wall across from him. After a while, I said, "Brian?" He gradually turned his head, nodded, and entered my office. Settling into the couch, he resumed his silent rigid posture. After what seemed like a very long time, he looked at me and said, "What do *you* think you can do for me?" His tone suggested it was more a challenge than a question.

I imagined what this experience must be like for Brian. Going from doctor to doctor, never finding the help he needed, and now meeting with me was surely another disappointment waiting to happen. Wanting to avoid focusing on his problem too quickly, I broke the silence by asking him what he did for a living. "Baseball," was his response. "First base." Here was something I knew a little about, and it was with baseball that we started. My interest in baseball opened a window into his world, and our first meeting became a locker room session on strategy, history, and trivia. In the process, I also learned a little about his education, family history, his wife, and their 4-year-old son. Brian made sure to tell me that he was only seeing me on his wife's insistence. "Personally," he said, "I don't see any point in it." After all, there was something wrong with his head that the "real" doctors were too stupid to find. After he left, I wondered what had happened to make him so angry and cause him constant pain.

During our next session, I discovered that all of Brian's doctors, managers, coaches, teachers, and the police—in fact, anyone in a position of authority over him—were incompetent and of questionable moral repute. This rejecting stance seemed like good evidence of a powerful implicit social memory that Brian experienced when he looked at me. I know that when clients take this stance toward authority figures, they have usually been betrayed, disappointed, or hurt by someone they depended upon, usually a parent or caretaker. One of my goals as a therapist was to sidestep his transference enough to form a working alliance. Another was to make this transference conscious so that Brian and I could discuss it and explore its origin. Talking about baseball, and especially letting him guide the discussion with his expertise, minimized the power differential and the activation of his resentment and distrust to the point where we created a zone of connection.

After a few months, Brian felt safe enough to share his most painful and important memories with me. Brian's father was a harsh, abusive man who regularly became violent after a few drinks. A typical evening consisted of Brian's father locking him in his room and then beating his mother while Brian listened. Brian would lie on the floor in front of his door and see the reflection of the beating on the polished oak floor.

While his mother yelled to him for help, he would scream at his father to stop. Unable to go to his mother's aid, he gradually began to scratch the skin off his face so that he could share her suffering. After innumerable violent episodes, Brian grew large enough to stop his father. Still, he was never able to forgive himself for taking so long to protect his mother.

For a number of years, he and his father had maintained an uneasy truce and things remained peaceful at home. His physical symptoms remitted, he did well at school, and he became immersed in playing baseball at increasingly higher levels. He was accepted to college on full scholarship and excelled in his sport, becoming known for his athletic abilities. He made good friends and even met a girl and fell in love. Brian seemed to have a bright future, his painful past only a distant memory, until his junior year of college when he received the call that his mother was dying of cancer.

Brian immediately went home and cared for his mother until her death 2 months later. In the procession to the cemetery, Brian experienced a debilitating headache. The pain was so strong that he had a hard time distinguishing the reason for his tears. In the 10 years since her death, Brian graduated from school and became a professional baseball player. He met Sharon soon after college and they had a son 5 years later. Through this entire time he had struggled with headaches and other physical symptoms, visiting doctors and experimenting with all kinds of legal and illegal drugs. Over the years, scratching his face evolved into dermatitis, gastritis, asthma, and now headaches. He managed as best he could until his son reached the same age that Brian was when he had become aware of his father's violence. Since then, Brian struggled to suppress violent urges toward his wife and child. After dedicating so much of his life to trying not to be like his father, Brian discovered that his father was within himself. He was devastated.

From the perspective of Brian's conscious experience, he suffered from an undiagnosed neurological problem and had had a great deal of bad luck with doctors and other authority figures throughout his life. His array of stomach, skin, and respiratory problems was inherited from his mother, and his anger at his wife and child were a result of his headaches and work stress. Brian's implicit social memory, demonstrated through his behaviors, feelings, and symptoms, told quite a different story. Here are some of my impressions about Brian's situation:

- The betrayal and violence from his father established implicit networks of emotional activation in the face of authority figures, who were reflexively experienced as dangerous and incompetent. Early, amygdala-based memory systems remained vigilant for threat and revictimization. Fast appraisal circuits skewed his conscious experience of men in authority as being untrustworthy.
- The rage and sadness from his childhood, always cloaked in silence, were converted into a variety of bodily symptoms and physical illnesses. Unable to be processed by conscious, cortical circuits that could have helped him express and process his negative experiences, these emotions were converted into dysregulation of arousal, immunological functioning, and physical illnesses.
- The birth of his child and his current family situation contained many cues that triggered painful and violent memories from his childhood. Implicit emotional memory circuits could be triggered by crying, the smell of baby powder, and the intense feelings of love for, and even the dependency of, his child.
- His harsh superego resulted in his need to put intense pressure on himself to succeed. The internalization of abuse resulted in a background affect of shame and humiliation. These feelings intensified his emotional dysregulation and led him to avoid seeking help, for which he felt unworthy due to his failure to protect his mother.
- He hated authority, not only because he was betrayed by his father, but also because he had to hold his need for a kind and loving father at an emotional distance.

The opportunity to talk about his childhood, express his emotions, and establish conscious connections between past trauma and his present life relieved most of Brian's physical symptoms. Teaching Brian how to discern and express his emotions was as vital as teaching him alternative ways of coping with negative emotions when they arose. He also was able to reestablish a strong connection with his wife and bond in a deeper way with his son. Because his ability to trust had been so damaged by his father's behavior, building a positive relationship with him was a necessary first step in the therapeutic process. His implicit social memories, reactivated in the transference relationship, allowed us to examine his feelings first hand, and more fully appreciate their original source. The emotional quality of our relationship and the nature of our interactions set the biological and interpersonal stage for positive neuroplastic changes in his brain (Cozolino, 2002).

Chapter 10

Ways of Attaching

All of us, from cradle to grave, are happiest when life is organized as a series of excursions, long or short, from the secure base provided by our attachment figures.
—John Bowlby, 1988, p. 27

We are born with immature brains and cling to our mothers long after the umbilical cord is cut. Our mothers and other caretakers are the most salient aspects of our new world, becoming the central axis of our early learning. The first things we learn about our caretakers are how well they are able to make us feel safe and warm. Their skills as parents will depend on their empathic abilities, emotional maturity, and how they themselves were parented as children. Because these traits are embedded within implicit social memory and transferred to the same systems in their children, we can say that caretaking transmits the childhood experiences of parents to their children, making a parent's unconscious a child's first reality.

As we learned in the last chapter, attachment schemas are a category of implicit social memory that reflects our early experience with caretakers. Our best guess is that these schemas reflect the learning histories that shape experience-dependent networks connecting the orbital frontal cortex, the amygdala, and their many connections that regulate arousal, affect, and emotion. It is within these neural networks that interactions with caretakers are paired with feelings of safety and warmth, or anxiety and fear. How attachment schemas are established has widespread ramifications for both our children and *their* children. Positive attachment schemas enhance the formation of a biochemical environment in the brain conducive to regulation, growth, and optimal immunological functioning. Negative attachment schemas have the opposite effect, correlating with higher frequencies of physical and emotional illness throughout life.

Monkeys show consistent patterns of attachment across generations, with adult maternal behavior being predicted fairly well by the amount of contact received as an infant (Champoux et al., 1992; Fairbanks, 1989). Although attachment schemas in humans also show consistency over time, research and everyday experience suggest that they are also capable of change (Cicchetti & Barnett, 1991; Waters et al., 2000). And while human parenting shares similar biological determinants to monkeys and apes, in humans these more primitive systems are combined with later evolving cognitive and emotional elements of bonding and love (Mason & Mendoza, 1998). Thus, humans may be able to use conscious processing and decision making to alter their attachment schemas and relationship behaviors (Suomi, 1999).

John Bowlby and Attachment Schema

John Bowlby, an anthropologist and psychoanalyst, observed primates in the wild, children in orphanages, and mother–child interactions in his clinical practice. He recognized that both primate and human children thrive in the context of consistent and caring adults. Fascinated with the delicate balance between bonding and exploration, Bowlby developed the concepts of *attachment schema, proximity seeking,* and a *secure base.* His work, highlighting the importance of both physical contact and consistent caretakers, resulted in a shift in the care of institutionalized children. Children who had previously been cared for by whomever was available were now assigned to specific caretakers to encourage attachment. Bowlby's insights also worked against the cultural biases that resulted in the devaluation of parenting.

Bowlby believed attachment schema to be summations of thousands of experiences with caretakers that become unconscious reflexive predictions of the behaviors of others. These schema become activated in subsequent relationships and lead us either to seek or avoid proximity. They also determine whether we can use relationships to maintain physiological homeostasis and regulate our emotions. Attachment schemas are especially apparent under stress because of their central role in affect regulation. These implicit memory schema are obligatory; that is, they are automatically activated before we are even conscious of the people with whom we are about to interact. Schemas shape our conscious experience of others by activating rapid and automatic evaluations *hundreds of milliseconds* before our perception of others reaches consciousness. Decades of work inspired by Bowlby's theories provide a window to the implicit social memory of attachment.

Measuring Attachment I: In-Home Observations of Mothers and Children

The first step for attachment researchers was to develop observational strategies that could reliably measure interactive behaviors. They began by going into the homes of young families to carefully watch and try to categorize the ways in which mothers and children interact in their natural setting. These observations eventually led to the development of four broad categories of mother–child attachment patterns: (1) free/autonomous, (2) dismissing, (3) enmeshed–ambivalent, and (4) disorganized (Ainsworth et al., 1978; Main & Solomon, 1986). Each of these categories describes characteristics of mothers' behaviors, attitudes, and style of communication with their children.

The *free/autonomous* mothers were available, sensitive, and perceptive of their children's feelings and needs. These mothers were seen as effective in their interactions with their children. *Dismissing* mothers were rated as unavailable, rejecting, and distant. *Ambivalent* mothers demonstrated inconsistent availability that fluctuated with overinvolvement with their children. Mothers in the *disorganized* category appeared to create conflictive situations for their children. They often seemed to be both frightened by, and frightening to, their children. Many of these mothers were subsequently shown to be suffering from trauma and/or unresolved grief.

Measuring Attachment II: Abandonment, Stress, and Reunion

The next stage of exploration was to see if the children of these mothers demonstrated different kinds of attachment behaviors. The research method developed to study the attachment behavior of children was the infant strange situation (ISS). The ISS takes place in the laboratory and consists of first placing a mother and child in a room and allowing them some time to settle. Then a stranger joins them (usually one of the researchers), taking a seat off to the side. After a period of time, the mother exits the room, leaving the child alone with the stranger, and then returns after a set amount of time. When the mother returns, she sits back in her chair, allowing the child to respond in his or her own way. This method was chosen based on Bowlby's experience with mother and child primates in the wild. Bowlby observed that the absence of the mother combined with the presence of a stranger would create anxiety and evoke a distress call from the child (Ainsworth et al., 1978). This situation was chosen to measure attachment schemas based on the assumption that they would most likely manifest under the stress of separation.

The ISS rates reunion behavior, which is the child's reaction to the mother upon her return. Researchers observed these interactions, wanting to know upon reunion:

- Does the child seek comfort from the mother, or does the child ignore her?
- Does the child go over to the mother or remain distant?
- Is the child easily comforted, or does he or she have a hard time being soothed?
- Does the child go back to play or remain anxious, clingy, or withdrawn?

These and other behaviors became the focus of the ISS scoring system and are thought to reflect the child's implicit prediction of the mother's capacity to soothe and serve as a safe haven.

From these observations, four categories of behavior were identified: (1) secure, (2) avoidant, (3) anxious–ambivalent, and (4) insecure–disorganized. Strong correlations were found between these categories of childrens' reunion behavior and the attachment styles of their mothers. Children rated as *secure*—about 70% of the sample—generally had mothers who rated as free/autonomous. When their mothers returned, these children sought proximity, were quickly soothed, and soon returned to exploration and play. These children seemed to expect that their mothers would be attentive, helpful, and encouraging of their continued autonomy. They had learned that when they were distressed, interacting with their mothers would help them to regain a sense of security. Securely attached children seem to have internalized their mothers as a source of comfort, using them to feel safe while they seek stimulation elsewhere (Stern, 1995b).

Avoidantly attached children tended to have dismissing mothers; in turn, the children ignored their mothers when they came back into the room. These children might glance over toward their mothers or would avoid eye contact all together. Despite their anxiety about the stranger, these children appeared to lack an expectation that their mothers would be a source of soothing; they seemed to decide that it would be easier to regulate their own emotions. They may have learned that whatever stress they were experiencing may well be compounded by their mothers' inattention or dismissal.

Children rated as *anxious–ambivalent* sought proximity but were not easily soothed and were slow to return to play. Anxious–ambivalent children often had enmeshed or inconsistently available mothers and their stress seemed to be worsened by their mothers' distress. Their slow return to play and continued emotional dysregulation may reflect the internalization of their mothers' anxiety and their lack of a safe haven. These children tended to be clingier and engaged in less exploration of the room.

The children rated as *disorganized* were interesting yet sad to observe. Upon reunion, these children often engaged in chaotic and even self-injurious behaviors: They would spin, fall down, hit themselves, and not know what to do to calm themselves. They seemed overcome by trance-like expressions, froze in place, or maintained uncomfortable bodily postures. It was as if they were attempting to simultaneously approach the mother for security and avoid her for safety. The resulting inner turmoil dysregulated these children to the point that their adaptation, coping, and even their motor abilities appeared to crumble.

It was later described that these chaotic behaviors were often demonstrated by children with mothers who were suffering from unresolved grief or trauma. These mothers suffered from a variety of posttraumatic-like symptoms and employed dissociative and other primitive defenses. It appears that the chaos of the mother's internal world can be witnessed in the child's behavior even when it is not evident in the behavior of the mother. Consistent with this observation is the finding that frightening behavior on the part of a mother, regardless of the mother's attachment style, can result in disorganized types of behavior (Schuengel et al., 1999).

Measuring Attachment III: Mothers Talk about Their Childhoods

What about the relationship between a mother's parenting style and how *she* was parented? This is much trickier to study because we can't observe interactions from long ago, and we know that the conscious memory of childhood is prone to many gaps and distortions. The family, after all, is a cradle of misinformation, so we need an indirect measure of the impact of childhood on the quality of adult cognitive and emotional functioning. A research tool that seems to have succeeded in this tricky and difficult task is the Adult Attachment Interview (AAI; Main & Goldwyn, 1998).

On the face of it, the AAI is a set of open-ended questions about childhood experiences and relationships. The real goal, however, is to obtain a narrative that can be subjected to an analysis of coherence. Coherence analysis does not focus on the content of what is said but on its logic, structure, linearity, and understandability. Scoring takes into account the integration of emotional and experiential materials, gaps in memory and information, if the story can be understood by the listener, and the overall quality of the subject's presentation (Hesse, 1999). These qualities are believed to reflect the development and integration of neural systems, which, in turn, are an indirect measure of the quality of early social experience, bonding, and attachment (Cozolino, 2002; Siegel, 1999).

Again, four categories were correlated with parenting behaviors seen during in-home observations of mothers. Mothers (and fathers) who were rated as *free–autonomous* tended to have detailed episodic memories of their childhoods and a balanced perspective between the good and the bad aspects of their parents and childhoods. They were able to describe these experiences in a coherent narrative, free of significant gaps in information and emotional intrusions. The childhood narratives of free–autonomous parents were understandable, consistent, and believable to the listener (Main, 1993). These parents are better able to access, organize, and integrate cognitive and emotional memory. They are able to remember their own childhoods, have processed negative and traumatic experiences, and are more fully available to their children. This research suggests that parents' emotional availability to their children parallels their emotional availability to themselves (Siegel & Hartzel, 2003).

The *dismissing* group demonstrated a lack of recall for childhood events. They tended to idealize their parents and dismiss the importance of their early relationships, just as they were dismissive of their own children. The narratives of these mothers were incoherent, usually due to significant gaps of time and information. Dismissing parents seem to cope through denial and repression to a degree that interferes with adequate integration of cognitive and emotional processing. The lack of recall suggests encoding deficits due to trauma, chronic stress, or a lack of assistance in regulating affect and reinforcing memory early in life.

Mothers rated as *enmeshed–ambivalent* also had incoherent narratives but for different reasons than the dismissing group. Enmeshed–ambivalent mothers demonstrated an excess of verbal output which they had difficulty organizing. They were also lacking boundaries between past and present events, further confusing their listeners. These mothers appeared preoccupied, pressured, and had a harder time keeping the listener in mind. Lastly, the *disorganized* group had highly incoherent narratives with content suggestive of unresolved trauma and grief. The coherence of their narratives was disrupted by emotional intrusions and missing information about experiences of trauma and loss. Their narratives not only reflected the disorganization of verbal and emotional expression, but also the devastating impact their unresolved trauma had had on the development and integration of the networks of their social brain. Table 10.1 summarizes the findings from these three phases of attachment research.

Table 10.1. Summary of Findings from Attachment Research

In-home Observations of Mothers	Infant Strange Situation	Adult Attachment Interview
Free–Autonomous Emotionally available, perceptive, and effective	**Secure** Infant seeks proximity, is easily soothed/returns to play	Detailed memory, balanced perspective, narrative coherency
Dismissing Distant and rejecting	**Avoidant** Infant does not seek proximity and does not appear upset	Dismissing/denial, minimizing, idealizing, lack of recall
Enmeshed–Ambivalent Inconsistent availability	**Anxious–Ambivalent** Infant seeks proximity, is not easily soothed, and is not quick to return to play	Excessive verbal output, intrusions, pressured, preoccupied, idealizing or enraged
Disorganized Disorienting, frightening, or frightened sexualized behaviors	**Disorganized** Chaotic, self-injurious	Disoriented, conflictive behavior; unresolved loss and traumatic history

The power of the relationship between mother and child attachment patterns was demonstrated when AAIs were administered to women before they became pregnant with their first child. When these children reached their first birthdays, their attachment patterns were rated in the ISS. In 75% of these cases, the child's attachment pattern was predicted by the mother's AAI rating (Fonagy et al., 1991).

Relationships Become Biological Structure

Through this remarkable sequence of studies, we gain insight into how early experience is internalized, shapes the way we process information, and gets transmitted from one generation to the next. Attachment schemas reflect the transduction of interpersonal experience into biological structure. This transduction is accomplished through the construction of the OMPFC, its linkages with the amygdala, and the regulatory systems (fear, vagal, HPA, social motivation) these structures control (Bugental et al., 2003). This system processes the punishment and reward value of complex stimuli (i.e., parents and other environmental factors relevant to survival) and mediates emotional and visceral responses based on past learning (Hariri et al., 2000; O'Doherty et al., 2001; Price et al., 1996; Tremblay & Schultz, 1999). Remember, the social brain and fear circuitry share the amygdala as a core structure, so the early negotiation of relationships and the modulation of fear become one and the same (Panksepp, 2001).

Secure attachments build the brain in ways that optimize network integration, autonomic arousal, and positive coping responses. The regulation of these systems becomes established early in life and organizes enduring patterns of arousal, reactivity to stress, and interpersonal behavior. Insecure and disorganized attachment styles reflect less than optimal development and poor coping strategies. If the polyvagal regulation of the social engagement system is underdeveloped due to insecure attachment, we may come to depend on the utilization of more primitive autonomic regulation (fight/flight/splitting) in relationships. This primitive regulation results in dramatic and long-lasting emotional and bodily reactions to interpersonal stress, as seen in insecure and disorganized children and borderline adults (Porges, 2001).

Securely attached children successfully use other people to modulate their stress and do not produce an adrenocortical response when attachment figures are available. In contrast, those with insecure attachment schema do show an HPA stress reaction in the same situations. Thus, the behavior of insecurely attached individuals is better described as a measure of arousal than as a form of coping (Izard, Heynes, et al., 1991; Nachmias et al., 1996; Spangler & Grossman, 1993; Spangler & Schieche, 1998). An ANS that is biased toward parasympathetic arousal might result in an avoidant style, a low level of emotional expression, and an avoidance of eye contact. It is a bodily mode of withdrawal from others that blocks proximity seeking, exploration of the environment, and positive interpersonal regulation. Avoidant children develop a bias toward parasympathetic states, as reflected in helplessness, lower heart rate, and decreased activity. These children might present interpersonally and clinically as depressed, withdrawn, or unmotivated.

Sympathetic dominance of the ANS corresponds with anxious–ambivalent attachment patterns, which are characterized by irritability, dependency, acting-out behavior, and a decreased ability to recover from stress. These children receive unregulated doses of affect from their caretakers that are overstimulating and underorganized. They, in turn, experience difficulties with impulse control, hostility, and fears of abandonment (Schore, 1994). Children with a bias toward sympathetic arousal may exhibit high levels of activity and unmodulated emotional expressions, appearing hyperactive or manic.

Attachment schemas are implicit memories that are known without being thought. Because they are stored in the architecture of the social brain as predictions of the behaviors of others, they "create" the people we meet and unconsciously guide our reactions to them. Early attachment schemas persist into adulthood, impacting our choice of partners and the quality of our relationships. Their impact goes beyond the ability to shape our relationships; they also influence our emotional life, immunological functioning, and our experience of self.

Lori & Larry—The Fog of Abandonment

Lori and Larry had met 2 years before while on vacation in Hawaii. They hit it off immediately and were both surprised by their compatibility and shared interests. Six months ago they married, and that's when the trouble began. At the beginning of their courtship, Lori was quite insecure about the relationship. Her first husband had left her a few years earlier, after almost 20 years of marriage. Even today, she described herself as still being in a state of "abandonment shock." She would watch carefully to see if Larry looked at other women or said anything that might suggest he was tired of her. Larry understood her insecurity and did his best to reassure Lori during the early months of their relationship. Gradually, she seemed to become confident that Larry wasn't planning on leaving her. For some reason, soon after their wedding, Lori's insecurities came back with a vengeance.

Although Larry was upset by the return of her fears and suspicions, he thought that the stress of the wedding or being a new bride might be to blame. At first, he worked again at reassuring her that he was with her for the "long haul," but eventually he lost his patience with her incessant questions. He began to ignore her; not surprisingly, she interpreted this withdrawal as a clue that he was preparing to leave. As Larry felt more distant from Lori and increasingly hopeless about making her feel safe, he began to wonder whether the marriage had been a bad idea. Lori sensed this shift in his emotional state, which felt to her as further evidence that he was planning to leave. She responded by demanding even more reassurance. In this way, the waves of insecure clinging and avoidant withdrawal washed back and forth across the social synapse, eroding their increasingly fragile bond.

At the beginning of our work together, I asked Lori and Larry questions about their parents, childhoods, and attachment histories. Larry had a somewhat avoidant attachment history and coped with his anxiety by becoming preoccupied with work. Not surprisingly, Lori's early attachment history was anxious and ambivalent. Her parents were pragmatic, distant people who had little understanding of Lori's emotional needs. Their lack of understanding was experienced by Lori as rejection and abandonment, and she developed a variety of fears and phobias that persisted into adulthood. When she married her high school sweetheart the day after her 17th birthday, she finally felt she had found a safe haven and put all of her energy into making him happy. For the almost 20 years of their marriage, she felt safe and secure. When, over the course of a few days, her husband told her he had met someone else and was leaving by the end of the week, she found herself in a state of shock, thrown back into her childhood turmoil.

In the weeks and months that followed her husband's departure, Lori endlessly searched her memory for clues as to why he left. Simultaneously she recalled countless experiences of feeling like a worthless child and being repeatedly abandoned by her parents. As she described it, her present suffering was a mixture of the loss of her first marriage, her troubled early life, and her expectations of being abandoned over and over again for the rest of her life. She slowly recovered and began to feel like she was on firm ground. By the time Lori met Larry in Hawaii, she thought that she was "over" her marriage and her painful childhood. Unfortunately, they had now both returned full force.

I decided to gather this information with Lori and Larry in the consulting room at the same time. As they both talked about their families and histories, they gained a better understanding of their respective attachment histories and how those histories affected their relationship. We also discussed the unfortunate dance of approach and avoidance that gets set up when anxious and avoidant people start to have problems in their relationship. Together, we did a considerable amount of learning about implicit memory, attachment, fear circuitry, and what was driving Lori's suspiciousness. We instituted a number of practical strategies, such as Lori sharing her suspicions with her individual therapist rather than Larry. For his part, Larry contracted with Lori that if he thought he might want to leave her, he would agree to bring it up in therapy and give her at least a year to discuss it. Lori was also encouraged to work on her early relationships with her individual therapist and to establish a set of stress-reduction strategies.

Maintaining weekly couples therapy gave Lori a place to share her concerns and Larry a place to stay aware of his need to share his feelings on a regular basis. In the process of our discussions, Lori saw a connection between her level of stress, diet, quality of her sleep, and the amount of suspiciousness she experienced. Fortunately, things turned out well for Lori and Larry. Although their relationship was never simple or easy, they found in each other a partner with whom they could become more open and secure. Larry became a bit better at expressing his feelings, which made Lori more confident that he wouldn't suddenly fall out of love with her. Lori eventually stopped sifting through the memories of her first marriage to find out what she had done wrong. Together, they consciously strove to create a secure base and safe haven for one another.

An understanding of implicit social memory, attachment schema, and how they impact our experience of one another is an important tool in psychotherapy. Knowledge of these unconscious processes provides a language and logic with which to discuss thoughts and feelings that are automatic, overwhelming, and destructive of intimacy. It also helps us understand the importance of consistent caretaking, emotional availability, and self-insight in raising our children.

Part IV

Social Vision: The
Language of Faces

Chapter | |

Linking Gazes

She was born with a face that would let her get her
way, he saw that face and he lost all control . . .
—Bob Seger, 1978

Over millions of years, primates evolved from four-legged denizens of the night to two-legged creatures of the day. Standing upright was monumental: The human range of sight grew broader, and during the day we were able to see both prey and predator from a much greater distance. Upright, we were no longer dependent on the direction of the wind to carry scent molecules to us. With these changes, vision gradually came to replace smell as our primary sense. This "simple" act of standing also greatly increased the distance of our heads from the radiating heat of the ground, allowing our brains to stay cooler and grow larger.

Large portions of the brains of reptiles and more primitive mammals remain dedicated to olfaction. For dogs, rats, and cats, scents contain detailed information about spatial mapping, mating, social hierarchy, approach, and avoidance (Duvall, 1986). In primates, and especially in humans, the olfactory system is now largely confined to taste and gustation. If you look at the amount of the human brain dedicated to smell versus sight, it seems clear that evolution selected for vision over olfaction as our primary social sense. The chemical transmitters involved in smell have been superseded by electromagnetic waves of light that travel far faster, in all directions, and are not dependent upon the wind (Emery, 2000). The amygdala, initially an olfactory cortex, has greatly expanded to evaluate visual social information. Still, the question of how much chemical signaling occurs in humans via smells and pheromones remains unclear.

Thus, whereas more primitive animals secrete chemicals to communicate across the space between them, human beings use complex visual information to bridge the social synapse. We watch each other's faces, bodies, and behaviors, constantly monitoring them for information about safety and danger, acceptance and rejection, love and fear. Yet all visual stimuli are not created equal. The faces of others may be the single most important source of information in our world (Brothers, 1992). One of the most amazing things about our faces is the sheer quantity of information they communicate. Some of this information is sent intentionally via conscious facial expressions and gestures, while other forms of information such as blushing and pupil dilation are involuntary "readouts" of our internal states. As sophisticated and complex as neural transmission, these multiple channels of communication bridge parent and child, lover and beloved, therapist and client. In the next few chapters, we explore some of the visual messenger systems central to human communication.

First Sight

In the first hours of life, we begin to search out the faces and eyes of those around us and show a preference for our mothers' faces (Fantz, 1961, 1963, 1965; Field et al., 1984; Goren et al., 1975; Hood et al., 1998; Johnson et al., 1991a, 1991b). Prolonged eye contact early in life is of such great importance that evolution has left nothing to chance. The fixation on the mother's face is an obligatory brainstem reflex that ensures the "imprinting" of this vital social information (Stechler & Latz, 1966). Meanwhile, being gazed at by her child makes a mother feel calm and stimulates nurturing behaviors. Children and parents engage in prolonged periods of mutual gazing that calm and relax them both. Take a moment to look at the picture of the sleeping infant on the cover of this book. For most people, the sight of an infant affects them physically and emotionally, drawing them toward the child with increased openness and sensitivity.

The initial priming of the visual system to attend to faces stimulates and builds networks designed to enhance bonding and the growth of neural systems. Visual engagement and the constant reciprocal flow of information between child and parent also encourage the growth of social brain systems dedicated to attachment and affective attunement (Reissland et al., 2002; Serrano et al., 1992). In later months, the cortex develops the ability to break gaze, allowing the child to develop neural systems dedicated to the timing and pragmatics of communication, as well as sharing a direction of gaze with others (Beebe, 2000; Cohn & Tronick, 1989; Tomonaga et al., 2004). Throughout our lives we build on these early visual experiences as we attune to peers, gaze at loved ones, and develop increasingly subtle abilities to receive and send social signals. Most of us soon learn to modify what we say, do, and feel based on the facial expressions of those around us.

Vision Basics

Like other neural systems, the visual system is immature at birth and continues to develop through the first years of life (Atkinson, 1984; Bronson, 1974; Brown, 1961; Burkhalter, 1991; Diamond & Hall, 1969; Huttenlocher, 1994; Johnson, 1990b). The increasing sophistication of visual processing during development reflects the growing participation and integration of cortical with subcortical visual systems and cross-modal association with our other senses. Despite the developmental immaturity of many cortical networks, early experience activates regions that will eventually be dedicated to face processing. In fact, the areas that adult brains use for face processing have been found to be active in children as young as 2–4 months old (Acerra, Burnod, & de Schonen, 2002; Tzourio-Mazoyer et al., 2002).

Visual experience is constructed in multiple stages and utilizes many areas of the brain. Light is converted into chemical and electrical signals by the rods and cones of the retina and sent, via the optic nerve, first to the thalamus and then to the visual cortex (occipital lobe). The first area of the visual cortex (striate cortex) processes information such as orientation and curvature before sending it on to the other four layers of the occipital lobe for the analysis of color, motion, depth, and texture

(Finkel & Sadja, 1994; Goebel et al., 1998). These layers, in turn, send it forward through the rest of the cortex via three tracks of visual processing for more complex analysis.

A dorsal "where" visual stream projects up into the parietal lobes to assess spatial relationships and location, and a ventral "what" stream heads to the temporal lobes to assist with object recognition and identification (Burkhalter, 1991; Schneider, 1969; Ungerleider & Haxby, 1994; Ungerleider & Mishkin, 1982). A third visual stream, which specializes in the analysis of motion, projects forward to areas of the frontal lobes involved with attention and the direction of eye gaze. Identifying others, monitoring their whereabouts, and predicting their intentions require the participation of all three visual processing streams, represented in Figure 11.1.

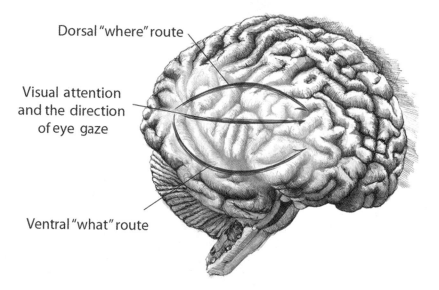

Dorsal "where" route

Visual attention and the direction of eye gaze

Ventral "what" route

Figure 11.1. **Beginning at the back of the brain in the occipital lobes, the three streams of visual processing proceed forward through the parietal and temporal lobes to the frontal lobes.**

Direct Eye Gaze

Eye gaze plays a central role in social communication: It provides information, regulates interactions, expresses intimacy or threat, exercises social control, and facilitates coordination and cooperation (Freire et al., 2004; Kleinke, 1986). As we discussed earlier, the role of eye gaze in human communication is apparent in the unique morphology and coloration of our eyes. The visible portion of the human eye consists of the colored iris and the surrounding white sclera, which is elongated instead of round. This extreme color contrast and distinct shape, not found in our primate ancestors, emphasizes the importance of gaze direction in human communication.

When we look at others gazing at something around us, there is an increased correlation of activity in the dorsal "where" visual stream (between the fusiform gyrus and the intraparietal sulcus) as we turn our attention to a shared processing of the external environment. In these situations, our brains are analyzing both the direction and object of the gaze (George, Driver, & Dolan, 2001; Wicker et al., 1998). As another's gaze shifts to us, brain activation increases in the amygdala, as well as the insula, cingulate, frontal, and temporal cortices (Calder et al., 2002; Kawashima et al., 1999; Kingstone et al., 2004; Pelphrey et al., 2004). The analysis of this direct eye gaze is very rapid because of the significance eye-to-eye contact has for physical safety and reproductive success (von Grünau & Anston, 1995). If people maintain eye contact for more than a few seconds, they are likely to fight, have sex, or both. You can actually feel this shift as you experience yourself go "on alert" as someone's gaze—especially someone who looks particularly threatening or attractive—finds your own (Senju & Hasegawa, 2005).

To test the power of direct eye contact, Whalen and his colleagues (2004) took images of fearful and happy faces and removed all of the information except for the eyes. What remained of the eyes were the pupils and sclera (Figure 11.2). Despite the fact that these images were presented to subjects so quickly that they were unaware of even having seen them, a highly significant degree of amygdala activation was recorded when they were presented with the eyes from a fearful versus a happy face. These findings suggest that the ratio of pupil to sclera visible to others provides an immediate, automatic, and unconscious measure of safety or danger.

The language of the eyes is also influenced by cultural values. In the West it is a sign of respect and interest to look at whomever is speaking to us. However, if we look *too* intently, it can be experienced as an insult or a sign of aggression. We monitor the gaze of our listeners to see if they are paying attention and are likely to become offended if they look away too often. In

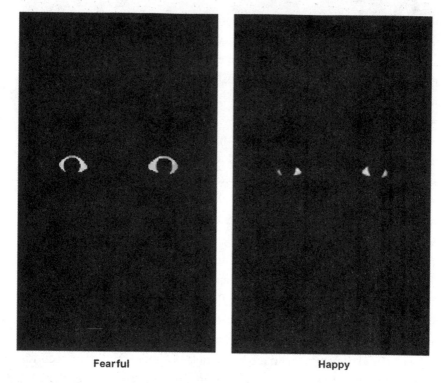

Fearful   **Happy**

Figure 11.2. **The eyes of fearful and happy faces used in the Whalen et al. (2004) study. Image courtesy of Dr. Paul Whalen; reprinted with permission.**

many other cultures, gaze aversion is a sign of respect to higher-ranking people and something that is expected between the sexes. Thus, eye contact is also used to establish social dominance. How many of us know "the look" our father gave us that could freeze us in our tracks! In a similar way, kids engage in "staring contests" to see who breaks their gaze or laughs first from nervousness. How many times have you heard the expression "If looks could kill"? On the other hand, maintaining direct eye contact with someone of potential romantic interest can be interpreted as a sign that an approach will be accepted. Movie stars have become icons because of their ability to convey a "come hither" look with their "bedroom eyes."

Jewel—Predator and Prey

"Stop staring at me!" Jewel shouted, startling me. "I'm sorry," I said. "I didn't realize I was staring. I felt like I was just listening and paying attention to you." She sat with her legs crossed, looking off into the corner of my office, avoiding my eyes. She glared at me and said, "Well, just stop, it freaks me out." Unsure where to look, I sat back and studied the painting on the wall behind her. I believe that most of my clients would get offended or feel rejected if I didn't maintain eye contact. Jewel was an exception.

Jewel suffered from almost constant anxiety. She had a difficult time sleeping and often awakened during the night in a sweat, worrying about her son's health, her lack of productivity, or her relationship with her husband. Being extremely tense already, Jewel probably had a high baseline level of amygdala arousal. Most of us can tolerate and even enjoy direct eye contact, but in Jewel's case, even an empathetic gaze was enough to push her over the edge. I usually don't resort to the old analytic technique of having my clients lie down on the couch, but here was a possible working solution. Of course, this, too, caused Jewel anxiety. "That's great," she complained, "if I lie down, I can't keep my eye on you!"

Jewel grew up with abusive, alcoholic parents who ignored her except when they became violent. She was conditioned to avoid their eyes, remain invisible, but stay on alert. She lacked the experience of warm and loving gazes to activate positive emotions and the calming neurochemicals of attachment and bonding. Despite her tall stature and strong athletic physique, she experienced life as a defenseless animal of prey. For her, the very condition of being seen was to be placed in danger. Her response to being seen was to go on a state of high alert, making the kind of relaxed openness needed for successful psychotherapy difficult to impossible.

Eventually, Jewel accepted my suggestion to lie down. What came out of this shift was both odd and instructive. She described a monthly ritual in her household: the day her son drops a live mouse into his snake's terrarium. When the mouse first drops in, it looks a bit dazed but knows something is terribly wrong. As it comes to grasp the gravity of its situation, it begins to run frantically around the cage, even running over the back of the snake in its panic to escape.

Eventually, the mouse seems to accept its fate and comes to rest in front of the snake, staring into its eyes. Jewel described being transfixed by the eye contact between predator and prey and feeling like the mouse. She always turns away before she hears the *thump* in the cage and the cheers from her children. Like that mouse, Jewel lived in a world where her fear circuitry froze her in terror. Her early experiences with her parents created an association between visibility and danger that, decades later, became activated by the eye contact of others. The first steps in psychotherapy were focused on retraining her brain to learn to relax while being seen by another. This foundation of trust needed to be accomplished before we could move forward.

Pupil Dilation

Although the contrast between pupil and sclera gives us clear information about the direction of gaze, the pupils have a language all their own. Ongoing changes in the size of our pupils serve as a direct readout of the state of our arousal and interest, fluctuating along with brain activity (Bitsios et al., 2004; Hess, 1965; Partala & Surakka, 2003). Activation of the sympathetic nervous system stimulates the radial dilator muscles of the pupil, causing them to increase in diameter, whereas inhibition of the parasympathetic nervous system can have the same result. Parasympathetic activation stimulates the sphincter muscle of the iris to constrict the pupil in reaction to bright light (Granholm & Steinhauer, 2004; Thompson, 2004). Although pupil dilation occurs in response to both positive and negative social situations, positive emotions and sexual attraction appear to result in greater and more consistent pupil dilation (O'Neill & Hinton, 1977). Pupils become smaller while we evaluate what we are looking at and larger when we have already accepted and appreciate what we are seeing. For example, viewing a pleasurable image, listening to music, or solving a problem all result in pupil dilation (Hess, 1965; Siegle et al., 2004).

It seems that large pupil size is a signal to others that we are having positive feelings and are interested in them. People with larger pupils are judged to be more sympathetic, happier, and warmer. They are more likely to be chosen as partners and found to be more sexually attractive (Hamel, 1974; Stass & Willis, 1967). Although this finding seems to be true for men, one study found that this is not the case for all women: Only those women who are attracted to the proverbial "bad boys" prefer men with dilated pupils (Tombs & Silverman, 2004). Whereas men have one strategy for attraction, perhaps women have two: the "nice guys" for the long haul and the "bad boys" for other purposes.

Figure 11.3. **Dilated and undilated pupils.** These two images are identical except for the size of the pupils. Do you have a different reaction to these two pictures? Reprinted with permission of Michelle Walker.

The two photos in Figure 11.3 are identical except that one has enlarged pupils. For most people, the picture of the woman with dilated pupils will result in more positive feelings. You may feel more attracted, drawn in, or compassionate toward her. Children tend to have larger pupils, which may contribute to the urge we have to take care of them. Not surprisingly, seeing dilated pupils makes our own pupils dilate. Larger pupil size generally leads us to judge others' eyes as soft, warm, and attractive (Hess, 1975). Historically, women put belladonna (beautiful woman) in their eyes because atropine (the active ingredient in belladonna) causes pupil dilation. Dilated pupils are a compelling "approach" signal to caretakers, friends, and potential mates, saying we are excited to see them, welcome their presence, and will accept their advances.

Blushing

Like pupil dilation, blushing is a visual readout of the state of our autonomic arousal. Blushing is caused by the dilation of the small capillaries of the face, triggered by sympathetic arousal (Gerlach et al., 2003). We blush in situations in which (1) our social identity is threatened, (2) we are being scrutinized, (3) we are being overpraised, or (4) we are told we are blushing even when we aren't (Leary et al., 1992). Blushing, a social signal unique to humans, demonstrates that we are aware that others are aware of us (Crozier, 2004). In fact, it has been found that staring at one side of a person's face while she is singing results in more blushing on that side of the face (Drummond & Mirco, 2004). The fact that blushing almost always occurs in the presence of others speaks to its role as a form of social communication. Because blushing can't be controlled voluntarily, it cannot be used for conscious deception.

The fear of *looking* anxious is, in and of itself, an additional source of anxiety for socially anxious people. When they experience increases in their heart rates due to anxiety, they fear they are blushing, feel "outed," and are embarrassed by their embarrassment, making them even more anxious (Drummond et al., 2003; Gerlach et al., 2001; Mulkens et al., 2001). There is even a clinically recognized fear of blushing in social situations (erythrophobia) that is linked to social phobia and anxiety disorders (Bögels et al., 1996; Laederach-Hofmann et al., 2002; Mulkens et al., 1999).

Blushing is associated with feelings of shame and guilt; it is an "involuntary apology," more likely to elicit sympathy, conciliatory behavior, and positive evaluations from others (Castelfranchi & Poggi, 1990; de Jong, 1999; de Jong et al., 2003; Keltner & Buswell, 1997; Stein & Bouwer, 1997). When we blush after doing something wrong, we communicate to others that we are aware of their rules, despite our transgression (Tangney et al., 1996; Semin & Manstead, 1982). When people violate a rule accidentally, blushing signals that they are ashamed of their mistake, in response to which we tend to be more forgiving. Blushing is charming. It suggests that rule-breaking creates an internal conflict and is not a self-accepted aspect of our character. In a similar way, the blush of inexperienced public speakers tells us they are nervous, and we tend to be more encouraging and supportive in our response.

When it is unclear whether a rule violation is intentional or unintentional, blushing has been found to undermine the actor's trustworthiness (de Jong et al., 2002, 2003). In these situations, blushing becomes a warning signal that individuals are aware of what they are doing but have chosen to do it anyway (Bögels & Lamers, 2002). The absence of blushing when it seems called for can also undermine trustworthiness. Antisocial individuals, often lacking autonomic arousal in social situations, may make us feel uneasy by their lack of blushing. With the evolution of private thought, blushing may have been a way to "tip off" others about what might be on our minds. Thus, involuntary blushing, like the increasing contrast between pupil and sclera and pupil dilation, becomes an example of how the value of social communication and the well-being of the group came to override strategies of individual survival.

Direction of Attention

Have you ever walked down a street, noticed someone looking up, and suddenly felt compelled to look up yourself? This is actually a reflex triggered by the gaze of others. Our direction-of-attention reflex is a broad social signal, automatically transmitted via constant interpersonal monitoring, that increases the survival value of being in a group. Perhaps a predator was approaching, a clan member had discovered food, or a member of the troop was in trouble. Through this linking of visual attention, a collection of individuals becomes a super organism whose senses expand in both range and sensitivity.

The need for rapid social information is so vital that the direction of gaze has been found to influence the earliest stages of visual processing (Kimura et al., 2004; Klucharev & Sams, 2004; Schuller & Rossion, 2004). From the first moments of life, primates and humans begin to orient to the direction that caretakers are looking and facing (Itakura, 2004; Langton & Bruce, 1999; Okamoto et al., 2002; Phillips et al., 2002; Taylor et al., 2001; Tomasello, 1998; Waitzman et al., 2002). Monitoring the direction of attention recruits all three visual processing streams as we analyze head and body direction, the identity of the individual, facial expressions, and the layout of the environment (Ashbridge et al., 2000; Bayliss et al., 2004; Hoffman & Haxby, 2000; Perrett et al., 1992; Senju & Hasegawa, 2005; Symons et al., 2004). This orienting reflex, maintained throughout life, is so powerful that it even occurs when we try to resist it (Driver et al., 1999).

Direction of eye gaze is also a key component of what is known as "theory of mind." Theory of mind is an idea of what the other knows, wants, and is likely to do next. The theory is based on observable behavior, the direction of attention, other environmental variables, and the attribution of our own drives and motives to those we observe. The evolutionary advantage of such a theory lies in having a predictive (or early warning) system of how others are likely to behave (Phillips, Baron-Cohen, & Rutter, 1992). An analysis of brain activity during theory-of-mind tasks suggests that the direction of gaze is a key component of "mind reading" and our ability to predict others' behaviors and feel safe with them. We depend on eyes as "windows to the soul" when judging someone's trustworthiness. Prejudice against Asians in Caucasian groups tends to focus on their "inscrutability" and may be related to the different anatomical shape of their eyes. On a more mundane level, salesmen are trained to maintain eye contact and not wear sunglasses while interacting with clients. A person who averts his or her eyes, especially while engaging in behavior designed to influence us, is almost always judged to be less trustworthy.

Focus on the Amygdala

Primates appear to have evolved from moles, shrews, and hedgehogs: animals for whom the amygdala plays a central role in smell and social communication. In these mammals, where feeding and social communication are guided by olfaction, the amygdala is chiefly involved with the sense of smell (Zald et al., 1998). As primates became increasingly social and visual, the amygdala became involved in the sending and receiving mechanisms for facial expressions, as well as hearing and touch, thereby facilitating more rapid and subtle social interactions (Brothers, 1997; Dolan & Vuilleumier, 2003; Schore, 1994). Through all of these evolutionary changes, the amygdala (see Figure 11.4) retained the seat of executive function in the rapid appraisal of threat and in triggering the fight/flight response in dangerous situations (Hamann et al., 2002; Yang, 2002).

The amygdala is a key component of emotional memory throughout life; it associates survival value, based on experience, with the object of the senses (Brodal, 1992; Davis, 1992, 1997; LeDoux, 1986). The direct and rapid neural connections of the amygdala with the hypothalamus and limbic–motor circuits rapidly translate these appraisals into bodily states and action (Amaral, Veazey, & Cowan, 1982; Kalin et al., 2004).

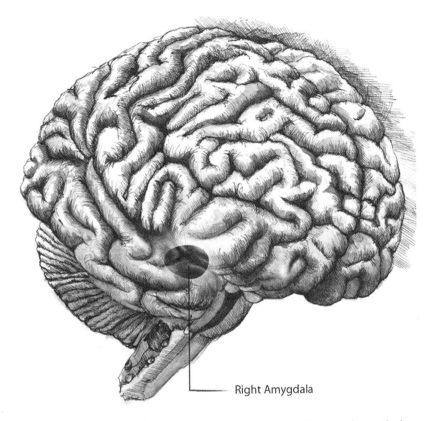

Right Amygdala

Figure 11.4. **The amygdala is located toward the brain's center, beneath the temporal lobe.**

The amygdala becomes active in response to pleasant or positive stimuli but in a less consistent manner than it does to negative and threatening experiences (Davis & Whalen, 2001; Garavan et al., 2001; Zald, 2003). The amygdala also enhances memory storage by stimulating the release of norepinephrine and glucocorticoids in negative emotional situations (Hamann et al., 1999; McGaugh, 1996; McGaugh et al., 1993; Paré, 2003; Paré et al., 2004). Damage to the amygdala in humans causes deficits in visual memory as well as to the auditory recognition of fear and anger (Scott et al., 1997; Tranel & Hyman, 1990).

The amygdala has reciprocal interconnections with the ventral striatum, hippocampus, and the prefrontal cortex (see Figure 11.5; Rosenkrantz et al., 2003). Together, these structures create a network connecting sensory stimulation (striatum) with motivational value (amygdala) and

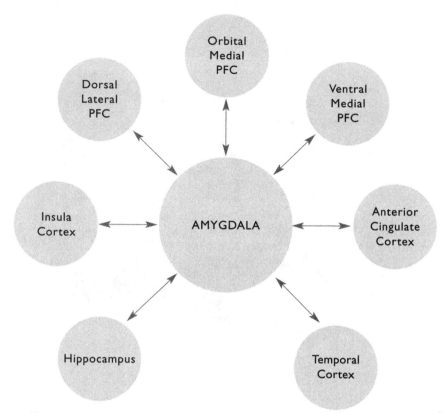

Figure 11.5. **Amygdala connections to the primary structures of the social brain.** The amygdala is the hub of emotional processing among the primary structures of the social brain. Reciprocal connections provide the amygdala with information about the inner and outer environment, which, in turn, provides information to cortical and limbic structures to guide their orientation, attention, and ongoing processing. The projection from the amygdala downward into the lower regions of the brain regulates bodily responses to threat and fear. *Note:* PFC = prefrontal cortex.

emotional awareness (orbital medial cortex/hippocampus) (Adolphs, 2003; Barrett et al., 2003; Winstanley et al., 2004). Activity within the fusiform gyrus (an area dedicated to face recognition) is modulated early by emotional facial expressions, which is likely due to amygdala influence (Etkin et al., 2004; Pizzagalli et al., 2002).

In its role in the social brain, the amygdala couples the senses and somatic states with the reward value of contact with others (Bechara, Damasio, & Damasio, 2003; Dolan, Morris, & de Gelder, 2001; Murray &

Mishkin, 1985). The primary role of the amygdala in the social brain is to modulate vigilance and attention in order to gather information, remember emotionally salient events and individuals, and prepare for action (Adams et al., 2003; Anderson et al., 2003; Fanselow & Gale, 2003; Gallagher & Holland, 1994; Hariri et al., 2002; Kahn et al., 2002). When a stimulus is understood to be nonthreatening, amygdala activation decreases until another potential threat arises (Schoenbaum et al., 1998; Whalen, 1998). These appraisal processes are automatic and do not require conscious or directed attention (Dolan & Vuilleumier, 2003; Williams & Mattingley, 2004).

As the emotionally expressive face became an increasingly important transmitter of information across the social synapse, the amygdala networked with circuits throughout the brain to "read" information from eyes, faces, direction of attention, gestures, body postures, and facial expressions (Adolphs et al., 1994, 1995; Hamann et al., 1996; Young et al., 1995). The amygdala becomes activated to both sad and happy faces but appears vital for recognizing fear (Baird et al., 1999; Breiter et al., 1996; Calder et al., 1996; Yang et al., 2002). Faces judged to be untrustworthy, as well as verbal and written threats, automatically activate areas of the amygdala (Elliott, Friston, & Dolan, 2000; Isenberg et al., 1999; Phelps et al., 2001; Winston et al., 2002). Subjects asked to evaluate emotions and communicate back to an experimenter show increasing bilateral involvement of the amygdala (Adolphs, Damasio, & Tranel, 2002).

Damage to the amygdala in monkeys results in a loss of status in the group hierarchy, loss of judgment in relation to fear, and even abnormal friendliness to experimenters (Kluver & Bucy, 1938). In both monkeys and humans, amygdala damage is followed by a similar loss of judgment regarding group etiquette, appropriate social behavior, and potential social danger (Bauman et al., 2004; Hayman et al., 1998; Lee et al., 1998). Amygdala deficits result in difficulties in social judgment, communication, reading emotional facial expressions, directing eye gaze, and estimating trustworthiness (Adolphs et al., 1994, 1998; Gur et al., 2002; Whalen et al., 2004; Young et al., 1995).

Concerning laterality of amygdala functioning, differential roles of the left and right amygdala most likely fall in line with overall hemispheric differences (Markowitsch, 1998). The left may be more involved with the analysis of specific (and verbal) threats, whereas the right may provide more global activation and autonomic triggering in dangerous situations (Gläscher & Adolphs, 2003). The left amygdala is involved with the implicit learning of a new face and judging it to have positive or negative (approach/avoidance) value (Baas, Aleman, & Kahn, 2004).

The evolution of the social brain revolves around the increasing participation of the amygdala in the evaluation of visual information. Through time, more and more channels of visual communication linked the brains of primates, leading to more efficient behavioral coordination, emotional coherence, and mutual cooperation. Information gleaned from the direction of eye gaze, pupil dilation, blushing, and, as we will see, the wealth of information contained in facial expressions, built a growing vocabulary of conscious and unconscious interpersonal communication. The interconnection of inner experience with visual social information was very clear in Jewel's strong emotional reaction to my gaze. And there is no greater evidence of the power of visual social communication than all we can say with *just a glance*.

Chapter | 2

Reading Faces

Love takes off masks that we fear we can't live
without, and know we cannot live within.
—James Baldwin, 1962, p. 95

Back in graduate school, I had a classmate with an unusual problem. Andy had been a competitive bicycle racer for many years until he took a serious fall. He hit his head on a fence post, part of which penetrated the right side of his skull. Days later, after regaining consciousness, he was lucid and communicative, leading his doctors to believe that he had avoided serious brain damage. His problem was discovered only when his loved ones were finally allowed to see him. Andy didn't recognize any of them and became frightened when they approached to kiss him. His lack of recognition of his wife and parents was first explained as a transient aftereffect of the accident. Unfortunately, as his other symptoms cleared, his inability to recognize faces (prosopagnosia) remained.

In the weeks following his accident, Andy came to gradually recognize his family and friends by their clothes, mannerisms, and the sounds of their voices. In class he seemed completely normal; he was bright, engaging, and had a good sense of humor. However, each week we had to reintroduce ourselves to him until we all decided to wear name tags. Andy had lost his rapid, automatic shorthand for identifying others: face recognition. He had to work hard to gather the information about those around him that the rest of us took for granted.

As for less familiar faces, we remember them in the context in which we usually encounter them. Think about our confusion when we run into someone we know in an unfamiliar context, say, the grocery clerk at the gas station, or an acquaintance from home while on a trip to another country. These encounters are usually accompanied by confusion and disorientation caused by a juxtaposition of strangeness and familiarity. "Where do I know you from? What are you doing here?" In these experiences it becomes clear that networks of face recognition interact with other networks of memory dedicated to context and location.

Whereas the *visual* recognition of facial features depends on cortical processing networks, the *feeling* of recognition relies on networks of emotional processing. From time to time, these two networks can become dissociated from one another. For instance, in déjà vu experiences, we experience an activation of networks of familiarity but without concurrent visual recognition. Thus, we look around at a new environment with a feeling of familiarity but no visual memory, leading some to postulate the existence of past lives or clairvoyant abilities. On the opposite end of the spectrum lies the phenomenon of Capgras syndrome. Capgras syndrome is the feeling of unfamiliarity with very familiar people (usually family) that leads the person to believe that his or her loved ones have been replaced by impostors: "They look just like my parents, but I just know they aren't." In both déjà vu and Capgras, the left-hemispheric networks, attempting to make sense out of nonsense, construct (or confabulate) an explanation for a seemingly "paranormal" experience. Interestingly, it may be that what is lost in prosopagnosia is the *conscious* memory of faces, even as unconscious recognition remains intact (de Haan et al., 1987). This idea is supported by the fact that people with this problem have different physiological reactions to familiar and unfamiliar faces.

Face Recognition

Half a century ago it was proposed that memories of individuals were contained within single neurons. It was thought that these so called *grandmother cells*, if stimulated, would produce a memory of your grandmother or other familiar people. This idea was probably triggered by the work of Roger Penfield, who, during brain surgery, asked his patients what they were experiencing while he stimulated different areas of their brains with small electrical currents. A few recalled vivid memories, an emotional piece of music, or an image from childhood of their grandma cooking at the stove. We now know that memory is far too complex to be contained in a single cell: a memory is a coming together of the activation patterns of multiple neural networks. It turns out that our grandmothers live throughout our brains.

Research has found that our prefrontal lobes, the upper portion of the temporal lobes, and the amygdala become active as we recognize faces, track facial expressions, or try to figure out if a face looks trustworthy. In primates and humans, however, specific neurons in these structures appear to selectively respond to faces (Brothers, Ring, & Kling, 1990; Gauthier & Logothetis, 2000; Leonard et al., 1985; Ojemann et al., 1992; Perrett et al., 1982, 1992). It has since been proposed that this specialized system in the human cortex is responsible for the processing of face recognition, facial features, and gaze direction (Kanwisher et al., 1997; Uchida et al., 2000). Whether the areas involved in face processing are specific to faces or utilized in face recognition because they are good at making fine visual distinctions with all kinds of familiar stimuli is a matter of current debate (Diamond & Carey, 1986; Farah, 1996; Farah et al., 1998; Gauthier & Logothetis, 2000; Kanwisher, 2000; Tarr and Gauthier, 2000).

Focus on the Face Recognition System

Seeing faces activates three cortical areas outside of the occipital lobe in humans: the occipital–temporal junction, the inferior parietal lobe, and the temporal lobe (Lu et al., 1991). This tract is part of the identification, or the "what," visual stream described earlier. The areas of the brain that are primarily responsible for face recognition are the fusiform face area, the superior temporal sulcus (STS), and the amygdala (see Figure 12.1; Gauthier et al., 2000; Puce et al., 1995; Puce et al., 1996). Jellema and colleagues (2000) suggested that separate populations of cells within the STS respond to features such as body posture, eye gaze, and faces, whereas a second group responds to the limbs moving in certain directions. They further suggested that these different groups of cells modulate one another as we automatically analyze and predict the intentions of others through combinations

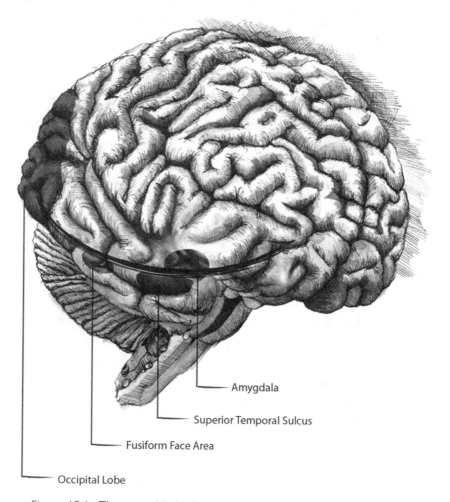

Amygdala

Superior Temporal Sulcus

Fusiform Face Area

Occipital Lobe

Figure 12.1. The ventral "what" route of visual processing contains a network hypothesized to be specialized for faces.

of facial and postural information, contextual variables, and biological motion (Jellema et al., 2000; Jellema et al., 2004; Jellema & Perrett, 2003). Neurons within the primate STS have been shown to be sensitive to gaze direction, head direction, and different parts of faces (Puce, et al., 1998; Perrett et al., 1982; Hasselmo et al., 1989; Allison, Puce, & McCarthy, 2000).

Depending on the task, face recognition recruits a variety of brain regions. As faces become familiar and memory begins to consolidate, there is a reduction of bilateral activation of networks in the anterior temporal and left frontal regions required for memory encoding (Sugiura et al., 2001).

Later, accessing the memory of a familiar face activates the right pre-frontal cortex (Haxby et al., 1994, 1996; Katanoda et al., 2000). Given the social and emotional significance of familiar faces, it is no surprise that bilateral activation to familiar faces is seen in the amygdala, hypothalamus, and medial frontal areas. Tasks requiring naming, cate-gorization, or instrumental gestures appear more left lateralized and re-sult in higher levels of hippocampal activation as language and memory networks become involved (Andreasen et al., 1996; Gallagher et al., 2004; Sergent et al., 1992). As you reflect on memories of your grandmother, networks throughout the brain become activated as all of the components of your many experiences with her are brought together.

Inverted Faces

When I was a kid, it was popular to paint an inverted face on our chins and watch ourselves speak as a sort of upside-down puppet. Toy stores even sold a little set of mirrors and a makeup kit with which to create various chin characters and watch them speak right-side-up. I found it both fascinating and unsettling to watch these chin puppets: The result-ing creatures appeared frightening, and I've always wondered why. As it turns out, face processing networks are shaped specifically for right-side-up human faces and are not activated by objects, animals, or upside-down faces (Kanwisher, Stanley, & Harris, 1999).

A normal human brain uses an "obligatory" face processing network that does not become active when faces are inverted (Farah et al., 1995; Kilts et al., 2003). Turning faces upside-down makes them much more difficult for us to process because they are analyzed using object pro-cessing networks (see Figure 12.2; Aguirre et al., 1999; Haxby et al., 1999; Moscovitch et al., 1997). We are experts in face recognition when they are right-side-up but inverted they are new, unusual, and unpre-dictable objects. In fact, individuals with damage to specific face recog-nition centers perform as well or better than normal subjects when faces are inverted, suggesting that their brains may have organized an alterna-tive face processing strategy.

Autistic individuals analyze faces with these same object-processing circuits (Pierce & Courchesne, 2000). Could it be that my discomfort

Figure 12.2. These are identical images, one rightside-up, the other upside-down. Notice how much easier it is to process the face as a whole when it is rightside-up. When a face is upside-down, we tend to examine its component parts and have much greater difficulty in identifying who we are looking at. Reprinted with permission of Chris Howells.

with chin people had to do with my brain's struggle to make sense of a talking, animate object processed in circuits designed for inanimate objects? Perhaps anxiety is triggered in the brain when what are supposed to be inanimate objects move around, make sounds, and approach us. Could part of the anxiety autistic individuals experience in social interactions come from their use of object-processing networks for people?

Facial Expressions

Centuries before Darwin (1872/1998), facial expressions were a focus of those studying emotion. The vast array of human facial expressions is the result of millions of years of evolutionary handiwork. The amount of cortical area dedicated to the face, the straps of muscles beneath the surface of our skin, and the neural fibers connecting them have all increased in complexity as facial expressions have become more important to social communication. As you can see in the drawing of the muscles of facial expression in Figure 12.3, most of the surface of the face is able to move as a result of one or more of these six muscle groups (Huber, 1931). As the need for more detailed and accurate social communication has increased, so has our ability to articulate varied and more precise expressions though combinations of muscle movements.

Although infinite subtleties of facial expressions are possible, and each culture has its own unique facial idioms, there appear to be a group of facial expressions that are primary to all people regardless of age, gender,

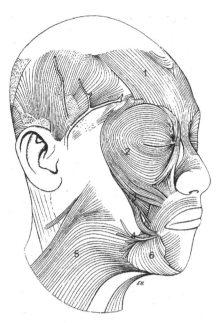

Figure 12.3. **The muscles of facial expression: (1) frontalis; (2) orbicularis oculi; (3) zygomaticus major; (4) risorius; (5) platysma; (6) depressor anguli oris.** Original drawing from Huber (1931).

or culture (Ekman, 2003). These basic facial expressions—disgust, fear, joy, surprise, sadness, and anger—represent fundamental emotions tied to our basic survival, primitive neural systems, and our long evolutionary heritage (Figure 12.4). The many layers of more complex emotional expressions unique to cultures, regions, and individuals are likely elaborations on these basic expressions.

Reading Facial Expressions

Emotionally expressive faces appear to be a primary transmitter of information across the social synapse, and our ability to read facial expressions is integral to social bonding and physical survival (Blair, 2003; Wicker et al., 2003). From birth, our interactions with others gradually make us experts in reading facial expressions. We use the constant stream of obvious, subtle, and often contradictory messages we receive from other faces to navigate our complex social environment. An angry look might make us back away and prepare for flight. A sad or hopeless look might evoke feelings of nurturance and soothing, resulting in moving toward another.

Figure 12.4. **The basic facial expressions of (1) disgust, (2) fear, (3) joy, (4) surprise, (5) sadness, and (6) anger. Reprinted with permission from Kanade et al. (2000).**

Both the value and complexity of facial expressions as a form of communication are attracting growing attention. A number of scoring systems have been developed to expand our understanding of the role of facial expressions in social interactions (Bartlett et al., 1999; Ekman & Friesen, 1978; Ekman, Friesen, & Hagar, 2002). But in our day-to-day lives, we rely on automatically detecting, processing, interpreting, and reacting to the facial expressions of others on a moment-to-moment basis. Our monitoring of faces sometimes becomes conscious, for example, in situations where we are speaking to a group and look into their faces to see if we are holding their interest. Evaluating facial expressions may become our sole focus if we find ourselves in an emotional discussion with a lover or feel physically threatened.

Knowing how to interpret the meaning of facial expressions requires lots of practice. This practice requirement is illustrated by monkeys raised in isolation who are unable to send or comprehend socially useful facial expressions (Miller et al., 1967). Reading facial expressions calls on diverse brain systems: bottom-up mechanisms of imitation and resonance contribute to emotional recognition, whereas top-down input modulates the analysis of emotion based on contextual variables and learned behavioral strategies (Adolphs, 2002a; Wallbott, 1991). Based on a sample of over 100 patients with lesions to various parts of their brains, Adolphs and his colleagues (2000) demonstrated that recognizing emotions from facial expressions requires the participation of the right somatosensory cortices. Their findings suggest that the recognition of facial expressions is based on the creation of an internal somatosensory map corresponding to the experience of witnessed emotions (Adolphs et al., 2000). We draw on these inner emotions to hypothesize about the internal state of the other.

Although we tend to imitate other peoples' facial expressions while interacting with them, such imitation is not necessary to understand the meaning of their expressions (Dimberg, Thunberg, & Elmehed, 2000). In a study of three patients with Mobius syndrome, a form of facial paralysis, none were impaired in the ability to recognize facial expressions (Calder et al., 2000). This finding does not imply, however, that those of us who can imitate facial expression don't use this ability to assist us in face reading. Facial expressions of anger and sadness activate the networks of the social brain and speed up heart rate in preparation for action, even as they modulate the mood of others (Critchley et al., 2004; Heisel & Mongarin, 2004). When it comes to emotional facial expressions we have a wide span of attention, a low threshold for detection, and obligatory and automatic processing (Calvo & Lang, 2004; Calvo & Esteves, 2005).

People who have been physically or emotionally abused, like my client Jewel, often become hypersensitive to facial expressions. A small change in eye gaze, the raising of an eyebrow, or a constriction of the pupil can signify potential danger. These individuals often learn to be so good at unconsciously reading the internal states of others that they begin to believe they have clairvoyant powers. Although the belief in these powers can help them cope with their victimization, hypersensitization to the nonverbal communication of others can lead to consistent misunderstandings and high levels of stress in relationships.

Haxby and his colleagues (2000) proposed that different neural systems are involved in processing the invariant and changeable aspects of the human face. The starting point for both of these systems is a central region in the inferior occipital lobe involved with analyzing the basic elements of facial features. The *invariant* aspects of a face are involved with recognition of familiar faces, whereas the *changeable* aspects include gaze direction and emotional expression. Invariant aspects of faces are represented in the lateral fusiform gyrus, whereas the changeable ones are processed in the STS. At the next level of processing, the amygdala and anterior cingulate are recruited for connecting faces with emotional and survival value. The parietal lobe contributes an evaluation of the environmental aspects of direction of attention. The anterior region of the STS is selectively activated during the analysis of emotion through eye contact (Wicker et al., 2003), suggesting that being the object of another's emotions recruits additional processing regions. Figure 12.5 provides a diagram of the various face processing systems.

Studies measuring electrical brain activity have detected maximum activation at 110 milleseconds in the occipital lobe and a 165 milleseconds maximum reading in the fusiform face area, reflecting the timing and direction of face processing (Halgren et al., 2000). Complex visual processing of faces can occur within 100 milleseconds and is impacted by emotional expressions (Eger et al., 2003). This finding suggests that feed-forward and feedback mechanisms constrain and guide the processing of faces very early on (Lehky, 2000). The early influence of facial expressions (even before conscious recognition) provides an advantage in the timely prediction of the behaviors of others, especially when danger is potentially involved.

Alexithymics, individuals with a reduced ability to identify and describe their own feelings, have been shown to process faces more in the left hemisphere, with less activation in the anterior cingulate and medial frontal regions than normals (Berthoz et al., 2002; Kano et al., 2003). One of the theories regarding the underlying neurology of alexithymia is that there is deficient interhemispheric transfer of information between the right and left cerebral hemispheres. Results from these studies suggest a

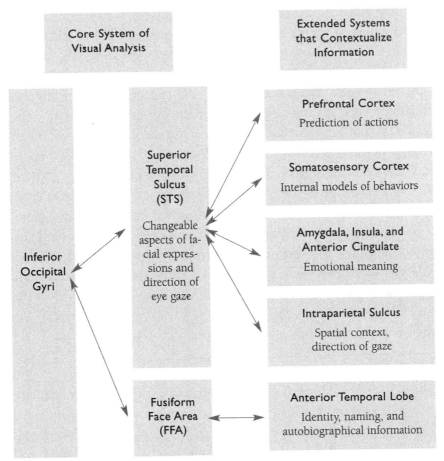

Figure 12.5. **Diagram of face processing systems.** Adapted from Adolphs et al. (2000); Calder (2000); Haxby et al. (2000); and Wicker et al. (2003).

lack of reliance on the usual right-hemisphere systems of emotional and facial processing. Perhaps these patients, lacking an inner somatic model on which to base their judgments about others, rely more on logical, left-hemispheric processes.

Fear and Trustworthiness

In keeping with its role as the core of our fear circuitry, the amygdala generates more activity in response to fearful faces than to other expressions (Whalen et al., 2001). Faces judged as untrustworthy also activate the amygdala in both hemispheres as well as the right insula cortex

(Winston et al., 2002). The right amygdala appears to be part of a right-biased system that is specialized for facial expressions of fear and the activation of avoidance and withdrawal responses (Adolphs, 2002b; Anderson et al., 2000; Broks et al., 1998; Vuilleumier et al., 2001). These functions suggest that there has been an evolutionary choice for fear cues to interpret and override ongoing behavior. In other words, seeing fear in the faces of others or the appearance of untrustworthiness in others triggers our own brains to be on alert and beware of danger.

Other brain areas, such as the insula and anterior cingulate cortices, also become activated in response to fearful faces (Morris, Friston et al., 1998). The contribution of different cortical structures places the fear reaction into personal, interpersonal, and spatial–temporal contexts. Thus, when someone looks fearful of *us,* we may feel dominant and therefore safe. On the other hand, if a child sees a fearful expression on the face of his or her father in response to something in the environment, the child may feel unsafe. In this case, the father's fearful expression is placed in the context of the child's reliance upon him for safety.

Disgust

The facial expression of disgust—pushing out our tongue, wrinkling our face, and moving our head backward—seems to be designed to expel food from the mouth and move the face away from an object of repulsion. This expression is also a signal to others to stop eating shared food or approaching a potentially dangerous area (Erickson & Schulkin, 2003). Current evidence suggests that gestures and feelings of disgust are mediated via the insula and the putamen (a structure in the ventral striatum) (Phillips et al., 1997; Sprengelmeyer et al., 1997, 1998). One study also found right striatal and left amygdala activation when subjects were asked to make judgments about a disgusted facial expression (Gorno-Tempini et al., 2001). Individuals with Huntington's disease or OCD are particularly impaired in the recognition of disgust, supporting the role of the amygdala and ventral striatum, both of which function abnormally in these illnesses (Sprengelmeyer et al., 1996).

Surprise

The typical expression of surprise—eyes and mouth wide open—may rest in an evolutionary-selected reaction to unexpected situations. The expression of surprise signals heightened attention and increased processing of the environment. Open eyes allow us to see more fully, and an open mouth may be a preparation for eating, biting, or rapid oxygen intake if the surprise is threatening. Not surprisingly, when we witness surprise on another, there is an increased activation in the right parahippocampal gyrus of our own brains, an area that is associated with the detection of novelty (Schroeder et al., 2004). As part of the analysis of novelty, both the medial prefrontal cortex and the right amygdala become involved. When the surprise is evaluated to be negative, right amygdala activation dominates, whereas positive surprise results in more medial prefrontal activation (Kim et al., 2003).

The importance of surprise may be seen in how much delight children take in games of anticipation. We can also see how unpredictable a child's reaction can be to being surprised, highlighting the role of contextual and relationship variables in his response (Kim et al., 2004). Children are drawn into games of "predictable surprise," such as playing peek-a-boo or watching a jack-in-the-box. These games may then serve as stimulation for the growth and development of their young brains and better prepare their neural systems to cope with the unexpected eventualities of real life.

Anger and Sadness

At present, the findings about angry and sad expressions have shown mixed results. OMPFC and anterior cingulate activation were found in reaction to angry facial expressions, with no signal recorded in the amygdala. In response to sad faces, the left amygdala and right temporal pole showed activation (Blair et al., 1999). This research contradicts other findings showing that individuals with amygdala lesions were impaired in their ability to read angry facial expressions, frequently mistaking expressions of anger for smiles (Adolphs & Tranel, 2003). The activation of the right temporal pole may trigger sad personal memories, assisting us in attuning to others and accounting for the contagious nature of depression (Mineka & Cook, 1993).

Happiness and Joy

What about our positive emotions? How we read positive expressions has been studied less and appears less clear from a neurophysiological perspective. We have no good animal model for happiness. Evolution, with its emphasis on survival, doesn't appear to have been very concerned with whether animals enjoy themselves while they are surviving. Bilateral activation in response to happy faces generally has been found in the OMPFC and right anterior cingulate (Gorno-Tempini et al., 2001; Phillips et al., 1998). We know that looking at positive *and* negative facial expressions activates the amygdala bilaterally (Williams et al., 2004; Yang et al., 2002). The response of the left amygdala is significantly greater to fearful faces (Blair et al., 1999; Morris et al., 1996; Morris, Friston et al., 1998), with level of activation being positively correlated with the degree of fearfulness and negatively correlated with the degree of happiness.

Interestingly, it has been found that left-hemisphere activation in response to happy faces varies as a function of extroversion. Whereas all subjects show amygdala activation in response to fearful faces, extroverts show left-hemisphere activation in response to happy faces associated with positive emotions and approach behaviors (Canli et al., 2002). Introverts don't appear to be rewarded in the same way as extroverts by approaching others. Overall, it appears that the foundation of happiness is largely dependent upon the absence of fear. After that, activation of the OMPFC, anterior cingulate, and other social brain structures driven by the biochemistry of the reward systems take over.

Biological Motion

Although faces are data-rich, posture, orientation, proximity, and movement are also full of information. Whether at a cafe, marketplace, or a parade, people-watching is a time-honored tradition around the world. We are fascinated by how people look, how they walk, their gestures, and what they are doing. It is almost reflexive for us to create scenarios about other people: who they are with, what's on their minds, and what they are up to (Pavlova et al., 2005). This popular human "hobby" most likely rests in the evolution of networks initially designed to monitor and predict the movements of potential predators and, later, those in our expanding social groups. By 4 months, infants show a preference for biological over inanimate motion, similar to our reflex to seek out faces (Fox & McDaniel, 1982; Neri, Morron, & Burr, 1998). By 2 years of age, children are able to recognize others by their gait, gestures, and other behaviors (Cutting & Kozlowski, 1977). Like eye gaze and facial expressions, body movements and postures are important sources of information.

There is considerable evidence for the existence of an additional processing network for biological movement. This evidence relies on the high-level analysis of patterns in motion from an area of the occipital cortex called V5, a region that specializes in the perception and analysis of movement (Battelli, Cavanagh, & Thornton, 2003). Damage to V5 can result in an inability to perceive objects or people while in motion. In addition to V5, other regions of the occipital lobe, the fusiform face areas, superior temporal sulcus (STS), and the left parietal cortex become activated when movement is from a biological source (Allison, Puce, & McCarthy, 2000; Bonda et al., 1996; Grèzes et al., 2001; Grossman & Blake, 2002; Pelphrey, Mitchell et al., 2003; Puce & Perrett, 2003).

It has been proposed that a specialized body area exists at the junction of the temporal and occipital lobes that focuses on monitoring and analyzing biological motion, especially the walking human body (Downing, Jiang, Shuman, & Kanwisher, 2001). Support for separate processing networks of biological motion versus other visual–spatial analysis comes from people with William's syndrome, who suffer from profound visual–spatial deficits when processing inanimate objects but perform as well as, or better than, normals in the perception of biological motion (Jordan et al., 2002).

When biological motion involves gestures or expressiveness, the right STS, adjacent temporal cortex, and amygdala also become activated (Bonda et al., 1996; Jellema & Perrett, 2003a, 2003b). This neural circuit may allow us to imply motion from static postures; that is, certain postures are associated with a likely movement to follow, allowing us to react without having to wait until the action is initiated (Castelli et al., 2000). It appears that humans have evolved to be experts in reading motions *and* emotions. We don't just read facial expressions but the expressions of the entire body (Decety & Grèzes, 1999).

The Power of a Pretty Face

From the beginning of life, we are treated differently based on how attractive others find us. Thus, attractiveness and beauty are interpersonal realities that shape our brains because they impact our development, self-image, successes, and failures. Even the most sacred of relationships between mother and child is affected by the infant's attractiveness. Mothers are more affectionate and playful with attractive children and will turn their attention to the more attractive children of other mothers (Langlois et al., 1995, 2000). Even infants will tend to look at more attractive faces when given the choice (Langlois et al., 1987).

As they grow, the misbehaviors of unattractive children are seen as the result of negative character traits, whereas attractive children are seen to misbehave because of factors external to themselves (Dion, 1972). If the way we are treated is affected by how we look, and the way we are treated builds our brains, it stands to reason that the brains of attractive people come to be different from the brains of unattractive people. This would be stark evidence of the fact that the brain is a social organ and that vision is a powerful social sense. Beauty may be in the eye of the beholder, but it is also in the brain of the beheld.

Why is it so exciting when someone attractive looks our way? Why do attractive people get better jobs and talk their way out of more traffic tickets? The answer may lie in what is evoked in our brains when we see them. Put simply, the sight of an attractive face is to humans what a food pellet is to a rat: a reward. When we see an attractive face, especially when it turns our way, there is considerable activation in the OMPFC, ventral striatum, and nucleus accumbens, key structures of the dopamine circuitry related to the expectation of reward (Aharon et al., 2001; Kampe et al., 2001; O'Doherty et al., 2003). By juxtaposing their products to attractive faces, advertisers condition consumers to experience activation of this reward system when they see automobiles, breakfast cereal, and bars of soap. Not surprisingly, this is the same circuitry activated in substance abuse and other addictive behaviors. After all, isn't it the business of advertisers to get us addicted to the products they have to sell?

The activation of reward circuitry biases our judgment in a positive direction. This "halo effect" results in attractive people being judged as smarter, kinder, more honest and deserving, more familiar, and more like us (Monin, 2003). When attractive people are defendants in court, they receive less severe sentences, jurors are less certain of their guilt, and they are judged to have committed less serious crimes (Stewart, 1980); as plaintiffs, they receive higher damage settlements (Efran, 1974). Attractive people win more political elections, garner more assistance from others, and are taken more seriously in discussions. Unfortunately, like other implicit, automatic processes (e.g., attachment, transference, projection) we are unconscious of this bias and attribute our judgments not to the appearance of those we judge but to our sense of fairness and our good common sense. If a pretty face can topple "blind justice" and impact a mother's "unconditional love," something powerful must be happening. As Philip Roth suggested, "The authority of beauty is a very irrational thing."

What makes a face attractive to us is a matter of debate (Perrett et al., 1994). Some think it is in the geometry of the features, while others suggest that we find more feminine and childlike features to be more attractive (Grammer & Thornhill, 1994; Langlois & Roggman, 1990; Perrett et al., 1998). Faces that are considered attractive by adults are also preferred by infants regardless of race, age, or gender. This finding suggests that what is attractive to us may, in part, be guided by innate dispositions, though this has yet to be proven (Kirkpatrick & Ryan, 1991). We may, however, find some clues in other species. For example, female swallows prefer males with larger and more symmetrical sexual ornaments, whereas female widowbirds prefer bigger tails (Andersson, 1982; Enquist & Arak, 1993). Size isn't everything, but apparently it doesn't hurt. Although we may like to believe that we are not so superficial as to evaluate others based on their appearance, research suggests that when it comes to the social brain, the book *is* judged by its cover.

Chapter 3

Imitation and Mirror Neurons: Monkey See, Monkey Do

When people are free to do as they please,
they usually imitate each other.
—Eric Hoffer, 1955, p. 16

The tendency for primates to imitate one another is well known and probably accounts for the fact that "aping" is synonymous with imitation. But humans are also primates, and we also imitate one another (we're just a little subtler). Within hours of our birth, we begin to reflexively imitate adults when they open their mouths, stick out their tongues, or make happy or sad faces (Field et al., 1982; Meltzoff & Moore, 1992). Why has evolution selected the automatic imitation of facial expressions, gestures, and body movements? The most likely explanations are that imitation is central to learning and important for the coordination of group behavior. The discovery of mirror neurons and the neural networks they coordinate provides clues to the mechanics of these vital social processes.

Mirror Neurons

Using arrays of microsensors, researchers have recorded the firing of hundreds of neurons in the brains of monkeys while they are alert and observing the behaviors of others. These microsensors revealed that neurons in the premotor areas of the frontal lobes fire when another primate is observed engaging in a specific behavior, such as grasping an object with a hand. These are the same neurons that fire when the subject engages in the identical task. Because these neurons fire both when observing and performing a particular action, they have been dubbed *mirror neurons* (di Pellegrino et al., 1992; Gallese, 2001; Gallese et al., 1996; Gallese & Goldman, 1998; Jeannerod et al., 1995; Rizzolatti et al., 1999).

Some of these neurons were found to be so specific that they fired only when a particular object was grasped in a certain way by particular fingers, such as picking up a banana with the right hand at a certain angle or peeling it with the thumb and forefinger (Rizzolatti & Arbib, 1998). These neurons are all the more interesting because they are sensitive to goal-directed behaviors. In other words, they don't fire in response to the hand or the banana or even the two presented together; they fire only when the hand is acting on the banana in a specific way for a specific purpose.

The structures of mirror neurons are not special in and of themselves; they serve this mirroring function due to their location. They reside in association areas of the frontal cortex where networks converge to process high-level information. Mirror neurons lie at the crossroads of the processing of inner and outer experience, where multiple networks of visual, motor, and emotional processing converge (Iacoboni et al., 2001). It is because of their privileged position that mirror neurons are able to bridge observation and action. Mirror systems have helped us to understand how our brains link together in the synchronization of such group behaviors as hunting, dancing, and emotional attunement (Jeannerod, 2001). They are most likely involved in the learning of manual skills, the evolution of gestural communication, spoken language, group cohesion, and empathy.

Motor Learning and Gestural Communication

It is common knowledge that we can learn by observation. It is likely that mirror systems first developed as a way for skills and abilities to be transferred from one animal to another. When we watch someone else performing an action, such as breaking the hard shell of a nut between two rocks, we not only see what is occurring, but the motor circuits involved in performing the same action become activated. In procedural memory, our brain records how the nut is held in the hand, how it is placed on the rock, and the movements involved in hitting the nut. It then connects these behaviors with the desired outcome of eating what's inside. Observing the attainment of the goal then serves to motivate and reinforce the learning of the sequence of behaviors necessary for attaining it. In this way, our brains practice doing while watching and associate action–object relationships with rewards. Because mirror neurons link observation and motor programs, observing becomes a way to rehearse.

As bands of primates grew in size and the demands for social communication increased, mirror systems were likely recruited for the development of gestural communication (Rizzolatti et al., 1996; Wolf et al., 2000). How did this happen? Gallese (2001) proposed that the intention of an action triggers mirror neurons to activate a pattern of motor behavior associated with achieving the desired goal. Dialing a phone number, playing a piece on the piano, or serving a tennis ball are good examples of how this mechanism works. The first number, first note, or tossing the ball in the air sets the entire sequence of procedural motor memory in motion. In support of this theory, it has been shown that the imitation of a goal-directed action activates the prefrontal cortex, the area of the brain that connects the behaviors with memory for future outcomes (Chaminade, Meltzoff, & Decety, 2002). In this way, a gesture can become a "prefix" for a set of movements and intentions that can evolve into a symbol for communication (Rizzolatti & Arbib, 1998).

In a chimpanzee, this prefix might be a gesture that mimics the bodily reaction to seeing a snake, activating other members of the troop to scurry up a tree. For the troop of chimps, the gesture of escape comes to represent both the danger and the action required. Millions of years would turn this gesture into a grunt, and then a sound like "snake" in imitation of the snake's hissing sound, and finally just the use of the word. A human who spots a friend on a passing escalator can hold her hand to her head, extending fingers to her mouth and ear to let him know that she wants him to call her. If she shakes her hand rapidly with emphasis and widens her eyes, she also lets him know that she wants this to happen, *Oh my God! Really, really soon!* Thus, the gesture of an action becomes a prefix of a set of actions and an intended outcome. As with chimps and snakes, gestures can eventually be linked with sounds, and the sounds become words associated with actions and objects. Ultimately, as language becomes more sophisticated, the gestural part of the message become secondary or eliminated (except for Italians). If you pay attention to people's gestures while they are talking, it soon becomes clear that all of these gestures are a vital part of communication.

Language

As the number of individual primates in a social group expanded, so did the ratio of the size of the neocortex to the entire brain (Dunbar, 1992). The expansion of the neocortex and hemispheric specialization created the neural space for the development of increasingly more com plex forms of social communication. This expansion and differentiation provided the computational power necessary for gestures and sign language to be adapted into verbal communication (Wilson, F. R., 1998).

The region in the frontal lobes of monkeys (F5) where the most mirror neurons have been found is analogous to Broca's region in humans. This overlap suggests that they are likely involved in the recognition and expression of phonetic gestures and actions (Gallese et al., 1996; Petitto et al., 2000). It is reasonable to assume that mirror systems might also aid us in learning lip reading and spoken language and may explain why it is easier to follow speech when we can see the speaker's lips—and why lip reading without hearing is even possible (McGurk & MacDonald, 1976). If watching is equivalent to learning, then mirror neurons would contribute to the evolution of language by providing a vital link between language, gestures, and internal experience (Liberman & Mattingly, 1985; Rizzolatti & Arbib, 1998).

There is considerable evidence in humans that our words and gestures are linked. The observation of hand movements, even in imagination, result in activation of Broca's area, as does the attempt to use paralyzed hands (Bonda et al., 1994; Chollet et al., 1991; Parsons et al., 1995). It has been demonstrated that listening to speech activates our tongue muscles, which may aid not only in learning to speak early in life but in our understanding of what we are listening to throughout life (Fadiga et al., 2002). Having a schizophrenic client hold his or her mouth wide open can even inhibit auditory hallucinations. Aphasic patients are unable to recognize hand actions and have difficulty understanding pantomime, and the gestures of people who stutter freeze when their words become blocked and then resume simultaneously along with their words (Bell, 1994; Mayberry et al., 1998). These observations all offer evidence of the intimate connection between language and action: Verbal expressions related to physical actions activate motor areas linked to what is being described (Nyberg et al., 2001).

Some have hypothesized that mirror neurons were vital to the evolution of language by creating social interactions based on grasping, sharing, and using objects. These interactions evolved into hand gestures and then into the symbolic code of language (Arbib, 2002). The use of the word *grasp* to mean *understand* may reflect the primitive linkage between the somatic and the semantic in the action-based origin of speech. Our ubiquitous use of physical metaphors to describe our inner experiences may also betray the sensory–motor core of both our subjective experience and abstract thought. When we use expressions such as "She's *devastatingly* beautiful, he's *strikingly* handsome, she'll *knock you off* your feet, he *bowled* me *over*, she's a *bombshell*, or he *blew me away*, we both feel *and* understand what is being said (Johnson, 1987). It is our shared visceral and physical experiences that make this kind of metaphorical discourse meaningful. In the same way, many believe that human reason is not derived from abstract logic but rather emerges from our bodily experience within our social and physical environments (Damasio, 1994; Greenspan & Shanker, 2004; Lakoff, 1990).

Based on our present knowledge, it is logical to assume that observing the actions, gestures, and facial expressions of others will result in the reflexive activation of motor systems. These motor systems will, in turn, activate thoughts and emotions associated with these behaviors. Seeing children cry makes us reflexively frown, tilt our heads, say "aawwhhhh" and feel sad with them. Watching a defeated athlete walk slowly off the field, head in her hands, can not only lead us to feel sad but also trigger a memory of a time when we, too, suffered defeat. In these and countless other ways, mirror neurons may bridge the gap between sender and receiver, enhancing emotional resonance, empathic attunement, and mutual understanding (Wolf et al., 2000). Although mirror systems are only one small component of the social brain, they are, in and of themselves, an evolutionary masterpiece.

Nelson—The Sincerest Form of Flattery

When I first saw Nelson in my waiting room, I thought Popeye had come to life. He was a thin, wiry man of 75, with a short beard, bulging biceps, and a full head of wild silver hair. His daughter Nancy sat next to him, noticeably anxious, her eyes searching the room for some comforting distraction. In contrast, Nelson was "holding court" with the other patients, telling stories, dispensing advice, and asking very personal questions. He seemed entirely pleased to have a captive audience in an enclosed space.

I brought Nancy into my office to find out why she had brought her father into the clinic. Nelson had moved in with Nancy after the death of her mother 2 years ago. She noticed he was acting a bit odd, but attributed his behavior to the loss of his wife, on whom he had been quite dependent. As the months went by, she became increasingly concerned with his behaviors. His memory seemed to be getting worse, and he easily got lost when away from home. Nelson, historically a conservative and reserved man, began telling Nancy off-color jokes and seemed unaware of how uncomfortable they made her. Nancy knew that these were symptoms of dementia and suspected that her mother's careful attention had protected the family from discovering his illness. But there was something else at work as well.

I brought Nelson into the office, offered him my hand, and said, "Hello, sir, I'm Dr. Cozolino." He took my hand and replied, "Hello, I'm Dr. Cozolino. You could really use some new furniture and magazines in your waiting room." Nancy turned red and shook her head as I looked over to her and smiled. It appeared that Nelson felt he was having a completely normal conversation as he mimicked the words he heard from others. He also seemed to have stopped filtering his thoughts. For Nelson, to *have* a thought was to *express* it with no editing or consideration of his audience. I imagined him interacting this way with strangers in the community and understood why Nancy was concerned with his welfare.

Voicing his unedited opinions violated one set of social norms, and repeating what others said might be considered mocking. These behaviors added up to a bad combination for an older man living in a tough neighborhood.

During the day while Nancy was away at work, Nelson would sit on the steps in front of their building. He would feed the pigeons, talk to the neighbors, and play checkers with some of his friends. However, Nelson had been recently getting into trouble. Through friends in the neighborhood, Nancy heard that her father had been making people angry and, a few weeks ago, someone had actually slapped him. She found out that Nelson had begun to repeat back what they were saying almost simultaneously as the words were coming out of their mouths. He didn't do it all the time. When his attention was focused on some activity he enjoyed, such as eating or working in his shop, it didn't happen. But when he was bored or distracted, he took to imitating as if it were an acceptable form of communication.

After being examined by the neurology team, it was determined that Nelson was in the middle stage of dementia. His reflexive imitative behavior is called *echolalia,* or the tendency to repeat (or echo) the words and sounds of others. Because of our mirror systems, we all have the automatic tendency to echo the sounds and words made by others. As we have seen, this reflexive imitation is in place immediately after birth. As we grow and our cortex develops, one of its primary roles is to inhibit early primitive reflexes so that we can be in greater control of our behaviors and make choices, especially about the interpersonal behaviors we exhibit. During the progression of dementia, the cortex slowly atrophies, resulting in the deficits of memory, problem solving, and orientation that Nelson had been showing for a number of years. It seems that sometime during the last few months, the dementing process began to decrease Nelson's ability to inhibit this primitive imitative reflex. His symptoms suggest that these early reflexes to imitate are never lost but are actively inhibited by the developing cortex.

Focus on the Mirror Neuron System

Although single-cell recording from healthy human subjects is far too damaging to perform solely for research purposes, scan data have demonstrated that areas in the human brain analogous to those containing mirror neurons in other primates (premotor cortex and Broca's area) are activated during the observation, imagination, empathy, and execution of hand actions (Bonda et al., 1994; Buccino et al., 2004; Decety & Chaminade, 2003a, 2003b; Nishitani & Hari, 2000). Current research supports that the human mirror system extends to the temporal, parietal, and frontal lobes as well as to the insula, amygdala, basal ganglia, and cerebellum. The areas of the brain that become activated depend on the task and whether it is observed, imagined, or involves emotions (Fadiga et al., 1995; Grafton et al., 1996; Ohnishi et al., 2004; Rizzolatti et al., 1996). When humans observe hand movements, subcortical motor areas such as the basal ganglia and cerebellum become more active. When asked to imagine the same movements, activations shift to the frontal and parietal lobes (Decety & Chaminade, 2003a).

Whether we imitate or just observe the facial expressions of another, the inferior frontal, superior temporal, amygdala, and insula become activated (Carr et al., 2003). Our tendency to imitate behavior on the same side of our bodies as the behavior we observe supports the fact that our brains are automatically primed to "mirror others" (Iacoboni et al., 2001; Koski et al., 2003). This finding suggests that we are not working off a cognitive map that corrects for left–right differences. Instead, imitation is controlled by automatic mirroring systems at lower levels of processing. This process may have been initially shaped to support the rapid reaction to physical threat from others on the same side as the threat. If someone is about to give you something or strike you with his or her right hand, it is most beneficial and efficient to respond with your left in order to grasp the object or block the attack.

Within mirror systems, multiple somatotopic and visual–spatial maps interweave, connect, and coordinate cognitive and emotional experience with motor behavior. Figure 13.1 identifies regions bridged by mirror neurons. During the execution of an observed action, Broca's area is activated first, followed by the left primary motor area, and then the right. During observation itself, the sequence is the same except that activation begins in the left occipital cortex (Nishitani & Hari, 2000). Visual input into F5 comes from the parietal lobes, where it has already combined

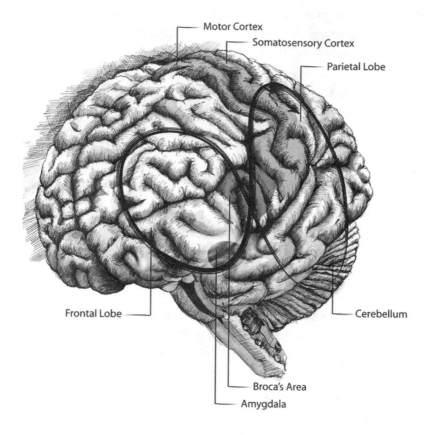

Figure 13.1. **Some of the regions involved in observation and action that are bridged by mirror neurons.**

with somatic, spatial, and auditory information. Audiovisual mirror neurons link sounds with actions that are seen and performed as well as heard (Kohler et al., 2002).

By the time a child is 18 months old, he or she is able to understand the goal of an action without seeing it completed (Meltzoff, 1995). This ability suggests that the action–goal connections are processed in implicit memory and do not require conscious recall of future goals. In their studies of infant imitation, Meltzoff and Moore (1989) predicted the existence of mirror systems in humans. They suggested that the perception of an act could be used directly for the execution of a motor plan in a process they described as "active inter-modal mapping." Inter-modal (sensory–motor) mapping, linked to emotional and cognitive processing, is essentially what mirror neurons and their circuitry provide. Table 13.1 summarizes the brain regions involved in mirror systems.

Table 13.1. **Brain Regions Involved in Perceptual–Action Mirror Systems**

1. **Premotor cortex, motor cortex, cerebellum, basal ganglia**
   Motor representation of motor actions
   Generation of action–motor sequences

2. **Somatosensory cortex**
   Integrating sensory, visceral, and motor aspects of experience

3. **Parietal lobe (self-management)**
   Visual-spatial organization and somatosensory information
   Pragmatic analysis of objects (Freund, 2001; Jeannerod et al., 1995)
   Linking objects and actions (Buccino et al., 2001)
   Global representation of action
   Patterns of motor behavior and limb position (Iacoboni et al., 1999)

4. **Broca's area (F5 in monkeys; BA44 and BA45 in humans)**
   Executive of mirror neuron system (Nishitani & Hari, 2000)
   Specific representation of particular actions
   Imitation (Heiser et al., 2003)
   Gestures (Cantalupo & Hopkins, 2001)
   Semantic representation of action

5. **Amygdala**
   Assigning a value to behaviors
   Emotional salience
   Expressing and reading facial gestures

6. **Frontal lobe (behavior–goal connection through time)**
   Planning and memory for the future (Decety et al., 1997; Ingvar, 1985)
   Anticipation of the consequences of actions
   Motor goals (Iacoboni et al., 1999)
   Action understanding and action monitoring
   Empathy
   Integration of somatosensory, motor–action plans, and value

Theory of Mind

In neuroscience the term *mind reading* does not refer to telepathy or clairvoyance but rather to the comprehension of what another knows and is about to do based on observation. Premack and Woodruff (1978) first used the term *theory of mind* (TOM) to describe the system of inferences primates utilize in attempting to predict the behaviors of others. A TOM starts out as a visceral–emotional sense of the intentions of others gained through the activation of mirror systems in response to direction of eye gaze, facial expressions, biological movement, posture, tone of voice, and other channels of social communication (Hobson, 1991). In humans it includes an understanding of what other people can see from their perspective, what they may know, and what motivates them. By employing our own action–goal networks, we automatically generate a TOM, which becomes an expectation about the other. Multiple neural systems, from primitive brainstem reflexes to abstract abilities, contribute to our theory of what is in the mind of another. Children begin to have an unconscious awareness of a TOM somewhere between 3 and 5 years of age (Povinelli & Preuss, 1995).

It is logical to assume that we may use an internal model of motivation and means–end relationships as a template to predict the actions and intentions of others. In fact, simulating, anticipating, and predicting the actions of others are key components of social interactions (Grèzes & Decety, 2001). These processes involve primitive resonance and identification with others as well as the abstract ability to create a mental representation of their thoughts, feelings, needs, and motivations. It has been demonstrated that when we attempt to predict the actions of others, we employ some of the same neural networks that become activated when we are planning for our own future (Ramnani & Miall, 2004).

Although TOM may have initially evolved to cooperate with or keep us safe from others, it has come to contribute to other aspects of bonding and social communication. When we interact with others, our nervous systems resonate, activating the emotional and intentional associations to what we are observing. In this way, we come to know others by creating internal working models of facial gestures, body language, and the direction of their attention and movement (Platek et al., 2004). Our own internal state, generated via mirroring, becomes our theory of what others are feeling. Mirror systems supporting social cognition not only enhance the survival of an individual through the anticipation of the behavior of others, they also enhance the individual's desirability as a collaborative member of the group and reproductive mate.

Frith and Frith (1999) proposed a TOM system comprising three major nodes: (1) medial prefrontal organizing (self-related mental states), (2) superior temporal sulcus (analyzing agents, goals, and outcomes), and (3) inferior frontal (representations of actions and goals). The overlap of activation in superior and medial temporal areas during TOM and eye-gaze processing tasks suggests that the analysis of eye gaze may have been one of the earliest evolutionary components of a TOM (Calder et al., 2002).

Modeling other minds requires multiple areas of the prefrontal cortex (Goel et al., 1995). The right OMPFC is especially important in decoding mental states, whereas the left specializes in the ability to reason about mental states (Sabbagh, 2004). Developing a theory of other minds also appears to require the amygdala, insula, and anterior cingulate (Siegal & Varley, 2002). The parietal lobes, somatosensory cortex, and the cerebellum are involved in the organization of the nonconscious internal model connecting actions, intentions, and goals (Carlage, Andreasen, & O'Leary, 2003). Our frontal lobes use this internal model to generate a working model of others. Our awareness of the relationship between our intentions and actions creates a sense of "will" that we may use as a working model to perceive will in others (Frith, 2002). Table 13.2 summarizes the brain regions involved in TOM.

TOM has yet to be measured in a naturalistic situation. Task responses in the laboratory are often verbal or based on selecting a choice, which activates semantic processing that may not be central to TOM processing (Varley & Siegal, 2000; Bloom, 2000). For example, when subjects were asked to perform a storytelling task that necessitated attributing mental states, activation was primarily on the left side of the brain (Carlage et al., 2003; Fletcher et al., 1995). It would make sense that the core components of a TOM circuitry would organize a form of social intelligence that we share with other primates that would be biased toward the right hemisphere (Povinelli, Bering, & Giambrone, 2000).

Disorders on the autistic spectrum are characterized by an impairment of mentalizing, especially about social relationships (Fletcher et al., 1995). When patients with Asperger's disorder were compared with normals on TOM tasks, it was found that the center of activation within the left frontal region differed (Happé et al., 1996). This finding parallels research that found that faces are processed in an adjacent area of the

Table 13.2. **Brain Regions Involved in Theory of Mind**

Region	Action/Function
Medial prefrontal cortex	Subtle social reasoning[1] Self-related mental states[2] Analysis of deception[3] Deception of others[4]
Dorsal lateral prefrontal cortex	Actions and goals Abstraction from given data[5] Visual perspective taking[6]
Anterior cingulate	Deception of others[7]
Superior temporal sulcus	Agents, goals, outcomes[8] Eye-gaze analysis[9]
Amygdala	Perspective taking, affective arousal[10] Creating an internal model of the other[11]
Right hemisphere	Mentalizing about subject[12] Visual perspective taking[13]
Left hemisphere	Reasoning about subject[14]

[1] Stone et al., 1998; [2] Frith & Frith, 1999; [3] Happe et al., 1999; [4] Kozel et al., 2004; [5] Frith & Frith, 1999; [6] Gallagher et al., 2000; [7] Kozel et al., 2004; [8] Frith & Frith, 1999; [9] Calder et al., 2000; [10] Siegal & Varley, 2002; [11] Stone et al., 2003; [12] Frith & Frith, 1999; [13] Stuss et al., 2001; [14] Sabbagh, 2004.

temporal lobes in autism. Both of these studies suggest that the neuroplastic adaptations made by the brain in autism and Asperger's disorder recruit adjacent neural structures not specialized for social tasks. Unfortunately, these nonspecialized regions do not work as well as those sculpted through countless generations of natural selection for social specialization.

Mirror neurons and the neural networks they coordinate work together to allow us to automatically react to, move with, and generate a theory of what is on the mind of others. Thus, mirror neurons not only link networks within us but link us to each other. They appear to be an essential component of the social brain and an important mechanism of communication across the social synapse.

Chapter | 4

Resonance, Attunement, and Empathy

I do not ask the wounded person how he feels . . . I myself become the wounded person . . .
—Walt Whitman, 1855/1931, p. 40

When I was growing up, Friday night was boxing night. The living room would glow from the *Gillette Fight of the Week* as my grandfather sat at the edge of his chair (in boxer shorts, of course), bobbing and weaving, jabbing and upper-cutting, ducking and covering. He would groan, grunt, and shout with abandon as my grandmother retreated to the kitchen. I remember feeling both frightened and fascinated as I looked on. In an attempt to gain reassurance, I would ask, "What are you doing, Grandpa?" Without taking his eyes off the screen, he would say in his Brooklyn accent, "I'm watchin' the fights, whadda-yatink I'm doin'?"

A similar thing would occur when we went to a baseball game. He would jump from his seat when bat met ball, yell at some fly balls to help them gain distance, or curse at others to get them into the gloves of *his* outfielders. He was no dispassionate observer: When a punch landed he felt dazed, when a batter was hit by a pitch he would cry out in pain, and when the Yankees won, he was jubilant. He participated in these events through what looked like a complete resonance with the athletes. His mirror neurons fired, and he went with them. By the end of the Friday night fights, he was physically and emotionally spent. Rising slowly, he would hang his towel around his neck and head off to the showers.

If sports are sublimated combat and athletes are our modern day glad-iators, it is easy to see how our resonance with others may have evolved to enhance survival through coordination and cooperation. These reso-nance reactions are yet another example of our innate interconnection through reflexive communication. Have you ever seen an aerial shot of a herd of hundreds of impalas running across a savanna in Africa? One animal on the periphery suddenly changes direction after sensing a potential danger. Instantaneously, this reaction spreads through the herd, resulting in a massive wave of directional shift. Mob mentality in humans may, in some ways, represent an eclipse of conscious control by reso-nance behaviors, stimulated by being surrounded by others engaging in emotionally driven behaviors.

Resonance Behaviors

Resonance behaviors triggered by mirror systems are automatic responses that are reflexive, implicit, and obligatory. They communicate potentially important information, advance social cohesion, and enhance group identification and safety. Resonance behaviors also serve learning by pro-viding an automatic core for imitative learning and the organization of procedural memory (Rizzolatti et al., 1999). Reflexively looking up when we see others doing it, yawning in response to the yawns of oth-ers, and my grandfather's reactions watching boxing and baseball are all examples of resonance behaviors (Platek et al., 2003).

Whereas resonance mechanisms may have originally evolved to syn-chronize group behaviors such as hunting, gathering, fighting or flee-ing, they appear to have been adapted to support the development of gestural communication, language, and other aspects of social relating (Rizzolatti et al., 1999). Resonance behaviors occur in all kinds of so-cial situations. Research with therapist–client dyads has shown that therapists unconsciously mirror the facial expressions, tone of voice, and body postures of their clients. With greater control over mirror sys-tems in the course of evolution, we can now inhibit some resonance be-haviors, choose to emit others voluntarily, and use the information provided by our mirror circuitry in increasingly strategic ways (Rizzolatti & Arbib, 1998).

For example, I practice aikido, a martial art based on the traditions of Japanese sword fighting. Of course, the first thing you need to learn to do when sword fighting is to stay away from your opponent's blade. Thus, even though there are no swords involved, the ultimate move in aikido would be to throw your opponent without actually having to touch him. For years I had heard there were aikido masters who could do this seemingly metaphysical act (of which I was extremely skeptical). As fate would have it, one day I found myself standing across from the man who many considered the world's premiere aikidoist.

When it was my turn with the master, I stood about 10 feet away from him trying to overcome my fear. My role as his uke (opponent) required that I run at him and hit him. Well past 70 and slight of build, he stood calmly awaiting my approach. With some hesitation, I set out across the mat, arm raised, going for his head. As I took my first step, he adjusted his body in a way that led me to turn slightly to the right. On my next step, he shifted his posture again, leading me to reflexively react and become even more off-balance. By my third step, he moved again and I twisted a bit to the left. When I was close enough to strike him, he took a quick, compact step to my right. As I tried to rotate and hit him, my feet were tangled. He suddenly raised both of his hands toward my face, startling me, and making my head shoot back.

The next thing I knew, I was lying on the mat, listening to the other students laughing in the background. I was too amazed to feel shame; I just lay there, my eyes wide, my head shaking with disbelief. I now know that being thrown without being touched is far from metaphysical. My teacher was a master at activating and manipulating balance, reflexes, mirror systems, and resonance behaviors. He was playing my body like a familiar instrument, and I understood his calm in the face of attack; I was easy prey. It was a humbling lesson on both my lack of skill as an aikidoist and of the power of these automatic and unconscious resonance reactions.

Attunement and Emotional Contagion

In addition to physical movements, mirror systems and resonance behaviors appear to be involved in our ability to attune to the *emotional* states of others. They provide us with a visceral–emotional template of what the other is experiencing, allowing us to know another from the inside out. One example of this phenomenon occurs when we look at pictures of emotionally expressive faces: our facial muscles become activated in imitation of the perceived expressions (Lundqvist & Dimberg, 1995).

In building and shaping her child's brain, a mother relies on resonance to stay entrained with her child while generating ideas about his or her internal state. The ability to access and use resonance behaviors in parenting will likely correlate with the security of attachment relationships. When mothers are asked to sing to their infants, attuned mothers sing less playfully to a distressed child in order to match the child's affective state more closely. Mothers with dismissing attachment do not adjust in this way to their child's emotional state (Milligan et al., 2003). Emotional resonance between mother and child correlates with the child spending more time in social engagement, better affect regulation, symbolic play, verbal IQ, and the child's ability to comment on his feelings and inner experience (Feldman et al., 1997; Feldman et al., 1999; Penman et al., 1983). Of course, a mother does not exist in isolation, and support for a mother not only decreases her stress but correlates with more positive behaviors with, and attitude toward, her child (Crnic et al., 1983).

Because resonance reactions occur before we are consciously aware of them, our awareness of others comes into consciousness "prepackaged" with an activation of our resonance circuitry (Wild, Erb, & Bartels, 2001). Resonance behaviors also have a downside; they make us susceptible to emotional contagion: that is, being "infected" by what we see being acted out by others. Fears, anxiety, and phobias can all be passed from one person to another, especially from parents to children, through observation (Hornik et al., 1987; Mineka & Cook, 1993; Platek et al., 2003; Walden & Ogan, 1988).

Other less benign forms of social contagion include trauma and suicide. The faces of the grief-stricken are matched by the expressions on the faces of those attempting to assist them. Suicides of celebrities often trigger "copycat" suicides, especially by adolescents who have overidentified with them. A wave of suicides swept through Europe after the publication of Goethe's *The Sorrows of Young Werther*, in which the lovelorn

Werther commits suicide (Marsden, 1998). Each in their own generation, Rudolph Valentino, Marilyn Monroe, and Kurt Cobain triggered contagious suicides in the weeks and months following their deaths.

On the other hand, there is an aspect of social contagion that is best described as inspiration. There are some people who make a statement through words and deeds that inspires us to change our thinking, have courage in the face of danger, and behave in new and more life-affirming ways. Think of the pictures we have all seen of the young man in Tienneman Square standing in front of the advancing tanks, Rosa Parks refusing to surrender her seat on a bus, or Winston Churchill's radio addresses during the bombing of London. Their actions and words send a chill up our spine, warm our hearts, and make us reconsider our acceptance of the status quo. This visceral reaction to the inspirational behavior of others is another aspect of social contagion that serves group coherence and positive change.

Empathy

The everyday understanding of empathy consists of a muddle of resonance, attunement, and sympathy. Empathy is actually a *hypothesis* we make about another person based on a combination of visceral, emotional, and cognitive information. Mirror and resonance circuits combine with visual–spatial, cognitive, and abstract networks to allow us to place others in context as we try to "get inside their head." Thus, empathy requires many levels of neural processing and integration beyond resonance behaviors.

According to Kohut (1984), empathy is an attempt to experience the inner life of another while retaining objectivity. In other words, we hold our own perspective in mind while simultaneously imagining what it is like to be the other. In order to have empathy, we need to maintain an awareness of our inner world as we imagine the inner world of others. Shuttling back and forth between my head and what I imagine to be in yours, I generate hypotheses about your inner state based on my own thoughts and inner experiences, and these hypotheses are added to other forms of communication. This process is at the core of the therapeutic relationship. When boundaries become blurred and resonance experiences are assumed to be identical to the inner state of the other, empathy is re-placed by identification or fusion. This primitive and often pathological state is not the same as empathy because it lacks perspective and an awareness of boundaries.

Measuring neural firing in a monkey's brain while she observes an-other monkey grasping a grape is relatively straightforward when com-pared to examining the complexities of human emotional experience. Not only do we lack a clear definition for complex emotions, but we also lack the technology to directly measure human brain activity in natura-listic settings. Although we are just beginning to explore the neurobiol-ogy of empathy, some clues are beginning to emerge. Given that the cortex first evolved to guide motor behavior, it makes sense that more primitive somatic and motor activation serve as the infrastructure of emotion, cognition, and abstract thought. Utilizing mirror circuitry as a core system and expanding it to include additional systems of the social brain, we may be able to begin looking for a fundamental network of res-onance and empathy. Table 14.1 summarizes the circuitry involved in imitation, resonance, and empathy.

Table 14.1. **Neural Circuits Involved in Imitation, Resonance, and Empathy**

Structure	Function
Broca's Area	Frontal mirror neurons code action/outcome linkage
STS	Early visual description/imitation/action feedback
Posterior parietal cortex	Kinesthetic aspects of face and body movements and differentiation of self and other
STS/post parietal connections	Match visual description, predict sensation, and plan imitative movements
Anterior cingulate and amygdala	Emotional relevance/physical pain and social exclusion
Insula	Bridging internal and external experience
Autonomic and motor networks	Beginning of imitation/empathy
Primary sensory cortex	New stimuli redirects attention

Note: STS = superior temporal sulcus. Sources: Botvinick et al. (2005); Carr et al. (2003); Decety & Chaminade (2003a): Eisenberger et al. (2003); Iacoboni (1999); Ruby & Decety (2001).

Suzanne—A Selfless Life

Suzanne came to therapy complaining of exhaustion and depression. She was raising two children, holding down a part-time job, and supporting her unemployed husband. Although she said that she understood her husband's difficulty in finding work—"Middle-aged middle managers are not very employable"—she resented the fact that he didn't seem to be looking very hard and that she would come home from a long day to find that he hadn't done much around the house. Suzanne would do all the cooking, feed the kids, clean the house, put the kids to bed, then get up early the next morning, get the kids fed and ready, and then take them to school. Her weekends consisted of catching up on all of the tasks she lacked the time to complete during the week. She knew she was tired, and she understood why. However, she had become concerned about her depression and recent suicidal thoughts. "My life is good," Suzanne told me. "I have children, a husband, a good job, my health, so why do my thoughts drift to killing myself? It must be some chemical imbalance."

During our first few sessions I noticed that Suzanne would always ask me questions about how I was feeling. She seemed very sensitive to my facial expressions, movements, and gestures. A couple of times she asked me if I was eating right and getting enough rest. She then began bringing me coffee and a muffin because she thought I wasn't eating enough. One day, when I had to change the time of an appointment, she responded very quickly by saying that we could skip the session if I was too busy or tired to see her that week. It became clear that despite the fact that she paid me to take care of her, she, in fact, had made it her job to be *my* care-taker. She had added me to her list of responsibilities.

Suzanne grew up the only girl in a large traditional family. Her family never addressed her needs and feelings, and they evaluated her each day based on her ability to help her mother attend to the needs of the men and boys they served. Suzanne's cultural and religious beliefs also reinforced this kind of family structure. As she grew older, her primitive and reflexive imitative, resonance, and mirror systems had been reinforced and fine-tuned to the point where she prided herself on being able to "read the minds" of others. At times, she suspected she might be clairvoyant because she could predict the needs of others moments before they would ask her for something, "just like that guy Radar on M.A.S.H." Unfortunately, she never learned to know herself, to be aware of her own feelings, or to articulate her needs.

In Suzanne's mind, to be needed was to be loved, to be loved was to be connected, and to be connected was to survive. She came to realize that she was attracted by, and attractive to, dependent men who fit her need for caretaking, and that she had shaped her children to be dependent so that she would always feel needed—and, hence, loved. Suzanne's experience suggests that whereas resonance systems are automatic, having a sense of self and being conscious of our own needs and emotions requires a mirroring relationship that helps us to come to know ourselves. Suzanne's brain had been shaped to serve as an adjunct to others.

Through the course of therapy, Suzanne learned about the source of her depression. She discovered many things she needed: a vacation, more help from her husband, an easier schedule, and some time each week to relax, have her hair done, or spend time with friends. Her intrusive suicidal thoughts came to be understood as her desire to kill the part of herself that lived completely for other people. Many psychotherapy clients experience a common condition: an inadequate boundary between self and others in tandem with an inability to be aware of their own feelings and needs. The awareness, exploration, and conscious articulation of the self are core components of most forms of psychotherapy.

Focus on the Insula Cortex

At the crossroads of the cortex and limbic system, the insula has been described as the limbic integration cortex (Augustine, 1996). It appears to play an important role in both the experience of self and our ability to distinguish between ourselves and others. The insula begins life on the surface of the brain but is soon hidden as the frontal and temporal lobes expand to cover it. To find the insula cortex on an adult brain, you have to separate the lateral fissure, pushing the frontal and temporal lobes aside. Here you find the insula, the fifth cortical lobe. In Figure 14.1 the lower side portion of the right frontal lobe has been cut away to reveal the surface of the insula. As you can see, its surface appearance is identical to the rest of the cortex.

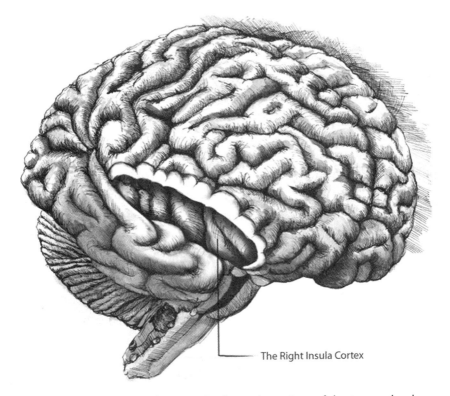

The Right Insula Cortex

Figure 14.1. **The insula cortex lies beneath portions of the temporal and frontal lobes.**

Like the motor and sensory cortices, the insula is somatotopically organized and links together networks that process primitive bodily states with those mediating emotional and behavioral reactions. The insula serves as an interface between our sense of self and our self-control capabilities (Garavan, Ross, & Stein, 1999). Its working relationship with the ventral striatum integrates foraging, feeding behavior, and gastric functions with memory and reward circuitry (Chikama et al., 1997; Gray et al., 1997; Penfield & Faulk, 1955). When the posterior insula is electrically stimulated, patients report a wide range of somatic sensations, with painful sensations lateralized primarily to the right (Ostrowsky et al., 2002). The insula also becomes activated by multiple stimuli such as taste, soothing touch, smell, nausea, lack of oxygen, and changes in temperature (Banzett et al., 2000; Craig et al., 2000; Royet et al., 2003; Singer et al., 2004; Small et al., 1999).

Beyond these basic sensations, the left insula is involved in the evaluation of the direction of eye gaze, responding to fearful faces, and observing the facial expressions of another (Carr et al., 2003; Kawashima et al., 1999; Morris, Friston et al., 1998). Faces that come to be judged as untrustworthy automatically activate areas of the right insula, demonstrating its involvement in the analysis of threat and reward (Elliott, Friston, & Dolan, 2000; Winston et al., 2002). Research suggests that the insula is involved with mediating the extreme limits of our emotions—everything from pain to disgust to passionate love (Andersson et al., 1997; Bartels & Zeki, 2000; Calder et al., 2000; Calder et al., 2003; Phillips et al., 1997).

In its role as an integration cortex, the insula bridges and coordinates limbic and cortical processing as well as somatic and visceral experience (Ostrowsky et al., 2000). This bridge may allow us to integrate somatic experience with conscious awareness. The newborn's ability to distinguish between his touch and the touch of another reflects one of the early contributions of the insula to development. Activation of the anterior portion of the insula, especially on the right side, correlates with the experience of emotions and the ability to accurately time our own heart rate. In a review study, Phan et al. (2002) found that the insula became activated (along with the anterior cingulate) during emotional recall and tasks involving imagery. Thus, the insula may play a central role in the development of our sense of self and the degree to which we are self-aware or can develop self-insight.

The role of the insula cortex and anterior cingulate in linking hearts and minds is best demonstrated by its activation while watching others experience pain. These two regions become activated either when we experience pain, or when a loved one experiences pain. The degree of activation of these two structures has been shown to correlate with measures of empathy (Singer et al., 2004; Jackson et al., 2005). Thus, whereas the insula cortex has played a small role in the history of neurology and neuroscience until this point, it appears to have a bright future as a central component of the developing social brain. When someone rejects us, we feel as if our heart is breaking. When someone we love is in pain, we can feel it in our own bodies. This sort of physical and emotional resonance serves as a foundation not only to connect our own bodies and minds, but to link us to the bodies and minds of those around us. See Table 14.2 for a summary of insula functions.

Table 14.2. **Functions of the Insula Cortex**

The insula cortex becomes activated in response to:

Bodily Processes

Offensive tastes, nausea	Phillips et al., 1997
Smell	Sander, Brechmann, & Scheich, 2003
Thermosensation, soothing touch, somatic, visceral, painful sensations	Ostrowsky et al., 2002; Singer et al., 2004
Monitoring own heart rate	Bechara & Naqvi, 2004; Critchley et al., 2004

Social Visual Processing

Eye gaze	Morris, Öhman, & Dolan, 1998
Seeing untrustworthy others	Elliot, Dolan, & Frith, 2000; Winston et al., 2002
Facial expressions	Carr et al., 2003; Kawashima et al., 1999
Expressions of disgust in others	Phillips et al., 1997

Emotional States of Self and Others

Frustration	Ahler et al., 2005
Feeling in control of an action	Farrer & Frith, 2002
Hearing laughter or crying	Sander & Scheich, 2001
A loved one's experience	Singer et al., 2004; Jackson et al., 2005

Thinking back to Suzanne, I wonder if her childhood experiences shaped her brain to be unaware of her own needs. We all know of people who are caretakers *to a fault*, denying their own needs while attending to those around them. Perhaps for some people, a childhood without help in developing a self narrative that includes their own experiences, results in a disconnection of the insula and adjacent structures. Can identity be "disembodied" such that it coalesces outside of one's own body? I thought about this during my interactions with Suzanne. When I would ask her how she was feeling, she would go through a mental checklist of her family and friends and think about whether they were all okay. When she couldn't think of anyone having any difficulty, she would respond, "I'm fine, and you?" One of the first goals of therapy for Suzanne was to become aware of her own thoughts and feelings. She then had to learn that they mattered to me. Only after this could her own inner experiences become important to her.

Part V

Disorders of the
Social Brain

Chapter | 5

Impact of Early Stress

A child can come to feel terribly guilty about not making a good mother.

—Justin Call

Imagine a large, poorly lit room filled with 30 cribs. Each crib contains a silent child. To your left, a 4-year-old girl stands in her crib shifting her weight from foot to foot as she flaps her hands. Some children drink from bottles propped on pillows, some rock in place, most just sit and stare. The walls are bare and white; the smell of antiseptic burns your nostrils and throat. There are no toys, few visitors, and little physical contact. One person cares for 30 children, her time filled with keeping them clean and fed. This scene might sound like something out of a horror film, but, sadly, it is the typical situation in a contemporary Romanian orphanage (Fisher et al., 1997). These children may be clean and fed, but they are suffering from severe social deprivation. Overwhelmed by the stress of their deprivation, their brains and hearts slowly waste away.

Orphans confined to their cribs and starved for human contact during critical periods become incapable of molding early reflexive movements into complex patterns of crawling and walking. Repetitive movements such as rocking, hand flapping, and headbanging offer a modicum of soothing, reflecting the natural tendency of our bodies to be involved in activity. We know that human contact stimulates neural circuits to grow, drives gene transcription, shapes sensory–motor functioning, and helps regulate the autonomic nervous system (Kuhn & Schanberg, 1998; Parker & Nelson, 2005). The vital importance of early interactions to the building of the brain helps us to explain the death of institutionalized children, otherwise healthy, who have been deprived of physical contact and love (Spitz, 1946).

The stress response was designed by evolution as part of the conversion of threat into adaptation. In the best-case scenario, low and moderate levels of stress are soon resolved through adaptive behavior. In these situations, stress hormones initiate biological changes that enhance neural plasticity, learning, and adaptive coping responses (Huether, 1998). When stress is extreme, prolonged, or we are too young to adapt, however, it becomes a problem. In these conditions, brain functioning and behavior become organized around fear, rigidity, and an avoidance of stimulation and exploration. In this chapter we focus on the consequences of prenatal stress, maternal depression, and maternal deprivation, especially when these stressors are too great and last too long.

Prenatal Stress

A growing body of research has demonstrated how development and behavior are influenced by intrauterine experience. Some studies show that a high level of maternal stress during pregnancy has a negative effect on a child's development. Although the full mechanisms of this process remain unknown, stress hormones are thought to impact the developing brain via HPA functioning, alterations of neurotransmitter levels, and disturbances in cerebral lateralization (Gunnar, 1992, 1998; Schneider, 1992; Seckl, 2004).

During pregnancy, highly anxious women tend to have higher levels of norepinephrine and lower levels of dopamine. Increased norepinephrine is related to high levels of arousal and agitation, and less dopamine correlates with less positive mood and reward expectation. Their newborns have lower levels of serotonin and dopamine, greater right frontal activation, lower vagal tone, and experience a variety of growth delays (Field et al., 2003). These changes correlate with emotional dysregulation, depression, anxiety, and attachment difficulties in these children (Field et al., 2002).

Prenatal stress has also been associated with congenital malformations, spontaneous abortions, reduced head circumference, irritability, hyperactivity, speech and language difficulties, lower IQ . . . the list goes on and on (Hansen et al., 2000; Hobel, 2004; Hobel et al., 1999; Lou et al., 1994; Mancuso et al., 2004; Mulder et al., 2002; Neugebauer et al., 1996). Depression during pregnancy results in similar biochemical profiles in both mother and child and correlates with higher levels of cortisol, premature birth, and lower birth weight (Field et al., 2004). Studies with rodents show similar results, and prenatally stressed rhesus monkeys were found to exhibit more clinging, self-directed behavior, and an increased need for sleep. This group also engaged in less environmental exploration, climbing, and gross motor movements.

Is all prenatal stress necessarily detrimental to the development of the brain? Could brief, mild stress actually *enhance* brain development, adaptation, and learning (DiPietro, 2004, Gunnar & Donzella, 2002)? When mother rats experience mild stress during pregnancy, their offspring show weaker emotional responses to stressors, enhanced learning, and less structural buildup in the amygdala (Fujioka et al., 2003). Brief intermittent maternal separation in newborn squirrel monkeys results in a significant increase in the size of right prefrontal structures, diminished negative emotionality, increased affiliation toward peers, and less reaction to stress in adolescence and adulthood (Lyons et al., 2002; Parker et al., 2004). These studies suggest that brief, mild prenatal stress or brief postnatal maternal separations in the context of generally positive maternal behavior may serve to build a brain that is better able to cope with stress. Before we accept this notion unconditionally, we should note that opposite findings have also been found in other studies, suggesting that there is more to this story yet to unfold (Fride & Weinstock, 1988; McClure et al., 2004).

Maternal Depression

Although depression is common in the normal population, it is more prevalent in women and can certainly be exacerbated by the added stress, sleep deprivation, and hormonal consequences of childbirth (National Institute of Mental Health, 2001; Garrison & Earls, 1986). Maternal depression after childbirth results in attitudes, beliefs, and behaviors that negatively impact infant development (Lyons-Ruth et al., 1986; Murray, 1992). It manifests not only in silent withdrawal but also in explosive anger and dysregulated states that impair a mother's ability to help regulate her child and disrupts the child's ability to self-regulate (Tronick & Gianino, 1986). The mother's expressive face, her ability to attune to the feelings and needs of her child, and her level of energy are all deficient at a time when her child needs her active and attuned engagement the most (Gur et al., 1992; Mikhailova et al., 1996; Rubinow & Post, 1992; Zuckerman et al., 1990). Overall, research that has observed mother–infant pairs suggests that both positive and negative synchronous states are self-perpetuating and synergistic (Field et al., 1990). Based on these findings, the prevalence and impact of postpartum depression makes it a significant public health issue (Cohen et al., 1986; McLennan & Offord, 2002). Table 15.1 summarizes the effects of maternal depression on both child and mother.

The importance of the mother's expressive face is nowhere more apparent than in what has been called "still-face" research. In this paradigm the mother shifts from interacting with her infant to a blank expression for a period of time before resuming normal interactions. In research in

Table 15.1. **Effects of Maternal Depression on Child and Mother**

Characteristics of Depressed Mothers (in relation to their children)	Characteristics of Children of Depressed Mothers
Less active	Spend more time in states of protest
Exhibit more gaze aversion	Spend less time exploring
Less likely to speak "motherese"	Show longer habituation times
Express more anger	Exhibit fewer positive facial expressions
Imitate their childrens' vocalizations less often	Fail to show face and voice preferences
Slower to respond to their infants' vocalizations	Less likely to look at others
Less likely to modulate the tone of their voice to their childrens' auditory abilities	Interact less well with strangers
More likely to poke and prod their children	Spend less time playing
More likely to disengage	

Sources: Bettes, (1988); Field et al. (1988); Hernandez-Reif et al. (2000); Hernandez-Reif et al. (2002).

which nondepressed mothers assumed a still-face, 3-month-olds quickly reacted with wariness and protest (Cohn & Tronick, 1983, 1989); 6-month-old infants reacted with negative affect, a drop in vagal tone, and an increase in heart rate (Gusella, Muir, & Tronick, 1988; Weinberg & Tronick, 1996). After the resumption of normal facial expressions by the mothers, there was an increase in fussiness and crying. Even under normal conditions, a flat, withdrawn maternal expression is associated with distress in the infant (Cohn & Tronick, 1989).

Children of depressed mothers have been reported to show a disruption in the development, connection, and integration of the frontal lobes (Dawson, Frey et al., 1997; Diego et al., 2004), with activation biased toward the right hemisphere, which correlates with more negative and dysregulated emotional states. As mothers get more depressed, their children have less left frontal activity and demonstrate increasing depression and withdrawal. These infants also fail to produce the typical pattern of increased right frontal activation during separation (Dawson, Klinger et al., 1992) and are at increased risk for poor self-control, affective regulation, academic performance, and empathic attunement (Dawson, Panagiotides et al., 1997; Jones et al., 2000).

Depression disrupts the ability of the mother–child pair to form optimal attunement, which, in turn, impacts the child's ability to develop adequate internal emotional regulation and states of interpersonal synchrony (Tronick & Weinberg, 1997; Weinberg & Tronick, 1998). An additional danger is that maternal depression will evoke caretaking behaviors in the child, creating a *reversal of the mirroring process* (Radke-Yarrow et al., 1994). Children with depressed mothers are at risk of becoming arrested in their own emotional development as they attempt to regulate their parents' affect. Thus, the outwardly competent and "adultlike" child may only be able to regulate his or her own emotions by distracting him- or herself through caring for others.

Overall, maternal depression results in neurological, biological, and behavioral patterns that correlate with stress and distress (Essex et al., 2002; Field et al., 1988; Halligan et al., 2004; Lupien et al., 2000). It downregulates neuroplastic processes in both mother and child and locks them into stereotyped patterns of interaction that mutually maintain their negative states of mind (Field et al., 1990). Dysregulation of emotional and endocrine processes, if chronic, can result in long-term emotional, physical, and cognitive difficulties (Henry & Wang, 1998; Kaufman et al., 2000). Good-enough mothering correlated with lower cortisol levels and increased exploratory behavior, socialization, and sooth-ability in 3- to 6-month-old human infants (Spangler et al., 1994). These early experiences appear to have a long-lasting effect in humans. In one study the physical and emotional health of men at midlife correlated significantly with their descriptions, 35 years earlier, of the amount of warmth they experienced from their mothers and fathers (Russek & Schwartz, 1997).

Of Dams and Pups

The relationship between mother rats (dams) and their babies (pups) has taught us a great deal about the biology of mother–child interactions. Mother rats show natural variations in the amount of maternal behavior they show their pups, and their easily observed licking, grooming, and nursing provide a measurable way to connect maternal attention to differences in brain structure and behavior later in a pup's life. Tracking this behavior into adulthood is made easier by the fact that the rat develops, lives its life, and dies of natural causes in only 2 years. Similarities between the biology and behavior of rodents and humans make rats a valuable source of information, especially regarding the biological foundations of caretaking.

A mother rat responds to the cries of her pups if they are moved from, or roll out of, the nest. She licks them while they are in the nest and arches over them (*kyphosis*) so that they can attach to her teats (Magnusson & Fleming, 1995). Through physical contact with her pups, maternal behaviors are reinforced via the dopamine reward system (Fleming, Korsmit, & Deller, 1994; Fleming et al., 1979). It is likely that heightened levels of dopamine and prolactin stimulate neuroplastic processes in the mother's brain to help her learn about, and take care of, her newborns (Bridges & Grattan, 2003; Grattan, 2002; Shingo et al., 2003).

Despite the differences in our outward appearance, rats and humans have brains that are strikingly similar. Both have neurons and glial cells that communicate, organize, and function in the same fashion. Both have babies that are immature at birth, develop within the context of relationships, and are shaped by social interactions. There is also evidence of considerable overlap between the neuroanatomy underlying maternal behavior in rats and humans (Lorberbaum et al., 2002). Rat pups demonstrate enhanced metabolic activation in the precentral medial cortex and anterior cingulate in response to their mother's nursing calls (Braun & Poeggel, 2001). Damage to the cingulate cortex causes disruptions in the efficiency and organization of maternal behaviors but does not lessen maternal instinct or motivation (Slotnick, 1967). Damage to the medial cortex, the ventral tegmental area, or the substantia nigra results in impairment in the cleaning and gathering of pups after birth, and the construction of their nest (Stamm, 1955; Numan & Nagle, 1983; Numan & Smith, 1984). These structures are analogous to the social brain structures in humans that control maternal behavior and influence the quality of attachment.

Mothers of both species quickly learn to identify their own young, find reinforcement in their children, and work hard to feed and protect them (Stern, 1997). Human mothers demonstrate sympathetic arousal to pictures of their own children but not the children of other parents (Wiesenfeld & Klorman, 1978). Pictures of their own children trigger bilateral activation of the OMPFC, reflecting both the reinforcement value of their children and a mechanism that enhances selective bonding with their own children (Nitschke et al., 2004). Of course, rats and humans aren't identical. Whereas maternal behavior in rats is fairly routinized, in humans it is more flexible, changes with time, and is modified by feedback from the child (Beeghly, Bretherton, & Mervis, 1986; Corter & Fleming, 1995; Stern, 1997). These differences speak to both our larger cortices and an increased degree of experience-dependent brain plasticity.

Rats "stress out" just as we do. Because they can't tell us how they feel, we estimate their stress by measuring their cortisol levels. We can also measure the number of cortisol receptors that develop during early nurturing experiences and serve to diminish the impact of stress on the brain and body. The adult offspring of mother rats who engaged in a high level of maternal behavior have higher levels of mRNA in the medial prefrontal cortex, hippocampus, and basolateral regions of the amygdala.

Heightened mRNA levels reflect an increased ability of the brain to learn and serve as a protective factor against the catabolic (destructive) effects of stress hormones (Caldji, Diorio, & Meaney, 2003; DeKosky et al., 1982; Francis D. et al., 1999; Liu et al., 1997; Plotsky & Meaney, 1993). Well-parented rats show more benzodiazepine receptors in the amygdala and locus coeruleus, which contribute to decreased levels of anxiety; they are less anxious, more exploratory, less fearful of novelty, and better learners (Caldji et al., 1998; Caldji, Francis et al., 2000). The findings of these studies are essentially identical to what we observe in securely attached human children.

On the other hand, maternal deprivation in rats, mice, and primates can result in permanent dysregulation of the HPA axis and increasing levels of adrenal hormones that damage brain structures (Anisman et al., 1998; Dettling et al., 2002; Schmidt et al., 2002; Tanapat et al., 2001). The long-term social and emotional development of physically ill young mice correlated with the responsiveness and attention of their mothers (Hood et al., 2003). When rat pups are deprived of their mothers, they demonstrate increased death of neurons and glial cells, lower rates of synaptogenesis (new synapses), and decreases in the expression of neural growth factors in the hippocampus. They also perform more poorly on tasks of memory and learning (Bredy et al., 2001, 2003; Liu et al., 2000; Weaver et al., 2002; Zhang et al., 2002).

Early touch is so important that even the handling of rat pups by human researchers results in increased density of cortisol receptors and lower levels of cortisol in the bloodstream (Smythe et al., 1994). The positive effects of handling were not present when pups were stressed prenatally, suggesting again that stress before birth modulates the effects of postnatal nurturance and stress (Smythe et al., 1996). Table 15.2 summarizes the effects of early handling and attention on rat pups. The changes noted in Table 15.2 were maintained well into the adult lives of the rats, suggesting that the establishment of these early physiological setpoints may be stable over a lifetime. The negative effects of early stress, avoided by adrenalectomy in middle-aged rats, supports the theory that these negative changes are mediated via high levels of cortisol.

Table 15.2. **Effects of Early Handling and Attention**

The more rats are handled, groomed, and attended to during infancy, the greater their:

Open field activity	Levine et al., 1967
Gene expression	Meaney et al., 1989
Concentrations of cortisol receptors	Meaney et al., 2000
Resistance to stress	Liu et al., 1997
Cortisol feedback sensitivity	Liu et al., 1997
Positive HPA changes in reaction to stress	Jacobson & Sapolsky, 1991; Viau et al., 1993
Hippocampal cell retention	Sapolsky, 1990
Spatial memory	Sapolsky, 1990
Mothering behavior with their own pups	Fleming et al., 2002

Positive maternal attention impacts the brain in two very important ways. First, it decreases the impact of subsequent stress on the brain. By generating more cortisol receptors in many regions of the brain, it creates a kind of biochemical buffer to future challenges. Second, it enhances brain growth and the development of brain systems that support attachment, affect regulation, and problem solving (Davidson, 2000). These transpositions of maternal behavior into the biological structure of the brain are the mechanism underlying the correlations between positive attentive parenting and subsequent physical and mental health. Good parenting tells the child he or she is loved, accepted, and valued; fortifies the body for growth; and strengthens immunological functioning. From an evolutionary perspective, being touched (or licked, if you're a rat) tells the brain that you are part of the group, that you are safe, and to live long and prosper!

Focus on the Hypothalamic–Pituitary–Adrenal Axis

The HPA axis is a central component of the body's stress response system. Its role is to convert the perception of danger into a bodily state of arousal, attention, and a fight/flight response. At best, a threat is perceived, responded to, and resolved in short order, allowing a return to homeostatic balance. In conditions of chronic and irresolvable stress, the components of the HPA axis may establish a style of functioning that is not conducive to long-term physical and psychological health.

At the apex of the HPA system is the hypothalamus, specifically, the periventricular nucleus (PVN) of the hypothalamus. When stimulated by the amygdala, the role of the PVN is to release two peptides: corticotrophin-releasing factor (CRF) and arginine vasopressin (AVP). Remember, the amygdala combines input from all over the brain to make a "decision" about whether something is a source of danger. The amygdala can become stimulated by real or imagined threat from the environment, from conscious thought, or from unconscious processing.

When a threat is detected, projections from the central nucleus of the amygdala activate the PVN of the hypothalamus, which, in turn, triggers the pituitary gland (attached to its lower surface) to secrete adrenocorticotropic hormone (ACTH) into the blood. When ACTH reaches the adrenal glands located down on the kidneys, the adrenal glands secrete cortisol and other stress hormones. Glucocorticoids (cortisol) play a supporting role in the stress response by shifting the body from a state of homeostatic conservation to an all-out effort for immediate survival. Energy usually directed toward internal processes (e.g., digestion) and fighting internal threats (e.g., bacteria and viruses) are redirected to maximizing available energy. See Figure 15.1 for a diagram of the HPA system.

Two processes are affected most by prolonged stress. First, prolonged stress inhibits protein production in order to maintain higher levels of metabolism. Proteins are, of course, the building blocks of the immunological system (e.g., leukocytes, B cells, T cells, natural killer cells) and the suppression of protein synthesis also suppresses the ability of the body to fight off infection and illness. This mechanism is one of the primary reasons for the high correlations that are found between prolonged stress and disease (see Table 15.3). Second, sustained higher levels of metabolism continue to pump sodium into neurons, eventually overwhelming the ability of cells to transport it out again, resulting in destruction of the cell membrane and cell death. This process has been found to be particularly damaging to cells within the hippocampus, leading to a variety of memory deficits. Sustained high levels of stress partly explain why early negative experiences in parenting and attachment have a lifelong impact on physical health, mental health, and learning.

Table 15.3. **Summary of Cortisol Actions**

- Breaks down fats and proteins for immediate energy
- Inhibits inflammatory processes
- Inhibits protein syntheses within the immune system
  (e.g., leukocytes, B & T cells, natural killer cells)
- Suppresses gonadal hormones

When the HPA system is repeatedly activated, such as in the case of a neglected child, an air traffic controller, or a person suffering from chronic anxiety, sustained levels of cortisol continuously break down the body for an immediate threat that never resolves. As we have seen, one of the ways that early nurturance is translated into biological processes is by stimulating the growth of glucocorticoid receptors in many locations within the brain and body. The more receptors, the more negative feedback the system can receive in order to shut down glucocorticoid production. In the opposite case, deprivation and abuse correlate with fewer receptors, higher circulating levels of cortisol, and more damage to the brain and body. Early contact can also downregulate the sensitivity of the PVN, making the system less responsive to stress (Levine, 2001).

Resting cortisol levels, the reaction of the cortisol system to stress, and the number of receptors all work together to establish the ability of the body to respond and cope with stress. The lower the resting levels, the less activation there is to subsequent stress. The more receptors that exist at sites that get activated, the easier it is to roll with life's punches. Early stressful experiences in rats also correlate with their later vulnerability to ulcers and hypertension. When we are traumatized early in life, we are far more likely to experience serious physical problems that, in turn, serve as a continued source of stress.

Secure and mutually supportive attachments, whether between parents and children or husbands and wives, provide security and reduce arousal. The presence of a loving and attuned other reduces uncertainty and stress—or, to put it another way, HPA and sympathetic nervous system activity (Sachser et al., 1998). Receiving a caring touch from a significant other elicits positive changes in neurotransmitters and improves

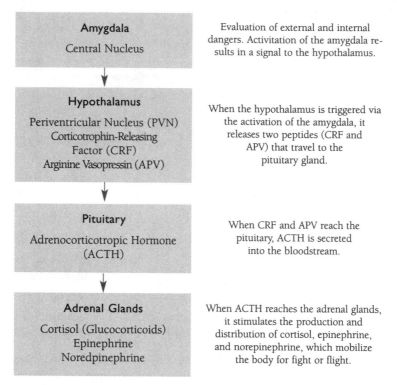

Figure 15.1. **Diagram of the hypothalamic–pituitary–adrenal axis.**

immunological functioning (Goodfellow, 2003; Hernandez-Reif et al., 2004; Lund et al., 2002). Relationships are a source of stress for individuals who are avoidantly and insecurely attached, and therefore they are unable to receive the positive physiological benefits of intimacy and attachment (Temoshok, 2002).

Stephan—Coming Home

An example of this circumstance would be 8-year-old Stephan. He was brought to the clinic by his adoptive parents, Paul and Susan, who wanted to know whether Stephan's early emotional development was negatively impacting his current intellectual functioning. They had adopted Stephan 2 years ago after having tried to have a child of their own for many years. A friend had told them about the many orphans in Romania, and both of them felt that they could bring home the child they always dreamed of having. Of course, they knew they were taking on a challenge, adopting a child who might very well have special needs, but they decided they were up to the task.

Paul and Susan's phone calls and letters to the Romanian orphanage did not prepare them for the subtly disturbing conditions they found upon their arrival. They were greeted at the door by a kindly nurse and uncanny silence. Before taking a tour of the building, they were asked to interact with the children as little as possible. As they walked past sterile rooms containing rows of cribs and small beds, they saw precious little of what we might think of as healthy childhood behavior. At the far end of the building was a playroom. The children were brought there for short periods each day while their rooms were being cleaned and disinfected. Here they sat, looked at books, or handled toys while ignoring one another.

The couple looked into the face of each child, searching for a spark of interest, anything to help them make a choice. It was then that they spotted Stephan. Both Paul and Susan took a liking to him right away. "It was something about the way he looked at us," they said. Little Stephan also shared their skin coloring and had thick dark hair, like Paul's. To the best of anyone's knowledge, Stephan had come to the orphanage soon after birth. Left on the orphanage doorstep by a family that could not afford to raise him, he was one of the few children there who was thought not to have experienced neglect or abuse prior to arrival. Stephan was behind in his language development but generally at the same level as other children his age at the orphanage. He seemed to have a special talent for drawing, and some of his works had been pinned up in the nurses' office.

When Paul and Susan brought Stephan home, they immediately began investing their time and energy in tutoring him in English and exposing him to their world. When they brought him in to see me at the clinic, Stephan spoke fluent English and had only a slight accent, which his parents said made him special, in a positive way, to the other kids at school. The new testing done at the clinic revealed that Stephan's intellectual development had basically caught up to his 8-year-old American classmates. Paul and Susan were certainly happy to hear the good news and were gratified that the clinic staff recognized the value of all their dedication and hard work.

But there were still troubling questions about Stephan's interpersonal skills. When Stephan was left alone with me, he seemed listless and withdrawn. He responded to questions with short answers and seemed to avoid me by occupying himself with toys and books. Paul and Susan had described similar behavior at home, and at school he tended to shy away from group activities. In fact, the general level of elementary school chaos appeared to unnerve him. His parents realized that these interpersonal behaviors were probably the result of his early deprivation but had no idea how to help Stephan grow up to be a healthy and well-adjusted person.

Stephan's deprivation came at a time when the brain relies on human contact and attuned relationships to help build circuitry dedicated to emotional regulation. In later years these neural networks help to filter and modulate stimulation, thereby allowing us to better navigate our complex social worlds. At the same time, interactions build networks dedicated to eye contact, face recognition, interpretation of facial expressions, and the monitoring of the infinite number of cues that we receive from those around us—the constant flow of information and stimulation across the social synapse. Later developing networks dedicated to language and abstract abilities were stimulated during appropriate sensitive periods after Stephan's adoption, but he was still lagging behind in his emotional development.

Over the course of a few weeks, I listened, watched, and interacted with Stephan and his family. There were a number of things I wanted to try to accomplish: helping Stephan feel more comfortable around others, increasing his eye contact, and easing him into interactive play. I thought he might benefit from learning some coping strategies for dealing with the sensory overload of school, parties, and other social events, where there were many people and lots of stimulation. But he needed something more, something that could reach inside and help him come out of himself. He needed a way of expressing his feelings that was safer and more predictable than a group of rambunctious 8-year-olds.

During one of our sessions in the courtyard, I noticed that a dog caught his attention. Later in the session he drew a dog similar to the one that he had seen. I asked his parents if Stephan had ever had a dog. They said they once took him to a breeder to find a puppy, but when all the dogs ran after him, jumping and licking and doing all the things puppies do, Stephan became afraid and ran away. Paul and Susan assumed that they had made a mistake and didn't bring it up again. I suggested that they might try again, but perhaps with a well-socialized older dog.

Soon thereafter, they found a dog at an animal rescue sanctuary that had been orphaned by the death of its elderly owner. It was calm, gentle, well past puppyhood, and accustomed to sitting quietly next to someone who didn't move much. Max the dog had come to the shelter disoriented and depressed but gradually bonded with some of the volunteers. So here were Stephan and Max, two beings who had been orphaned. Perhaps, with some luck, they might understand and connect with one another. When Max was brought home, Stephan's eyes widened. He seemed anxious and confused about what to do. Fortunately, Max had no such problems. As Paul and Susan told me later, Max walked slowly over to Stephan, sat next to him, and put his head gently under Stephan's hand. "It was as if Max knew exactly what to do," they told me. That night, as Paul and Susan listened at Stephan's door, they heard him teaching Max the names of his friends, the teachers he liked best, and the neighbors to avoid if you wanted to stay out of trouble. "I wasn't born here either," Stephan told Max, "but you don't have to worry because Mom and Dad won't make you go away."

Max was now a member of the family and went most everywhere with Stephan. Of course, there's nothing like a big friendly dog to attract other children, and Stephan soon found himself surrounded by potential friends. Max not only soothed Stephan but created a bridge between Stephan and the world around him. With the help of a perfect four-legged therapist, Stephan slowly crossed that bridge, came out of his shell, and grew brave enough to begin the long and often painful process of learning to look the world in the eye.

All of our brains rely on a protected and gradual introduction to the world. We depend on the attention and nurturance of our caretakers, as they depend on those who surround them for support and loving care. Stress and depression in a mother or early abuse or neglect of a child (such as that experienced by Stephan) are severe challenges to the developing social brain. I am hopeful about Stephan's future, based on the care and concern I could see being provided by his mom and dad. On the other hand, I struggle with the vast sea of unmet nurturance I come across every day in my practice and in the news from around the world. My hope is that as the evidence of the impact of early experience mounts, it will begin to have an effect on public policy and the allocation of resources. We need to invest in our children and our childrens' children, even before they are born.

Chapter 6

Interpersonal Trauma

Everything can be acquired in solitude—except sanity.

—Friedrich Nietzsche

Our brains rely on other brains to remain healthy, especially under stress. When faced with illness, catastrophe, or loss, we turn to each other for comfort, regulation, and stability. Resiliency—our ability to cope with life's ups and downs—is closely tied to the extent and quality of our support systems. We appear to be capable of coping with just about anything when we are connected to those for whom we care and who care for us. But what happens when we experience trauma at the hands of those we love and depend on? Interpersonal trauma is an especially difficult challenge, particularly for children, because it creates competing responses within them: They simultaneously want to cling for support and push away for protection. It is precisely this approach- avoidance conflict that can make interpersonal trauma so damaging.

Learning to hold ourselves away from others cuts us off from the beneficial effects of relationships we need to assimilate trauma and move on with our lives. Thus, interpersonal trauma is more likely to be self-perpetuating and resistant to healing. When interpersonal trauma occurs early in life, this approach-avoidance conflict can become a consistent state of being around which our personalities are formed. We can witness this inner conflict in the behavior of children with frightened and frightening parents. When these children are stressed, they run toward their parent while simultaneously averting their gaze, fall to the floor, or engage in other types of apparently irrational behavior. For a child, the experience of simultaneous impulses to run toward and away from a parent is crazy-making. Adults who find themselves in relationships that include physical and emotional abuse often turn to drugs and alcohol, become physically ill, or develop severe psychological problems while they struggle to stay close to those who dysregulate them.

Early interpersonal trauma in the form of emotional and physical abuse, sexual abuse, and neglect shape the structure and functioning of the brain in ways that negatively affect all stages of social, emotional, and intellectual development. Early trauma, especially at the hands of caretakers, begins a cascade of effects that result in a complex posttraumatic reaction. The effects often manifest in what we call personality disorders, which impact many aspects of a person's functioning and are resistant to change.

The tenacity of personality disorders rests in an approach–avoidance conflict. If you need to feel connected in order to heal but are too afraid to trust because you become fearful and dysregulated in relationships, you are stuck. This "Catch-22" keeps many people in a constant cycle of loneliness➤approach➤terror➤avoidance➤loneliness, and so on. Many people come to therapy for years but are too afraid to trust their therapists enough to share themselves openly. They desperately need to establish a relationship in order to heal, but their fears overwhelm them and they flee back into a safe isolation.

This basic biological principle is seen in cold-blooded animals that regulate their body temperature by changing locations. They lack the inner mechanisms that regulate body temperature so they are forced to use actions to survive. When we lack the ability to regulate our internal emotional state, we attempt to regulate by "acting out" or through geographical solutions. When we can't move away physically, we learn to dissociate our reality from consciousness. For example, abused children learn not to look at faces and are less skillful in decoding facial expressions (Camras et al., 1983). When they do look at faces, they are hypervigilant to any sign of negativity or criticism.

In the face of early interpersonal trauma, all of the systems of the social brain become shaped for offensive and defensive purposes. Instead of the social synapse being used for free and flexible exchange of information between individuals, it becomes a "no-man's land" fraught with difficulties and dangers. We stare at others trying to predict when they will become dangerous and require us to fight or flee. Mirror systems are employed to defend instead of cooperate; attachment schemas are used as battle plans instead of ways of connecting. Faces are explored for signs of disapproval. Regulatory systems become biased toward arousal and fear, priming our bodies to sacrifice well-being in order to stay on full alert at all times. Reward systems designed to make us feel good through contact with loved ones are manipulated with drugs, alcohol, compulsive behaviors, and self-harm. When the brain is shaped in this way, social life is converted from a source of nurturance into a mine field.

Child Abuse and Neglect

Abused children have a high rate of disorganized attachment, demonstrate higher resting levels of stress hormones, and have strong physiological reactions in response to brief separations from their mothers (Carlson et al., 1989; Hertsgaard et al., 1995; Spangler & Grossman, 1993). By far, the most disturbed children examined in attachment research are those rated as having disorganized attachment. These children usually have mothers who suffer from unresolved trauma, passing it along through their actions and reactions. A powerful example of this intergenerational traumatic transfer is shown in the children of Holocaust survivors, who come to share their parents' trauma-based biochemistry in the absence of having any traumatic experiences themselves (Yehuda & Siever, 1997; Yehuda et al., 2000). A child with a traumatizing mother has no choice but to stay with, and depend upon, the source of the trauma. The safe haven is now a source of fear and emotional dysregulation, creating a new generation of victims.

The ability to link feelings and words does not come automatically but relies on relationships to build connections between separate neural networks dedicated to affect and language. A child needs to experience parents who connect their own emotions and thoughts and can help them do the same by asking questions such as, "Are you sad because Grandma is leaving?" or "Are you worried that we won't get to school on time?" Questions such as these guide a child's attention to his or her inner thoughts and feelings. Parental concern and curiosity make children aware that they have an inner experience of their own and it can be different from what others may think and feel. Because this inner experience can be understood, discussed, and organized through a coconstructed narrative, it becomes available for conscious consideration. As one of my young clients once said, "Talking about stuff makes it kinda real."

Language, in combination with emotional attunement, creates the opportunity to support neural growth and network integration. When a child is left in silence due to parental inability to verbalize internal experience, the child does not develop the capacity to understand and manage his or her world. The ability of language to integrate neural structures and organize experience at a conscious level is mostly unavailable. When children are abused and neglected, both neural growth and integration are impaired.

Over the last decade, we have learned that multiple structures and communication networks within the developing brain are impacted by abuse and neglect. Most striking are the abnormal development of experience-dependent structures such as the cerebral cortex, corpus callosum, and hippocampus. These abnormalities are likely the result of the negative biochemical effects of severe and prolonged early stress combined with inadequate stimulation and regulation, required by the developing social brain. Table 16.1 summarizes some of these findings.

Parent–child talk in the context of emotional attunement provides the ground for the coconstruction of narratives. When verbal interactions include references to sensations, feelings, behaviors, and thoughts, they provide a medium through which the child's brain is able to integrate the various aspects of experience in a coherent manner. The organization of autobiographical memory in a manner that includes processing from multiple neural networks enhances self-awareness, increases the ability to problem solve, and allows us to cope with stress and regulate affect.

As you might expect, there is a relationship between caretakers' own attachment history and their parenting abilities. This relationship was shown clearly in rhesus monkeys who were raised in isolation and

Table 16.1. **Abnormal Brain Development Due to Child Abuse/Neglect**

Abnormal cortical development	Perry & Pollard, 1997
Diminished corpus callosum size	De Bellis et al., 1999b; Teicher et al., 1997; Teicher et al., 2004
Diminished left-hemisphere development	Bremner et al., 1997; Ito et al., 1998
Diminished left hippocampal volume and development	Bremner et al., 1997; Ito et al., 1998; Vythilingam et al., 2002; Brambilla et al., 2004
Decreased right–left cortical integration	Schiffer et al., 1995; Teicher et al., 2002
Increased EEG abnormalities	Ito et al., 1993

demonstrated neglectful or atypical maternal behaviors (Champoux et al., 1992; Suomi, 1997). As with monkeys, human mothers with atypical and conflictive parenting styles usually have traumatic histories. However, research also suggests that adults can create secure attachment for their children, despite their own negative experiences as children. Earned autonomy, or the attainment of secure attachment later in life, results in the ability to develop secure attachments and serve as a safe haven for one's children. Thus, the powerful shaping experiences of childhood can be modified through subsequent personal relationships, psychotherapy, and self-awareness (Siegel & Hartzel, 2003). The ability to consciously process stressful and traumatic life events creates the possibility for positive change via the growth and integration of neural networks.

Shame

While most of us aren't physically or sexually abused during childhood, all of us experience shame. During the first year of life, parent–child interactions are mainly positive, affectionate, and playful. The limited skills and mobility of infants keeps them in close proximity to the caretaker, who provides for their many bodily and emotional needs. As the infant grows into a toddler, increasing motor abilities and exploratory drives confront caretakers with new challenges. A parent's role comes to include protecting toddlers from themselves as they run with abandon in whatever direction their impulses direct them. The positive parent–child interactions of the first year of life give way by the beginning of the second year to an almost constant cry of "No!" (Rothbart et al., 1989). Thus, the affection and attunement that were experienced as unconditional during the first year become tied to appropriate *behavior* as parents try to teach children to inhibit dangerous and forbidden impulses. The same face-to-face interactions that stimulated excitement, exhilaration, and brain growth during the first year now include information on the recognition of disapproval and disappointment. This is the context of the emergence of shame.

At its heart, shame is the visceral experience of being shunned and ex-pelled from social connectedness. Social exclusion is painful and even stimulates the same areas of our brains that become active when we ex-perience physical pain. In small doses, shame can be useful in the de-velopment of conscience and a sense of social responsibility. Because shame is powerful, preverbal, and physiologically based, the overuse of shame can predispose children to problems with affective regulation and self-identity. Schore (1994) rightly differentiates shame from the later-occurring phenomenon of guilt. Guilt is a more complex, language-based, and less visceral reaction that exists in a broader psychosocial context.

Guilt is more closely related to unacceptable behaviors whereas shame is an emotion about the self that is internalized before the ability to dis-tinguish between the action and the self is possible. You can take action to alleviate guilt, but shame offers no redemption. At its core, shame is the emotional reaction to the loss of attunement with the caretaker. The power of shame comes from the experience of attunement as life sustain-ing, in part, because, for young primates, separation and rejection equal death. Prolonged and repeated shame states result in a physiological dys-regulation that negatively impacts the development of networks of affec-tive regulation and attachment circuitry.

The return from a state of shame to attunement with parents creates a return to a balance of autonomic functioning, supports affective regula-tion, and contributes to the gradual development of self-regulation. Re-peated and rapid return from shame to attuned states consolidates into an expectation of positive outcomes during difficult social interactions. These repeated repairs are stored as visceral, sensory, motor, and emo-tional memories at all levels of the central nervous system, making the internalization of positive parenting a full-body experience.

Shame is represented physiologically in a rapid transition from a positive to negative affective state and from sympathetic to parasympathetic dominance. This shift is triggered by the expectation of attunement in a positive state, only to find disapproval and misattunement in the face of the caretaker (Schore, 1994). A person in a shame state looks downward, hangs his head and rounds his shoulders. This same state of submission is not unlike that of a dog when he hunches over, pulls his tail between his legs, and slinks away after a scolding for committing a canine faux pas. Similar postures reflect loss, helplessness, and submission in virtually all social animals.

Because shame is neurobiologically toxic for older infants, these early preverbal experiences can have lifelong effects. Prolonged shame states early in life can result in permanently dysregulated autonomic functioning and a heightened sense of vulnerability to others. When parents use shame as their primary socialization tool, children spend too much time feeling anxious, dysregulated, and fearing for their safety. When these children grow up, they can usually find criticism, rejection, and abandonment in every interaction. Their lives are marked by a chronic anxiety, exhaustion, depression, and a losing struggle to achieve perfection (Bradshaw, 1990).

Focus on the Hippocampus

Why discuss the hippocampus in a chapter on interpersonal trauma? Very simply, because research suggests that the hippocampus is extremely vulnerable to sustained stress (Benes, 1989; Geuze et al., 2005). The biological link between prolonged stress and hippocampal damage appears to be mediated via glucocorticoids such as cortisol. Glucocorticoids (GCs) are hormones secreted by the adrenal gland as part of the body's response to stress. Prolonged high levels of GCs result in dendritic degeneration, cell death, and inhibited hippocampal functioning (Sapolsky, 1987; Watanabe, Gould, & McEwen, 1992). GCs trigger hippocampal neurons to work harder and harder, until they eventually run out of energy, collapse, and die. Loss of volume in the hippocampus appears to be related to long-term, cumulative GC exposure (Sapolsky et al., 1990).

The quality and amount of maternal care, handling, and soothing touch stimulates the creation of GC receptors, allowing the hippocampus to downregulate GC exposure (Meaney et al., 1989; Plotsky & Meaney, 1993). The result is a decreased reaction to subsequent stress and greater protection of the hippocampus. If this is the case, one of the important biological effects of secure attachment would be to protect the hippocampus from stress. As we come to understand the processes that translate trauma into neurobiological structure, we will be able to move swiftly to treat individuals who have experienced—or are about to experience—trauma by blocking the impact of GCs (Cohen et al., 2002).

The hippocampus and related structures are essential for the encoding and storage of our explicit memory for spatial, semantic, and temporal information (Edelman, 1989; O'Keefe & Nadel, 1978; Selden, Everitt, Jarral, & Robbins, 1991; Zola-Morgan & Squire, 1990). The hippocampus is necessary for the consolidation and contextualization of new episodic and autobiographical learning (Eichenbaum, 1992; Squire, 1987). Severe damage to the hippocampus will result in anterograde amnesia, which is the inability to learn new information that is available to conscious awareness.

Because explicit memory requires networks involving the hippocampus and higher cortical structures, the development of conscious memory parallels the maturation of these systems over the first years of life (Fuster, 1996; Jacobs, van Praag, & Gage, 2000; McCarthy, 1995). Unconscious learning and conditioning that utilize alternate memory systems continue to occur, even though we have no conscious recollection of the experience. Take, for example, a fearful memory: Whereas the hippocampus is required for the conscious memory of the experience, the amygdala is necessary for the visceral response to fear (Williams, L. M. et al., 2001). The sight of a dog that once bit you might elicit a bodily fear response via the amygdala, but hippocampal damage would leave you with no conscious memory of *why* you were afraid.

The hippocampus and amygdala have an important relationship to one another. The amygdala has a central role in emotional and somatic experience, and the hippocampus participates in conscious, logical, and cooperative social functioning. Because both the emotional and cognitive components are vital to relationships, their proper development, functioning, and reciprocal regulation are essential. Impairment of the hippocampus from early chronic stress can impact virtually every aspect of development. Decreases in hippocampal volume have been shown to correlate with deficits of encoding short-term into long-term memory (Bremner et al., 1993). Adult women who experienced childhood abuse have reduced left hippocampal volume and increased dissociative symptoms. This relationship suggests that the hippocampus plays a role not only in memory encoding but also in integrating our memories into a cohesive narrative about our past and personal identity (Stein et al., 1997).

Catherine—The Fabric of Life

Catherine was a woman in her late 30s who came to therapy complaining of anxiety and panic attacks. She was an accomplished writer who had published many successful novels, traveled widely, and lived an interesting and adventurous life. As she sat across from me, her posture overerect, never taking her eyes off of me, I became aware of how attentive she was to my every move, be it a shift in posture or reaching for my coffee. More than this, I noticed that her every hair was in place, her clothes were perfectly pressed, and each word was carefully chosen. Possessing none of these attributes myself, I smiled at the thought of what an interesting contrast we presented. Catherine made it clear from the outset that it was difficult for her to share her feelings and that she needed to proceed slowly. I assured her that I was in no hurry and that she could take all the time she needed. She decided to start by telling me about her family history, upbringing, and education.

The only child of an aristocratic English family, Catherine was sent off to a Swiss boarding school at the age of 6. She only saw her parents when they would meet at a resort for vacation or during an infrequent visit to their home in England. She was primarily raised by nannies, nurses, and tutors and had spent a good deal of time alone. She offhandedly mentioned that her parents didn't seem to like children, and that they couldn't wait to have her out of the house. She became interested in literature at an early age, and had loved to write "old-fashioned" stories in the style of Thomas Hardy. Even when Catherine discussed topics that she claimed made her happy, she showed a noticeable lack of emotion. She acted like a disinterested reporter discussing the life of a stranger.

Over the next few weeks, Catherine described her many travels, her brief and superficial romantic relationships, the plots of some of her stories, and other facts of her life. She avoided talking of any of the things that had brought her to therapy, occasionally reminding me that she would get to them in her own time. Meanwhile, I began to notice something quite odd. From time to time, I found small pieces of material on the sofa, floor, or out in the waiting room. About 2 inches square, they appeared to have been cut out of some larger piece of cloth. I threw the first two away, but the third made me wonder whether someone was playing a joke on me, so I tucked it into my desk drawer. A few weeks went by as Catherine continued to provide me with factual information about her life. As she came in for one session, I held up one of the small pieces of cloth and asked her if she had ever seen anything like it. Abandoning her aristocratic stance, she lunged toward me, grabbed the material from my hand, and ran out of the room. I sat there stunned. She was gone before I could say anything. I looked down at my hand and saw that her nails had broken through my skin. What was the connection between Catherine and the fabric and why did she have such a strong reaction?

In the days that followed I left a number of messages for her, suggesting that she come in for a session so we could talk about what had happened. After avoiding me for a few weeks, she finally called back and we set up another session. Taking a seat across from me, she started out by apologizing for running away and said that she realized the time had come to talk about what was really bothering her. As it turned out, the small pieces of material were patches of a baby blanket that Catherine had carried with her for years. When she grew too old to carry her blanket, she carefully cut it into small pieces and carried those with her. She would always keep one in her pocket and rub it with her thumb and index finger to help remain calm. This had been a lifelong secret about which she was very ashamed. When she saw me holding a piece of her blanket, she felt completely exposed.

This disclosure helped us move forward into much darker childhood secrets. Her father had sexually molested her every time she came home from boarding school. When she told her mother and asked for protection, her mother refused to believe her and told her she was only trying to make trouble. "From then on," Catherine said, "my mom always found a reason to keep me away from her and my dad." Catherine, desperate for help, approached one of the teachers at school. Again, she was rebuffed. Later, as a teenager, a female coach on whom she had a bit of a crush molested her. After they had sex, this coach also distanced herself from Catherine.

As with many children who are sexually molested by parents and teachers, Catherine felt deeply ashamed. In Catherine's case, the fact that her parents essentially abandoned her at such an early age left her feeling unloved and unlovable. She was overwhelmed by emotions and had no one to help her contain or process them. When she did ask for help, she was called a liar—another layer of victimization that compounded her shame. She had no place to feel safe, yet she longed for a relationship where she could discover what it would be like to trust someone. Through her novels, Catherine created worlds full of people who kept her company and of whom she was totally in control. Through our work, Catherine realized that she unconsciously tried to test me by dropping the pieces of cloth. She shared her fantasy that if she came to trust me, I would also molest her. Then she would lodge a complaint against me, but no one would believe her. After all, I was the "great doctor" and she was only a "crazy patient." Catherine had also created an even deeper fantasy that she would come to depend on me and I would send her away, banishing her to loneliness.

My primary job in therapy was to disconfirm her expectations. By being available, by listening, believing, and, most importantly, not exploiting or abandoning her, I created a safe haven for her to be able to become aware of and modify her interpersonal conditioning. Catherine had been abandoned and violated, a situation paired in her mind with anxiety, panic, and death. All she had to comfort herself for all of these years were squares of aging fabric. The countless nights she spent alone in a dark dormitory room in the Swiss mountains, overwhelmed with fear and loneliness, had imprinted her trauma deep into the wiring of her social brain. I explained to her the effects that this sort of conditioning has on neural systems related to fear, anxiety, and panic. Her symptoms were no accident, nor were they a weakness of character. They were but a natural consequence of a child forced to grow up without loving parents in a frightening, overwhelming, and dangerous world. When your abuse comes at the hands of those who are supposed to protect and care for you, you truly feel adrift in an alien universe.

The depth of the harm caused by neglect, abuse, and inadequate nurturance rests on the fact that the human brain is a social organ. Relationships that cause pain teach children that their role in the group is tenuous, their existence is unnecessary, and their future survival is in question. Negative interpersonal experiences not only impact an individual's ability to relate to others, they also damage the body's ability to maintain and heal itself in response to physical illness and subsequent psychological stress. When stress is early and prolonged, neurons, neural structures such as the hippocampus, processes of immunological functioning, and the construction of the self can all be compromised. Raising a child is a daunting responsibility, one that includes building a brain that will last a lifetime—for better and for worse.

In the next four chapters we will look at different ways in which dysfunctions of social brain networks can result in well-recognized mental disorders. First we explore social phobia and borderline personality disorder to examine those who have a heightened sense of fear and shame when interacting with others. We then look at antisocial personality disorder and autism to examine two different ways in which a lack of social connection and attunement can manifest in human behavior. There is considerable debate concerning all four of these disorders over the relative influence of experience versus predetermined genetic programming that makes someone vulnerable to them. Although the answers to these questions remain to be discovered, what we do know about these social disorders can teach us much about the functions and dysfunctions of the social brain.

Chapter 17

Social Phobia: When Others Trigger Fear

*Always expecting the worst, he was never disap-
pointed for long. Never caught off guard either. All
of which goes to show that . . . worrying works.*
—Philip Roth, 1997, p. 385

Anxiety and fear are the conscious aspects of our body's ongoing appraisal of danger. They can be triggered by countless conscious or unconscious cues, and they have the power to shape our thoughts, behavior, and feelings. At their most adaptive, anxiety and fear encourage us to step back from the edge of a cliff, cross the street when unsavory characters are coming our way, or check to see if we signed our tax forms before sealing the envelope. At their least adaptive, they prevent us from taking appropriate risks, engaging in relationships, and exploring our world.

Just about everyone experiences some kind of social anxiety. A blind date, a job interview, or public speaking are all situations where it is normal to experience some level of anxiety. However, up to 12% of us experience social anxiety at some point in our lives that significantly impacts our functioning (Charney, 2004; Wittchen & Fehm, 2001). Social phobia appears to have both inheritable and learned components (Lieb et al., 2000; Mannuzza et al., 1995; Marcin & Nemeroff, 2003), and although a variety of differences in the brains of social phobics have been found, it is not known whether these differences are a cause, an effect, or simply correlates of social phobia (Li et al., 2001; Stein, 1998).

In this chapter we focus on ways in which our fear circuitry becomes activated in social situations. Keep in mind that what triggers social anxiety is not a direct threat to our physical survival. Rather, it is usually related to the *anticipation of shame,* the social correlate of physical danger. As an infant, shame is an emotional disconnection with caretakers that is experienced as a threat to survival. The automatic and unconscious activation of shame continues to shape our self-image and social behavior into adulthood. For some, coping with shame and the anxiety it evokes is a crippling and lifelong struggle.

Samantha—In the Eyes of the Jury

Samantha, a woman in her 30s, came to therapy with the complaint that "my life is going nowhere!" At the beginning of our relationship, I had a difficult time following her. Her feelings, thoughts, and beliefs seemed so tenuous and vague that it was difficult to understand what she was saying. Even Samantha realized this, saying, "I don't know what to think, who I am, or what I'll do next." The one thing that seemed clear from her day-to-day life was that she was uncomfortable around people. Even though she insisted that she loved people, she did anything and everything to avoid them. The only people she felt safe and comfortable around were her immediate family and whatever man she was dating. She tried hard to go out into the world and do things, but usually something would trigger her to "get the hell home," and she would retreat to her bed and television.

Thinking back on Samantha, I'm still struck by her physical agitation, her furtive glances, and, most especially, her tendency to interpret nearly everything I said as criticism. There seemed to be no statement neutral enough to avoid making her defensive. If I asked her how she was feeling, her first response was, "Do you think I look bad?" When I commented on her arms and legs being crossed, her response was to apologize profusely, saying that she knew she had poor posture. She cancelled our initial appointment twice and when we finally did meet, I asked if she had been nervous about meeting me. Samantha apologized over and over again, pulled out her checkbook, and offered to pay for the two cancelled sessions. Her tension was contagious; I found myself growing increasingly hesitant to say anything to her.

My gaze made her uncomfortable. "People looking at me make me freeze. It feels like they can look right through me and see my thoughts. When I see someone looking at me, I begin to shake. Sometimes it feels like their eyes are hurting me. I'm like a scared rabbit; all I can think about is how to hop away." During high school, Samantha sat alone at a table in a far corner of the cafeteria. If someone sat near her, she would act as if she was finished eating, nervously gather up her things, and leave. She told me about a time when she had to make a presentation at work. She organized the chairs in the conference room, set up her materials, and put her first slide up on the screen. As everyone came in and seated themselves, she excused herself to go to the restroom. Samantha said that "I walked right out of the building, drove home, got in bed, and watched TV until I fell asleep that night. I just left them all staring at my first slide. I never even called to tell them what happened."

Even when seemingly relaxed, Samantha's anxiety always lurked just beneath the surface. "I have good people skills, " she told me, "and I'm good at fooling everyone, but they usually figure out that I'm stupid and have nothing to offer. I can tell by the way they look at me. If I say something and I see someone rolling their eyes, I just freeze and can't talk anymore. I can't tell you how many times I get up in the morning, get dressed, get in the car, and head for work. At some point during the ride, I just turn around and go back home. It's as if I'm possessed, like I'm not in control of my body. It just does what it wants to do." Unfortunately for Samantha, a steady supply of money from her family kept her from having to overcome these fears.

While growing up, Samantha's family never discussed any feelings except positive ones, as if putting words to negative feelings allowed them to become real. She remembered that when she was sad or afraid, her parents would tell her that she had nothing to worry about and the subject would be dropped. As a sensitive and shy young woman, this approach left her victimized by her own unspoken anxiety with no way of understanding or controlling it. All these years later, she experienced her emotions as alien forces that directed her actions.

The first focus of our treatment plan was to help Samantha become aware of her negative feelings and to describe them as clearly as she could. Once she was able to connect her inner emotional world with her conscious thoughts, we were able to explore and question them. It was gratifying to be part of her growing ability to learn a language for her anxiety and fear, forming narratives about their origins, triggers, and ways of coping with them. During one session, we did a "psychological autopsy" on her flight from her presentation at work. Samantha came to realize that she hadn't run off because she was possessed by some alien force; rather, her anxiety had been triggered by noticing that someone had yawned. This yawn triggered shame and produced the thought that her audience was bored with her even before she began! This, in turn, led to a chain of thoughts and feelings that ended with the fantasy that she would be laughed at and humiliated—causing her to leave the room and not return.

Being shamed was, in fact, a common experience in Samantha's early life. Her father, an extremely successful businessman, had a sarcastic sense of humor that he often directed at his family. Samantha recalled many painful comments he made to her that made her flee to her bed in tears. Samantha came to see clearly how preparing to speak in front of her boss and coworkers created the same expectation of humiliation. She reacted the way she had as a child, retreating to her room and distracting herself with television, story books, or imaginary friends. This reflexive withdrawal, used as a defense to modulate anxiety as a child, continued seamlessly into adulthood. Sadly, without anyone to help her gain awareness of her emotions, her inner experience remained a painful mystery that resulted in her "going nowhere." Her thinking remained confused and vague, keeping her from focusing on the realities of her life.

Through the Eyes of a Social Phobic

Social anxiety disrupts our ability to have relationships through a variety of mechanisms. It alters how we gather and process information across the social synapse and how the networks of the social brain respond to experience. For example, social phobics have an attentional bias toward information that is socially evaluative in nature: They are biased toward anticipating, detecting, and remembering negative and angry responses by others (Amir, Foa, & Coles, 2000; Asmundson & Stein, 1994; Clark & McManus, 2002; Eastwood et al., 2005; Mogg et al., 2004; Musa & Lépine, 2000; Spector, Pecknold, & Libman, 2003; Straube et al., 2004).

They also tend to orient to anxiety-provoking stimuli and, once locked in, have a difficult time disengaging, even when it is irrelevant or harmful to their personal well-being (Amir et al., 2000; 2003; Fox et al., 2001; 2002; Georgiou et al., 2005; Yiend & Mathews, 2001).

Social phobics employ visual avoidance and elaborate processing strategies to modulate the fear evoked by being seen (Chen et al., 2002; Mansell et al., 1999; Van Ameringen et al., 1998; Wenzel & Holt, 2002; Wik et al., 1996). The combination of increased orientation to, and fixation on, social evaluation makes the experience of social phobics one of constantly being on trial: Every interaction is experienced as a negative evaluation of their worth. Thus, the memories and emotional impact of negative interpersonal responses cut deeper and last longer.

Children with social phobia have poor recognition of emotional facial expressions and experience greater anxiety while looking at faces (Simonian et al., 2001). On the other hand, socially phobic adults demonstrate a better memory for facial expressions than normal subjects, especially for those that are negative or critical (Foa et al., 2000; Lundh & Ost, 1996). It makes sense, then, that social phobics avoid looking directly at faces, especially eyes, preferring to focus on other aspects of those with whom they interact (Horley et al., 2003).

Turning away from others cuts down the amount of available information and results in the use of their own negative self-image when making self-judgments (Hirsch & Mathews, 2000; Hirsch et al., 2003). This is why social phobics come to conclusions faster in social situations—their social brains recycle old shame experiences and fail to gather new information. Based on their inner certainty of the inevitability of criticism and shame, they know that if they are "seen," they will be disliked. This interlocking set of thoughts, emotions, and behaviors maintains and reinforces their fear and avoidance of stress.

Orienting toward, and locking into, the negative expressions of others evolved due to its potential survival value. An angry look in our direction is a good indication that we need to pay increased attention to that person, and a frightened look in another direction suggests the presence of potential danger somewhere nearby. Social phobia, when not the result of sustained early stress or a specific traumatic experience, is most likely the result of an imbalance of the alarm and feedback systems that regulate the approach and avoidance responses in social situations. This theory parallels our present understanding of obsessive–compulsive disorder, in which adaptive concerns about contamination and disorganization go unchecked, resulting in intense anxiety and disruptive rituals.

The Socially Phobic Brain

The triggering of these physiological and emotional reactions in response to other people leads to an experience of the social world as a dangerous place. Although people with social phobia may have an intellectual understanding that a situation is not dangerous, the power of their body's fear response makes it difficult for them to believe their own thoughts. When social phobics prepare to engage in public speaking, it is not surprising that they experience more anxiety and negative emotions than others without social phobia. They have an increased heart rate and right-sided electrical activation in anterior temporal, lateral frontal, and parietal lobes (Davidson, Marshall et al., 2000; Tillfors et al., 2002). Remember that right-sided bias correlates with emotional arousal and negative affect.

A right-hemispheric bias has also been found in other kinds of anxiety disorders (Nordahl et al., 1998; Rauch et al., 1995, 1997, 2003). Right-hemisphere activation has been shown to result in decreased metabolism in Broca's area, suggesting that the more anxious someone becomes, the more likely he or she will have difficulty speaking (Bruder et al., 2004; Rauch et al., 1997). This physiological pattern may explain why a fear of public speaking is particularly common. In fact, one group of researchers found that a combination of right prefrontal and left parietal activation was specific to social phobia, hypothesizing that this pattern of activation may be related to a unique interaction between the processing of autobiographical memory and social presentation (Bell at al., 1999). Perhaps such neural wiring makes it difficult or even impossible to overcome self-consciousness and the expectation of negative evaluation about the self. This theory is still highly speculative and we cannot yet say with any certainty that social phobia demonstrates a unique pattern of brain activation (Malizia et al., 1997).

For the most part, social phobics share the neurochemical profiles of those with other anxiety disorders: heightened (adrenergic) excitatory neurochemistry combined with decreased gamma-aminobutyric acid (GABA) inhibitory regulation (Argyropoulos et al., 2001; Bell et al., 1999; Papp et al., 1988). What distinguishes social phobia from other anxiety disorders is evidence of dysfunction in serotonin and dopamine systems (Nutt et al., 1998; Potts et al., 1996). Lower dopamine (D2) binding has been found in the striatum of social phobics, which in animals correlates with a lack of exploration and novelty seeking and lower social status (Schneider et al., 2000; Tiihonen et al., 1997). Remember, dopamine is an important neurochemical in the social reward system, related to approaching others, sustaining attachment, and creating a sense of well-being.

As with so many other findings, we don't know if biological differences are a cause or effect of social phobia. They could reflect an innate inability to compete socially or an experience-dependent shutdown of activity in the face of anxiety and shame. When parents dominate children through physical or psychological punishment, some young brains may be shaped to experience persistently lower social rank. The symptoms of hypervigilance and avoidance seen in social phobia may be an evolutionary continuation of the behavior of lower-ranking individuals in primate groups who "know their place" and stay in it. It would be an interesting and sad social reality if those of lower rank in the world came home and "took it out" on their children, only to create children shaped to remain of lower social rank.

The Role of the Amygdala in Anxiety and Fear

From an evolutionary perspective, many of our complex neural systems have evolved in the service of keeping us safe. The amygdala plays a central role in the evaluation and expression of fear and safety and has been conserved and expanded during evolution to accommodate increasingly complex cognitive, sensory, and emotional input into survival decisions. Its central role in appraisal and the triggering of the biochemical cascade of the fight/flight response involve it in networks of memory, affective regulation, and social relatedness. Electrical stimulation of the central nucleus of the amygdala results in the experience of fear, whereas destruction of the amygdala results in an inability to acquire conditioned fear and possibly an elimination of fear reactions altogether (Carvey, 1998). It appears that the amygdala is indispensable for the association of sensory experiences with the fear response (Bechara et al., 1995).

As the center of our fear circuitry, the amygdala is capable of learning to pair any thought, feeling, or sensation with a fear reaction. Under the proper conditions, we can have a conditioned fear response to everything from lions, tigers, and bears to success, attachment, and even love. Social phobia, if nothing else, is a conditioned fear of social interactions that produces activation of the amygdala. Projections from the amygdala to the lateral hypothalamus result in sympathetic activation responsible for increased heart rate and blood pressure, and the amygdala's connection to the trigeminal facial motor nerve causes the facial expressions we identify with fear (Davis, 1992).

Although the amygdala has been the focus of intense study for many decades, another structure has attracted increasing attention in the neuroanatomy of anxiety. The *bed nucleus of the stria terminalis* (BNST) is a structure that is separate from the amygdala but appears to project to most of the same neural targets. Unlike the amygdala, it does not activate a fight/flight response to specific stimuli but results in a lower level of diffuse arousal we think of as anxiety (Davis et al., 1997). Whereas the amygdala is the center of fear conditioning to specific sensory cues, the BNST appears to be involved in activating a sense of concern over a longer period of time. Perhaps this is the structure responsible for a sense of foreboding, long-term anxiety, and making some of us "worry warts."

The BNST may be a later evolving companion structure to the amygdala, allowing us a longer event horizon for the prediction of trouble than the amygdala. The amygdala has been viewed as the center of both fear and anxiety. When we discuss the amygdala in humans, however, we may, in fact, be discussing the functions of both the amygdala and the BNST. Figure 17.1 shows just a few of the target areas that are activated by both of these structures.

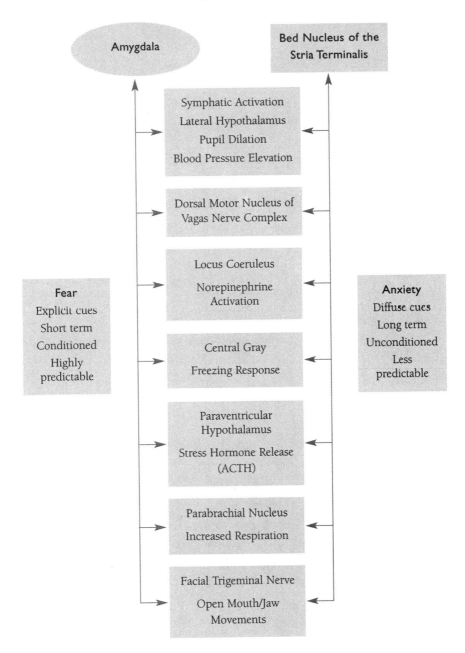

Figure 17.1. The amygdala and the bed nucleus of the stria terminalis: Target sites in the regulation of fear and anxiety. Adapted from Davis et al. (1997).

The prime directive of the amygdala is to protect us at all costs, and although it's good at its job, its successes come with some considerable downsides. The amygdala is stealthy in its appraisal, assessing situations based on past learning in small fractions of a second, way before conscious awareness. The tendency of the amygdala toward generalization, however, results in the triggering of panic by an ever-increasing number of internal and external cues (Douglas & Pribram, 1966). Aaron Beck put it best when he suggested that evolution favors anxious genes (Beck et al., 1990, p. 4). Unfortunately, that anxiety leaves us vulnerable to thoughts and feelings that are unnecessary and often destructive. Table 17.1 summarizes characteristic functionings of the amygdala.

Table 17.1. **The Amygdala**

- Appraises inner and outer environments much faster than conscious awareness.
- Does not require conscious awareness.
- Is well-formed before birth.
- Retains early learning and unconsciously weaves it into ongoing experience.
- Resists inhibition.
- Tends to generalize from specific instances.

The development and connectivity of the amygdala have many implications for both early child development and psychotherapy. Because the amygdala is operational at birth, the experience of fear may be the strongest early emotion. Without the inhibitory impact of the hippocampal–cortical networks, early fear experiences are likely to be overwhelming. Part of the power of early emotional learning may come from the intensity of these uninhibited and unregulated negative affects in shaping neural infrastructure. The infant is very dependent on caretakers to modulate these powerful experiences. What we call attachment schema reflect the power of early interpersonal experiences to condition the brain to approach or avoid other people as a way to regulate fear.

Amygdala dysfunction has been tied to all forms of anxiety disorders (Shekhar et al., 2003). Social phobics show greater amygdala activation during aversive conditioning to neutral faces and even greater activation in response to angry and contemptuous faces (Schneider et al., 1999; Stein et al., 2002). The amygdala is also essential in the reading of fearful facial expressions; it may be that a hyperactive amygdala leads to sustained interpersonal vigilance and an overestimation of danger (Baird et al., 1999; Schwartz et al., 2003). When treated successfully with either medication or psychotherapy, a decrease in fear correlates with a decline in amygdala activation (Furmark et al., 2002).

One of the primary roles of the amygdala is to act as a social brake against random approach, inhibiting interaction with unfamiliar others until their safety can be evaluated (Amaral, 2002; Amaral et al., 2003b). In fact, it has been discovered that cells in the amygdala of macaque monkeys are selectively sensitive to approach movements (Brothers et al., 1990). When the amygdalas of macaque monkeys are destroyed, they begin to approach objects they should fear, including monkeys of higher rank. Human subjects whose brains were electrically stimulated in the region of the amygdala reported a sense of being reprimanded by an authority or of being an unwanted participant in a social group (Gloor, 1986). This finding certainly suggests that an emotional awareness of being where you are unwanted exists at a primitive level of processing and induces feelings of anxiety and shame.

The Fast and the Slow

In order to understand fear, the amygdala needs to be placed in the broader context of the human experience of fear. The response to, and evaluation of, fear involves two interconnected systems with different functions (LeDoux, 1996). So far, we have been discussing the fast system. With the amygdala at its core, this system makes rapid, reflexive, and unconscious decisions to provide for immediate survival reactions. This system develops first in the child and organizes learning related to attachment and affective regulation. The fast system sends information immediately and directly from the sense organs (eyes, ears, skin, tongue) through the thalamus to the amygdala. The amygdala then translates this "danger" information into bodily responses related to fight/flight reactions via its connections to the various structures described in Figure 17.1.

The slow system, involving the hippocampus and cortex, contextualizes and makes conscious what is being experienced. Its job is to balance the reflexive activation of the amygdala with inhibitory input after the stimulus is judged to be safe. The slow system sends sensory information from the thalamus to hippocampal and cortical circuits for more detailed evaluation. This system is slower because it contains many more synaptic connections and involves complex conscious processing. Cortical circuits of memory and executive processing examine the information, compare it to memories of similar situations, and make voluntary decisions concerning how to proceed. This slow system in humans has the additional task of making sense of the behavioral and visceral reaction already set into motion by the fast systems. Figure 17.2 juxtaposes the fast and slow fear circuitry.

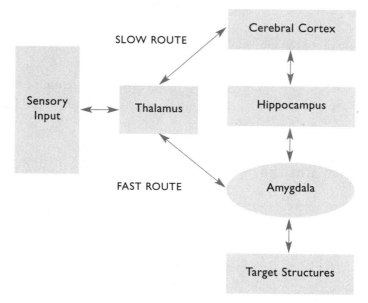

Figure 17.2. **The fast and slow networks of fear processing. Based on Ledoux (1994).**

From moment-to-moment, our fast system (organized by past learning) shapes the nature of our present experience. This is a key mechanism through which early social learning and attachment schema shape our experience. By the time we become conscious of others, our brains have already organized ways to think about them. At one extreme, "love at first sight" involves the triggering of positive associations and projection of them onto another person, thereby creating a sort of positive prejudice. In the opposite case, as in situations of racial prejudice, salient aspects of a person's skin color trigger the fast system, which unconsciously shapes our experience as based in fear and other negative feelings.

Racism as a Form of Social Phobia

History is plagued with examples of racism, hate crimes, and "ethnic cleansing." An objective study of racism is difficult because emotions run high and usually cloud our judgement. And *why* do emotions run high? What would make hundreds of European-American adults threaten the lives of a handful of African-American children walking into a school-house during the early days of integration?

What would allow concentration camp guards to order millions of innocent people into gas chambers? The cause of our inhumanity to others is an enduring and vital question. Racism seems so endemic in human history that it may not be "inhuman" but rather "all too human." On the other hand, countless examples of interracial cooperation and harmony seem to contradict the notion that racism is a basic human truth.

As we project our imaginations back to the prehistoric bands of our ancestors, we can easily see the benefit of quickly spotting unfamiliar others. Those from another tribe were potentially dangerous and not to be trusted. If this scenario of natural selection is true, it would make sense that the neurobiology of racism would be related to the fear circuitry in the brain. So is racism hard-wired into our brains, learned, or some combination of both? A number of studies have examined brain activation during exposure to pictures of same/other group faces in an attempt to identify the neural substrate of prejudice. (Because these studies have been conducted at U.S. universities, and our most salient racial struggle is between African-Americans and European-Americans, the studies reviewed here focus on these two populations.)

Recognition memory is superior for faces of same-race individuals and greater activation occurs in brain areas involved in the recognition (left fusiform cortex and right hippocampal area) for faces of our own race (Brigham & Barkowitz, 1978; Malpass & Kravitz, 1969). In these studies, African-American participants were better at recognizing European-American faces than European-Americans were at recognizing

African-American faces. This difference is likely due to greater exposure of African-Americans to European-American faces in the media and in most college environments (Golby, Gabrieli, Chiao, & Eberhardt, 2001). When European-American subjects are shown African-American faces, they demonstrate more left amygdala activation and enhanced startle response (Phelps et al., 2000). For African-American and European-American subjects, there is greater amygdala habituation to same-race versus other-race faces (Hart et al., 2000).

Because neither conscious awareness nor attention are required to condition a fear response, the body's reaction to individuals of other races is unrelated to the individuals' conscious experience or stated attitudes. Consistent with these neuroanatomical findings, social psychologists have found that stereotypes are automatically activated and require conscious inhibition to produce low-prejudice responses (Devine, 1989). Increased implicit prejudice is related to increased sensitivity to facial expression (Hugenberg & Bodenhausen, 2004). These emotional–visceral activations may relate to findings from other studies that suggest that other-race speakers are seen as more forceful or powerful than same-race speakers (Hart & Morry, 1996, 1997; Hass et al., 1991; Linville & Jones, 1980). In fact, anger results in greater expressions of prejudice even when the anger has nothing to do with a member of the other race, suggesting that negative affect can prime or activate prejudice (DeSteno et al., 2004).

Research with African-American children dating back to 1950 showed that they would choose white dolls over brown ones. When asked why, they described the brown dolls as "ugly," "not pretty," or labeled them with racial epithets. White dolls were described as "good," "pretty," and "the best looking because they're white" (Clark & Clark, 1950, p. 348). Given that the self emerges from relationships, cultural prejudice becomes woven into the core of the developing psyche. What a sad state of affairs.

So back to our question about whether prejudice is learned or innate. To explore this question, Phelps and her colleagues (Phelps et al., 2000) showed pictures of well-known and well-liked African-Americans to European-American subjects. These subjects demonstrated the same pattern of results as in previous studies except that amygdala activation was absent! These results suggest that exposure to, and knowledge about, a person of a different race can teach the brain to be less afraid.

Although the interpretation of these results has been contested (Dasgupta et al., 2000), it does make intuitive sense that positive exposure is capable of inhibiting the activation of fear circuitry. For European-Americans, amygdala activation may be reinforced by the consistent pairing of African-American faces with criminal behavior on the nightly news. The pairing of these images with criminal behavior may not have the same impact on African-American viewers because of their increased ability to differentiate same-race faces in conjunction with greater general exposure. For African Americans, real and suspected racial prejudice may consistently reinforce the brain to remain vigilant and suspicious of European-Americans.

Segregation and other forms of prejudice embedded in culture may keep us from becoming experts about the faces of those from other groups. Segregation may shape our brains to analyze the faces of people from other races using less efficient alternative circuitry, thus making us more vulnerable to cultural stereotypes and media representations. Like the social phobic, we may all employ avoidance strategies to modulate our anxiety with those of other races. We know from studies of affect regulation that labeling activates neural networks (dorsal lateral prefrontal/hippocampal) that inhibit emotional reactivity. So it may be that prejudicial labeling of others decreases our anxiety and creates the illusion of control. The lessons of history appear to support this interpretation.

Prejudice is so automatic and unconscious that its manifestations need to be continually uncovered right before our eyes. It does seem clear, however, that once stereotypical attitudes and beliefs are inculcated, change requires intention, attention, and time (Devine, 1989; Phelps & Thomas, 2003). People from other cultures, with different degrees of exposure, proximity, and prejudice, need to be studied before we can arrive at any conclusions about the origins of racial prejudice in the human brain. With the science of genetics revealing that race is more of a cultural construct than a biological reality, future study of how our brains react to one another can help to shed light not just on the nature and etiology of the neuroscience of prejudice, but also on how all of us who live on this increasingly crowded planet may learn to overcome our differences and discover the true wealth of human diversity.

Chapter 8

Borderline Personality Disorder: When Attachment Fails

I just love torturing people for not loving me enough.

—An anonymous poet

People with borderline personality disorder live on an emotional roller coaster. They inexplicably spin from fear, anguish, and pain into a sense of calm, only to lurch, once again, into an overwhelming sense of fear and anger. They experience criticism, shame, and abandonment from all directions as they hang on for their emotional lives. When confronted with even a hint of criticism or rejection, these people become emotionally overwhelmed and catapulted into drastically fluctuating moods, unstable perceptions, and rocky relationships. Friends and family suffer with them: They are targets of rage, accused of sadistically causing pain, and bewildered by unpredictable shifts in mood and behavior. Borderline personality is truly an interpersonal disorder, created in a social milieu, triggered by close relationships, and destructive to social connectedness.

What we witness in the lives of borderline clients is the result of a profound disruption of the development and integration of social brain systems and the ability to regulate emotion. The histories and symptoms of borderline clients strongly suggest that early attachment was experienced as highly traumatic and sometimes life-threatening (Fonagy, Target, & Gergely, 2000). Attachment trauma can result from physical and/or sexual abuse, neglect, or profound misattunement between parent and child.

Mood disorders have also been shown to occur at above-average rates in these patients and their parents, a likely contributing factor to difficulties in emotional regulation. Whatever the cause, the child is unable to utilize others in the development of secure attachment and to regulate overwhelming anxiety and fear. The result is that real or imagined abandonment triggers a state of terror, similar to what any young primate experiences when physically abandoned by its mother.

Jasmine—An Emotional Roller Coaster

Jasmine was an attractive woman in her late 20s who had moved to the West Coast about a year earlier to take a job in an advertising firm. She came to see me complaining of depression, anxiety, and estrangement from her family, as well as repeated failures in relationships. She seemed nervous about discussing personal issues, so we focused on her job during our early sessions. She was fun to talk to and easy to get along with, making me wonder why she had so much difficulty in relationships; I would soon find out. Jasmine came into my office for our fifth session with a big smile, bubbling over with enthusiasm about what had happened in the days since our last meeting. She was working on a new advertising campaign that she found challenging and exciting. This campaign was important to her company, and her boss was counting on her to do a good job. She was touched and honored by the faith he seemed to be placing in her.

As we had gotten to know each other, she described some of the specifics of the ad campaign, interactions with her coworkers, and the feedback they were getting from clients. Jasmine made sure to include details about her contributions to the project and how much better she was at many aspects of the job than her coworkers, despite the fact that they seemed to receive the kudos she deserved. She also mentioned that her stress levels were high and that she found it difficult to sleep and find time to rest and exercise. After a year of living in her apartment, she still hadn't found the time to empty the last few boxes or hang up her pictures. In passing, I mentioned that she might consider taking some time off to relax for a day or two.

As I finished making this suggestion, Jasmine's expression changed. At first she seemed to recede behind her eyes, and then they became tearful as her expression turned soft and vulnerable. I barely had time to grow accustomed to her sadness when rage began to emerge through her tears. When I broke the silence by asking her what she was feeling, it was as if someone else were now in the room. She sprang from the couch like a cat and paced the floor in front of me.

"My boss knows that I can't handle this job," she yelled. "That bastard is just setting me up to fail so he can fire me! I know he doesn't respect my work. He treats me like shit! He never asks me to go out after work like the others and I know they talk behind my back. They all think I'm pathetic." She sat and glared at me. I was flabbergasted, but she wasn't through yet. Pointing her finger at me, she shouted, "You! You're just as bad! You think I'm some pathetic bimbo who has to pay you to be her friend. You don't want me to succeed, so you don't lose your cash cow. You have mortgage payments to make and vacations to take. You tell me to take some time off like it's nothing. What? You don't think my job means anything? You want me to go home to live with my parents so you won't have to see me anymore? Is that it?"

If looks could kill, I wouldn't be telling this story. Still, I hung on in silence as she fell back onto the couch, threw the pillows at the wall, and proceeded to curl up like a child. I tried to remain centered and not allow my own feelings of anxiety and defensiveness to interfere with my availability to her. I focused on my breathing and tried to stay in an open and receptive state of mind. The word *borderline* may have flashed through my head, but my role as her therapist was to remain connected, accepting, and not to punish Jasmine for punishing me. I knew better than to focus on her attacks. Something had triggered a feeling of abandonment within her, and I was seeing just how overwhelming and profoundly frightening that experience was to her.

We sat in silence together for a few minutes. Finally, when it felt right to reach out to her, I said quietly, "I'm sorry you feel so rejected, so alone. I know your work is difficult and that you're under a lot of pressure. When I suggested you take time off, I really was only thinking of how it might be good for you and even help you do a better job in the long run." Another few minutes went by in silence. I watched her face gradually work through the different expressions I had seen before, this time in reverse order.

Jasmine looked over to me with a gentle smile. "Guess what I did yesterday?" Her voice was that of a coy young girl. "My sister dropped my niece off while she was having her hair done. We put on our bathing suits, went down to the beach, and made sandcastles. We had ice cream and she sat on my lap, and we rocked back and forth and sang songs. I love spending time with her. She thinks I'm the greatest thing in the world. All she wants to do is play and talk to me." I nodded my head and asked, "Did it feel good for you?" She opened her eyes wide, pushed out her lower lip in a child's pout, and slowly nodded.

I asked Jasmine if she was worried about going back to work the next day, given the things she had said about her boss. She dismissed my concern with a wave of her hand and said, "Naw, he's a really good guy, and I think he likes me." Our time was about up, so we scheduled our next appointment. As I walked her to the door, she stopped and picked up the pillows and put them back on the couch. When we got to the door, she reached out, squeezed my arm affectionately, and said, "You're the greatest."

When Borderlines Attack

Jasmine complained of a wide range of compulsive symptoms, including substance abuse, hypersexuality, eating disorders, and excessive shopping. She seemed unable to regulate anything she did. When she dieted, she would grow dangerously thin. When she went off the diet, she would expand many dress sizes. She tried all sorts of solutions, including changing religions, having relationships with women, and moving around the country. Each attempted solution led to a realization that there was no escape. As Jasmine put it, "I keep running into myself wherever I go."

Although what she talked about changed from session to session, the emotional pattern remained the same. She came into the session in a positive state of mind. After a while, some association of hers or something I would say triggered a feeling of rejection, criticism, or abandonment. This was followed by a period of anger, rage, and withdrawal. If I argued with her or tried to talk her out of her feelings, her anger escalated and I became part of the problem. If I accepted her anger and was able to make an empathic response, she became reregulated and shifted into a contrite mode. She would then share an experience of a positive connection with someone, a disclosure apparently triggered by my empathy for her.

This pattern of connection, disconnection, and reconnection occurred many times in our relationship. I think of what Jasmine and I experienced as paralleling what happens with children and their parents countless times during childhood. It is the outward expression of the day-to-day experience of young children as they go through cycles of regulation, dysregulation, and reregulation, their parents serving as external frontal lobes, helping them to navigate the emotional ups and downs of life. Repeating this process thousands of times creates an unconscious expectation of regulation. Therapy is an attempt to build new memory later in life when it was not successfully established early on. This is "a memory for the future," a pattern that contains the thought, "I can survive these feelings" and that reregulation is "just around the corner." This positive background affect allows us to feel that the glass is half full, to have the confidence to take risks, and to stay on course when things don't go our way.

This was not the memory pattern laid down during Jasmine's childhood. Her mother, a rigid and distant woman (who may have suffered from obsessive–compulsive disorder) had little tolerance for any negative feelings. She had no idea how frightened and ashamed Jasmine felt, and if she did, she was incapable of soothing her. Jasmine's brother was usually off playing sports, and her father was away at work. She spent many days playing alone, intensely focused on her activities in order to avoid any interaction with her mother, who only seemed to make things worse. Her primary memory from childhood was of being frightened and lonely while doing everything she could to keep from interacting with the people around her. Jasmine's glass was perpetually half empty. Each new connection between us evoked old patterns that became the work of therapy, the foiling of anger and fear, and the rebuilding of regulation and trust.

The Brain of the Borderline

Although Jasmine's brain has never been scanned, the brains of patients who share her symptoms have been explored. Traditional neuropsychological testing has demonstrated frontal and temporal lobe dysfunction in borderline patients (Paris et al., 1999; Swirsky-Sacchetti et al., 1993). When the actual structure and functioning of their brains are examined, patients such as Jasmine demonstrate abnormalities in size, activation patterns, and neurochemical levels in several brain regions (Cowdry et al., 1985; Johnson et al., 2003; Lange et al., 2005; Lyoo et al., 1998).

As we might expect, the ways in which borderline brains differ from normal brains are found in networks of the social brain and those involved in regulating impulses and emotions (Bazanis et al., 2002; Dinn et al., 2004; Johnson et al., 2003). Borderline patients have smaller hippocampi, amygdala, left orbital medial and right anterior cingulate cortices (Brambilla et al., 2004; Driessen et al., 2000; Schmahl et al., 2003b; van Elst et al., 2003). And although smaller hippocampi have been discovered in many psychiatric and medical disorders, this pattern of abnormalities in multiple structures of the social brain may be more specific to borderline personality disorder (Bremner et al., 2000; Johnson et al., 2003).

At rest, the brains of borderline patients demonstrate hypometabolism in prefrontal and anterior cingulate cortices. These individuals are under-aroused on measures of heart rate, skin conductance, and pain sensitivity (Bohus et al., 2000; de la Fuente et al., 1997; Goyer et al., 1994; Herpertz et al., 1999). But when borderline patients are shown slides of emotionally adverse situations, they show greater than normal activation in the amygdala, prefrontal cortex, temporal and occipital lobes, and the fusiform gyrus (Herpertz et al., 2001a; Johnson et al., 2003; Juengling et al., 2003). Interestingly, higher levels of neurotoxins have also been found in the frontal lobes of these patients (van Elst et al., 2001). Simultaneously, the hippocampus, which is required for reality testing, new learning, and amygdala modulation, becomes hypometabolic (Juengling et al., 2003).

These findings suggest that interpersonal situations result in hyperactivation of networks throughout the social brain, putting the brain on high alert for danger while simultaneously decreasing inhibition, reality testing, and emotional control—a potent one–two punch to the social brain. When borderline patients experience negative feelings, they are overwhelmed and unable to use conscious cortical processing to test their reactions or to solve problems. They lose perspective, the ability to remember ever feeling good, or the idea that they may ever feel good again. Overwhelming fear and lack of perspective combine to create the experience that their very life is at risk. As one client put it, "When I get that way, I get so upset that I set off a bomb when a fly swatter would be enough."

The neurotransmitters regulating the social brain are also abnormal in borderline patients, who demonstrate low serotonin synthesis and diminished serotonin regulation in their frontal cortices (Leyton et al., 2001; Soloff et al., 2000). These findings correlate with increased impulsivity, depression, difficulty being soothed, and decreased emotional inhibition. Borderline patients also have heightened and/or unstable levels of norepinephrine, triggered by unregulated activation of the amygdala. A number of neurotransmitter systems within the social brain, including serotonin, norepinephrine, dopamine, and GABA, are most likely involved in the affective and behavioral instability experienced by borderline patients (Gurvits et al., 2000). Table 18.1 summarizes some of the possible neurodevelopmental dysfunctions in someone with borderline personality disorder.

There certainly exists the possibility that there is a genetic predisposition to the formation of this disorder, and, for some, this genetic bias may override the availability of good parenting. This may be what occurs when a mood disorder is present in the family, especially in the child who will come to have borderline personality disorder as an adult. The evidence is quite strong, however, that what we see in borderline symptoms is related, at least in part, to early attachment failures, and that these failures are translated into lasting neurodevelopmental damage.

One of the central tools of the psychotherapist is the interpretation. Simply put, an interpretation is a statement that attempts to make unconscious material conscious. Borderline clients often demonstrate extreme negative emotional reactions to interpretations. They may become violent, leave the consulting room, and engage in self-injurious behavior. Early in my relationship with Jasmine, I suggested that she used her anger to hold others at a distance, resulting in her being rejected. She screamed at me, shook her head, and stormed out of the room. It took days before she would answer my calls, and then only to tell me that she felt I was blaming her for all her problems. This was just one of many times that she told me that I would never see her again.

Table 18.1. **Possible Neurodevelopmental Dysfunctions in Borderline Personality Disorder**

Inadequate development and integration of hierarchical systems of the social brain that organize attachment schema and affect regulation (*orbital medial prefrontal, anterior cingulate, insula, amygdala*)

Inadequate development of the social engagement system (*vagal brake*), resulting in gross sympathetic responses (vs. subtler vagal regulation) in social situations (bomb vs. fly swatter)

Dysregulation of systems supplying and modulating *serotonin, norepinephrine, dopamine,* and *endogenous opioids,* neurotransmitters that regulate arousal, mood, well-being, and reward

Inadequate development of *spindle cells* in the *anterior cingulate,* resulting in a lack of integration between internal and external experience, boundary development, and identity formation

Heightened and prolonged stress creating *dysregulation of cortisol secretion* and *receptor development,* resulting in cell loss and decreased immunological functioning

Hippocampal compromise, resulting in decreased reality testing, memory functioning, and affective regulation; immunological compromise contributes to physical difficulties and ongoing physical distress and medical trauma

Anterior cingulate, insula, and hippocampal compromise, affecting the development and organization of the *parietal lobes,* affecting the somatic sense of self and boundary formation (Swinton, 2003)

Amygdaloid memory systems are primed to scan for, and react to, an ever-increasing number of abandonment cues through words, facial expressions, eye movements, and all other social behaviors (Schmahl et al., 2003a; Schmahl et al., 2003b)

Amygdaloid dyscontrol heightens the impact of early memory on adult functioning, decreases reality testing, and increases the impact of early bonding failures on contemporary relationships

Conditioned secretion of *endogenous endorphins* through self-harm is reinforced as a way of down-regulating overwhelming fear states

Decompensation in the face of interpretations may reflect a rapid shift from frontal to subcortical (amygdala) dominance, manifesting in an emotional storm and functional regression. Borderline patients lack the ability to be mindful of their own thoughts when they are emotionally aroused. That is, they lose the ability to think about their own thinking—which makes self-monitoring across emotional states almost impossible. The ability to self-reflect and regulate affect—two requirements of being able to benefit from interpretations—are severely impaired.

Activation of the amygdala (and the related physiological and biological changes) is at the heart of the modulation of emotional and traumatic memory (Cahill & McGaugh, 1998). The release of norepinephrine during the stress response serves to heighten the activation of the amygdala, inhibiting the neural networks (frontal–hippocampal) that could contextualize and attenuate the response (McGaugh, 1990). Both interpretations and abandonment cues trigger a kind of post traumatic flashback of life-threatening proportions for borderline patients. Patients become consumed and overwhelmed with fear and desperately try to stop their pain by any means possible. This disproportionate reaction is one reason why they have a catastrophic reaction to separation and are so afraid of being alone. These reactions in borderline patients may be our best window to the chaotic emotional world of early childhood.

Self-Harm

Adults who engage in repeated self-harm almost always describe childhoods that included abuse, neglect, cruel teasing, and shame at the hands of caretakers (Mazza & Reynolds, 1998; Pfeffer et al., 1997; Zoroglu et al., 2003). This correlation has led many theorists to explore the significance of self-harm as an ongoing psychic involvement with destructive parents. Abuse experiences are kept alive within networks of implicit social memory and intrude into conscious awareness when cued by criticism, rejection, or loss. Because of the correlation between negative attachment experiences and self-harm, suicide has been hypothesized to be a final act of compliance with the parents' perceived wish for the death of the child (Green, 1978).

Repeated suicide attempts are often unintentionally reinforced by the rapid attention of health care professionals, family, and friends (Schwartz, 1979). This form of attention becomes a means of affective regulation that parallels the distress calls of young primates, whose endorphin levels drop in the absence of the mother, then raise when the mother returns and calms her young. The appearance of health care professionals may do the same. I have worked with a number of clients who automatically and unconsciously translated their abandonment panic into suicidal thoughts and self-destructive behaviors.

Endogenous opioids also appear to be involved in severe cases of self-harm and suicide (van der Kolk, 1988; Villalba & Harrington, 2003). In case of injury, endorphins provide analgesia for pain to allow us to continue to fight or flee (Pitman et al., 1990). This endorphin system, originally used to cope with pain, was adapted by later evolving networks of attachment and bonding to reinforce affiliative behavior with positive emotional states. As we saw in Chapter 8, endorphin levels rise and fall and rise again in both infant and mother as they draw near one another, separate, and reunite. The endorphin system and its role in the modulation of attachment and proximity may be central to borderline pathology and account for the lack of treatment success with antidepressant medications, which target serotonergic and dopaminergic neurotransmitter systems (Corrigan et al., 2000; Winchel & Stanley, 1991).

The analgesic effects of these morphine-like substances may also account for the reports of reduced anxiety and sense of calm after cutting or burning. Research has demonstrated that self-harm decreases or terminates completely when patients are given a drug to block the soothing and reinforcing effects of endogenous opioids (Pitman et al., 1990; van der Kolk, 1988). Their release in response to fear and stress may help most individuals modulate emotional states and enhance coping and problem solving (Fanselow, 1986; Kirmayer & Carroll, 1987). This system may not become activated under normal conditions in borderline individuals, and self-harm might be a way to move past a higher threshold for endorphin release. This idea is supported by the fact that those who report analgesia during self-mutilation also show less pain sensitivity, even in states of calm (Bohus et al., 2000).

Self-Loathing

It seems clear that borderline personality has early psychological and neurobiological origins that result in fundamental disturbances of identity and emotion. The core of borderline experiences may be organized and stored within the early formation of the insula, anterior cingulate, OMPFC, and amygdala. One of the most fundamental emotional realities for the borderline client is a sense of profound shame. Shame, as we talked about in the previous chapter, is the experience of the self as defective, bad, and worthy of rejection. This feeling is almost never based on recalled behavior but rather on a bodily intuition that is more *felt* than thought. Many people with borderline personality disorder are exceptionally conscientious, careful to abide by the law, and keep their agreements with others to a fault. It seems as children, however, they experienced themselves as objects of disgust. This experience then becomes the core sense of self. To become aware of the self for a borderline patient is to feel repulsive and unlovable, and launches him or her into a spiral of internal chaos. When these patients look within, all they feel is pain. To feel is to feel badly about the self.

Organized like a map of the body, the insula cortex and anterior cingulate connect primitive bodily states with the experience and expression of emotion, behavior, and cognition; both structures are involved with mediating the gamut of emotions from disgust to love (Bartels & Zeki, 2000; Calder et al., 2003; Carr et al., 2003; Phan et al., 2002). It appears that the insula is central to the organization and experience of our core sense of self in space and our ability to distinguish between self and others (Bechara & Naqvi, 2004; Critchley et al., 2004; Farrer & Frith, 2002; Gundel et al., 2004). Interestingly, both the insula and anterior cingulate become activated when subjects are asked to recall behavior for which they felt ashamed (Shin et al., 2000).

Disgust is a very primitive emotion shaped by evolution to make us reflexively retreat from potential danger. The facial expressions of disgust depict an attempt to expel food from the mouth and back away from the object of our distaste. Our aversion to corpses and bodily damage puts us on guard and makes us wary of both potential predators and toxic microorganisms. Overall, the emotion of disgust is one of avoidance and expulsion, either from the body or from one's presence. Given what we have learned thus far, the possibility exists that the early experiences of borderline individuals may lead them to pair the sense of self with disgust. This pairing could occur when feeling pushed away, abandoned, or seeing a look of disgust on a caretaker's face. The extreme reactions seen in borderline individuals may be a function of the need to escape an unbearable self.

Given its functions and early development, the insula may be responsible for the basic associations between a sense of one's bodily states and what come to be labeled through language as emotions. For example, in the context of secure attachment, the insula may associate feelings of love with the organization of self-awareness. These early neural connections may establish a lifelong sense of self-love, well-being, and an expectation of positive outcomes. On the other hand, if the infant experiences neglect, abuse, or sees disgust or despair in the eyes of caretakers, the insula may come to associate the experience of self with disgust, shame, pain, discomfort, and rejection. For these individuals, to become self-aware would trigger despair, rage, and self-loathing; in these instances, the self would be something to avoid at all costs.

Disorders of Extreme Stress

Van der Kolk and his colleagues have made a compelling argument for the possibility that borderline personality disorder shares a common etiology with other disorders in terms of early and severe stress. They (and others) cite somatization disorder, dissociative identity disorders, alexithymia, and borderline personality disorder as different symptomatic outcomes of early traumatic experiences (Maaranen et al., 2004; Maaranen et al., 2005; Nijenhuis et al., 2003; van der Kolk et al., 1996). In field trials for the *DSM–IV* (American Psychiatric Association, 2000), they found that all these patients shared difficult histories and suffer from anxiety, identity disturbances, blocked affect, and severe emotional and cognitive dysregulation, as seen in PTSD. This finding led them to propose a broader category that cuts across previous diagnostic lines. Their new diagnosis, called disorders of extreme stress not otherwise specified (DESNOS), is described as containing the following symptoms (Luxenberg et al., 2001):

- Impairment of affective regulation
- Compulsive and self-destructive behaviors
- Amnesia and dissociation
- Somatization
- Distorted relations with others
- Loss of sustaining beliefs

Each of the disorders subsumed by DESNOS in the DSM represents different strategies of adaptation to early and overwhelming impingements. Dissociators employ the imaginative capacities of the frontal lobes to shut off the experience of emotional pain, creating alternate experiences, worlds, and identities. Those with PTSD suffer from the oscillating dysregulation of emotional arousal when cued by both conscious and unconscious associations. Somatizers and alexthymics demonstrate a disconnection between the cognitive and emotional processing that is centered in the left and right cortices (Spitzer et al., 2004). Alexithymia in adulthood correlates with having been an unwanted child, and attachment patterns tend to be insecure, either avoidant/dismissing or preoccupied and fearful (Fukunishi et al., 1999; Taylor & Bagby, 2004). The degree of emotional facial expressions is negatively correlated with somatic symptoms. Put another way, the less a person reveals emotions in his or her facial expressions, the more somatic symptoms they tend to experience (Malatesta, Jonas, & Izard, 1987).

DESNOS offers a unifying construct that ties together multiple diagnoses with similar causes and symptoms. Examining the process of the brain's adaptation to early interpersonal trauma may provide a way of understanding borderline personality disorder that will help us better treat this painful and debilitating social condition. Early stress disrupts the growth, integration, and regulation of the many neural networks that contribute to healthy cognitive and emotional functioning. The fact that interpersonal trauma results in a higher risk of DESNOS than natural disasters and accidents points to the vital importance of early relationships and the profound impact that disruptions of bonding, attachment, and loving care have on the developing social brain.

Chapter 19

Psychopathy: The Antisocial Brain

To measure a man, measure his heart.
—Malcolm Forbes

Some kids don't play fair! They tell lies, cheat at games, and play too rough. These kids have trouble at home, trouble at school, and gravitate toward other kids with similar problems. Unfazed by rules, they challenge authority at every opportunity and seem incapable of engaging in positive relationships. If you meet the parents of some of these kids, it is easy to see that the cause of their behavior stems from the way they are treated at home. Sadly, such parents are often harsh and neglectful over-aged children themselves. Like the proverbial acorns, schoolyard bullies merely demonstrate what they have learned while standing in the shadow of their parents. Still, we must be careful not to use too broad a brush: Often, from the harshest, most deprived and abusive homes come the most tender and loving people. On the other hand—and to the heartbreak of those closest to them—the cruelest killers sometimes can come from loving homes.

Although most children grow out of bullying and settle down to become good citizens, some continue on this destructive course into adulthood. As children and adolescents, they were labeled delinquents or diagnosed as suffering from conduct disorder or oppositional defiant disorder. As adults, they are labeled as psychopaths or sociopaths or diagnosed as having antisocial personality disorder. Regardless of the label, we can agree that the phenomenon of antisocial behavior exists and that its cost to society is high.

Think about the characteristics that make for "good citizens." We expect individuals to be aware of, and adjust to, the needs of others, recognize and conform to the social norms, and live by the rules. The needs of an individual are weighed against the needs of others, and negotiations are employed to create the most good for the most people. Antisocial individuals, in contrast, are a tribe of one, conforming to the primitive mandate of personal survival. In some ways, they haven't participated in the eons of social evolution but remain in a premammalian world, disconnected from the social mind of those around them. Although thinkers such as Machiavelli, Nietzsche, and Rand have extolled the virtues of the "*Ubermensch*," and society even lionizes those who gain prominence and success through use of force, the antisocial personality has not proven to be a successful strategy for survival. For humans, a sole focus on personal goals does not correlate with broad evolutionary success.

Antisocial Personality Disorder

As a diagnostic category, antisocial personality disorder has been an admixture of scientific theory, metapsychology, and moral judgments. Murderers, criminals, and delinquents have been lumped together with victims of trauma and prejudice who engage in criminal acts for emotional, socioeconomic, and political reasons. Because the nonscientific nature of what we call antisocial personality has become increasingly obvious, there have been recent attempts to clarify and refine the diagnosis (Hall et al., 2004). The focus has been on the kinds of behaviors and attitudes engaged in by these individuals, such as the following:

• Failure to conform to social norms, the law, or work requirements
• Deceitfulness
• Lack of empathy
• Lack of remorse for actions that have harmed others
• Impulsive behavior and lack of foresight
• Aggressiveness and irritability
• Reckless disregard for the safety of self and others

Even within a narrower definition this is not a homogeneous group; patients identified as antisocial differ on physiological and neuropsychological measures as well as in their cultural, educational, and economic backgrounds (Ishikawa & Raine, 2001; Lindberg et al., 2004; Seguin, 2004). Although antisocial behavior is a complex phenomenon, correlations exist between antisocial types of behavior and deficits in affect regulation, impulse control, and the ability to relate to the experiences of others. Many antisocial individuals have childhood backgrounds of neglect and abuse, often with parents who seem to be antisocial themselves. The relative impact of template genetics in predisposing an individual to antisocial personality disorder and the negative neurodevelopmental impact of aversive parenting and abuse are unknown. Thus, determining a causal etiology of antisocial personality disorder at this point is simply impossible. However, it is clear that both nature and nurture certainly appear to play a role in the creation of the antisocial individual (Rutter, 1997).

Antisocial behavior and incarceration are modulated by a number of broader social factors within families and cultures. More sophisticated antisocial individuals with business degrees are able to steal millions of dollars, stash them in foreign bank accounts, and bribe those who would hold them accountable (Thornquist & Zuckerman, 1995). People in prison, on the other hand, tend to be from ethnic minority backgrounds and of lower socioeconomic status. However, income and education do not immunize a person from antisocial personality disorder. In searching for subjects with antisocial personality disorder for his research, Adrian Raine found that he was more likely to find such people at a temporary employment agency than in prison.

When neuroscientists look at the symptoms of antisocial personality disorder, they often find deficits in the orbital medial prefrontal cortex. However, different frontal structures, when compromised, may lead to different symptomatic expressions (Bigler, 2001; Dolan & Park, 2002). Although OMPFC damage usually correlates with antisocial problems, physical aggression often results from damage to dorsal lateral prefrontal areas (Bernstein et al., 2000; Kosson, 1998; Seguin, 2004), while convicted murderers demonstrate lower glucose metabolism in both lateral and medial prefrontal cortex (Raine et al., 1994). At this early stage of exploration, we need to be cautious about assigning "blame" to the OMPFC for antisocial behavior, keeping in mind that most dysfunctions result from the failure of multiple systems to develop, integrate, and function properly.

Arousal

Although antisocial individuals generally don't appear to differ from others in terms of anxiety, they have been shown to have distinctly different patterns of autonomic arousal (Schmitt & Newman, 1999). Those who believe that a lack of arousal is at the root of antisocial behavior make the case that a lack of bodily reaction to environmental cues and punishment keep a person from learning from experience and behaving in prosocial ways. Antisocial individuals appear to have less activation to aversive stimuli when either they or others are experiencing it. The studies in Table 19.1 all demonstrate differences between antisocial and normal individuals in automatic reactions to punishment and negative stimulus cues.

These studies report deficits not only in arousal but also in the networks involved in mirroring and resonance, which would allow these individuals to connect at a visceral level with their interpersonal worlds. Functional magnetic resonance imaging (fMRI) scans of criminal antisocial

Table 19.1. **Abnormal Physiological Measures in Antisocial Personality Disorder**

Antisocial individuals show deficits in:	
Autonomic arousal	Raine, 1996
Attention to meaningful social cues	Patrick et al., 1994
Orienting response	Raine, 1987
Sustained attention	Raine, 1987
Electrodermal responses to distress cues[1]	Hare, 1972
Lack of fear to adverse events	Herpertz et al., 2001b
Antisocial individuals tend to have:	
Lower heart rates following punishment	Arnett et al., 1993
Fewer skin conductance responses following punishment[1]	Arnett et al., 1993

[1] One aspect of autonomic nervous system arousal is perspiration, which can be measured through increases in the skin's electrical conductance.

individuals reveal significantly less affect-related activation in limbic regions of the social brain—including the amygdala, hippocampus, ventral striatum, and cingulate—than nonpsychopathic criminals (Kiehl et al., 2001). The scans also demonstrate lower levels of activation in the amygdala and lateral frontal areas during habituation using visual or verbal stimuli (Patrick et al., 1994; Schneider et al., 2000; Williamson, Harpur, & Hare, 1991).

Whereas antisocial people react normally to simple unconditioned stimuli such as an unexpected loud noise, they react with abnormally low autonomic activation to social stimuli such as faces and expressions of emotions (Damasio, Tranel, & Damasio, 1990). For most individuals, pictures of faces activate multiple areas of the social brain, including the orbital frontal cortex, insula, anterior cingulate, and amygdala. These are the circuits discussed in earlier chapters that are involved in the recognition of faces, facial expressions, and monitoring direction of gaze. By contrast, antisocial individuals demonstrate only superficial amygdala activation in response to faces and are less accurate in recognizing fearful faces (Blair & Coles, 2000; Blair et al., 2004; Montagne et al., 2005; Veit et al., 2002). Because there is no evidence of basic visual or language deficits in these people, the failures must lie in circuits that process social information (Lykken, 1957).

Empathy

Many see antisocial personality disorder primarily as the result of a lack of empathy (Soderstrom, 2003). Empathic thinking not only requires access to one's own emotions but also the cognitive flexibility and affect regulation to pull back from the environment, put our needs aside, and imagine the feelings of others. Because empathy requires conceptual understanding, emotional attunement, and the ability to regulate one's own affect, damage to either the dorsal lateral or orbital frontal areas impairs different aspects of empathic behavior (Eslinger, 1998). When damage to orbital frontal areas happens early in life, behavioral deficits coincide with a lack of factual knowledge about social and moral norms (Anderson et al., 1999) In fact, general damage to the prefrontal cortex at any time during life can result in a loss of empathic capacities (Dolan, 1999).

Children with antisocial tendencies have difficulty recognizing and understanding fear and sadness in the facial expressions of others (Blair et al., 2001; Richell et al., 2003; Stevens et al., 2001). This ability, central to developing a theory of the emotional state of another, may be a key component of antisocial symptomatology. The ability to read facial expressions rests on the functioning of the OMPFC and amygdala in conjunction with properly functioning visual processing systems.

Patients with traumatic damage to the OMPFC or to the right posterior frontal lobes show impaired emotional resonance, whereas damage to the dorsal lateral prefrontal areas results in a loss of the cognitive flexibility required for empathy (Eslinger, 1998; Shamay-Tsoory et al., 2003). Antisocial patients do have a theory of mind of the other, but instead of using it to connect, they use it to get their way. Their lack of empathy allows them to objectify and use others for their own needs. Homicides committed by antisocial individuals are not crimes of passion. The folk term "cold-blooded killer" reflects our instinctual understanding that some kill without emotion or arousal—the ultimate disconnection from the social mind (Woodworth & Porter, 2002).

Chuck—What's the Problem?

When I first met Chuck, he was an inmate in a maximum security prison in Western Massachusetts. He had grown up in a tough neighborhood in South Boston, one of six children of an alcoholic mother and violent father. He recalled nights sleeping on the front steps or wandering around the neighborhood waiting for his father to fall asleep—the only way he could avoid being beaten. He never did well in school and found it impossible to sit still or pay attention in class. The nuns punished him constantly, but it never affected his behavior. People in the neighborhood never liked him, and mothers kept their kids away from him, so he mostly played alone. Chuck spoke of his history of alienation blithely, as if he could see no connection between his behavior and the reactions others have to him. In fact, he accepted his behavior, social isolation, and punishment as simple facts of life.

"I got a bad rep early in life," he laughed. "When I was about 8, I put some lighter fluid on a big dog that hung around the block and lit him up. The dumb bastard just kept yelping and running, fanning the flames higher and higher. It was a warm day, a Sunday afternoon, and everybody was hanging around the block. They all knew I did it. Some guys tried to catch the dog to put out the fire, but it just kept running away. Some guys from the neighborhood came over and kicked the shit out of me, called me Crazy Chuck from then on. That's what they call me in here." When I asked him why he set the dog on fire, he replied, "I don't know. I guess I wanted to see what would happen." There seemed to be no evidence of reflection, remorse, or a perceived connection between his actions and the dog's experience.

Chuck was serving consecutive life sentences for a double murder. He had broken into a home to steal money so he could go out drinking. While he was looking through the dresser drawers, the elderly couple who lived in the house came home. "They started yelling at me, sayin', 'What are you doing in our house, get out of here.' It pissed me off, being yelled at, so I started wailing on them. I didn't mean to kill them, but they were old and I thumped them pretty good. I guess that's what did it." From Chuck's perspective, they had insulted him and got what they deserved.

He had never had a close friendship or a romantic relationship. He always worked alone whenever he engaged in any criminal activity and experienced only brief sexual relationships with women. He seemed to know he was different from other people. "I know people feel things that I don't. Like at the trial, the judge asked me if I had any remorse about killing those folks. I said I didn't understand what he meant. He asked me if I felt bad, or guilty, or sad about what I had done. I thought about it for awhile and told him I didn't think so. I don't think I know what those feelings are. The judge told me he pitied me. I told him I didn't get that one either."

Another memory he shared with me was from a time when he was working on a gardening crew. Chuck was standing near a road with a shovel, digging a trench for underground pipe, when he saw a motorcycle driving toward him down the road. He felt a rush of anger as the rider approached. "When he was just about to pass me, I held the shovel up in front of his face and knocked him off the bike. He was knocked out, and the bike crashed into one of our trucks. What a shame, that bike was perfect before the accident. If I ever get out of here, I'm gonna get a bike like that and ride to California." I never challenged his perceptions—and I always sat close to the door. I never developed a sense of connection with Chuck. I had encountered many tough people in my life, but he was the first one who left me convinced that, in his eyes, my humanity held no value.

Listening to Chuck's stories, it was hard not to shake my head in shock and surprise. His reactions to salient aspects of a situation and how he assessed consequences were always at an oblique angle to my expectations. His behaviors were triggered by impulses and emotions that were acted upon with no conscience, inhibition, or memory for the future. For Chuck, only the present moment existed. Most strikingly, he had no sense of how his actions impacted other people, or that they had feelings, needs, or experienced pain.

Chuck seemed to live a life of restless prowling, a cracked mirror of consciousness in a world of distorted objects. Lacking a sense of direction or any kind of plan, he moved through his days like a shark, swimming forward and finding food. Chuck helped me to understand the poverty of an antisocial life. Without resonance, attachment, or empathy, Chuck had never been, nor could he ever be, part of the social world.

Focus on the Prefrontal Cortex

The frontal lobes, along with all of the other systems of the social brain we have explored, allow us to have a theory of the minds and hearts of others. They allow us to use this information to modulate and guide our interactions with those around us. The array of socioemotional abnormalities found in antisocial personality reflects the range of functions that are organized and regulated by frontal–limbic circuits (Müller et al., 2003). Research with antisocial, delinquent, and violent individuals has contributed to our understanding of socially destructive behavior in relation to brain functioning. Adolescent delinquents show delayed frontal lobe development (Bauer & Hesselbrock, 2003; Ponitus & Ruttiger, 1976), and violent psychiatric patients demonstrate lower metabolism in medial temporal and prefrontal regions than nonviolent patients (Juhasz et al., 2001; Rule et al., 2002; Volkow et al., 1995).

Studies of adult antisocial individuals reveal fewer neuronal cell bodies in the frontal lobes and hippocampi suggesting either inadequate growth or too much cell loss during development (Laakso et al., 2001, 2002; Raine et al., 2004). Serotonin, a key neurotransmitter in frontal systems, is also found in low levels in violent criminals and correlates with spontaneous aggression, impulsivity, and thrill seeking (Brown et al., 1989; Mehlman et al., 1994; Soderstrom et al., 2001). Murderers demonstrated significantly lower glucose metabolism in both lateral and medial portions of the frontal lobes in the absence of either brain damage or decreased metabolism in other areas (Raine et al., 1994).

The neurology literature is replete with examples of "acquired pseudo-psychopathic personality" individuals who behave in antisocial ways after sustaining a brain injury (Meyers et al., 1992). The classic case from the 19th century is that of Phineas Gage, a young New Hampshire railroad foreman known for his maturity, leadership skills, and "well-balanced" mind. An accident sent a one-and-a-quarter-inch-wide iron rod through his head, obliterating much of his orbital medial prefrontal cortex. Although free of "neurobehavioral" deficits such as aphasia, paralysis, or sensory loss, Gage was "no longer Gage" (Harlow, 1868). After the accident, he was unable to control his emotions, sustain goal-oriented behavior, or adhere to the conventions of social behavior. He went from being a young man with a promising future to an aimless and unsuccessful drifter (Benson, 1994; Damasio et al., 1994; Stuss et al., 1992).

An intact and well-developed prefrontal cortex enables us to maintain a simultaneous sense of self and others that is necessary for interpersonal strategizing and decision-making (McCabe et al., 2001). Tasks of moral reasoning simultaneously activate the prefrontal lobes and most of the centers of the social brain (Berthoz et al., 2002; Mah et al., 2005; Moll, de Oliveira-Souza, Bramati et al., 2002; Moll, de Oliveira-Souza, Eslingler et al., 2002). Whereas the dorsal lateral and orbital frontal regions are physically contiguous, they differ in their connectivity, neural architecture, biochemistry, and function (Morgan & LeDoux, 1995; Wilson et al., 1993). The orbital frontal areas, first to evolve and develop in our species, perform executive functions biased toward the right hemisphere (Barbas, 1995; Schore, 1994). The dorsal lateral prefrontal areas specialize in problem solving and maintaining attention to a task through time.

Research with primates has demonstrated that whereas both dorsal lateral and orbital frontal areas play a role in inhibition and control, the dorsal lateral areas are involved when decisions involve how to deploy attention, and the orbital frontal regions take over when decisions are based on affective information (Dias et al., 1996; Teasdale et al., 1999). The medial regions appear to monitor whether what we are doing is leading to desirable outcomes. If not, it signals the dorsal areas to redeploy attention, adjust behavior, and try something different (Ridderinkhof et al., 2004). In the other direction, stimulation of the lateral areas can inhibit attention to emotional problems, such as occurs in the commonplace defense of distracting ourselves from difficult emotions (Yamasaki et al., 2002). In its respective affiliations with the right and left hemispheres, the OMPFC is strongly activated along with negative emotional right-hemispheric processing, whereas the lateral regions become more active in positive emotional states processed in the left hemisphere (Northoff et al., 2000).

At present, most research seems to support the idea that the OMPFC is at the heart of antisocial pathology (Dolan, 2002). We know that this structure is vital to the interpretation of complex social events, linking them with emotional value, and activating the autonomic nervous system (Hariri et al., 2000; Mah et al., 2004). It has been hypothesized that one role of the OMPFC is to generate an expectation of the reaction of others, which we use to direct and modulate our behavior (Blair & Cipolotti, 2000). The orbital regions mediate primary reinforcers such as taste and touch, sustaining a representation and expectation of reward that maintains goal-directed behavior (Gallagher et al., 1999; O'Doherty et al., 2001, 2002; Rolls, 2000a; Schultz, Tremblay, & Hollerman, 2000). The OMPFC also calculates the magnitude of reward or punishment value, such as winning or losing money while gambling or using others as soothing objects, as in the development of attachment schema (Damasio, 1994; O'Doherty et al., 2001; Rolls, 2000b; Tremblay & Schultz, 1999; Wantanabe, 1996).

Many studies with antisocial individuals have found impairments of the OMPFC but not the dorsal lateral areas (LaPierre et al., 1995; Mitchell et al., 2002). For example, patients with intermittent bouts of explosive anger show the same test results as those with damage to the OMPFC. People with damage to either orbital medial or dorsal lateral regions have difficulty recognizing facial expressions, gambling successfully, and identifying smells (Best, Williams, & Coccaro, 2002; Mitchell et al., 2002).

Neither group is good at inhibiting responses that result in monetary punishment or using subtle cues that others give to modulate or guide behavior (Newman & Kosson, 1986; Newman et al., 1990; Newman et al., 1997).

We also need the OMPFC to appreciate humor. Frontal damage, especially on the right side, often deprives its victim of the ability to comprehend jokes (Goel & Dolan, 2001; Shammi & Stuss, 1999). To "get" a joke we have to both appreciate the juxtaposition of information and get an emotional jolt from our reward system. The OMPFC, at the interface of emotional and cognitive processing, is the likely candidate for the job. The role of humor is vast in social functioning: We enjoy laughing, making others laugh, and we inject all sorts of chuckles and smiles while we interact. Laughter in conversation, in the absence of anything funny, greases the wheels of social communication, tells others that we are safe to relax with, and to let our guard down. Chuck never laughed.

Antisocial people lack a sense of humor, and, tragically, there is nothing funny about being antisocial. They also lack emotional resonance, empathy, and any sense of how their behavior is experienced by others. Based on our present knowledge, the prefrontal cortex is a vital component of the systems responsible for receiving, sending, and interpreting messages across the social synapse. Whatever the cause of antisocial personality disorder is eventually discovered to be, the answer will almost certainly involve the prefrontal cortex.

Chapter 20

Autism:
The Asocial Brain

The more I became aware of the world around me,
the more I became afraid. Other people were my en-
emies, and reaching out to me was their weapon . . .
—Donna Williams, 1992, p. 5

When you work in a psychiatric clinic for young children, you are often faced with having to assess whether a child is autistic. Spotting autistic symptoms is not all that difficult. What is difficult is making an educated guess about whether the symptoms amount to a diagnosis or are simply an aspect of a particular child's pattern of neurological growth. Many children who do not turn out to be autistic have some autistic symptoms during development. I was trained to believe that it is best to err on the side of diagnosing autism so that a child could get the earliest intervention possible if, in fact, he or she does turn out to be autistic. What is most difficult is giving the bad news to anxious and frightened parents.

Jason—A World Apart

I arrived at work one morning to find that I had been scheduled to evaluate a 4-year-old boy. Because of her son's unusual behaviors and increasing silence, Jason's mother had called a few weeks earlier at the encouragement of her best friend. As I sat in my office looking over the intake form, I found that Jason's parents were concerned about his disinterest in playing with them and were particularly upset because he didn't like to be touched. The Avilas also had a 6-year-old daughter who was "doing fine," according to the paperwork. I looked up at the clock and saw that it was just about time for their appointment.

As I approached the waiting room, I saw a young girl singing and bouncing a ball. Spotting my approach, she ran to greet me. "Are you the doctor?" she asked. "We're here because my brother won't talk. That's my family over there. Do you have candy in your office like *my* doctor?" By the time she stopped asking me questions, I had no idea which one to answer first. Fortunately, her parents approached, and Mrs. Avila quieted Sonia by gently pulling her close and letting her snuggle between them. Smiling, Mrs. Avila said, "I have one that won't talk and one that never stops." I liked this family immediately and was touched by the warmth and concern I could see in their faces.

Out of the corner of my eye, I noticed Jason lying on the floor under a chair. He was on his stomach with one eye at carpet level. With his hand, he was rolling a toy car back and forth in front of his face. He was slow and deliberate in his actions, completely content and oblivious to the rest of us. Mr. Avila shrugged and said, "He can do that all day long. If it isn't the car, it's turning the lights on and off, kicking his closet door, or stacking and unstacking his blocks. He's in his own world." As we all walked back to my office, Jason stayed focused on his car as Sonia described what was on Jason's mind, how excited he was about taking the tests, and that he really wanted some candy. As the Avilas and I smiled at one another, I wondered whether Sonia was trying to distract her parents from the pain of their son's increasing distance from them.

From his parents' perspective, Jason appeared to develop normally for the first 2 years. At a certain point, however, his language seemed to start "going backwards" and he seemed to care less and less about other people. "He stopped looking at us," said Mr. Avila. "Even if I hold his head and point his eyes at me, he just looks away." He seemed to prefer to sleep in the space between his bed and the wall and would often push his head into the corner. He would also sit and rock, repeatedly tap his head, and sometimes scream for no apparent reason. Sonia added, "That's really scary when he does that!" By the end of the testing sessions, it was clear that Jason had many symptoms of autism and I would have the job of telling this to his parents. Of course, they had already suspected as much, so it was not a complete shock. Even so, it was upsetting for all of us to face the reality of the diagnosis and the long road ahead.

Autism is a developmental brain disorder characterized by a radical withdrawal from others. Autistic children have problems with language, motor movement, and sensory processing, but nothing is as devastating to their parents as their difficulties with bonding and attachment. Although the cause of autism remains a mystery, it appears that victims suffer from multiple neurodevelopmental deficits that impact many networks of the social brain. Children with autism have difficulties with such basic building blocks of attachment as cuddling, eye contact, and being soothed by another's touch, decimating their ability to connect with those around them. The primary symptom clusters of autism include (1) deficits in social interaction, (2) restricted and repetitive patterns of behavior, interest, and activity, and (3) dysfunctions in communication. Children with mild to moderate deficits in the first two categories are often diagnosed with Asperger's disorder. The clinical features of Asperger's focus on a lack of empathy, one-sided social interactions, and intense absorption in circumscribed topics (Aronowitz et al., 1997).

Individuals with Asperger's disorder are often socially isolated but not "unaware" of the presence of others, whereas those with severe autism seem to be oblivious to others. Although they are often self-described "loners," individuals with Asperger's express an interest in making friends but are thwarted by their social awkwardness and insensitivity to interpersonal communications (Klin & Volkmar, 1995). Although the relationship between autism and Asperger's is unclear, many feel that Asperger's represents a less severe form of autism (Bishop, 1989; Lotspeich et al., 2004; Schopler, 1985; Szatmari, Tuff, Finlayson, & Bartolucci, 1990; Tantum, 1988; Wing, 1988). Epidemiological variables related to sex ratio, family history, and the presence of neurological disease suggest similar etiologies (Szatmari, Bremner, & Nagy, 1989). Whether autism and Asperger's are discrete disorders or reflect degrees of severity along a continuum of a common, undetermined neuropathology, remains unknown.

Deficits of Social Perception

Individuals suffering from autism or Asperger's disorder have difficulty reading facial expressions and are especially deficient in recognizing fear (Grossman et al., 2000; Pelphrey et al., 2002). It is unknown at the present time whether face processing deficits are a cause or an effect of their social withdrawal (Grelotti et al., 2002). When the brains of autistic individuals are scanned while they are asked to assess facial expression, they demonstrate significantly different brain activation patterns than normal subjects: They tend to analyze separate features of a face rather than processing the face as a whole. Autistic subjects also demonstrate either weak or absent activation in the usual face recognition system and show idiosyncratic activation in a variety of sites normally used for the recognition and analysis of inanimate objects (Pierce et al., 2001; Schultz et al., 2000). When given a stack of pictures of peoples' faces with varying expressions, nonautistic children sorted them into piles based on facial expressions, whereas autistic children tended to sort them based on the type of hat they were wearing (Weeks & Hobson, 1987).

Individuals with autism show deficits in reading biological motion but not in reading the movement of geometric forms (Blake et al., 2003). Mirror systems are also impaired in autistic individuals; it is easy to see that damage to mirror systems could be a severe handicap to learning through observation, verbal and nonverbal communication, and emotional attunement and empathy (Williams, Whiten, Suddendorf, & Perrett, 2001). Imagine what it would be like to utilize brain systems designed for simple stationary objects to analyze the overwhelming amount of moment-to-moment information coming from another person across the social synapse. This deficit may account for some of the anxiety and confusion experienced by autistic and Asperger's patients in interpersonal situations. What would it be like for you if the objects around you began to make sounds, interacted with each other, and approached you in unpredictable and frightening ways? For those with autism, human behavior is the stuff of nightmares.

Children with autism tend to avoid making eye contact with other people and are relatively blind to the significance of the direction of eye gaze (Baron-Cohen, Baldwin et al. 1997; Charman et al., 1997; Phillips,

Baron-Cohen, & Rutter, 1992; Richer & Coss, 1976). When autistic individuals are asked to look at the eyes of another person and judge what he or she might be thinking, there is no activation of the amygdala. This and other research findings have led to an amygdala-based theory of the cause of autism (Baron-Cohen et al., 1999, 2000; Howard et al., 2000; Sweeten et al., 2002). Although amygdala dysfunction is a component of autism, its diverse symptomatology speaks against the amygdala being the only cause of the illness.

The Autistic Brain

Dysregulation of sensory, motor, cognitive, and affective processing suggests the presence of compromise in multiple cortical and subcortical neural networks. Despite this wide dispersement of change, neuroscientists search for a "home" for autism somewhere in the brain (Rapin, 1999). Could it be the frontal lobes? The amygdala? The brainstem? The answer appears to be yes, yes, and yes! Table 20.1 outlines some of the brain abnormalities found in autism thus far.

Based on the current research, it appears that if we are to come to an understanding of the neurobiological causes of autism, we will first have to learn how the many systems of the brain grow and interconnect with one another. Making sense of an illness that simultaneously involves disturbances of gait, language, eye contact, and abstract reasoning requires a working model of the central nervous system (CNS) that addresses the interrelationship of systems through many levels of neural processing. In the meantime, this system-by-system exploration is an important first step in unraveling the mystery. As we have seen above, many areas of the social brain have already been found to be abnormal in autism, as are the neural networks connecting the cortex, limbic system, and cerebellum (Baron-Cohen et al., 2000).

The cerebellum is interesting to explore because the diversity of symptomatology found in autism matches the wide range of computational, timing, and regulatory functions this structure provides to the rest of the CNS. Let's take a closer look at the cerebellum not because it is necessarily the key to autism, but because it is a structure we have not yet discussed as a hub of social processing. This exploration will also illustrate

Table 20.1. **Abnormalities Found in the Brains of Autistic Individuals**

Reduced brainstem size	Hashimoto et al., 1995; Ornitz, 1985, 1988
Abnormalities of the ventricle system	Damasio et al., 1980; Hauser et al., 1975
Lower levels of cingulate activity	Haznedar et al., 2000
Hypometabolism in limbic structures	Haznedar et al., 2000
Structural abnormalities of the cerebellum and limbic forebrain	Bauman & Kemper, 1988; Ciaranello & Ciaranello, 1995; Courchesne et al., 1995; Gaffney et al., 1987
Reduced corpus callosum size	Egaas et al., 1995
Delayed maturation of the frontal cortex	Zilbovicius et al., 1995
Abnormal right orbitofrontal development	Sabbagh, 2004
Abnormal neuronal growth and pruning in the cortex, limbic structures, cerebellum, and brainstem	Abell et al., 1999; Aylward et al., 1999; Bachevalier, 1994; Courchesne et al., 2003; Levitt et al., 2003; Piven et al., 1990; Saitoh et al., 2001
Amygdala dysfunctions	Amaral, 2002; Baron-Cohen, 1995; Grelotti et al., 2005; Rojas et al., 2004; Schultz, 2005; Schumann et al., 2004
Glial guidance abnormalities	Courchesne, 2001
Lack of cerebral coordination	Chiron et al., 1995; Deb & Thompson, 1998; Escalante-Mead et al., 2003; Herbert et al., 2002; Horwitz, 1988
Left-hemispheric deficits	Dawson, 1983; Hoffman & Prior, 1982
Right-hemispheric deficits	Weintraub & Mesulam, 1983

how many of the networks of the social brain discussed thus far depend on the proper functioning of subcortical structures. There is considerable evidence of structural irregularities in the cerebellums of autistic individuals, and two genetic-based disorders—fragile X and Joubert syndrome—result in impaired cerebellar growth and symptoms of autism (Holroyd, Reiss, & Bryan, 1991; Joubert et al., 1969; Reiss, 1988; Reiss et al., 1988).

Focus on the Cerebellum

Located beneath the occipital lobes and behind the brainstem, the cerebellum is a vastly complex structure. It contains almost as many neurons as the cerebral cortex, and each cell is designed to have as many as 1,000,000 connections to adjacent neurons (Stein, 1986). This neural architecture speaks to the cerebellum's remarkable computational capacity. The cerebellum evolved from the vestibular system and is concerned with the coordination of motor function, the control of muscle tone, and the maintenance of equilibrium (Brodal, 1992). The core of the cerebellum is called the *vermis,* and it is still central to functions related to balance and equilibrium. As the brain evolved, so did the need and capacity for increasingly precise motor movements, expressions in communication, and symbolic representations.

The outer lobes of the cerebellum evolved and work in partnership with the association areas of the cerebral cortex (Junck et al., 1988; Leiner et al., 1991; Passingham, 1975). The evidence suggests that the cerebellum is involved in the neural networks of higher-order processes via modular processing loops that provide timing functions for a diverse set of perceptual and emotional tasks (Keele & Ivry, 1990; Leiner et al., 1991; Raymond, Lisberger, & Mauk, 1996). It is believed that the cerebellum duplicates its role in the motor system in the other hierarchical systems in which it participates (Berntson & Torello, 1982). Its coordinating role may be important in the modulation and timing for language and affective regulation. In fact, many of the nonmotor dysfunctions caused by damage to the cerebellum are often attributed to the frontal lobes (Barinaga, 1996; Ghez, 1991; Schmahmann, 1991).

The cerebellar projections to the prefrontal cortex include Brodmann's area 8, which contains frontal eye fields, and areas 44 and 45, which comprise Broca's area on the left side of the brain. Disturbances of eye contact, eye tracking, shared gaze, shifting attention, and language are all symptoms of autism. Both stimulus regulation and smooth temporal sequencing are impaired in autism and Asperger's, resulting in a dysregulation of the experience of the body in time and space. Loss of sensory regulation would result in the avoidance of unpredictable stimulation (especially from other people) and the preference for sameness and predictability. The rhythmic self-stimulation and need for predictability seen in these individuals could provide an internal substitute for an absent or chaotic internal regulation of sensory input. Table 20.2 summarizes the effects of damage to the cerebellum.

The cerebellum would be a likely structure in which to store the procedural elements (sequences) of learned experience, which serve as building blocks for the experience of bodily coherence and time sequencing

Table 20.2. **Functions Affected by Damage to the Cerebellum**

Mental imagery	Decety et al., 1990
Emotion and cognition	Schmahmann, 2004
Anticipatory planning	Leiner et al., 1986
Shifting attention	Akshoomoff & Courchesne, 1994
Language	Silveri et al., 1994
Affective regulation	Gutzmann & Kuhl, 1987; Heath, 1977

(Inhoff et al., 1989). The sequential organization of sensory, motor, and autonomic state transitions organized by, and stored within, the cerebellum may serve ongoing affect-regulation, attachment, and positive self-image (Gutzmann & Kuhl, 1987). This automatic visceral regulation may contribute to the maintenance of positive emotional states, especially when we are under stress, paralleling how an intact vestibular system frees us from focusing on balance so we can learn to dance. It has been suggested that the cerebellum contains early sensory–motor memories of "good mothering" that contribute to later emotional well-being and affect regulation (Levin, 1991).

The Brain of Temple Grandin

Temple Grandin shared her experiences of Asperger's disorder in her autobiography, *Thinking in Pictures* (Grandin, 1995). Despite the challenges of Asperger's, she holds a doctorate in animal science and is a professor at Colorado State University. I had the pleasure of meeting Dr. Grandin at a conference and having lunch with her. She was enthusiastic, interested in sharing her experiences and ideas, and extremely articulate. What was most striking, however, was her complete blindness to social signals. For example, immediately following lunch I had to present a talk in another part of the building. As the time approached for me to leave, Dr. Grandin continued to talk as I shifted in my seat, gathered my papers, and stood next to my seat. Despite all of these overt cues and my distracted facial expressions, she continued to speak without a hint of awareness of my nonverbal signals. Eventually, I put out my hand to her and said I had to be going. Ignoring my extended hand, and without another word, she turned to her neglected lunch and dove in.

In her book Dr. Grandin reports great difficulty not only in reading social signals but also in comprehending sequential language. She describes adapting to this deficit by translating verbal communication into visual images. She writes that she can hear words one at a time but has difficulty following ongoing conversation. She can, however, hold and work with visual images indefinitely. This deficit and adaptation could reflect the transfer of information from the cerebellum-dependent language areas to the visual system, which has little direct neural connectivity with, or reliance upon, the cerebellum. Thus, she may have found a means to find cognitive stability through the use of an unimpaired neural system. This neurobehavioral "detour," combined with exceptional visual–spatial memory, allows her to perform very complex tasks in her well-functioning visual cortex.

Another well-publicized adaptation to her Asperger's is what she refers to as her "squeeze machine." Through the use of an air compressor, padding, and hand controls, Dr. Grandin has created a chamber in which she can experience a constant, gentle, and nondemanding holding. She reports that time in the squeeze machine results in a decrease in agitation and an increased sense of well-being (which she hypothesizes that normal people are able to get from each other). The machine also seems to free her from having to read and react to the subtle nonverbal social cues that are a mystery to her. Her squeeze machine gives her the kind of hug that can make her feel good. Dr. Grandin states that after a while in the machine, she has thoughts of the love she has received from others and the love she feels for them. Her squeeze machine may create a condition of sensory–motor regulation that allows her to gain a window into her own emotional world, closed under her normal bodily conditions.

Attunement in early relationships is based on the ability of both caretaker and child to engage in positive physical and emotional interactions, eye contact, shared gaze, and a variety of other reciprocal interactions. Cerebellar damage appears to disrupt many of the very functions that serve as the basis for vital interpersonal attunement. Such damage could lead to deficits in later developing frontal circuits involved in affect regulation, social judgment, and empathy, which rely on close relationships to take shape. Many of the interventions with autistic children designed to increase eye contact, interpersonal interaction, and physical activity serve to enhance the development of these experience-dependent circuits.

Smooth and reflexive vestibular, sensory, motor, and temporal functioning frees the normal child to become unconscious of his or her body and escape the autistic world. Reliable, replicable, and automatic bodily experience allows normal children to connect with the environment in a flexible and receptive manner, enabling them to learn to understand and cope with the infinite amount of information they must process. Some individuals with autism or Asperger's may not have a "theory of mind," therefore, because they lack a "theory of body" and consistent emotional experience on which to build a cohesive sense of self. The pattern of Dr. Grandin's strengths and weaknesses, along with her ingenious invention, reflects the adaptation of a gifted *and* impaired brain. Her strengths result from a combination of a supportive family, a superior intellect, creativity, and an intact visual system. Her weaknesses lie in sensory processing, social awareness, and affect regulation. Her openness to sharing her struggles serves as a window into a pattern of CNS disturbances that is highly suggestive of early deficits in cerebellar development.

Williams Syndrome

Williams syndrome (WMS) is a rare genetic disorder resulting in deficits in a variety of cognitive, spatial, memory, and executive functions. But unlike autism, WMS does not result in a breakdown of the networks of the social brain. In fact, individuals with WMS are often unusually affectionate and seem to rely on their social abilities to compensate for their considerable intellectual deficits. They have even been described as *overfriendly and engaging* by some (Jones et al., 2000). Although typically mentally retarded, they show strengths in language functioning, musical abilities, facial processing, and often have a sweet, simple sense of humor (Bellugi et al., 2000; Galaburda et al., 1994; Levitin et al., 2003).

WMS is a caused by a series of missing genes on chromosome 7, resulting in abnormalities in the cerebellum, right parietal cortex, and left frontal cortical regions (Galaburda et al., 2001; Galaburda & Bellugi, 2000; Jernigan & Bellugi, 1994; Jones et al., 2002; Schmitt et al., 2002).

This pattern of brain abnormalities is consistent with the visual–spatial disabilities and problems with behavioral timing often seen in WMS. Frontal–cerebellar circuits are involved in the timing of behavior, and the parietal–dorsal areas of the neocortex contain a stream of visual processing that supports visual–spatial analysis of the environment (but not faces). Individuals with WMS are often gregarious and hyperverbal, reflecting decreased inhibitory capacity stemming from dorsal–frontal deficits (Adolphs et al., 1998; Galaburda et al., 2001).

People with WMS have none of the deficits in reading biological motion, eye contact, or facial expressions seen in those suffering with autism. In fact, they are as good as or better than normal subjects in reading biological motion and recognizing faces (Jordan et al., 2002; Mills et al., 2000; Tager-Flusberg et al., 1998). These abilities of social brain networks stand in stark contrast to their profound visual–spatial deficits. Because individuals with WMS often demonstrate unusual empathic abilities, they are of particular interest to our exploration of the social brain (Francke, 1999). The frontal and temporal regions involved in the processing of social information are spared in WMS, allowing individuals with this condition to retain many of their social abilities and perform well on theory of mind tasks.

The brain systems compromised in WMS are those that process the more abstract aspects of relationships and social interactions. Despite their abilities to connect and resonate with others, individuals with WMS are still impaired when it comes to understanding the complexities of social interactions, social concepts, and friendship (Gosch at al., 1994). They do quite well with caretakers who provide the structure, direction, and care they require, and their empathic abilities and interpersonal concern are appreciated by those around them. What is most impressive about these individuals is that although they have difficulties navigating the most basic functions of day-to-day life, they appear to have a heightened capacity for emotional attunement.

The symptoms, strengths, and disabilities in autism and WMS emphasize the functional modularity of neural networks and how genetic disruptions can impair some systems but spare others. Autism, in particular, demonstrates how dependent social relatedness is on intact social brain networks.

The overwhelmingly complex symphony of signals we process from microsecond to microsecond, which are completely taken for granted by most of us, requires an incredible amount of neural computation, the integration of multiple neural networks, and an intact social brain.

Part VI

Social Neural Plasticity

Chapter 21

From Neurons
to Narratives

*When we try to pick out anything by itself, we find
it hitched to everything else in the universe.*
—John Muir, 1911, p. 110

We began this book with the assumption that larger, more complex, and more experience-dependent brains allow for increasingly adaptive responses to environmental challenges. To accomplish this goal, we found that evolution selected for bonding, attachment, and caretaking to provide the necessary scaffolding for the prolonged extrauterine development required to build such brains. This "socialization" of the brain laid the foundation for increasingly sophisticated forms of communication, the emergence of language, and the birth of culture. The evolution of culture, in turn, allows for higher levels of biological, behavioral, and technological complexity, which emerge not simply within select individuals but through the group as a whole (Bonner, 1988).

A clear example of the role of culture in natural selection comes from a tsunami-ravaged island of Southeast Asia. After the floodwaters abated, rescue workers found most coastal populations decimated. On one island, however, a community was found totally intact. Apparently, this island tribe's narrative history included a story of the ground shaking, followed by a giant wave, after which only those living on the mountain survived. The moral of the story was that when the ground gets moving, so should you! When the earthquake struck, the coastal inhabitants remembered this story and fled to the nearby hills. After the waters receded, they returned to their village and were in the middle of rebuilding when the "rescuers" arrived. This memory, which spanned generations, could not have been remembered by any one individual. It became part of the culture, contributed to the diversity and adaptability of behavior, and saved many lives. This is one of the ways in which interwoven individuals become more than the sum of their parts.

Relationships among humans have allowed for role specialization, symbolic functioning, and culture to emerge from the collected efforts of millions of individuals over countless generations. Further, the more interrelated individual organisms become, the more a large group begins to behave like an individual being. Think of a swarm of bees, a herd of impala running across the savanna, or thousands of humans following the latest fad. From neurons to insects, from monkeys to humans, joining together in new and creative ways can enhance survival.

As evolution combines organisms to gain increasing biological complexity and behavioral flexibility, basic biological strategies such as neural transmission and metabolic homeostasis are conserved. These ancient biological mechanisms continue to oversee the government of systems that comprise our brains and bodies. Because complex social phenomena are so compelling, it is easy to overlook the fundamental themes of evolutionary strategies. Why might looking back at basic biological principles that connect our component parts be important to an understanding of our social brains? Given evolution's penchant for conservation, it makes sense to suspect that the strategies that govern our component structures (such as neurons and neural networks) may also guide how individuals function in social groups (Milo et al., 2004). In the past decade we have learned a great deal about how individual neurons communicate with and influence one another. I suggest that these discoveries may serve as a helpful model of how people connect with one another. First, let's take a look back at how neuronal "societies" communicate.

Three Messenger Systems in Neurons

You may recall from Chapter 3 that neurons communicate with and shape one another through chemical and genetic signals divided into three messenger systems. In the first messenger system, chemical neurotransmitters cross the small gaps between neurons (synapses) and cause adjacent neurons to fire. The second system consists of the internal biological and metabolic changes within the activated (efferent) neuron, based on how it is stimulated by adjacent neurons. In the third and final messenger system, internal cellular changes within the efferent neuron trigger genetic transcription in the neuron's nucleus to guide the building and reshaping of its dendrites. The resulting changes to the structure of the neuron modify its connectivity with other neurons and adjust its firing for better adaptation. Table 21.1 summarizes the functions of the three messenger systems.

Through these three messenger systems, neurons are stimulated to fire, grow, and interconnect with each other in an experience-dependent manner. Put another way, it is the firing patterns of neurons, based on environmental stimulation, that actually shape the neural circuitry of the brain. Through these three systems our brains are shaped by experience

Table 21.1. **The Three Messenger Systems**

First Messenger System

Multiple neurochemicals impact the receptor sites of neurons, resulting in the activation of surface proteins and neuronal firing. Receptor sites are sets of proteins that span the membrane of the cell to regulate communication between the outside and the inside of the cell. This is the messenger system we learn about in biology classes and see in commercials for antidepressants. When enough neurotransmitters stimulate the receptor sites, the neuron will fire.

Second Messenger System

The activation of proteins starts a cascade of chemical events that result in a number of biochemical changes within the receptor neuron. These internal changes alter metabolic homeostasis, effect activation patterns, and influence activity within the neuron's nucleus.

Third Messenger System

The third messenger system triggers genetic transcription via changes in the internal environment of the neuron. The transcription process guides the ongoing construction of the neuron. In this way neurons interact in a manner that guides gene transcription to maximize the formation of functional neural networks. This system also provides feedback to the second messenger system to further influence metabolic homeostasis and the continued growth of the neuron.

and become a reflection of our learning histories. Although this influence may seem obvious, given what we have discussed in the last 20 chapters, only since the 1990s has it been accepted that experience has such a large impact on the structure and function of the brain.

Three Messenger Systems in Humans

So how might these three physiological systems apply to people? In what way could this overall strategy to connect, grow, and gain increasing levels of complexity be occurring at the level of social interaction? As we explored the social brain, we found a myriad of ways in which we simultaneously send and receive signals in a constant flow of communication. Some of this communication is conscious and intentional, but most of it takes place outside of conscious awareness. Whereas neurons appear limited to chemical communication, humans (as more complex systems) not only maintain chemical transmission through olfactory and pheromonal communication, but also have developed senses that can detect and analyze mechanical vibrations and pressure through our ears and skin, as well as a complex visual system designed to receive and process patterns within waves of light. This multiplicity of sensory channels allows not only for all of these channels to be processed independently, but also for increased complexity through every kind of combination. Table 21.2 outlines some social transmitters we have discussed.

As experts in receiving and analyzing social information, our brains and bodies are primed to monitor and react to those around us. We accomplish these tasks through a variety of experience-dependent neural networks dedicated to receiving, interpreting, and sending information across the social synapse. The multiple means of social communication combined

Table 21.2. **Mechanisms of Communication across the Social Synapse**

Smell (olfactory and pheromonal systems): identification, attraction, repulsion

Sound (hearing): grunts, groans, sighs, laughter, volume, tone, prosody, rhyming, song

Touch (skin): affection, nurturance, grooming, sex, support, soothe/calm

Visual (vision): facial expressions, smiling, gestures, pupil dilation, blushing

with these receiving systems are analogous to the first messenger system we see at a neuronal level.

The second messenger system in humans begins with the activation of networks of the social brain by these multiple streams of information. These systems regulate bonding, attachment, proximity, and social motivation. As we have seen, these social systems are interwoven with those involved with the internal regulation of our bodily homeostasis. In this way, relationships regulate metabolic states, stress, and immunological functioning. Akin to the second messenger system in neurons, these systems support energy supply, metabolic homeostasis, and stimulate cell growth. Table 21.3 summarizes some of the systems we have discussed that are involved in both facilitating social connection and the regulation of internal states.

Table 21.3. **Internal Systems Facilitating Interpersonal Connection and Regulation**

Stress and Fear Systems: levels of arousal, fight/flight, approach–avoidance

Reward Systems: proximity seeking, bonding, attachment, soothing, social motivation

Engagement Systems: affective regulation, fear modulation, stress reduction, attachment schema

Social Visual Systems: orientation to faces, face recognition, direction of attention, facial expressions

Mirror Systems: imitation, learning, communication, coordination, resonance, empathy, theory of mind

Symbol Systems: internal objects, words, metaphors, narratives

---

We now know that our interactions with others, especially early in life and in intimate relationships, not only affect the ways in which our brains function but also shape their very structure. The three messenger systems at both the neuronal and human levels converge to change structures and connectivity of neural systems (see Table 21.4). From both animal and human research we have learned that positive social interactions result in increased metabolic activity, mRNA synthesis, and neural growth; in other words, relationships can create an internal biological environment supportive of neural plasticity.

Table 21.4. **The Three Messenger Systems in Neurons and Humans**

	Neurons	Humans
First Messenger System	Exchange of information via neurotransmitters and other neuromodulators across the synapse	Exchange of signals across the social synapse using the senses (smell, hearing, sight, touch, taste)
Second Messenger System	Activation and modification of internal biological state and homeostatic regulation of individual neurons	Activation of neural systems of regulation, homeostasis, stress, fear, reward, engagement, and attachment
Third Messenger System	Transcription mRNA and the modification of neural structure and connectivity of other neurons	Stimulation of brain growth, neural network growth and integration, and mutative changes in interaction with the social world

However much we focus on these internal biological processes, it is helpful to always remember that neurons are embedded within our brains, as our brains are embedded within our bodies, as our bodies are embedded in society, and so on up the chain of complexity. Stimulated by relationships within our social worlds, millions of changes within and between neurons combine to create our emotions, personalities, and the quality of our day-to-day lives. Through the three messenger systems, others around us activate our senses, regulate our brains and bodies, and, when called for, change the shape of our neuronal structures.

Why might this parallel between neurons and humans be important? It may be most important because the biases of Western science—the same science we have relied on for much of what we have discussed—lead us to think of each individual as a "unit" of study from which all things can be understood. But we now recognize that individuals are inseparable from the group, that groups themselves process information, and that we live in a field of mutual interpersonal regulation (Baumeister & Leary, 1995; Hinsz et al., 1997; Tronick & Weinberg, 1997). Trying to understand human experience by studying the words and behaviors of an individual may be like analyzing a film by counting the pixels in a tiny corner of a vast screen. We may come to know the flickers of light in that corner quite well but completely miss the meaning of the film.

The emerging parallels among neurons within neural networks and individuals embedded in the social world may help us to bridge the social and neurosciences with a common working model for process and change. Such a model could provide a means of integrating clinical and research endeavors in science, education, and mental health (Etkin et al., 2005). These are not new insights—systems theorists such as Bowen (1978) and Bateson (1972) were discussing these issues decades ago. However, science as a whole seems resistant to acknowledging the truth of our interconnectivity. Neuroscientists already know that an individual neuron does not exist in nature. When designing their experiments, they now need to remember that this is also true of rats, monkeys, and humans. From our side of the equation, psychotherapists and educators need to consider new ways of interacting with clients and students to account for the social embeddedness of human experience, learning, and the processes of neural plasticity.

Mental Illness and Social Trauma

In examining pathologies of social relating, we found disruptions in the development and integration of various components of the social brain. The breakdown of multiple systems within the brains of autistic individuals helps us understand their retreat from the world. Their inability to read facial expressions, regulate affect, and predict the movements and intentions of others produces an incomprehensible interpersonal world. The antisocial individual's lack of empathy, the emotional dysregulation of the borderline patient, and the fear of the social phobic all correlate with abnormalities of the neural networks that participate in affect regulation and attachment.

As our understanding of the brain continues to expand, we gain an increasing appreciation of the manner in which early experiences, both good and bad, become transformed into the substance of our nervous system via the three messenger systems. As we have seen, early neglect, stress, and trauma impact all of the developmental processes we have discussed in negative and destructive ways. Neglect and abuse decrease the growth of experience-dependent neural circuits, especially of the OMPFC, anterior cingulate, and insula cortex. Perhaps it may help us all to keep in mind that when we watch a child interacting with the world, we are witnessing the building and shaping of a brain in ways that will impact the individual throughout his or her life.

The following is an adult's recollection of her eighth birthday:

The Saturday morning before my eighth birthday, I was eating a bowl of cereal at the kitchen table. My mother informed me it had been a lean year for our family, and tuition at Saint Thomas Catholic School had gone up.

"Anyway," she said, "a good education is worth more than presents."

Just then my father ambled in unshaven, reached into the refrigerator, and came out with a can of beer for breakfast. He sat down at the table and motioned to me with the can.

"Come over here and tell me what you want for your birthday."

I stole a glance at my mother's back, hunched over the sink.

"Come on," he urged. "You must want something."

I sat on his lap but couldn't find the words. My mother loudly threw several plastic cups into the sink and added liquid detergent.

"Did she say we couldn't afford presents?" my father asked.

"A birthday is no reason to go into debt," my mother announced to the faucets, steam crawling up over her arms.

A vein bulged in my dad's neck. "So, old tightwad wants to spoil everything again."

"Easy for you to say," my mother muttered under her breath. "You're always out of town when the bills are due."

My father dumped me off his lap, and I hit the floor with a hard smack, sending a painful jolt from my tailbone to my head. I wanted to be picked up and hugged. Instead my father strode across the room, grabbed my mother's throat with his huge hands, and squeezed.

"Ask the goddamn pope for money if we are so goddamn poor!" he shouted. After a final shake, he released her. My mother's neck had red marks on it. She coughed and cried softly, in raspy sobs. I pulled myself up off the floor and stood between them. I wanted to hate them, but I couldn't. They had been fighting ever since I could remember; I just wanted the war to be over. I prayed for this every day at school, but my prayers were never answered. I could tell that round two was just minutes away. My dad was crushing his beer can with his fist, and my mother was sighing again. I was going to be 8 years old in a few days, and I didn't care. I screamed at the sky outside the kitchen window, "I hate my birthday! I don't want anything! I hate it! I hate it!"

How might a childhood filled with these sorts of interactions shape the social brain? It would be fair to assume that such experiences would result in a brain biased toward threat and danger. Attachment schemas may well be insecure and intimacy a source of ambivalence, anger, and fear. Direct eye contact, assertiveness, and "personal visibility" might be avoided. Emotions may be difficult to control because of dysregulation among frontal systems, resulting in depression, mood instability, and difficulties under stress. There may also be a tendency to convert emotional stress into physical symptoms. This kind of emotional dysregulation in the home will not help a child's brain grow and integrate. When this person comes to psychotherapy, we will see in her complaints and symptoms not only the disabilities of a single "organism" but the inherent pathology of their family's relationship history. Yes, we are individuals, but the architecture of our brains are records of our interpersonal histories.

Narratives and Neural Network Integration

As we have seen, the human brain co-evolved with increasing social complexity, the emergence of language, and the expansion of culture. Storytelling is obviously an ability that emerges from larger brains and sophisticated language capacities. While storytelling serves to teach the lessons of culture, it also serves as a means of homeostasis and integration of brain functioning. How so? As brains became more complex and developed modular networks dedicated to motor, affective, cognitive, and social functions, the challenge of organizing and integrating these systems also arose. Although we usually assume that these integrative functions should be located in later evolving frontal (executive) structures, social relationships and narratives also participate in these regulatory processes.

Narratives are heard sequentially but must be understood as a whole. Bringing together linear and Gestalt processing requires joint participation of the left and right hemispheres (Shumake et al., 2004; Tucker, Luu, & Pribram, 1995). It appears that, over time, narratives became a strategy for neural integration contained *within the group mind* (language and culture) that allowed the brain to grow further in size and complexity. The salient role of narratives in brain integration may be why we find a strong correlation between mental health, emotional regulation, and the coherence of the narratives individuals tell about themselves and their relationship histories (Beeghly & Cicchetti, 1994; Cozolino, 2002; Fonagy et al., 1996; Main et al., 1985). There is evidence that narratives foster emotional security while minimizing the need for elaborate psychological defenses (Fonagy, Steele, Steele, Moran, & Higgit, 1991). See Figure 21.1 for a graphic representation of the dimensions of neural integration that we all need to accomplish.

Because narratives require participation of multiple structures throughout the brain, they require us to combine, in conscious memory, our knowledge, sensations, feelings, and behaviors. In bringing together multiple functions from diverse neural networks, narratives provide the brain with a tool for both emotional and neural integration (Rossi, 1993). Think about little Joseph, a 4-year old boy with whom I worked in therapy. As he struggled with a part of a puzzle he was working on, I heard him chanting "I think I can, I think I can" under his breath. When he was finished, I asked him what he was saying while working on the puzzle. He told me he was repeating what *The Little Engine That Could* would say to "himself" as "he" worked to get up a big hill. Joseph was like the little engine—he knew he could do it, he knew he would succeed, but it was just hard. This is an excellent example of the regulatory function of narratives. This classic children's story provided Joseph with a memory of a positive outcome during a difficult situation and helped him maintain the use of language while under stress. It also served to regulate his emotions during a challenge through identification with a hero who encountered a difficult situation and prevailed. The Little Engine is a part of our culture that Joseph used to help regulate his emotions, integrate neural networks, and build his brain.

Think about the structure of a basic narrative in a novel, a children's book, or a Hollywood movie. It contains a hero who faces a series of

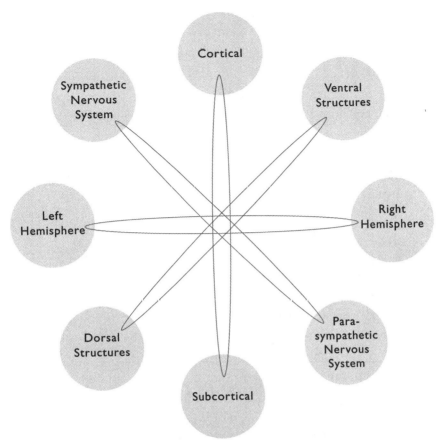

Figure 21.1. **Planes of neural integration. The integration of neural structures and networks occurs simultaneously on multiple planes of energy transfer and information exchange throughout the brain.**

obstacles and struggles to overcome them. Some obstacles are external, such as a natural disaster, winning a Gold Medal, or fighting an enemy. Other obstacles are internal, such as fear, anger, or emptiness that gets in the hero's way of obtaining his or her goals. The hero also brings a personal wound that causes emotional pain. In the process of the narrative things get bad and then get a little worse, but eventually the internal and external challenges are faced and surpassed. As the story proceeds, the hero matures, confronts his pain, succeeds, and usually gets the girl.

All stories contain trouble, and it is in this fact that their essential evolutionary value is contained. Narratives, just like our autonomic nervous systems at a more primitive level, have been shaped around getting out, or staying out, of trouble. Without conflicts and resolutions, good and bad, a story seems pointless. Of what interest is Red Riding Hood without the Wolf or Luke Skywalker without the evil empire? Why would we care about a man named Lear making good decisions about the succession of power in his kingdom? We are reflexively drawn in by the narrative process. By identifying with the heroes in stories, movies, and folklore, we enter into the conflict with them, struggle with different feelings, and learn about ourselves. Beyond the conscious lessons we learn from stories, the stories themselves become part of our internal emotional experience and are activated when we encounter similar situations. Joseph has a "little engine that could" inside of him.

A story well-told, containing conflicts and resolutions and thoughts flavored with feelings, connects people and integrates neural networks. An inclusive narrative structure provides the executive brain with the best template and strategy for the oversight and coordination of the functions of mind. Narratives allow us to practice facing challenging experiences in imagination as our brains learn to cope with the emotions they stimulate. The simultaneous activation of narratives and emotional experiences builds neural connection and coherence between easily dissociable networks of affect and cognition. Thus, although it may appear that storytelling, at best, may be teaching us cultural wisdom, the process of traveling with the hero is an experiential journey that serves to build our brains, regulate our emotions, and rehearse our skills. Later, when we train for an athletic event or prepare to go into a boardroom battle, we carry inside us the heros who live in our hearts.

Furthermore, our own personal narratives also contribute to our reactions, responses, and ways of engaging with others, as we look back on our unique stories to guide us in relationships and how we choose to live. Think of how different life would have been for the 8-year-old on her birthday to have had parents who were able to control their own emotions and *not* resort to alcohol, sarcasm, or violence. Imagine this same child sitting at the breakfast table talking over with her parents how they would celebrate her birthday. What if they could say, "We don't have much money to spend, and that makes us sad because we would love to buy you that beautiful doll you told us about. But how about taking a walk together, going to the zoo, and having birthday cupcakes in front of the elephants we know you love so much?"

This expression of feelings, coming up with solutions, sharing an adventure, and then retelling the story in the year to come would be a coconstructed narrative that would bring them closer together, help each to internalize the other two people in a positive way, and help them all to feel safer and happier in their lives and within themselves. These coconstructed narratives remind us that each unique story of our own contains elements of someone else's story, which contains elements of someone else's story. It has been said that there are only a few stories in literature, and these stories just kept getting retold in slightly different ways.

We need each other and our stories to discover ourselves, regulate our emotions, and heal from traumatic injuries. Humans serve as external neural circuits that we can use to help each other bridge dissociated neural networks, provide us with new ideas, and activate feelings within us that we may be unable to access or have forgotten to remember. When loving others link their brain with ours, the result is a vital integration. We can use our interpersonal resonance, intuition, and empathic abilities to help and heal one another. Human brains have vulnerabilities and weaknesses that only other brains are capable of mending. For human beings (and neurons), relationships are a natural habitat.

Implications of Interpersonal Neurobiology for Psychotherapy

We have seen a great deal of evidence supporting the impact of early nurturance on the shaping of the social brain. The brain is an organ of adaptation; it can adapt to any environment, including those that are not conducive to happiness and health. When our childhood relationships are frightening, abusive, or nonexistent, our brains dutifully adapt to the realities of our unfortunate situation. However, there is reason to believe that these circuits retain plasticity throughout life, especially in close relationships (Bowlby, 1988; Davidson, 2000). For example, research suggests that, in the transition from dating to marriage, there is a broad tendency for partners with insecure and disorganized attachment to develop increasingly secure patterns (Crowell et al., 2002). This retained plasticity in attachment circuitry makes sense from an evolutionary perspective, given the naturally occurring changes in our social situations over time. For many of us, adult relationships give us a second, third, and fourth chance at shaping our attachment circuitry and living a happy and satisfying life (Vaillant, 2002).

There are many clues to the nature of healing relationships that can be found by studying optimal parenting. After all, the networks of the social brain are first built in the interactive parent–child dyad and may be changed in similar ways. Because the core of the social brain is also the hub of our fear circuitry, negative early experiences can result in social relationships that act as a stimulus cue for troubling memories. Not surprisingly, the biggest challenge of therapy is the establishment of sufficient trust to allow attachment and healing to take place. In a previous book I outlined the aspects of successful psychotherapy that create the possibility for changing the brain (Cozolino, 2002). In that work I described the components of therapy that optimize neuroplasticity:

- A safe and trusting relationship with an attuned therapist.
- The maintenance of moderate levels of arousal.
- The activation of cognition and emotion.
- The coconstruction of narratives that reflect a positive, optimistic self.

In reviewing several psychotherapies, it appears that these common elements are necessary for treatment success, with each finding some degree of support in the neuroscience literature. An intimate relationship with the therapist reactivates attachment circuitry and makes it available to neuroplastic processes. Moderate levels of arousal maximize the biochemical processes that drive protein synthesis necessary for modifying neural structures. The activation of both affective and cognitive circuits allows frontal systems to reassociate and reregulate the various neural circuits that organize thinking and feeling—those most vulnerable to dissociation. Finally, the coconstruction of new narratives creates an evolving language for experience that can modify self-image, aid in affect regulation, and serve as a guide for positive behavior.

A number of important implications for the practice of psychotherapy arise from our expanded understanding of neuroscience. Perhaps the most crucial is that therapists need to integrate a brain-based understanding of human development, mental health, and mental illness into whatever theoretical orientation they practice. If psychotherapists are indeed neuroscientists, we need to use the underlying principles of neuroplasticity to guide treatment selection. This approach would require transcending professional rivalries or zealous devotion to a particular perspective in order to better serve our clients. Here are a few ways in which neuroscience might advance the practice of psychotherapy.

I. Utilizing Multiple Means of Influencing the Brain

We are living biological organisms with brains that continuously process thoughts, emotions, motions, and motivations. We live within our own experience of being human, embedded in a social world, but able to create through imagination and find comfort and clarity through spiritual beliefs. Thus, we are constructed of a fabric of all of these processes, and they all affect our experience and well-being. Therefore, we should not limit ourselves to a narrow set of clinical tools in our therapeutic work.

Everything from intimate relationships to medication to church attendance to having an affectionate pet has been shown to have a positive impact on physical and mental health. This wide range of solutions speaks to the multiple ways in which neuroplastic processes can be enhanced and healing achieved. It also suggests that therapists should expand their alliances with clergy, pharmacologists, spouses, and soccer coaches in order to maximize therapeutic leverage by utilizing as many ways of influencing the brain as possible.

II. Including a Brain-Based Perspective in Case Conceptualization

A brain-based perspective of change could become the underlying rationale for the selection and combination of specific treatments. For example, with any particular client, medication, lifestyle changes, or yoga classes may be utilized to reduce his or her level of arousal and maximize neuroplastic potential. The success of any of these interventions would be assessed based on its ability to assist the person in attaining and maintaining a moderate level of arousal. If we recognize the centrality of a caring relationship to positive change, and the psychotherapeutic context proves to be too threatening or artificial for some clients, new situations for contact should be explored. If all mental health practitioners had a brain-based conceptualization of their clients, it could serve as a common language among pharmacologists, occupational therapists, internists, social workers, and psychotherapists, aiding in communication and treatment coordination. With advances in technology, we may also find that measuring brain activity might someday aid in diagnosis as well as serve as a measure of treatment outcome.

III. Educating Clients about Their Brains

We have boxes full of owner's manuals for the many things we own but are clueless about the most important device we possess. Teaching clients about how the brain works, explaining to them the impact of early learning on the brain and body, the workings of memory, the biases of the amygdala, and our vulnerabilities to prejudice and phobias can go a long way to both "depathologize" their experience and create a shared conceptual model within the working relationship. Teaching someone with panic disorder about the autonomic nervous system, for example, not only helps her feel less "crazy" but also provides her with a conceptual tool to separate what she is experiencing from a heart attack and help her to stay calm the next time she becomes anxious. Not only is this potentially useful information, it also lends credibility to the therapeutic process and shows respect for clients by including them in an understandable discussion of theories and procedures relevant to their treatment.

IV. Fostering Ongoing Optimism Based on Lifelong Plasticity

We have a number of therapeutic and pharmacological tools, developed over the last century, that have taught us how to effect change in our clients. Our increasing knowledge of the mechanisms of ongoing plasticity throughout the lifespan, the impact of enriched and enriching relationships on the social brain, and our advances in the use of these processes can all serve as valuable tools in the therapeutic relationship. The power of what is called the "placebo effect" is not in a sugar pill or a client's gullibility; rather, it rests in the healing effects of the social brain to connect, to believe, and to internalize the doctor's optimism via the same neurochemical systems of attachment and bonding (Petrovic et al., 2002). The optimism of the healer parallels that of the encouraging parent who has dreams of her children's success and supports their well-being. The physiological reality of ongoing neuroplasticity and neurogenesis provides us with a solid foundation for ongoing optimism with any client at any time, regardless of his or her struggle.

V. The Malleability of Memory and Rewriting History

The trauma to the psychotherapeutic community created by the false memory debates still lingers, and many therapists are hesitant to approach the issue of memory head on. Although we know that the veridical truth of memory is always questionable, we have also learned that memory is quite malleable. Whereas this malleability is certainly a problem for our legal system, it can be extremely helpful for psychotherapy. Educating clients about the peculiarities of memory and giving them permission to play with and modify memories provides tools for rewriting history in a manner that supports mental health. As long as clients are capable of understanding the difference between accurate history and therapeutic coconstructed narratives, many clients may be able to transform their oppressive memories into healing stories.

VI. Emphasizing the Centrality of the Therapeutic Relationship to Positive Change

Research in social neuroscience and therapeutic outcome support the importance of the quality of the relationship to therapeutic success. This finding is true regardless of the theoretical orientation of the therapist and whether or not he or she considers the relationship to be an active ingredient in the change process. Therapists tend to undervalue the impact of the human relationship as they focus on diagnostics, treatment strategies, and management issues. The research suggests that the training

of therapists should include more emphasis on skills related to resonance, attunement, and empathic aspects of treatment, and that personal
psychotherapy should again become a mandatory part of training. This
is not to say that the technical aspects of therapy are unimportant, but
rather to counterbalance the trend toward understanding psychotherapy
as a set of interventions we do *to* clients, with a relationship we have *with*
clients (Cozolino, 2004).

Chapter 22

Healing Relationships

The biggest disease today is . . . The feeling of being unwanted.
        —Mother Teresa, 1971, p. 851

During decades of experiments, Harry Harlow and his colleagues studied the impact of social deprivation on young monkeys. In the most famous of these experiments, newborn monkeys were "raised" by wire and cloth surrogate mothers to examine the effects of maternal deprivation on social and emotional development. As you may have learned in Psychology 101, those monkeys raised by wire mothers engaged in autistic, self-abusive, and socially inappropriate behaviors. In another set of experiments, newborn monkeys were raised in total isolation for the first 6 months. They were then introduced into a colony of monkeys, having had no physical contact, nurturance, or social skill development. These isolate monkeys spent much of their time huddled in a corner or rocking in place. Furthermore, they failed to develop appropriate social, sexual, or maternal behaviors; they found the stimulation and complexity of the social world just too overwhelming.

In a subsequent set of experiments, before releasing these isolate monkeys into the larger group, they were given "therapists." The therapists were monkeys of the same species but only half the age of the isolates: true child therapists! And what good therapists they were! The therapist monkeys initiated contact out of interest, curiosity, and their instinct to connect. Though the isolates would initially freeze or withdraw from fear, the young therapists were persistent, continuing to approach and cling onto their "clients." Gradually, the isolates grew less afraid and began clinging back. Ever so slowly, they began to initiate play and learn positive social behaviors (Suomi & Harlow, 1972).

It turned out that these younger monkeys were the perfect therapists. Their stage of development led them to connect with the isolates at a very basic physical, visceral, and emotional level. More importantly, they wouldn't take *no* for an answer. Their clinging, cuddling, and soothing behaviors interrupted the isolates' autistic behaviors, allowing them to engage in movement, exploration, and social interactions. Whereas human therapists take years to learn how to facilitate these healing changes, these little monkey therapists did it reflexively. This small but eloquent study demonstrates that learning not to fear and learning to love are biologically interwoven (Bartels & Zeki, 2003).

There is no doubt that evolution has shaped us to love one another. This may be why so many of life's most gratifying experiences are those that are shared. Loving relationships help our brains to develop, integrate, and remain flexible. Through love we regulate each other's brain chemistry, sense of well-being, and immunological functioning. And when the drive to love is thwarted—when we are frightened, abused, or neglected—our mental health is compromised. Adults who thrive despite childhood neglect and abuse often describe life-affirming experiences with others who made them feel cared for and worthwhile. The potential for healing relationships is all around us: the caring martial arts teacher who takes an interest in a fatherless boy, the nurse who listens to the stories of her elderly client while placing a gentle hand on her shoulder, the anonymous act of kindness that takes us by surprise and melts our hearts. If we are fortunate enough to find someone who loves us, we have an opportunity to heal.

A strikingly beautiful example of healing occurs in Victor Hugo's *Les Miserables* (1985). Near the beginning of the story, we meet Jean Valjean, a homeless thief who is given food and shelter by a bishop. During the night, Valjean awakens, gathers up some of the bishop's silver, and runs off. He is later apprehended and brought to the bishop's door to be identified as a thief and returned to prison. Being a quick study, the compassionate bishop exclaims:

"So here you are! I'm delighted to see you. Had you forgotten that I gave you the candlesticks as well? Did you forget to take them?" Jean Valjean's eyes widened. He was now staring at the old man with an expression no words can convey. Valjean stood motionless, still held by the gendarme. He had never encountered kindness and was dumbfounded by it.

When the gendarme withdraws, the bishop speaks to Valjean in a low voice:

"Do not ever forget that you have promised me to use the money to make yourself an honest man. . . . Jean Valjean, my brother, you no longer belong to what is evil but to what is good." (p.111)

Valjean left town as if pursued, in crisis and total confusion. Obscurely he perceived that the priest's forgiveness was the most formidable assault he had ever sustained; that if resisted, his heart would be hardened once and for all, and that if he yielded, he must renounce the hatred which the acts of men had implanted in him during so many years, and to which he clung.

Valjean had suffered a life of poverty, neglect, and abuse, and in response, he expressed his rage at every turn. Receiving this act of compassion opened him to his own feelings of caring and acceptance, perhaps for the first time. The human warmth and genuine caring of the Rogerian therapist are analogous to the bishop's gift of the candlesticks to Valjean. It is the same gift we give when we absorb the rage of an angry adolescent, when we allow our spouses to do something that makes us insecure, or in the simple act of letting a stranger step ahead of us in line. When clients come to therapy, they carry the unconscious expectation that they will be treated as they have been treated before. One of the therapist's most essential acts is to thwart these negative expectations with kindness, empathy, and patience. Kindness pulls the rug out from under the defenses we have learned to use to protect ourselves from feelings of rejection and abandonment. Put in another way, compassion, warmth, and love have the power to change our brains.

The Loving Brain

What happens when we are in love? We know we feel euphoric, like we are floating on air, safe, optimistic, and positive. It is easy to imagine that brain systems involved in positive feelings become active, whereas those that organize negative emotional states are quieted. You would also expect that attention to the external environment would decrease as networks dedicated to social connection and reward become very active. As a matter of fact, when the brains of individuals who are deeply in love were scanned, that is exactly what was found.

When shown pictures of their loved ones, areas of the brain with heightened activation included the insula, anterior cingulate, caudate nucleus, and putamen. Subjects showed decreased activation in the amygdala, posterior cingulate, and the frontal, parietal, and temporal cortices on the right side (Bartels & Zeki, 2000). This study suggests that the experience of love is a combination of at least two processes. The first is that it greatly *decreases* activation of the fear systems, as demonstrated by the "standing down" of the amygdala and the environmental processing of the posterior cingulate and other cortical areas. Love is a relief from scanning the outer world for threat and our inner worlds for shame. Love turns off the alarm, cancels our insurance, and frees us from worry.

The state of being in love makes us happy by activating the brain's social engagement and reward systems: It creates positive feelings through the activation of biochemical networks throughout our brains. The sight, smell, and touch of our beloved make us glad to be alive. Love is a drug—in fact, a number of drugs—that includes endorphins and dopamine and results in similar patterns of brain activation as taking cocaine (Breiter et al., 1997; Schlaepfer et al., 1998). This parallel between the feeling of being in love and addiction may help those of us who have not taken drugs to understand their addictive qualities. Imagine being able to simulate the experience of falling in love at will and you can begin to grasp the hold some drugs have over the brain.

On the other hand, cocaine addicts have been found to have smaller frontal, cingulate, and insular cortices (Franklin et al., 2002). This shrinkage may be a result of drug use, or it may represent on inherent vulnerability to drug abuse. Given that these cortical regions are central to bonding and attachment, cocaine may provide a feeling that their brain is unable to generate on its own in relationships.

The Fearful Brain

Rejection and abandonment plunge us into states of fear, anxiety, and shame. The anguish of being spurned, the agony of separation, and the transient psychotic symptoms of bereavement all attest to the power of "withdrawal" from significant others (Irwin et al., 1988). Separation, divorce, or the death of a spouse increases risk for suicide, just as real or imagined abandonment triggers self-abusive and suicidal behavior in borderline patients. Paradoxically, it is the fear of abandonment, dysregulation, and shame that often keeps us from being able to love.

Based on what we know so far, the amygdala and OMPFC are major players in the regulation of our experience of safety and danger. On one side, the amygdala connects negative experiences with autonomic arousal, generating anxiety, fear, panic, and flashbacks (Adolphs et al., 1998; Furmark et al., 1997; LaBar et al., 1998; Maren, 2001; Morris, Buchel, & Dolan, 2001; Rogan & LeDoux, 1996; Sprengelmeyer et al., 1999). On the other, the OMPFC assesses the reality of the danger and is capable of inhibiting amygdala activation when a fear response is deemed unnecessary (Davidson, Jackson, & Kalin, 2000; Morgan, Romanski, & LeDoux, 1993).

Evidence that the OMPFC and amygdala have this sort of reciprocal regulatory relationship comes from the extensive interconnections of these two structures and their alternating patterns of activation (Abercrombie et al., 1996; Amaral et al., 1992; Shin et al., 2005). When we are exposed to angry faces and other fear-evoking stimuli, the amygdala becomes activated and the OMPFC become less active (Fredrikson et al., 1995; Kim et al., 2003; Nomura et al., 2004; Yamasaki et al., 2002). And when the OMPFC is underactive, the amygdala becomes more prominent in driving our behaviors, perceptions, and judgments (Drevets & Raichle, 1998). Anxiety disorders may result from an imbalance of this system in favor of the amygdala, with safety signals from the OMPFC failing to inhibit the activation and output of the amygdala. In fact, the size of the amygdala has been found to be larger in children with generalized anxiety disorder than in their less anxious peers (De Bellis et al., 2000).

Of course, fear regulation is not an "on/off switch"; rather, the OMPFC modulates the time course of emotional responding, particularly regarding recovery time from negative emotional states (Davidson, 2000). The intensity and duration of amygdala activation correlate with both the length and intensity of our subjective experience of negative emotions, anticipatory anxiety, and fear (Gur et al., 2002; Morgan, Romanski, & LeDoux, 1993; Rule et al., 2002; Schaefer et al., 2002; Simpson et al., 2001). The subtleties of how each of us deals with our emotional experience may be found in the experience-dependent shaping of these connections.

Based on the way our brains operate, evolution appears to have been far more interested in keeping us alive than making us happy. Overall, negative emotions trump positive ones and weigh more heavily in our evaluation of people and situations (Ito et al., 2002). A car accident, having a gun put to our head, or even seeing someone else seriously injured or killed can brand our memory. In a single highly charged affective moment, any of us can learn to be terrified of something for the rest of our lives. On the other hand, learning not to be afraid can take years of struggle.

All these elements of fear conditioning reflect primitive qualities of the amygdala that have been conserved by evolution. The amygdala is quick to learn and slow to forget. Learned fears are tenacious and tend to return when we are under stress (Davis, 2002). Fear is not easily forgotten, whereas learning *not* to fear is fragile and often dissipates over time. We don't even have to be conscious of a stimulus, either in the environment or within us, in order for it to become a conditioned cue for fear. As we saw in a previous chapter, a thalamic pathway to the amygdala becomes activated in response to "unseen" threats and controls reflexive and autonomic responses (Esteves et al., 1994; Hendler et al., 2003; Morris, Öhman, & Dolan, 1998, 1999). In other words, our amygdala is attending to things around us to which we are completely oblivious, guiding our thoughts and behaviors accordingly; it teaches us to fear without us even being aware of what is happening. Because the amygdala can respond in under 100 milliseconds, our fear networks can move through several processing cycles before a frightening stimulus even enters conscious awareness.

Based on our neurobiology, fear outranks and outwits love in a number of ways. Fear is:

- Faster
- Automatic
- Unconscious

- Spontaneously generalized to other stimuli
- Multisensory
- Resistant to extinction

Why is it so easy to forget someone's name but so hard to forget what scares us? One reason may lie in differences in neural plasticity between the hippocampus and amygdala. The hippocampus, central to explicit memory, varies in size depending on current learning requirements, and remains flexible to new learning (Nader, 2003; Phillips & LeDoux, 1992). In contrast, the amygdala demonstrates persistent (stable) dendritic remodeling triggered by stressful situations (Rainnie et al., 2004; Vyas et al., 2002, 2003, 2004). In other words, the amygdala is like an elephant: It doesn't forget. Whereas the hippocampus is constantly remodeled to keep abreast of current environment changes, the role of the amygdala is to remember a threat, generalize it to other possible threats, and carry it into the future. The combination of these neuroplastic proclivities leads us to be biased toward fear.

This OMPFC–amygdala circuit has evolved far beyond the ability to assess straightforward danger signals and can now evaluate the reward or punishment value of highly complex social interactions (O'Doherty et al., 2001). The positive shaping of this experience-dependent circuitry leads to the development of attachment schema, internal objects, and interpersonal affect-regulation that allow us to stay engaged and learn how to love.

Sasha—The Mine Field of Relationships

Sasha, a woman in her mid-30s, was referred to me by her brother, who had become concerned by her deepening depression and allusions to ending her life. They were the only children of a researcher and his wife who had moved every few years throughout their childhoods, following grant money and laboratory opportunities. Their parents were proud, efficient, and unemotional people, very concerned with appearances and reputation. As parents, they focused exclusively on how Sasha and her brother behaved and performed in school; emotional and social needs never appeared on their radar. Sasha grew up competing with her brother for the little attention their parents had to offer. To this day, their relationship reflected both the efficient cooperation and lack of emotional closeness they had witnessed in their parents' marriage. Sasha's parents seemed concerned only with avoiding being shamed in the eyes of others, so it was no surprise that Sasha's daily experiences were full of shame. She described finding it everywhere, in each interaction, reflected in the eyes of everyone she encountered.

It turns out that Sasha had suffered with serious bouts of depression throughout most of her life and had made a number of suicide attempts. She would take sleeping pills, drink a bottle of liquor, and pass out. Each time, she would wake up the next day with a terrible headache, surprised to be alive. The pain she felt seemed sufficient penance for her inadequacies, allowing her a few days of relief from shame. As I came to know her, I could see that she was always on trial; everyone was judging her, every comment became a condemnation, every gesture was a clue to her inevitable abandonment. Sasha had taken in her experiences as a child: they had shaped her brain, and now she projected them onto everything and everyone. Maintaining a positive connection with her felt like defusing a bomb with the timer rapidly working its way to zero.

Sasha asked me to help her find ways of improving the quality of her life. Together, we generated ideas about activities and goals that might be helpful. Somewhere during these discussions, our collaboration would invisibly shift into an evaluation of her worth as a person. I would notice that her face would become less expressive and her body would grow still. Soon she would stop interacting and simply nod her head, grunting in acquiescence from time to time. She would then stare at me, as if from a great distance. Within minutes she would tell me that she was tired of trying to please me.

Each time this sequence occurred, there was a turning point in our conversation, some trigger that resulted in a shift from something she wanted to do for herself to an external test she felt doomed to fail. Clearly, this pattern was burned into her networks of attachment through countless futile attempts to please her parents. When this emotional state became triggered, I became a judging parent. With this hair-trigger shame response, Sasha's moment-to-moment experience filled with negative evaluations of herself and those around her. She flipped back and forth between childish acquiescence and sarcastic anger aimed at anyone around her. Needless to say, her phone didn't ring, her mailbox was empty, and her messages were not returned. Naturally, this dearth of social reinforcement provided her with more evidence that her parents were right: She was a miserable disappointment and completely unlovable.

Given how few loving interactions she had with her parents, I suspected that Sasha never developed the regulatory functions necessary for smooth interpersonal interactions. She reacted with fight/flight responses to any imagined slight—a result of a poorly developed vagal system and OMPFC–amygdala network development. These brain abnormalities may, in part, have accounted for her extreme shifts in emotion during our sessions. She was unable to directly express even the most minor annoyance with me. When her negative feelings were triggered, she went into a full-blown arousal that would inhibit her language areas, further squelching her ability to talk through her interpersonal difficulties. When she got mad she would invariably overreact, even while knowing that her reactions were out of proportion. Any perceived criticism placed her in the position of a cornered animal. She was driven by fear, unable to think about the consequences of her behavior. This endless pattern left her ashamed and alone.

Sasha was a person whose avoidant attachment schema and poor self-image kept her from the positive regulatory effects of healthy relationships. She described her loneliness as painful, and it is true that isolation results in the activation of brain areas (insula and anterior cingulate) that mediate physical pain. Sasha's endorphins, dopamine, and serotonin levels were not stimulated by positive interactions with others. Her negative internal self-talk served to further decrease the levels of these soothing and rewarding biochemicals. She told me that as a child she was forced to go to bed right after dinner, usually around 6 P.M. Unable to sleep and not permitted to leave her room, she would stand next to her bed not knowing what to do, especially when she felt the urge to go to the bathroom. So entangled was she in this avoidance/avoidance conflict that on a number of occasions, she actually urinated standing next to her bed. She would try to clean it up before her mother noticed, but to no avail.

It never occurred to her to discuss this problem with her mother, who would only recite, again and again, "Good girls go to bed early and stay there till morning. Just close both your eyes, and soon you'll be yawning." In Sasha's words, talking to her mother was like talking to "a robot." Her experiences with her mother served as Sasha's unconscious assumptions about all relationships and all people. My work as her therapist was to disconfirm this expectation and help her to discover a newfound sense of trust in relationships. To give you some idea of the work and the time involved in this process, it took her more than a year before she could ask my permission to leave the session to use the restroom. Even the sensations from her bladder would catapult her back to childhood—and, in her mind, to her bedside—not knowing what to do.

Learning Not to Fear

Learning anything positive, including love, requires freedom from fear. We certainly can learn from traumatic experiences, but such learning has little to do with healthy attachment or real love. If we learn *not* to fear in early relationships, we will enter subsequent relationships assuming that others are trustworthy, caring, and dependable. If early relationships are problematic, we connect with others in a tentative way, anticipating that what has occurred will happen again.

The most important aspect of early attachment relationships is the establishment of a sense of safety. In the same way, establishing and maintaining trust is the first and most important order of business in a therapeutic or teacher–student relationship. Anxiety and fear are endogenous signals to help us stay clear of danger. The problem is that the amygdala has a great memory, loves to generalize, and is always adding to the "things to avoid" list. One of the most difficult challenges for a parent, educator, or therapist is to figure out how to encourage our charges to approach what they fear. As a therapist, I am always trying to get my clients to learn to use their anxiety as a navigation device. Anxiety needs to become a feeling that makes us approach rather than avoid a situation or challenge.

Let's put a human face on the problem. We know, for example, that when individuals with posttraumatic stress disorder look at fearful faces, they display increased amygdala activation and decreased activation in their OMPFC (Shin et al., 2005). We also know that when normal folks, especially those who tend to be more affiliative, experience hostile faces in the environment, their ability to learn decreases (Schultheiss et al., 2005). These studies support the notion that our ability to learn is related to social context and the relative activation of the OMPFC and amygdala. It stands to reason that the opposite social context—a kind and accepting face—may have the opposite effects on neuroplastic processes. It also makes sense that in order to learn to feel safe, we have to approach our anxiety by looking others in the eye.

But, how do you learn to not be afraid? How do you learn to feel safe with your husband when you had a father who would crash through your door in the dead of the night and beat you? When someone is raped, the amygdala will link the sights, sounds, smells, taste, and feelings of the experience with a powerful fight/flight response. Although completely appropriate for the rape experience, the same fear responses may be activated by the touch of a loved one, the smell of his cologne, or the sound of his breathing. How can you accept advice from a teacher when your mother took sadistic pleasure in publicly humiliating you? How do you take a deep breath and tell someone "I love you" even though you still haven't fully recovered from your last relationship?

Extinction research with animals is teaching us that whereas calcium plays a role in short-term extinction, long-term extinction requires gene expression and protein synthesis. This means that the structure and connectivity of neurons needs to be modified before we can learn not to fear. This finding is supported by research showing that the introduction into the amygdala of chemicals that promote neuroplastic changes facilitates extinction (Davis et al., 2003; Walker et al., 2002). NMDA (N-methyl-d-aspartate) receptors are necessary for the protein synthesis involved in both neural growth and long-term behavioral extinction (Davis & Myers, 2002; Ekstrom et al., 2001; Falls et al., 1992; Ghosh, 2002; Liu et al., 2004; Massey et al., 2004). The administration of D-cycloserine before treatment for fear extinction enhances NMDA production, leading to improved treatment response (Ledgerwood et al., 2003; Ressler et al., 2004). The implication of this research is that extinguishing fear involves structural changes in the amygdala, and that therapies may have enhanced efficacy when paired with the introduction of neurochemicals that promote the growth of new structures—and, hence, new learning.

Although we now know that learning or unlearning anything involves changing our brains, we have many more questions than answers. Does extinction involve increasing the inhibition from the OMPFC, the downregulation of certain connections among the various nuclei within the amygdala, or perhaps blocking the output from the amygdala to the autonomic nervous system? The importance of finding out how to eliminate unnecessary fear in our brains has inspired many researchers to search for an answer. What we think we *do* know is that the activation, maintenance, and modulation of fear occur somewhere within this circuitry (Garcia et al., 1999; Hariri et al., 2003; Maren & Quirk, 2004; Pitkänen et al., 1997, 2003; Quirk & Gehlert, 2003; Winstanley et al., 2004). It also seems clear that by employing conscious control of attentional processes, we are able to modulate anxiety (Derryberry & Reed, 2002).

One method of learning not to fear is allowing yourself to be exposed to a feared stimulus and not running away or dissociating it from consciousness. Your grandfather may have called it "getting back up on the horse that threw you" (LeDoux & Gorman, 2001). Cognitive therapists call it exposure, relaxation training, and response prevention. Gestalt therapists call it the "safe emergency" of psychotherapy. Parents do it while holding their child and telling him or her that everything will be okay. Teachers break down complex tasks into manageable parts and encourage their students along the way. All of these "interventions" combine a relationship, moderate levels of arousal, thinking, feeling, and a story. Stir and repeat over and over again. The repetition of this process encourages the reshaping and integration of neural circuits for emotional regulation and learning.

Learning to Love

Can attachment schema change for the better? In essence, can our social brains be healed by loving relationships? Despite all of the leverage evolution has given to the preservation of fear, the answer appears to be *yes!* Although there is consistency in attachment style from childhood into adulthood, many people show changes that reflect ongoing neural plasticity in attachment circuitry (Hamilton, 2000). Early secure attachments

do not immunize a child from later relationship difficulty, just as insecure attachments do not guarantee later psychopathology (Lewis et al.,
1984). Healthy relationships, life challenges, loss, and personal growth
seem capable of reshaping the circuits of the social brain in both positive
and negative ways.

Attachment research has demonstrated that children who do not have
safe and secure relationships with their parents can grow up to attain autonomous attachment status as adults and, in turn, provide secure attachment for their own children. These individuals are considered to
have accomplished what is called "earned autonomy." Somehow, they
have found a way to learn how to cognitively and emotionally process
negative experiences with their parents, find others with whom to connect, and regulate their inner emotional worlds. This is certainly an example of neural plasticity within the networks of the social brain.

Individuals who have accomplished earned autonomy often report
finding someone who was able to make them feel cared for and important and provided them with a feeling of well-being and safety. They
found someone who was curious and interested in their thoughts and
feelings. Sometimes it was a passion for some shared activity or interest
that connected them with others and provided a sense of belonging
and accomplishment. In short, later relationships and/or the working
through and integration of childhood experiences is possible. Earned autonomy appears capable of interrupting the transmission of negative attachment patterns from one generation to the next. It is what we hope
will happen through the process of psychotherapy.

Our inherent optimism about overcoming fear and altering attachment patterns for the better is repeated again and again in themes of redemption in Western literature. Stories of reclaiming admission to the
social world through personal struggle fill our hearts. We saw this theme
with Jean Valjean, and we see it in Charles Dickens's (1966) Ebenezer
Scrooge. The sad events of Ebenezer's early life—his mother's death and
being sent off to boarding school by an indifferent father—led him to a
life of misanthropy and isolation. While still a young man, Ebenezer's fi-
ancée left him with these words: "You fear the world too much. All your
other hopes have merged into the hope of being beyond the chance of
its sordid reproach."

When we meet Ebenezer after decades of isolation, loneliness, and penury, he is visited by his long-dead partner and three additional ghosts. What do these ghosts show Scrooge? They expose him to the kindnesses he had received from others in the past, the suffering and kindhearted-ness of those around him in the present, and the stark inevitability of his own death. He witnesses how he has hardened his heart in reaction to the pain he had to endure, and how this hardening makes him blind to both the love and suffering around him. Somehow, in the course of one night, the ghosts of Christmas past, present, and future rekindle within him a sense of connection and love for his fellow humans: Ebenezer is wonderfully transformed!

> He went to church, and walked about the streets, and watched the peo-ple hurrying to and fro, and patted the children on the head, and ques-tioned the beggars, and looked down into the kitchens of houses, and up to the windows, and found that everything could yield him pleasure. He had never dreamed that any walk—that anything—could give him so much happiness. [Ebenezer discovers] "I am not the man I was. I will not be the man I must have been but for this intercourse. . . . I will live in the Past, Present, and the Future. The Spirits of all Three shall strive within me. I will not shut out the lessons that they teach." (p. 211)

Therapists strive to embody all three ghosts: We explore the past, test the realities of the present, and imagine possible futures. We take this journey with our clients, supporting and nurturing them while ques-tioning assumptions and challenging defenses. Ultimately, it is the shar-ing of this journey that is at the heart of all relationships.

Chapter 23

Social Brain
and Group Mind

It is man's participation in culture and the realiza-
tion of his mental powers through culture that
make it possible to construct a human psychology
on the basis of the individual alone.
—Jerome Bruner, 1990, p. 12

Early in my training as a psychotherapist I spent a week with a Zen master in the mountains near Mt. Fuji. I'll never forget the tranquil beauty of the Japanese countryside and the small temple tucked into a hillside where I spent most of my time. The days consisted of meditation and physical labor, followed by evening discussions with Sensei (teacher) and his other students. Sensei had been a monk for decades and was now the Zen priest for his community. He also served as a healer of "troubled" individuals who would come to spend time with him. I was most interested in what he understood to be the active ingredients of healing and what he thought changed inside his "patients."

Although communicating through a translator was an obstacle, it was nothing compared to the challenge posed by our differing worldviews. I slowly came to understand that his decades of meditation were a way of getting to know himself and to see reality more clearly. His training consisted of physical labor, meditation, discussions with his master, and studying Buddhist teachings. In his own words, the "therapy" he performed consisted of allowing others "to live my life with me."

Illusion

Why did Sensei devote himself exclusively to prayer and meditation for so many years? The simple answer to this question was to become enlightened. Buddhists talk in terms of seeing through the illusions of the senses, the self, and the ego and detaching from beliefs and possessions. The goal, from a psychological perspective, is to overcome the anxiety that often overwhelms our experience. Although I can't pretend to know what it feels like to be enlightened, neuroscience has given me one way to understand what Buddhists have discovered through thousands of years of discipline and introspection.

The complexities and compromises of the brain's evolution—those things that gave rise to psychotherapy—also appear to be the ground for some Buddhist beliefs. Evolution has done a magnificent job shaping the social brain, but we are far from perfect, especially when it comes to an accurate understanding of the world and the people around us. As we have seen, our brain processes most information out of consciousness and far faster than we can comprehend. Within these same neural networks, early emotional learning continues to influence, shape, and distort our experience. We have also witnessed the energy evolution has devoted to reading the minds of others and how little attention it has paid to self-awareness.

Our brains are also biased toward monitoring and preventing fear in ways that minimize conscious anxiety. Unfortunately, one of the costs of safety is to often minimize exploration and openmindedness. We can easily become attached to thoughts and ways of being that continue to hurt us because we are too afraid to risk new ways of seeing ourselves or experiencing our world. The more afraid we remain, the more convinced we become that the way we see the world is the "right" way. Sensei was fond of saying that *suffering is caused by the avoidance of pain*. Although I had always thought that pain and suffering were essentially the same thing, for Sensei, pain was just a basic part of nature. Sensei's belief was that we are fragile beings who get battered around by nature and fate, experience disappointment, lose the ones we love, have illnesses, grow old, and inevitably die.

To feel pain in response to these experiences, according to Sensei, is simply a part of life. Suffering, he explained, occurs when we try to avoid pain. To do this we become attached to objects that we think will keep us safe, fool ourselves into believing we are invincible, and distort reality into something more palatable. It is the suffering caused by our estrangement from "what is" that causes us to suffer. While pain is transient, suffering can become a way of life; we exchange something that will pass for something that never ends. Sensei tried to teach his students to be open to the pain of life as well as any other emotions that might arise. In this way, he felt, the suffering created by our minds could be cleared away and replaced by the everyday pain that is a natural part of life.

Over his many years of meditation, Sensei became familiar with the workings of his mind, gaining increasing control over his thoughts and perceptions. This clarity allowed him to experience himself and the world more clearly. The result was that he was able to be more perceptive and emotionally available in the present moment. Meditation, psychotherapy, and spiritual journeys are but three tools that can help us expand our awareness, which, in turn, makes us more available to ourselves and to others. Like love and trust, simple presence is a nurturing aspect of human relationships. Sensei had learned to be present; profoundly and powerfully present.

Connection

Inherent in Japanese thinking is the idea that mental health is reflected in interdependence: a state of being in which we receive care from others and give care in return. From this perspective mental illness results from a disconnection from others and a retreat into selfishness. Some people suffer because of negative early experiences. Others get caught up in selfish pursuits later in life and use others for their own needs. In either of these cases, we learn to suppress memories of love and cut ourselves off from connection and intimacy. Treatment, such as Naikan therapy, focuses on establishing (or reestablishing) a person's connection with those around him or her, believing that when a person is able to surrender to a life of appreciation and self-sacrifice, he or she will gain a sense of belonging, balance, and peace (Reynolds, 1980).

Toshi, a Tokyo businessman who was staying at the temple during my visit, talked to me about his weeks in Naikan therapy. He described spending most of his time in a cell practicing guided meditation and journal writing. Toshi was visited four times a day by a teacher who would read his journal, discuss his thoughts and feelings, and give him new topics to think about. He was given assignments such as listing all of the people he had known in his life and everything he had received from each of them. No gift, kindness, or courtesy was too small. His room soon filled with stacks of these lists.

Toshi was often moved to tears as he remembered his grandparents and a favorite uncle. He recalled the time they dedicated to him as a child and their sacrifices for his education and career. He told me that with each passing day, his depression, anger, and anxiety gradually lifted. He described a growing feeling of wanting to get back to his family and work, to be more caring to those around him, and to attend more to honoring his ancestors. These were feelings and thoughts he hadn't experienced for many years. His essential warmth and humility were certainly evident in his behavior at the temple: Despite his wealth and status, I remember Toshi diligently sweeping the footpath up to the temple each evening before dinner.

My first impression of this perspective on psychotherapy was that it was an expression of the Japanese communal mind and hardly applicable to Western cultures. With my growing appreciation of the social nature of the brain, I've had some second thoughts. I've come to suspect that the radical individualism of the West is one reason why we experience a higher incidence of psychological distress, drug addiction, and violence (Kawakami et al., 2004; Kessler et al., 2003). I recently heard a young American woman describe her experience of returning to the United States after attending a Japanese secondary school. She came from an unemotional family who sent her away to school to "expand her horizons." She said at first she felt overwhelmed by all the people around her but gradually came to accept their constant presence. She was surprised to find herself enjoying doing everything in groups, always feeling watched over and cared for. After graduating and returning to the United States, she reported feeling depressed and lost, suffering from anxieties that grew into phobias and struggles with self-confidence in college.

Sensei believed in the healing power of living our lives together, and that was his treatment. He lived his life deliberately and intentionally, always working to minimize the interference from his own misunderstandings, illusions, and unresolved suffering. Sensei believed that living itself can be healing if you are able to connect with others and be productive. Like Freud, Sensei believed that *love and work* were at the center of human life.

Curiosity

Whereas Japanese culture emphasizes social obligation as a vehicle for connectedness, it also pressures individuals to conform to narrow group norms. Isolation may not be a problem, but many in this communal system also crave more diversity and autonomy. We are complex creatures craving both connection and independence, security and adventure. Half of us wants to stay safe in bed while the other half craves risk. This aspect of human nature is reflected in the structures of our brains; whereas some are dedicated to safety, others have been shaped to forage and explore new worlds.

Parents sometimes ask my opinion about what I think are the most important aspects of child rearing. The obvious first choices are love and secure attachment, but what comes next? A consistent theme of adult psychotherapy clients is that they had parents who were not curious about who they were but, instead, told them who they should be. This parenting stance often results in a child who creates a persona for his parents' benefit but who doesn't come to know himself. For these folks, the authentic self—the part of us that is open to feelings, experiences, and intimacy—remains undeveloped. What emerges from such conditional childrearing is a variety of symptoms that bring people to therapy. A straitjacket of expectation is a formula for rigidity; for a sensitive and creative child, it can constitute significant trauma.

It is so important to be curious about who your children are, to learn how to play with them, and to encourage their imaginations. All that we have learned about neural plasticity tells us that the brain is primed to grow in conditions of safety, positive excitement, shared openness, and exploration. These states of mind create the flexibility that lets *you* adapt to your children and helps *them* discover their inner worlds. Much psychological distress in adulthood stems from having parents who had a picture of their child that did not match who the child was. In these cases, the child either rebelled and separated or became a "good child," conforming on the outside while remaining empty on the inside. In other instances, there was just a bad match between the temperaments and personalities of parents and their children.

Every child is an experiment of nature. Children need their parents' curiosity about them as an avenue of self-discovery. Attunement, secure attachment, curiosity, affect regulation, and brain plasticity go hand in hand. Maximum neural plasticity for both parent and child is probably the optimal foundation on which both can live in the present moment and learn from (and about) one another. Parental mirroring helps guide children through the infinite number of steps from physical birth into full membership into the social mind. Along the way, these interactions come to serve as the infrastructure not only of the self but of our ability to have emotional and interpersonal experiences. Love may be best defined as the availability to change for another.

Telling Stories

Oral tradition has long been the means of transmitting history and culture among individuals and across generations. Group participation in the construction of memory embeds it within a social context and assists in linking feelings to actions and self to others. The cocreation and repetition of stories also helps children develop and practice memory skills as their memories are shaped by the input of others (Nelson, 1993). The coconstruction of narratives imparts culture and shapes a secure sense of our place within our tribe. Unfortunately, it also transfers a caretaker's fears, anxieties, and distortions to the child's emotional and abstract experience of the world (Ochs & Capps, 2001).

The photograph in Figure 23.1 is one of my favorites. I feel that it captures the way that people are brought together by a story. I imagine the elder telling a mythic tale of the forces of nature colliding with the will of men. I see him using his words, facial expressions, gestures, intonation, sound effects, and eye contact to capture the minds and emotions

Figure 23.1. **The storyteller. A wonderful depiction of communication across the social synapse. Courtesy of Getty images.**

of those gathered around him. I think of the story bringing the listeners closer together in a shared imaginary journey, creating a vivid point of reference in their connection to the social mind of the tribe. I imagine the children, huddled together later that night, retelling the story, taking on the role of the hero and absorbing the strength and knowledge contained in its teachings. I think, as we witness this process, we are observing messages being transmitted across the social synapse within the larger human organism.

It turns out that the memories contained in our stories are also evolving. Memories are not a file of notes; they are stories that are told, reorganized, and recreated with each telling. Each time a memory is accessed, it can be modified (both in its narrative and neurology) by new experiences that increase its relevance to current conditions (Duvarci & Nader, 2004; Nader, 2003). The upside is that difficult or confusing memories can be restructured. Revisiting and revising the past (and the related thoughts and beliefs) are central components of dynamic, cognitive, and systems therapies. I'm sure that as tribal elders tell the stories that they heard as children in these small circles, they intentionally or even unwittingly make them more relevant to the current life of their tribe.

Secure parents share information about their internal states and ask their children about what's on their minds. These discussions provide scaffolding for cognitive processing, emotional regulation, and an ability to think about our experiences. This connection can also occur with others. If a child is able to attach to someone other than the primary caretaker, he or she may be able to earn a higher level of integration and security than would be predicted by the parents' level of attachment (Siegel, 1999). This "learning ability" may be part of the explanation of why some parents who experienced negative childhood experiences are able to provide a safe haven for their children. Their earned autonomy is convincing evidence of ongoing neural plasticity and the repair of attachment schema later in life.

Narratives of frightening experiences can serve as the context for healing by stimulating cortical activation and increasing descending control over subcortically triggered emotions. Not surprisingly, it turns out that securely attached children have more complex narratives, engage in more self-talk, and make more spontaneous self-reflective remarks (Fonagy et al., 1996). Securely attached children appreciate that their thoughts are private and tend to "meta-communicate"; that is, they make comments about their thinking and their ability to remember things about their history (Main et al., 1985). They develop the capacity for self-reflection and alternate between acting and stepping back to consider their actions.

As you might expect, child neglect and abuse correlate with less secure attachment and a decreased ability to think about internal states. As a result, these children also possess a greater tendency to "act out" instead of being able to think about, discuss, and come to understand their feelings (Beeghly & Cicchetti, 1994). Narratives serve neural network integration and the health of the persons who tell them and hear them. When a child is abused and kept in silence, there is little neural integration and even less joy.

Melanie—My African Cinderella

"Hi, I'm Melanie. Melanie isn't my real name but Americans can't pronounce my real name, so just call me Melanie. Nice to meet you." When we had talked on the phone prior to our session, Melanie told me that she was always anxious and suffered from an eating disorder and sexual addiction. At 29, she had only recently found the courage to seek help. Melanie sat staring at my shoes, a look of distressed sadness on her face. Melanie's family had emigrated from Nigeria soon after she was born. Although her parents had brought their five older children with them, Melanie was left behind with her grandparents. When she was 6, her father came back to take her to America. She had never met him before, and no one had told her that he was coming to take her way.

One minute she was safe at home and the next she found herself on a plane with a strange man. When she arrived in her new home, she found five siblings and a mother who didn't want her. She learned that her father had brought her to this country against the wishes of his family. Melanie was teased relentlessly by her siblings and told she was fat, ugly, and disgusting. Her mother spoke to her only to criticize and give her orders. Melanie recalled how embarrassed she felt when a teacher read *Cinderella,* and she cried in front of her classmates. The teacher unfeelingly told her to be quiet and not ruin the reading for the other children. Somehow, Melanie managed to graduate from high school and move away a few days before her 18th birthday.

It came as no surprise that Melanie had difficulty sustaining relationships. She was fine being with men with whom she had superficial relationships. As long as she was having sex or performing some service for whomever it might be, she felt safe and secure. If she were at a man's house and she ran out of things to do, she would soon bolt out the door. "I realize this isn't normal," Melanie told me, "and I really would like to learn how to be with a man, even if we're just hanging out."

Melanie's negative experiences with her family didn't dampen her need to be close to others—if anything, they increased it. She continually searched the eyes of strangers trying to find the love and safety she had lost so long ago. Unfortunately, being close to people was linked with the anticipation of separation and rejection, and drove her to escape her fear by fleeing from the other person's presence. When she felt this fear, she could not fight, speak, or even think; she only knew she had to get away. The men she dated never understood why she seemed to suddenly disappear. Melanie looked at me with a wry smile and explained, "I guess it's harder to hit a moving target."

From time to time, she alluded to the fact that there had been physical and sexual abuse at the hands of her father, but she said it was too embarrassing to talk about. I suggested that instead of focusing on the past we work on learning to tolerate higher levels of anxiety in her present relationships. Our sessions focused on gradually increasing the amount of "nonactivity" time she spent with her boyfriend while learning to risk what felt like inevitable rejection. We worked on relaxation techniques for these situations and monitoring the chains of thoughts and feelings that existed between intimacy and flight. This assignment gradually allowed her to understand, and gain some control over, the cascade of emotions and behaviors that kept her from staying put.

Melanie was a bright and personable individual who was fun to spend time with. My best evidence for this statement was how much I enjoyed our sessions—a pleasure she could clearly see reflected in my face. I felt certain that if she could stay in the right relationship long enough, her partner would be happy to work at keeping her in his life. As therapy went on, the focus of treatment shifted from her fear of being rejected to her fear of being loved and accepted. Eventually, her boyfriend asked her to move in with him, which presented a new crisis with a different twist. During one session, I brought in a copy of Cinderella and we took turns reading to one another. Seeing Cinderella's sincerity and innocence, Melanie began to reconsider the shame she had internalized during her years of rejection and abuse. The fact that Cinderella eventually found her prince became a powerful image for her to hold in mind as she struggled with her intimacy anxiety. We were not trying to define her by her relationship with a man but to utilize a once painful narrative to rebuild her sense of security and trust in the social world.

This was an instance in which the power of fairy tales, myths, and other narratives, especially those that tap into early-life experiences, can consolidate a state of mind to help us cope with fear. The picture of Cinderella and the prince embracing on the last page of the book symbolized Melanie's struggles and a vision of a happy ending. She would strive to achieve a state of connection with another who would love and protect her. It served as a *memory for the future* that could soothe her in the present. Her pain could eventually be left behind as she created a life where she was no longer an outsider. Melanie liked to savor the final line, saying in a slow, quiet voice, "and they lived happily ever after."

The unifying functions of stories and the healing reflected in changing narratives rests upon the underlying physiological changes that occur during healing relationships. Gaze, pupil dilation, facial expressions, posture, proximity, touch, and mirror systems are all reflexive and obligatory systems that work below conscious awareness. These and other systems yet to be discovered create a high-speed information linkup between us, establishing ongoing physiological and emotional synchrony (Coleman et al., 1956; DiMascio et al., 1957; Field et al., 2002; Levenson & Ruef, 1992; Malatesta & Haviland, 1982; Robles & Kiecolt-Glaser, 2003).

Therapy and other healing relationships utilize all levels of connection— from metabolic regulation to narratives—to alter neural network activation and balance. For example, when successfully treated with psychotherapy, depressed patients have been shown to achieve metabolic normalization in their frontal and temporal lobes, and patients with anxiety disorders have shown reduced activation in cortical and subcortical areas (Brody et al., 2001; Furman et al., 2002; Paquette et al., 2003; Schwartz et al., 1996). Thus, the brain remains plastic into adulthood and can be changed for the better in the context of personal and professional relationships. This plasticity depends on both top-down changes captured in narratives and bottom-up changes we can measure through brain activity and experience in our bodies (Berntson et al., 2003).

Self and Internal Experience

It may seem a bit paradoxical to conclude a book about the social brain with a discussion of the self, but in fact, the self emerges from relationships. The creation of a self is a gift we receive from our parents, caretakers, teachers, and coaches who show interest, concern, and curiosity about us. How does the self come to develop within the social brain? It is safe to assume that the self consists of many layers of neural processing that develop from the bottom up as we grow. The first systems of internal bodily sensations are joined by sensory–motor systems, added to by emotional and cognitive processing, and later topped off with abstract ideas and beliefs. All of these systems are woven together in the context of our relationships. This entire multilayered experience is then described in a coconstructed life story and labeled with the term "I."

Because the self cannot be localized in one defined area of the brain, the experience of self is likely an *emergent function* of multiple systems of implicit and explicit memory (Greenwald & Banaji, 1989). The experience of self is born in early relationships that shape the many layers of function biased toward the right hemisphere, as the cerebral cortex goes through its first critical period. This bias is most likely the foundation of right-hemispheric dominance for negative emotion, unconscious processing, and affective regulation. It also reflects two "truths" from psychoanalysis: (1) our mother's unconscious is our first reality, and (2) the individual emerges from the dyad.

Some interesting research suggests that the insula and anterior cingulate cortices may be involved in the early development and ongoing organization of the self. As we have seen, they both process information at the interface of the cortex and limbic system, coordinating thought and emotion with bodily experience. As the earliest evolving portions of the cortex, they have sensitive periods early in life, develop in the context of intense caretaking, and are sculpted by relational experiences. When caretaking includes emotional attunement, self-reflection, and sharing about states of mind, our children learn to be better aware of themselves and include this awareness in their narratives about themselves and the world.

Just as violinists expand their motor cortex as they advance their playing skills, people who are encouraged to look within and articulate what they find will expand their insula, cingulate, and frontal cortices (Allman et al., 2001; Craig, 2004; Gundel et al., 2004). In fact, the size of the right anterior insula is correlated with the propensity to experience certain emotions (Bechara & Naqvi, 2004). Secure attachment, the inclusion of internal states into discussions, even a parent's curiosity about what his or her child feels—all stimulate the development and connectivity of neural networks throughout the brain. This integration may allow for an increased consciousness of internal states, better emotional regulation, and an improved ability to attain shared states of consciousness.

Wisdom

How does the brain change with advancing age? Does gaining wisdom over time involve changes in the brain? Research shows that we lose gray matter through most of life, and white matter begins to decline at midlife. Mix these facts together with our culture's bias against aging and we come up with a pretty grim picture of the maturing brain; we hit our peak in early adulthood, followed by an embarrassing decline into senility. But for the vast majority of people, this trajectory is far from true. Yes, it is true that our brains get smaller as we grow older, but is this necessarily a bad thing? Remember, programmed cell death is a vital aspect of brain development, as systems are shaped by experience to become more functionally efficient. Could a similar process be happening later in life?

To remember stories, older individuals tend to use both sides of their brain more than younger people, who rely more on one side or the other (Beason-Held et al., 2005; Cabeza et al., 1997; Maguire & Frith, 2003; Reuter-Lorenz & Stanczak, 2000). And although this change in processing strategy *may* be due to compensation for declining functioning (the commonly held belief), it may also provide older adults with increased hemispheric participation that can better integrate affect with cognition and increase perspective. Slower functioning may also allow older adults more time to think through things as opposed to going with initial impulses. Further, it has been found that older adults demonstrate greater complexity of brain wave patterns during information processing, suggesting that a greater number of better organized neural networks are participating in higher-order mental processes (Anokhin et al., 1996).

Thus, changes generally thought of as degenerative signs of aging appear to effect a reorganization in the way the brain processes information. Is this bad or does evolution have a card up its sleeve? Might older individuals have a role in the social order that matches changes in their brain? In reality, aging correlates with an increasing fund of knowledge, an improvement in the comprehension of meaning, and a preservation and even improvement of our narrative abilities (Levine, 2004). Given that written language is relatively new on the evolutionary scene, older individuals have historically been the keepers of knowledge, history, and value through storytelling. Specific facts grow less important over time, because they change, whereas the general social values and survival strategies remain vital. Thus, the way the brain ages may have been shaped by the needs of the group within an oral culture (Vaillant, 2002).

It has been found that the nature of gene transcription also changes over the lifespan, with as many as 540 genes showing different timing patterns related to brain-based events (Erraji-Benchekroun et al., 2005). The construction, maintenance, and shaping of the brain has been influenced over eons by the social demands on individuals. If a mother's brain changes to help her care for her child, than those who are to be the keepers of the culture and embody the tribe's long-term memory will have brains that are shaped to play their role; not that all individuals are destined to play this role. Wise elders will likely be those individuals who stay both mentally and physically vital throughout life (Danner et al., 2001). It may actually be their ongoing involvement and curiosity that trigger their brains to be shaped for wisdom later in life

Both physical and mental activity stimulate brain growth in ways that trigger neurogenesis, network connectivity, and enhanced vascularization. Research has shown that greater amounts of gray matter in the temporal, parietal, and frontal lobes later in life are related to what has been called "self-transcendence." In the context of this research, self-transcendence includes factors such as mature creativity, openness to divergent feelings and thoughts, and a sense of connectedness with others and the world (Kaasinen et al., 2005).

The wise elders, medicine men and women, and teachers who serve as the "glue" for their communities and are sought out for their knowledge, guidance, and comfort have been present in all cultures throughout recorded time. They are special people who have spent a lifetime thinking, studying, caring for others, and stimulating brain growth. These wise elders often have stronger support systems, which, in turn, support superior brain functioning (Baltes & Lang, 1997). I suggest that we take a new look at aging. What we call wisdom may be programmed into the way brains are selected and shaped to hold families and tribes together.

The Evolution of Consciousness

What's next? How will our brains adapt to the changing demands of the world we now inhabit? Remember the primacy of projection and how we tend to attribute our own unconscious processes, feelings, and motives to those around us? We have millions of years of evolution dedicated to refining systems for reading the intentions, behaviors, and thoughts of others. We are quick to think we know others because these processes—and the attributions and emotions they trigger—are automatic and unconscious. Although our brains have evolved to predict what others are thinking, they are lagging behind in self-knowledge. Whereas projection is reflexive and lessens anxiety, self-awareness requires effort and a willingness to tolerate the anxiety it can create. Expanding and enhancing self-awareness is an evolutionary frontier that stretches ahead of us.

A second evolutionary frontier relates to anxiety—how we experience and understand it. Evolution has shaped the fear response to help animals stay alive. This is a good thing, except when you add an ever-expanding cortex. The sheer brain power we now have for abstraction, conceptualization, and imagining the future leads us to the point where we are able to be afraid of things that are not even possible. We have also created a society that itself generates so many stressors that we can be in a state of constant anxiety that could last our entire lives.

As modern human beings we have these two automatic and implicit processes, projection and anxiety, that automatically and unconsciously shape our experiences of the world. Unfortunately, mindfulness and the ability to tolerate anxiety are far less common. If anything, our omnivorous consumerism and thrill-seeking behavior bind us ever more tightly to sources of stimulation outside of ourselves.

The evolution of consciousness will involve remembering who we are. On the one hand, we need to learn to use our intellectual capacity to find ways around the hazards of our still primitive brains (Ouspensky, 1954). On the other, we need to deepen our appreciation of our interconnection and learn better how to listen and to love. These two directions are actually one and the same, because expanding our mindfulness will involve those around us who remind us to stay on task, correct our misperceptions, and offer alternative perspectives to ours. In this way, human relationships serve as external neural circuits that feed information back to us in comprehensible ways and deepen our awareness of the organism called the human species.

Getting to know another person requires that we know who we are. Although this might seem obvious and simple, knowing who we are involves an extremely high state of awareness that includes self-insight, curiosity, wisdom, and a still point from which to experience the world. It took Sensei 10 years of silent meditation before he felt he could experience this still point clearly. Placing our individual views into a social perspective, knowing our limitations, biases, and prejudices, and appreciating the importance of human relationships have the potential to lead us to a more loving world.

References

Abell, F., Krams, M., Ashburner, J., Passingham, R., Friston, K., Frackowiak, R., et al. (1999). The neuroanatomy of autism: A voxel-based whole brain analysis of structural scans. *NeuroReport, 10,* 1647–1651.

Abercrombie, H. C., Schaefer, S. M., Larson, C. L., Ward, R. T., Holden, J. E., Turski, P. A., et al. (1996). Medial prefrontal and amygdalar glucose metabolism in depressed and control subjects: An FDG-PET study. *Psychophysiology, 33,* S17.

Abler, B., Walter, H., & Erk, S. (2005). Neural correlates of frustration. *NeuroReport, 16,* 669–672.

Acerra, F., Burnod, Y., & de Schonen, S. (2002). Modelling aspects of face processing in early infancy. *Developmental Science, 5,* 98–117.

Acolet, D., Modi, N., Giannakoulopoulos, X., Bond, C., Weg, W., Clow, A., et al. (1993). Changes in plasma cortisol and catecholamine concentrations in response to massage in preterm infants. *Archives of Disease in Childhood, 68,* 29–31.

Adams, R. B., Jr., Gordon, H. L., Baird, A. A., Ambady, N., & Kleck, R. E. (2003). Gaze differentially modulates amygdala sensitivity to anger and fear faces. *Science, 300,* 1536.

Adams, R. D., Victor, M., & Ropper, A. H. (1997). *Principles of neurology.* New York: McGraw-Hill.

Adler, H. M. (2002). The sociophysiology of caring in the doctor–patient relationship. *Journal of General Medicine, 17,* 883–890.

Adolphs, R. (2002a). Neural systems for recognizing emotion. *Current Opinion in Neurobiology, 12,* 169–177.

Adolphs, R. (2002b). Trust in the brain. *Nature Neuroscience, 5,* 192–193.

Adolphs, R. (2003a). Cognitive neuroscience of human social behaviour. *Nature Reviews Neuroscience, 4,* 165–178.

Adolphs, R. (2003b). Investigating the cognitive neuroscience of social behavior. *Neuropsychologia, 41,* 119–126.

Adolphs, R. (2003c). Is the human amygdala specialized for processing social information? *Annals of the New York Academy of Sciences, 985,* 326–340.

Adolphs, R., Damasio, H., & Tranel, D. (2002). Neural systems for recognition of emotional prosody: A 3-D lesion study. *Emotion, 2,* 23–51.

Adolphs, R., Damasio, H., Tranel, D., Cooper, G., & Damasio, A. R. (2000). A role for somatosensory cortices in the visual recognition of emotion as revealed by three-dimensional lesion mapping. *Journal of Neuroscience, 20,* 2683–2690.

Adolphs, R., & Tranel, D. (2003). Amygdala damage impairs emotion recognition from scenes only when they contain facial expressions. *Neuropsychologia, 41,* 1281–1289.

Adolphs, R., Tranel, D., & Damasio, A. (1998). The human amygdala in social judgment. *Nature, 393,* 470–474.

Adolphs, R., Tranel, D., Damasio, H., & Damasio, A. (1994). Impaired recognition of emotion in facial expressions following bilateral damage to the human amygdala. *Nature, 372,* 669–672.

Adolphs, R., Tranel, D., Damasio, H., & Damasio A. R. (1995). Fear and the human amygdala. *Journal of Neuroscience, 15,* 5879–5891.

Aguirre, G. K., Singh, R., & D'Esposito, M. (1999). Stimulus inversion and the responses of face and object-sensitive cortical areas. *NeuroReport, 10,* 189–194.

Aharon, I., Etcoff, N., Ariely, D., Chabris, C. F., O'Connor, E., & Breiter, H. C. (2001). Beautiful faces have variable reward value: fMRI and behavioral evidence. *Neuron, 32,* 537–551.

Ahern, G. L., Schomer, D. L., Kleefield, J., Blume, H., Cosgrove, G. R., Weintraub, S., et al. (1991). Right hemisphere advantage for evaluating emotional facial expressions. *Cortex, 27,* 193–202.

Ainsworth, M. D. S., Blehar, M. C., Waters, E., & Wall, S. (1978). *Patterns of attachment: A psychological study of the strange situation.* Hillsdale, NJ: Erlbaum.

Akshoomoff, N. A., & Courchesne, E. (1994). ERP evidence for a shifting attention deficit in patients with damage to the cerebellum. *Journal of Cognitive Neuroscience, 6,* 388–399.

Alexander, G. E., DeLong, M. R., & Strick, P. L. (1986). Parallel organization of functionally segregated circuits linking basal ganglia and cortex. *Annual Review of Neuroscience, 9,* 357–381.

Allison, T., Puce, A., & McCarthy, G. (2000). Social perception from visual cues: Role of the STS region. *Trends in Cognitive Sciences, 4,* 267–278.

Allman, J., & Brothers, L. (1994). Faces, fear, and the amygdala. *Nature, 372,* 613–614.

Allman, J. M., Hakeem, A., Erwin, J. M., Nimchinsky, E., & Hof, P. (2001). The anterior cingulate cortex: The evolution of an interface between emotion and cognition. *Annals of the New York Academy of Sciences, 935,* 107–117.

Allman, J. M., Watson, K. K., Tetreault, N. A., & Hakeem, A. Y. (2005). Intuition and autism: A possible role for Von Economo neurons. *Trends in Cognitive Sciences, 9,* 367–373.

Amaral, D. G. (2002). The primate amygdala and the neurobiology of social behavior: Implications for understanding social anxiety. *Biological Psychiatry, 51,* 11–17.

Amaral, D. G. (2003). The amydala, social behavior, and danger detection. *Annals of the New York Academy of Sciences, 1000,* 337–347.

Amaral, D. G., Bauman, M. D., Capitanio, J. P., Lavenex, P., Mason, W. A., Mauldin-Jourdain, M. L., et al. (2003b). The amygdala: Is it an essential component of the neural network for social cognition? *Neuropsychologia, 41,* 517–522.

Amaral, D. G., Bauman, M. D., & Schumann, C. M. (2003a). The amygdala and autism: Implications from non-human primate studies. *Genes, Brain, and Behavior, 2,* 295–302.

Amaral, D. G., Price, J. L., Pitkanen, A., & Carmichael, S. T. (1992). Anatomical organization of the primate amygdaloid complex. In J. P. Aggleton (Ed.), *The amygdala: Neurobiolgical aspects of emotion, memory, and mental dysfunction* (pp. 1–66). New York: Wiley-Liss.

Amaral, D. G., Veazey, R. B., & Cowan, W. M. (1982). Some observations on the hypothalamo–amygdaloid connections in the monkey. *Brain Research, 252,* 13–27.

American Psychiatric Association (2000). *Diagnostic and statistical manual of mental disorders* (4th ed., rev.) Washington, DC: Author.

Amir, N., Elias, J., Klumpp, H., & Przeworski, A. (2003). Attentional bias to threat in social phobia: Facilitated processing of threat or difficulty disengaging attention from threat? *Behavior Research and Therapy, 41,* 1325–1335.

Amir, N., Foa, E. B., & Coles, M. E. (2000). Implicit memory bias for threat-relevant information in individuals with generalized social phobia. *Journal of Abnormal Psychology, 109,* 713–720.

Amir, S., Lamont, E. W., Robinson, B., & Stewart, J. (2004). A circadian rhythm in the expression of PERIOD2 protein reveals a novel SCN-controlled oscillator in the oval nucleus of the bed nucleus of the stria terminalis. *Journal of Neuroscience, 24,* 781–790.

Anderson, A. K., Christoff, K., Panitz, D., De Rosa, E., & Gabrieli, J. D. E. (2003). Neural correlates of the automatic processing of threat facial signals. *Journal of Neuroscience, 23,* 5627–5633.

Anderson, A. K., & Phelps, E. A. (2000). Perceiving emotion: There's more than meets the eye. *Current Biology, 10,* R551–R554.

Anderson, A. K., Spencer, D. D., & Fulbright, R. K. (2000). Contribution of the anteromedial temporal lobes to the evaluation of facial emotion. *Neuropsychology, 14,* 526–536.

Anderson, G. C. (1991). Current knowledge about skin-to-skin (kangaroo) care for preterm infants. *Journal of Perinatology, 11,* 216–226.

Anderson, S. W., Bechara, A., Damasio, H., Tranel, D., & Damasio, A. R. (1999). Impairment of social and moral behavior related to early damage in human prefrontal cortex. *Nature Neuroscience, 2,* 1032–1037.

Andersson, J. L., Lilja, A., Hartvig, P., Långström, B., Gordh, T., Handwerker, H., et al. (1997). Somatotopic organization along the central sulcus, for pain localization in humans, as revealed by positron emission tomography. *Experimental Brain Research, 117,* 192–199.

Andersson, M. (1982). Female choice selects for extreme tail length in a widow bird. *Nature, 299,* 818–820.

Andreasen, N. C., O'Leary, D. S., Arndt, S., Cizadlo, T., Hurtig, R., Rezai, K., et al. (1996). Neural substrates of facial recognition. *Journal of Neuropsychiatry and Clinical Neurosciences, 8,* 139–146.

Anisman, H., Zaharia, M. D., Meaney, M. J., & Merali, Z. (1998). Do early-life events permanently alter behavioral and hormonal responses to stressors? *International Journal of Developmental Neuroscience, 16,* 149–164.

Anokhin, A. P., Birbaumer, N., Lutzenberger, W., Nikolaev, A., & Vogel, F. (1996). Age increases brain complexity. *Electroencephalography and Clinical Neurophysiology, 99,* 63–68.

Apicella, P., Scarnati, E., Ljungberg, T., & Schultz, W. (1992). Neuronal activity in monkey striatum related to the expectation of predictable environmental events. *Journal of Neurophysiology, 68,* 945–960.

Arbib, M. A. (2002). Language evolution: The mirror system hypothesis. In M. A. Arbib (Ed.), *The handbook of brain theory and neural networks* (2nd ed., pp. 606–611). Cambridge, MA: MIT Press.

Argyropoulos, S. V., Bell, C. J., & Nutt, D. J. (2001). Brain function in social anxiety disorder. *Psychiatric Clinics of North America, 24,* 707–722.

Arnett, P. A., Howland, E. W., Smith, S. S., & Newman, J. P. (1993). Autonomic responsivity during passive avoidance in incarcerated psychopaths. *Personality and Individual Differences, 14,* 173–184.

Aronowitz, B. R., DeCaria, C., Allen, A., Weiss, N., Saunders, A., Margolin, L., et al. (1997). The neuropsychiatry of autism and Asperger's disorders: Review of the literature and case reports. *CNS Spectrums, 2,* 43–60.

Ashbridge, E., Perrett, D. I., Oram, M. W., & Jellema, T. (2000). Effect of image orientation and size on object recognition: Responses of single units in the macaque monkey temporal cortex. *Cognitive Neuropsychology, 17,* 13–34.

Asmundson, G. J. G., & Stein, M. B. (1994). Selective processing of social threat in patients with generalized social phobia: Evaluation using a dot-probe paradigm. *Journal of Anxiety Disorders, 8,* 107–117.

Atkinson, J. (1984). Human visual development over the first six months of life: A review and a hypothesis. *Human Neurobiology, 3,* 61–74.

Augustine, J. R. (1996). Circuitry and functional aspects of the insular lobe in primates, including humans. *Brain Research Reviews, 22,* 229–244.

Aylward, E. H., Minshew, N. J., Goldstein, G., Honeycutt, N. A., Augustine, A. M., Yates, K. O., et al. (1999). MRI volumes of amygdala and hippocampus in non-mentally retarded autistic adolescents and adults. *Neurology, 53,* 2145–2150.

Baas, D., Aleman, A., & Kahn, R. S. (2004). Lateralization of amygdala activation: A systematic review of functional neuroimaging studies. *Brain Research Reviews, 45,* 96–103.

Bachevalier, J. (1994). Medial temporal lobe structures and autism: A review of clinical and experimental findings. *Neuropsychologia, 32,* 627–648.

Bagby, R. M., & Taylor, G. J. (1997). Affect dysregulation and alexithymia. In G. J. Taylor, R. M. Bagby, & J. D. A. Parker (Eds.), *Disorders of affect regulation: Alexithymia in medical and psychiatric illness* (pp. 26–45). New York: Cambridge University Press.

Baird, A. A., Gruber, S. A., Fein, D. A., Maas, L. C., Steingard, R. J., Renshaw, P. F., et al. (1999). Functional magnetic resonance imaging of facial affect recognition in children and adolescents. *Journal of the American Academy of Child and Adolescent Psychiatry, 38,* 195–199.

Baker, K. B., & Kim, J. J. (2004). Amygdalar lateralization in fear conditioning: Evidence for greater involvement of the right amygdala. *Behavioral Neuroscience, 118,* 15–23.

Baker, R., & Berthoz, A. (1977). *Control of gaze by brain stem neurons: Proceedings of the symposium.* New York: Elsevier.

Baldwin, J. (1962). *The fire next time.* New York: Vintage.

Baltes, M., & Lang, F. (1997). Everyday functioning and successful aging: The impact of resources. *Psychology and Aging, 12,* 433–443.

Banzett, R. B., Mulnier, H. E., Murphy, K., Rosen, S. D., Wise, R. J. S., & Adams, L. (2000). Breathlessness in humans activates insular cortex. *NeuroReport, 11,* 2117–2120.

Barbas, H. (1995). Anatomic basis of cognitive–emotional interactions in the primate prefrontal cortex. *Neuroscience and Biobehavioral Reviews, 19,* 499–510.

Barbas, H., Saha, S., Rempel-Clower, N., & Ghashghaei, T. (2003). Serial pathways from primate prefrontal cortex to autonomic areas may influence emotional expression. *BMC Neuroscience, 1,* 1–12.

Barinaga, M. (1996). The cerebellum: Movement coordinator or much more? *Science, 272,* 482–483.

Baron-Cohen, S. (1995). *Mindblindness.* Cambridge, MA: MIT Press.

Baron-Cohen, S., Baldwin, D. A., & Crowson, M. (1997). Do children with autism use the speaker's direction of gaze strategy to crack the code of language? *Child Development, 68,* 48–57.

Baron-Cohen, S., Jolliffe, T., Mortimore, C., & Robertson, M. (1997). Another advanced test of theory of mind: Evidence from very high functioning adults with autism or Asperger's syndrome. *Journal of Child Psychology and Psychiatry, 38,* 813–822.

Baron-Cohen, S., Ring, H. A., Bullmore, E. T., Wheelright, S., Ashwin, C., & Williams, S. C. R. (2000). The amygdala theory of autism. *Neuroscience and Biobehavioral Reviews, 24,* 355–364.

Baron-Cohen, S., Ring, H. A., Wheelright, S., Bullmore, E. T., Brammer, M. J., Simmons, A., et al. (1999). Social intelligence in the normal and autistic brain: An fMRI study. *European Journal of Neuroscience, 11,* 1891–1898.

Barrett, D., Shumake, J., Jones, D., & Gonzalez-Lima, F. (2003). Metabolic mapping of mouse brain activity after extinction of a conditioned emotional response. *Journal of Neuroscience, 23,* 5740–5749.

Bartels, A., & Zeki, S. (2000). The neural basis of romantic love. *NeuroReport, 11,* 3829–3834.

Bartels, A., & Zeki, S. (2003). Functional brain mapping during free viewing of natural scenes. *Human Brain Mapping, 21,* 75–83.

Bartels, A., & Zeki, S. (2004). The neural correlates of maternal and romantic love. *NeuroImage, 21,* 1155–1166.

Bartlett, M. S., Hager, J. C., Ekman, P., & Sejnowski, T. J. (1999). Measuring facial expressions by computer image analysis. *Psychophysiology, 36,* 253–263.

Bartzokis, G., Beckson, M., Lu, P. H., Nuechterlein, K. H., Edwards, N., & Mintz, J. (2001). Age-related changes in frontal and temporal lobe volumes in men. *Archives of General Psychiatry, 58,* 461–465.

Bateson, G. (1972). *Steps to an ecology of mind.* New York: Ballantine Books.

Battelli, L., Cavanagh, P., & Thornton, I. M. (2003). Perception of biological motion in parietal patients. *Neuropsychologia, 41,* 1808–1816.

Bauer, L. O., & Hesselbrock, V. M. (2003). Brain maturation and subtypes of conduct disorder: Interactive effects on P300 amplitude and topography in male adolescents. *Journal of the American Academy of Child and Adolescent Psychiatry, 42,* 106–115.

Bauman, M., & Kemper, T. L. (1985). Histoanatomic observations of the brain in early infantile autism. *Neurology, 35,* 866–874.

Bauman, M. D., Lavenex, P., Mason, W. A., Capitanio, J. P., & Amaral, D. G. (2004). The development of social behavior following neonatal amygdala lesions in rhesus monkeys. *Journal of Cognitive Neuroscience, 8,* 1388–1411.

Bauman, M. L., & Kemper, T. L. (1988). Limbic and cerebellar abnormalities: Consistent findings in infantile autism. *Journal of Neuropathology and Experimental Neurology, 47,* 369.

Baumeister, R. F., & Leary, M. R. (1995). The need to belong: Desire for interpersonal attachments as a fundamental human motivation. *Psychological Bulletin, 117,* 497–529.

Baxter, M. G., Parker, A., Lindner, C. C. C., Izquierdo, A. D., & Murray, E. A. (2000). Control of response selection by reinforcer value requires interaction of amygdala and orbital prefrontal cortex. *Journal of Neuroscience, 20,* 4311–4319.

Bayliss, A. P., di Pellegrino, G., & Tipper, S. P. (2004). Orienting of attention via observed eye gaze is head-centered. *Cognition, 94,* B1-B10.

Bazanis, E., Rogers, R. D., Dowson, J. H., Taylor, P., Meux, C., Staley, C., et al. (2002). Neurocognitive deficits in decision-making and planning of patients with DSM-III-R borderline personality disorder. *Psychological Medicine, 32,* 1395–1405.

Beason-Held, L. L., Golski, S., Kraut, M. A., Esposito, G., & Resnick, S. M. (2005). Brain activation during encoding and recognition of verbal and figural information in older adults. *Neurobiology of Aging, 26,* 237–250.

Bechara, A., Damasio, H., & Damasio, A. R. (2000). Emotion, decision making and the orbitofrontal cortex. *Cerebral Cortex, 10,* 295–307.

Bechara, A., Damasio, H., & Damasio, A. R. (2003). Role of the amygdala in decision-making. *Annals of the New York Academy of Sciences, 985,* 356–369.

Bechara, A., & Naqvi, N. (2004). Listening to your heart: Interoceptive awareness as a gateway to feeling. *Nature Neuroscience, 7,* 102–103.

Bechara, A., Tranel, D., Damasio, H., Adolphs, R., Rockland, C., & Damasio, A. R. (1995). Double dissociation of conditioning and declarative knowledge relative to the amygdala and hippocampus in humans. *Science, 269,* 1115–1118.

Beck, A. T., Emery, G., & Greenberg, R. L. (1990). *Anxiety disorders and phobias: A cognitive perspective.* New York: Basic Books.

Beebe, B. (2000). Co-constructing mother–infant distress. *Psychoanalytic Inquiry, 20,* 421–440.

Beeghly, M., & Cicchetti, D. (1994). Child maltreatment, attachment, and the self-system: Emergence of an internal state lexicon in toddlers at high social risk. *Development and Psychopathology, 6*, 5–30.

Beeghly, M., Bretherton, I., & Mervis, C. (1986). Mothers' internal state language to toddlers: The socialization of psychological understanding. *British Journal of Developmental Psychology, 4*, 247–260.

Beer, J. S., Heerey, E. A., Keltner, D., Scabini, D., & Knight, R. T. (2003). The regulatory function of self-conscious emotion: Insights from patients with orbitofrontal damage. *Journal of Personality and Social Psychology, 85*, 594–604.

Bell, B. D. (1994). Pantomime recognition impairment in aphasia: An analysis of error types. *Brain and Language, 47*, 269–278.

Bell, C. J., Malizia, A. L., & Nutt, D. J. (1999). The neurobiology of social phobia. *European Archives of Psychiatry and Clinical Neuroscience, 249*, S11–S18.

Bell, M. A., & Fox, N. A. (1992). The relations between frontal brain electrical activity and cognitive development during infancy. *Child Development, 63*, 1142–1163.

Bell, S. M., & Ainsworth, M. D. S. (1972). Infant crying and maternal responsiveness. *Child Development, 43*, 1171–1190.

Bellugi, U., Lichtenberger, L., Jones, W., Lai, Z., & St. George, M. (2000). The neurocognitive profile of Williams syndrome: A complex pattern of strengths and weaknesses. *Journal of Cognitive Neuroscience, 12*, S7–S29.

Bellugi, U., & St. George, M. (2000). Linking cognitive neuroscience and molecular genetics: New perspectives from Williams syndrome. *Journal of Cognitive Neuroscience, 12*(Suppl.), 1–6.

Benes, F. M. (1989). Myelination of cortical–hippocampal relays during late adolescence. *Schizophrenia Bulletin, 15*, 585–593.

Benes, F. M., Turtle, M., Kahn, Y., & Farol, P. (1994). Myelination of a key relay zone in the hippocampal formation occurs in the human brain during childhood, adolescence, and adulthood. *Archives of General Psychiatry, 51*, 477–484.

Benson, F. D. (1994). *The neurology of thinking.* New York: Oxford University Press.

Berg, S. J., & Wynne- Edwards, K. E. (2001). Changes in testosterone, cortisol, and estradiol levels in men becoming fathers. *Mayo Clinic Proceedings, 76*, 582–592.

Bergman, N. J., Linley, L. L., & Fawcus, S. R. (2004). Randomized controlled trial of skin-to-skin contact from birth versus conventional incubator for physiological stabilization in 1200- to 2199-gram newborns. *Acta Paediatrica, 93*, 779–785.

Berns, G. S., McClure, S. M., Pagnoni, G., & Montague, P. R. (2001). Predictability modulates human brain response to reward. *Journal of Neuroscience, 21*, 2793–2798.

Bernstein, A., Newman, J. P., Wallace, J. F., & Luh, K. E. (2000). Left-hemisphere activation and deficient response modulation in psychopaths. *Psychological Science, 11*, 414–418.

Berntson, G. G., Sarter, M., & Cacioppo, J. T. (2003). Ascending visceral regulation of cortical affective information processing. *European Journal of Neuroscience, 18*, 2103–2109.

Berntson, G. G., & Torello, M. W. (1982). The paleocerebellum and the integration of behavioral function. *Physiological Psychology, 10*, 2–12.

Berthoz, S. (2002). Effect of impaired recognition and expression of emotions on fron-tocingulate cortices: An fMRI study of men with alexithymia. *American Journal of Psychiatry, 159,* 961–967.

Berthoz, S., Armony, J. L., Blair, R. J. R., & Dolan, R. J. (2002). An fMRI study of intentional and unintentional (embarrassing) violations of social norms. *Brain, 125,* 1696–1708.

Best, C. T., & Queen, H. F. (1989). Baby, it's in your smile: Right hemiface bias in infant emotional expressions. *Developmental Psychology, 25,* 264–276.

Best, M., Williams, J. M., & Coccaro, E. G. (2002). Evidence for a dysfunctional prefrontal circuit in patients with an impulsive aggressive disorder. *Proceedings of the National Academy of Sciences, USA, 99,* 8448–8453.

Bettes, B. A. (1988). Maternal depression and motherese: Temporal and intonational features. *Child Development, 59,* 1089–1096.

Bigler, E. D. (2001). Frontal lobe pathology and antisocial personality disorder. *Archives of General Psychiatry, 58,* 609–611.

Bishop, D. V. M. (1989). Autism, Asperger's syndrome and semantic–pragmatic disorder: Where are the boundaries? *British Journal of Disorders of Communication, 24,* 107–121.

Bitsios, P., Szabadi, E., & Bradshaw, C. M. (2004). The fear-inhibited light reflex: Importance of the anticipation of an aversive event. *International Journal of Psychophysiology, 52,* 87–95.

Black, J. E. (1998). How a child builds its brain: Some lessons from animal studies of neural plasticity. *Preventive Medicine, 27,* 168–171.

Blair, H. T., Tinkelman, A., Moita, M. A., & LeDoux, J. E. (2003). Associative plasticity in neurons of the lateral amygdala during auditory fear conditioning. *Annals of the New York Academy of Sciences, 985,* 485–487.

Blair, R. J. R. (1995). A cognitive developmental approach to morality: Investigating the psychopath. *Cognition, 57,* 1–29.

Blair, R. J. R. (2003). Facial expressions, their communicatory functions and neuro-cognitive substrates. *Philosophical Transactions of the Royal Society of London, 358B,* 561–572.

Blair, R. J. R., & Cipolotti, L. (2000). Impaired social response reversal: A case of "acquired sociopathy." *Brain, 123,* 1122–1141.

Blair, R. J. R., & Coles, M. (2000). Expression recognition and behavioural problems in early adolescence. *Cognitive Development, 15,* 421–434.

Blair, R. J. R., Colledge, E., Murray, L., & Mitchell, D. G. V. (2001). A selective impairment in the processing of sad and fearful expressions in children with psychopathic tendencies. *Journal of Abnormal Child Psychology, 29,* 491–498.

Blair, R. J. R., Mitchell, D. G. V., & Peschardt, K. S. (2004). Reduced sensitivity to others' fearful expressions in psychopathic individuals. *Personality and Individual Differences, 37,* 1111–1122.

Blair, R. J. R., Morris, J. S., Frith, C. D., Perrett, D. I., & Dolan, R. J. (1999). Dissociable neural responses to facial expressions of sadness and anger. *Brain, 122,* 883–893.

Blake, R., Turner, L. M., & Smoski, M. J. (2003). Visual recognition of biological motion is impaired in children with autism. *Psychological Science, 14,* 151–157.

Blonder, L. X., Bowers, D., & Heilman, K. M. (1991). The role of right hemisphere in emotional communication. *Brain, 114,* 1115–1127.

Bloom, P. (2000). Language and thought: Does grammar make us smart? *Current Biology, 10,* R516–R517.

Blum, D. (2002). *Love at Goon Park.* Cambridge, MA: Perseus.

Bögels, S. M., & Lamers, C. T. (2002). The causal role of self-awareness in blushing-anxious, socially-anxious and social phobic individuals. *Behaviour Research and Therapy, 40,* 1367–1384.

Bögels, S. M., Alberts, M., & de Jong, P. J. (1996). Self-consciousness, self-focused attention, blushing propensity and fear of blushing. *Personality and Individual Differences, 21,* 573–581.

Bohus, M., Limberger, M., Ebner, U., Glocker, F. X., Schwarz, B., Wernz, M., et al. (2000). Pain perception during self-reported distress and calmness in patients with borderline personality disorder and self-mutilating behavior. *Psychiatry Research, 95,* 251–260.

Bonda, E., Petrides, M., Frey, S., & Evans, A. C. (1994). Frontal cortex involvement in organized sequences of hand movements: Evidence from a position emission tomography study. *Social Neuroscience Abstracts, 20,* 7353.

Bonda, E., Petrides, M., Ostry, D., & Evans, A. (1996). Specific involvement of human parietal systems and the amygdala in the perception of biological motion. *Journal of Neuroscience, 16,* 3737–3744.

Bonner, J. T. (1988). *The evolution of complexity by means of natural selection.* Princeton, NJ: Princeton University Press.

Booth, A., & Dabbs, J. M., Jr. (1993). Testosterone and men's marriages. *Social Forces, 72,* 463–477.

Booth, K. K., & Katz, L. S. (2000). Role of the vomeronasal organ in neonatal offspring recognition in sheep. *Biology of Reproduction, 63,* 953–958.

Borod, J. C. (1993). Cerebral mechanisms underlying facial, prosodic, and lexical emotional expression: A review of neuropsychological studies and methodological issues. *Neuropsychology, 7,* 445–463.

Borod, J. C., Koff, E., Perlman Lorch, M., & Nicholas, M. (1986). The expression and perception of facial emotion in brain-damaged patients. *Neuropsychologia, 24,* 169–180.

Botvinick, M., Jha, A. P., Bylsma, L. M., Fabian, S. A., Solomon, P. E., & Prkachin, K. M. (2005). Viewing facial expressions of pain engages cortical areas involved in the direct experience of pain. *NeuroImage, 25,* 312–319.

Botvinick, M., Nystrom, L. E., Fissell, K., Carter, C. S., & Cohen, J. D. (1999). Conflict monitoring versus selection-for-action in anterior cortex. *Nature, 402,* 179–181.

Bowen, M. (1978). *Family therapy in clinical practice.* New York: Jason Aronson.

Bowers, D., Bauer, R. M., & Heilman, K. (1993). The nonverbal affect lexicon: Theoretical perspectives from neuropsychological studies of affect perception. *Neuropsychology, 7,* 433–444.

Bowlby, J. (1988). *A secure base: Clinical applications of attachment theory.* London: Routledge.

Bradshaw, J. (1990). *Homecoming: Reclaiming and championing your inner child.* New York: Bantam Books.

Brambilla, P., Soloff, P. H., & Sala, M. (2004). Anatomical MRI study of borderline personality disorder in patients. *Psychiatry Research: Neuroimaging, 131,* 125–133.

Braun, K., & Poeggel, G. (2001). Recognition of Mother's voice evokes metabolic activation in the medial prefrontal cortex and lateral thalamus of *Octodon degus* pups. *Neuroscience, 103,* 861–864.

Bredy, T. W., Grant, R. J., Champagne, D. L., & Meaney, M. J. (2003). Maternal care influences neuronal survival in the hippocampus of the rat. *European Journal of Neuroscience, 18,* 2903–2909.

Bredy, T. W., Weaver, I., Champagne, F. C., & Meaney, M. J. (2001). Stress, maternal care, and neural development in the rat. In C. A. Shaw & J. C. McEachern (Eds.), *Toward a theory of neuroplasticity* (pp. 288–300). Philadelphia: Psychology Press.

Breiter, H. C., Etcoff, N. L., Whalen, P. J., Kennedy, W. A., Rauch, S. L., Buckner, R. L., et al. (1996). Response and habituation of the human amygdala during visual processing of facial expression. *Neuron, 17,* 875–887.

Breiter, H. C., Gollub, R. L., Weisskoff, R. M., Kennedy, D. N., Makris, N., Berke, J. D., et al. (1997). Acute effects of cocaine on human brain activity and emotion. *Neuron, 19,* 591–611.

Bremner, J. D., Innis, R., Southwick, S., Staib, L., Zoghbi, S., & Charney, D. (2000). Decreased benzodiazepine receptor binding in prefrontal cortex in combat-related posttraumatic stress disorder. *American Journal of Psychiatry, 157,* 1120–1126.

Bremner, J. D., Randall, P., Vermetten, E., Staib, L., Bronen, R. A., Mazure, C., et al. (1997). Magnetic resonance imaging-based measurement of hippocampal volume in posttraumatic stress disorder related to childhood physical and sexual abuse: A preliminary report. *Biological Psychiatry, 41,* 23–32.

Bremner, J. D., Scott, T. M., Delaney, R. C., Southwick, S. M., Mason, J. W., Johnson, D. R., et al. (1993). Deficits of short-term memory in posttraumatic stress disorder. *American Journal of Psychiatry, 150,* 1015–1019.

Bridges, R. S., & Grattan, D. R. (2003). Prolactin-induced neurogenesis in the maternal brain. *Trends in Endocrinology and Metabolism, 14,* 199–201.

Brigham, J. C., & Barkowitz, P. (1978). Do "they all look alike"? The effect of race, sex, experience, and attitudes on the ability to recognize faces. *Journal of Applied Social Psychology, 8,* 306–318.

Brodal, P. (1992). *The central nervous system: Structure and function.* New York: Oxford University Press.

Brody, A. L., Saxena, S., Stoessel, P., Gillies, L. A., Fairbanks, L. A., Alborzian, S., et al. (2001). Regional brain metabolic changes in patients with major depression treated with either paroxetine or interpersonal therapy. *Archives of General Psychiatry, 58,* 631–640.

Broks, P., Young, A. W., Maratos, E. J., Coffey, P. J., Calder, A. J., Isaac, C. L., et al. (1998). Face processing impairments after encephalitis: Amygdala damage and recognition of fear. *Neuropsychologia, 36,* 59–70.

Bronson, G. (1974). The postnatal growth of visual capacity. *Child Development, 45,* 873–890.

Brothers, A., & Ring, B. (1993). Mesial temporal neurons in the macaque monkey with responses selective for aspects of social stimuli. *Behavioral Brain Research, 57,* 53–61.

Brothers, A., Ring, B., & Kling, A. (1990). Response of neurons in the macaque amygdala to complex social stimuli. *Behavioral Brain Research, 41,* 199–213.

Brothers, L. (1992). Perception of social acts in primates: Cognition and neurobiology. *Seminars in the Neurosciences, 4,* 409–414.

Brothers, L. (1996). Brain mechanisms of social cognition. *Journal of Psychopharmacology, 10,* 2–8.

Brothers, L. (1997). *Friday's footprint.* New York: Oxford University Press.

Brothers, L., & Ring, B. (1992). A neuroethological framework for the representation of minds. *Journal of Cognitive Neuroscience, 4,* 107–118.

Brown, C. A. (1961). The development of visual capacity in the infant and young child. *Cerebral Palsy Bulletin, 3,* 364–372.

Brown, C. S., Kent, T. A., Bryant, S. G., Gevedon, R. M., Campbell, J. L., Felthous, A. R., et al. (1989). Blood platelet uptake of serotonin in episodic aggression. *Psychiatry Research, 27,* 5–12.

Bruce, H. M. (1959). An exteroceptive block to pregnancy in the mouse. *Nature, 184,* 105.

Bruder, G. E., Schneier, F. R., Stewart, J. W., McGrath, P. J., & Quitkin, F. (2004). Left hemisphere dysfunction during verbal dichotic listening tests in patients who have social phobia with or without comorbid depressive disorder. *American Journal of Psychiatry, 161,* 72–78.

Bruner, J. (1990). *Acts of meaning.* Cambridge, MA: Harvard University Press.

Buccino, G., Binkofski, F., & Riggio, L. (2004). The mirror neuron system and action recognition. *Brain and Language, 89,* 370–376.

Buccino, G., Binkofski, F., Fink, G. R., Fadiga, L., Fogassi, L., Gallese, V., et al. (2001). Action observation activates premotor and parietal areas in a somatotopic manner: An fMRI study. *European Journal of Neuroscience, 13,* 400–404.

Bugental, D. B., Martorell, G. A., & Barraza, V. (2003). The hormonal costs of subtle forms of infant maltreatment. *Hormones and Behavior, 43,* 237–244.

Burkhalter, A. (1991). Developmental status of intrinsic connections in visual cortex of newborn infants. In P. Bagnoli & W. Hodos (Eds.), *The changing visual system: Maturation and aging in the central nervous system* (pp. 247–254). New York: Plenum Press.

Bush, G., Luu, P., & Posner, M. I. (2000). Cognitive and emotional influences in anterior cingulate cortex. *Trends in Cognitive Sciences, 4,* 215–222.

Bush, G., Vogt, B. A., Holmes, J., Dale, A. M., Greve, D., Jenike, M. A., et al. (2002). Dorsal anterior cingulate cortex: A role in reward-based decision making. *Proceedings of the National Academy of Sciences, USA, 99,* 523–528.

Bushnell, I. W. R., Sai, F., & Mullin, J. T. (1989). Neonatal recognition of the mother's face. *British Journal of Developmental Psychology, 7,* 3–15.

Cabeza, R., Grady, C. L., Nyberg, L., McIntosh, A. R., Tulving, E., Kapur, S., et al. (1997). *Journal of Neuroscience, 1,* 391–400.

Cabeza, R., McIntosh, A. R., Tulving, E., Nyberg, L., & Grady, C. L. (1997). Age-related differences in effective neural connectivity during encoding and recall. *NeuroReport, 8*, 3479–3483.

Cacioppo, J. T., & Berntson, G. G. (2002). Social neuroscience. In J. T. Cacioppo, G. G. Berntson, R. Adolphs, C. S. Carter, R. J. Davidson, M. McClintock, et al. (Eds.) *Foundations in social neuroscience* (pp. 1–10). Cambridge, MA: MIT Press.

Cacioppo, J. T., & Gardner, W. L. (1999). Emotion. *Annual Review of Psychology, 50*, 191–214.

Cahill, L., & McGaugh, J. L. (1998). Mechanisms of emotional arousal and lasting declarative memory. *Trends in Neurosciences, 21*, 294–299.

Calder, A. J., Keane, J., Manes, F., Antoun, N., & Young, A. W. (2000). Impaired recognition and experience of disgust following brain injury. *Nature Neuroscience, 3*, 1077–1078.

Calder, A. J., Keane, J., Manly, T., Sprengelmeyer, R., Scott, S., Nimmo-Smith, S., et al. (2003). Facial expression recognition across the adult life span. *Neuropsychologia, 41*, 195–202.

Calder, A. J., Lawrence, A. D., Keane, J., Scott, S. K., Owen, A. M., Christoffels, I., et al. (2002). Reading the mind from eye gaze. *Neuropsychologia, 40*, 1129–1138.

Calder, A. J., Lawrence, A., & Young, A. W. (2001). Neuropsychology of fear and loathing. *Nature Reviews Neuroscience, 2*, 352–363.

Calder, A. J., Young, A. W., Rowland, D., Perrett, D. I., Hodges, J. R., & Etcoff, N. L. (1996). Facial emotion recognition after bilateral amygdala damage: Differentially severe impairment of fear. *Cognitive Neuropsychology, 13*, 699–745.

Caldji, C., Diorio, J., & Meaney, M. J. (2000). Variations in maternal care in infancy regulate the development of stress reactivity. *Biological Psychiatry, 48*, 1164–1174.

Caldji, C., Diorio, J., & Meaney, M. J. (2003). Variations in maternal care alter GABA(A) receptor subunit expression in brain regions associated with fear. *Neuropsychopharmacology, 28*, 1950–1959.

Caldji, C., Francis, D., & Sharma, S. (2000). The effects of early rearing environment on the development of GABA-sub(A) and central benzodiazepine receptor levels and novelty-induced fearfulness in the rat. *Neuropsychopharmacology, 22*, 219–229.

Caldji, C., Tannenbaum, B., Sharma, S., Francis, D., Plotsky, P. M., & Meaney, M. J. (1998). Maternal care during infancy regulates the development of neural systems mediating the expression of fearfulness in the rat. *Proceedings of the National Academy of Sciences, USA, 95*, 5335–5340.

Calvo, M. G., & Esteves, F. (2005). Detection of emotional faces: Low perceptual thresholds and wide attentional span. *Visual Cognition, 12*, 13–27.

Calvo, M. G., & Lang, P. J. (2004). Gaze patterns when looking at emotional pictures: Motivationally biased attention. *Motivation and Emotion, 28*, 221–243.

Camras, L. A., Grow, J. G., & Ribordy, S. C. (1983). Recognition of emotional expression by abused children. *Journal of Clinical Child Psychology, 12*, 325–328.

Canetti, L., Bachar, E., Galili-Weisstub, E., De-Nour, A. K., & Shalev, A. Y. (1997). Parental bonding and mental health in adolescence. *Adolescence, 32*, 381–394.

Canli, T., Desmond, J. E., Zhao, Z., Glover, G., & Gabrieli, J. D. E. (1998). Hemispheric asymmetry for emotional stimuli detected with fMRI. *NeuroReport, 9,* 3233–3239.

Canli, T., Sivers, H., Whitfield, S. L., Gotlib, I. H., & Gabrieli, J. D. E. (2002). Amygdala response to happy faces as a function of extraversion. *Science, 296,* 2191.

Cantalupo, C., & Hopkins, W. D. (2001). Asymmetric Broca's area in great apes. *Nature, 414,* 505.

Carlage, C., Andreasen, N. C., & O'Leary, D. S. (2003). Visualizing how one brain understands another: A PET study of theory of mind. *American Journal of Psychiatry, 160,* 1954–1964.

Carlson, V., Cicchetti, D., Barnett, D., & Braunwald, K. (1989). Disorganized/disoriented attachment relationships in maltreated infants. *Developmental Psychology, 25,* 525–531.

Carr, L., Iacoboni, M., Dubeau, M. C., Mazziotta, J. C., & Lenzi, G. L. (2003). Neural mechanisms of empathy in humans: A relay from neural systems for imitation to limbic areas. *Proceedings of the National Academy of Sciences, USA, 100,* 5497–5502.

Carter, C. S. (1998). Neuroendocrine perspectives on social attachment and love. *Psychoneuroendocrinology, 23,* 779–818.

Carter, C. S. (2003). Developmental consequences of oxytocin. *Physiology and Behavior, 79,* 383–397.

Carter, C. S., Braver, T. S., Barch, D. M., Botvinick, M. M., Noll, D., & Cohen, J. D. (1998). Anterior cingulated cortex, error detection, and the online monitoring of performance. *Science, 280,* 747–749.

Carter, C. S., Macdonald, A. M., Botvinick, M., Ross, L. L., Stenger, V. A., Noll, D., et al. (2000). Parsing executive processes: Strategic vs. evaluative functions of the anterior cingulate cortex. *Proceedings of the National Academy of Sciences, USA, 97,* 1944–1948.

Carvey, P. M. (1998). *Drug action in the central nervous system.* New York: Oxford University Press.

Castelfranchi, C., & Poggi, I. (1990). Blushing as a discourse: Was Darwin wrong? In W. R. Crozier (Ed.), *Shyness and embarrassment: Perspectives from social psychology* (pp. 230–251). Cambridge, UK: Cambridge University Press.

Castelli, F., Happé, F., Frith, U., & Frith, C. (2000). Movement and mind: A functional imaging study of perception and interpretation of complex intentional movement patterns. *NeuroImage, 12,* 314–325.

Chambers, R. A., & Potenza, M. N. (2003). Neurodevelopment, impulsivity, and adolescent gambling. *Journal of Gambling Studies, 19,* 53–84.

Chambers, R. A., Taylor, J. R., & Potenza, M. N. (2003). Developmental neurocircuitry of motivation in adolescence: A critical period of addiction vulnerability. *American Journal of Psychiatry, 160,* 1041–1052.

Chaminade, T., Meltzoff, A. N., & Decety, J. (2002). Does the end justify the means? A PET exploration of the mechanisms involved in human imitation. *NeuroImage, 15,* 318–328.

Champagne, F., Diorio, J., Sharma, S., & Meaney, M. J. (2001). Naturally occurring variations in maternal behavior in the rat are associated with differences in estrogen-inducible central oxytocin receptors. *Proceedings of the National Academy of Sciences, USA, 98,* 12736–12741.

Champoux, M., Byrne, E., DeLizio, R., & Suomi, S. J. (1992). Motherless mothers revisited: Rhesus maternal behavior and rearing history. *Primates, 33,* 251–255.

Charman, T., Swettenham, J., Baron-Cohen, S., Cox, A., Baird, G., & Drew, A. (1997). Infants with autism: An investigation of empathy, pretend play, joint attention, and imitation. *Developmental Psychology, 33,* 781–789.

Charney, D. S. (2004). Discovering the neural basis of human social anxiety: A diagnostic and therapeutic imperative. *American Journal of Psychiatry, 161,* 1–2.

Chen, Y. P., Ehlers, A., Clark, D. M., & Mansell, W. (2002). Patients with generalized social phobia direct their attention away from faces. *Behaviour Research and Therapy, 40,* 677–687.

Cheney, D. L., Seyfarth, R. M., & Smuts, B. (1986). Social relationships and social cognition in nonhuman primates. *Science, 234,* 1361–1366.

Chikama, M., McFarland, N. R., Amaral, D.G., & Haber, S. N. (1997). Insular cortical projections to functional regions of the striatum correlate with cortical cytoarchitectonic organization in the primate. *Journal of Neuroscience, 17,* 9686–9705.

Chiron, C., Jambaqué, I., Nabbout, R., Lounes, R., Syrota, A., & Dulac, O. (1997). The right brain hemisphere is dominant in human infants. *Brain, 120,* 1057–1065.

Chiron, C., Jambaqué, I., Plouin, P., & Dulac, O. (1999). Functional imaging of cerebral maturation and cognition. *Advances in Neurology, 81,* 89–96.

Chiron, C., Leboyer, M., Leon, F., Jambaqué, I., Nuttin, C., & Syrota, A. (1995). SPECT of the brain in childhood autism: Evidence for a lack of normal hemispheric asymmetry. *Developmental Medicine and Child Neurology, 37,* 849–860.

Chollet, F., DiPiero, V., Wise, R. J., Brooks, D. J., Dolan, R. J., & Frackowiak, R. S. (1991). The functional anatomy of motor recovery after stroke in humans: A study with positron emission tomography. *Annals of Neurology, 29,* 63–71.

Chugani, H. T. (1998). Biological basis of emotions: Brain systems and brain development. *Pediatrics, 102,* 1225–1229.

Chugani, H. T., & Phelps, M. E. (1991). Imaging human brain development with positron emission tomography. *Journal of Nuclear Medicine, 32,* 23–26.

Chugani, H. T., Phelps, M. E., & Mazziotta, J. C. (1987). Positron emission tomography study of human brain functional development. *Annals of Neurology, 22,* 487–497.

Ciaranello, A. L., & Ciaranello, R. D. (1995). The neurobiology of infantile autism. *Annual Review of Neuroscience, 18,* 101–128.

Cicchetti, D., & Barnett, D. (1991). Attachment organization in maltreated preschoolers. *Development and Psychopathology, 3,* 397–411.

Cirulli, F., Berry, A., & Alleva, E. (2003). Early disruption of the mother–infant relationship: Effects on brain plasticity and implications for psychopathology. *Neuroscience and Biobehavioral Reviews, 27,* 73–82.

Clark, D. M., & McManus, F. (2002). Information processing in social phobia. *Biological Psychiatry, 51,* 92–100.

Clark, K. B., & Clark, M. K. (1950). Emotional factors in racial identification and preference in Negro children. *Journal of Negro Education, 19,* 341–350.

Cohen, J. A., Perel, J. M., DeBellis, M. D., Friedman, M. J., & Putnam, F. W. (2002). Treating traumatized children: Clinical implications of the psychobiology of post-traumatic stress disorder. *Trauma, Violence, and Abuse, 3,* 91–108.

Cohen, J. D., Botvinick, M., & Carter, C. S. (2000). Anterior cingulate and prefrontal cortex: Who's in control? *Nature Neuroscience, 3,* 421–423.

Cohn, J. F., & Tronick, E. Z. (1983). Three-month-old infants' reaction to simulated maternal depression. *Child Development, 54,* 185–193.

Cohn, J. F., & Tronick, E. (1989). Specificity of infants' response to mothers' affective behavior. *Journal of the American Academy of Child and Adolescent Psychiatry, 28,* 242–248.

Cohn, J. F., Matias, R., Tronick, E. Z., Connell, D., & Lyons-Ruth, K. (1986). Face to face interactions of depressed mothers and their infants. In E. Z. Tronick & T. Field (Eds.), *New directions for child development: Vol. 34. Maternal depression and infant disturbance* (pp. 31–45). San Francisco: Jossey-Bass.

Coleman, R., Greenblatt, M., & Solomon, H. C. (1956). Physiological evidence of rapport during psychotherapeutic interviews. *Diseases of the Nervous System, 17,* 71–77.

Coren, S., & Porac, C. (1977). Fifty centuries of right-handedness: The historical record. *Science, 198,* 631–632.

Corina, D. P., Vaid, J., & Bellugi, U. (1992). The linguistic basis of left hemisphere specialization. *Science, 255,* 1258–1260.

Corrigan, F. M., Davidson, A., & Heard, H. (2000). The role of dysregulated amygdalic emotion in borderline personality disorder. *Medical Hypotheses, 54,* 574–579.

Corter, C. M., & Fleming, A. S. (1995). Psychobiology of maternal behavior in human beings. In M. H. Bornstein (Ed.), *Handbook of parenting: Vol. 2. Biology and ecology of parenting* (pp. 3–25). Mahwah, NJ: Erlbaum.

Courchesne, E., Carper, R., & Akshoomoff, N. (2003). Evidence of brain overgrowth in the first year of life in autism. *Journal of the American Medical Association, 290,* 337–344.

Courchesne, E., Karns, C. M., Davis, H. R., Ziccardi, R., Carper, R. A., Tigue, Z. D., et al. (2001). Unusual brain growth patterns in early life in patients with autistic disorder: An MRI study. *Neurology, 57,* 245–254.

Courchesne, E., Townsend, J., & Saitoh, O. (1995). The cerebellum and autism. *Neurology, 45,* 398–402.

Cowdry, R. W., Pickar, D., & Davies, R. (1985). Symptoms and EEG findings in the borderline syndrome. *International Journal of Psychiatry in Medicine, 15,* 201–211.

Cozolino, L. J. (2002). *The neuroscience of psychotherapy: Building and rebuilding the human brain.* New York: Norton.

Cozolino, L. J. (2004). *The making of a therapist: A practical guide for the inner journey.* New York: Norton.

Crabbe, J. C., & Phillips, T. J. (2003). Mother nature meets mother nurture. *Nature Neuroscience, 6,* 440–442.

Craig, A. D. (2004). Human feelings: Why are some more aware than others? *Trends in Cognitive Sciences, 8,* 239–241.

Craig, A. D., Chen, K., Bandy, D., & Reiman, E. M. (2000). Thermosensory activation of insular cortex. *Nature Neuroscience, 3,* 184–190.

Critchley, H. D., Daly, E. M., Bullmore, E. T., Williams, S. C., Van Amelsvoort, T., Robertson, D. M., et al. (2000). The functional neuroanatomy of social behaviour: Changes in cerebral blood flow when people with autistic disorder process facial expressions. *Brain, 123,* 2203–2212.

Critchley, H. D., Daly, E., Phillips, M., Brammer, M., Bullmore, E., Williams, S., et al. (2000). Explicit and implicit neural mechanisms for processing of social information from facial expressions: A functional magnetic resonance imaging study. *Human Brain Mapping, 9,* 93–105.

Critchley, H. D., Mathias, C. J., Josephs, O., O'Doherty, J., Zanini, S., Dewar, B. K., et al. (2003). Human cingulate cortex and autonomic control: Converging neuroimaging and clinical evidence. *Brain, 126,* 2139–2152.

Critchley, H. D., Wiens, S., Rotshtein, P., Öhman, A., & Dolan, R. J. (2004). Neural systems supporting interoceptive awareness. *Nature Neuroscience, 7,* 189–195.

Crnic, K. A., Greenberg, M. T., Ragozin, A. S., Robinson, N. M., & Basham, R. B. (1983). Effects of stress and social support on mothers and premature and full-term infants. *Child Development, 54,* 209–217.

Crowell, J. A., Treboux, D., & Waters, E. (2002). Stability of attachment representations: The transition to marriage. *Developmental Psychology, 38,* 467–479.

Crozier, W. R. (2004). Self-consciousness, exposure, and the blush. *Journal for the Theory of Social Behaviour, 34,* 1–17.

Cummings, J. L. (1993). Frontal–subcortical circuits and human behavior. *Archives of Neurology, 50,* 873–880.

Cutting, J. (1992). The role of right hemisphere dysfunction in psychiatric disorders. *British Journal of Psychiatry, 160,* 583–588.

Cutting, J. E., & Kozlowski, L. T. (1977). Recognizing friends by their walk: Gait perception without familiarity cues. *Bulletin of the Psychonomic Society, 9,* 353–356.

Dahl, R. E. (2004). Adolescent brain development: A period of vulnerabilities and opportunities. *Annals of the New York Academy of Sciences, 1021,* 1–22.

Damasio, A. R. (1994). *Descartes' error: Emotion, reason and the human brain.* New York: Putnam.

Damasio, A. R. (1995). Toward a neurobiology of emotion and feeling: Operational concepts and hypotheses. *The Neuroscientist, 1,* 19–25.

Damasio, A. R., Grabowski, T. J., Bechara, A., Damasio, H., Ponto, L. L., Parvizi, J., et al. (2000). Subcortical and cortical brain activity during the feeling of self-generated emotions. *Nature Neuroscience, 3,* 1049–1056.

Damasio, A. R., Tranel, D., & Damasio, H. (1990). Individuals with sociopathic behavior caused by frontal damage fail to respond autonomically to social stimuli. *Behavioural Brain Research, 41,* 81–94.

Damasio, A. R., & Van Hoesen, G. W. (1983). Emotional disturbances associated with focal lesions of the limbic frontal lobe. In K. Heilman & P. Satz (Eds.), *Neuropsychology of human emotion* (pp. 85–108). New York: Guilford Press.

Damasio, H., Grabowski, T., Frank, R., Galaburda, A. M., & Damasio, A. R. (1994). The return of Phineas Gage: Clues about the brain from the skull of a famous patient. *Science, 264,* 1102–1105.

Damasio, H., Maurer, R. G., Damasio, A. R., & Chui, H. C. (1980). Computerized tomographic scan findings in patients with autistic behavior. *Archives of Neurology, 37,* 504–510.

Danner, D. D., Snowdon, D. A., & Friesen, W. V. (2001). Positive emotions in early life and longevity: Findings from the nun study. *Journal of Personality and Social Psychology, 80,* 804–813.

Darwin, C. (1872). *The expression of the emotions in man and animals.* London: Murray.

Dasgupta, N., McGhee, D. E., Greenwald, A. G., & Banaji, M. R. (2000). Automatic preference for white Americans: Eliminating the familiarity explanation. *Journal of Experimental Social Psychology, 36,* 316–328.

Davidson, R. J. (1992). Emotion and affective style: Hemispheric substrates. *Psychological Science, 3,* 39–43.

Davidson, R. J. (2000). Affective style, psychopathology, and resilience: Brain mechanisms and plasticity. *American Psychologist, 55,* 1196–1214.

Davidson, R. J., Ekman, P., Saron, C. D., Senulis, J. A., & Friesen, W. V. (1990). Approach–withdrawal and cerebral asymmetry: Emotional expression and brain physiology: I. *Journal of Personality and Social Psychology, 58,* 330–341.

Davidson, R. J., & Fox, N. A. (1989). Frontal brain asymmetry predicts infants' response to maternal separation. *Journal of Abnormal Psychology, 98,* 127–131.

Davidson, R. J., Jackson, D. C., & Kalin, N. H. (2000). Emotion, plasticity, context, and regulation: Perspectives from affective neuroscience. *Psychological Bulletin, 126,* 890–909.

Davidson, R. J., Marshall, J. R., Tomarken, A. J., & Henriques, J. B. (2000). While a phobic waits: Regional brain electrical and autonomic activity in social phobics during anticipation of public speaking. *Biological Psychiatry, 47,* 85–95.

Davidson, R. J., Putnam, K. M., & Larson, C. L. (2000). Dysfunction in the neural circuitry of emotion regulation: A possible prelude to violence. *Science, 289,* 591–594.

Davis, K. D., Taylor, S. J., Crawley, A. P., Wood, M. L., & Mikulis, D. J. (1997). Functional MRI of pain- and attention-related activations in the human cingulate cortex. *Journal of Neurophysiology, 77,* 3370–3380.

Davis, M. (1992). The role of the amygdala in fear and anxiety. *Annual Review of Neuroscience, 15,* 353–375.

Davis, M. (1997). Neurobiology of fear responses: The role of the amygdala. *Journal of Neuropsychiatry and Clinical Neurosciences, 9,* 382–402.

Davis, M. (2002). Role of NMDA receptors and MAP kinase in the amygdala in extinction of fear: Clinical implications for exposure therapy. *European Journal of Neuroscience, 16,* 395–398.

Davis, M., & Myers, K. M. (2002). The role of glutamate and gamma-aminobutyric acid in fear extinction: Clinical implications for exposure therapy. *Biological Psychiatry, 52,* 998–1007.

Davis, M., Walker, D. L., & Myers, K. M. (2003). Role of the amygdala in fear extinction measured with potentiated startle. *Annals of the New York Academy of Sciences, 985,* 218–232.

Davis, M., & Whalen, P. J. (2001). The amygdala: Vigilance and emotion. *Molecular Psychiatry, 6,* 13–34.

Dawson, G. (1983). Lateralized brain dysfunction in autism: Evidence from the Halstead–Reitan neuropsychological battery. *Journal of Autism and Developmental Disorders, 13,* 269–286.

Dawson, G., Frey, K., Panagiotides, H., Osterling, J., & Hessel, D. (1997). Infants of depressed mothers exhibit atypical frontal brain activity: A replication and extension of previous findings. *Journal of Child Psychology and Psychiatry, 38,* 179–186.

Dawson, G., Klinger, L. G., Panagiotides, H., Hill, D., & Spieker, S. (1992). Frontal lobe activity and affective behavior of infants and mothers with depressive symptoms. *Child Development, 63,* 725–737.

Dawson, G., Panagiotides, H., Klinger, L. G., & Hill, D. (1992). The role of frontal lobe functioning in the development of self-regulatory behavior. *Brain and Cognition, 20,* 152–175.

Dawson, G., Panagiotides, H., Klinger, L. G., & Spieker, S. (1997). Infants of depressed and nondepressed mothers exhibit differences in frontal brain electrical activity during the expressions of negative emotions. *Developmental Psychology, 33,* 650–656.

Deb, S., & Thompson, B. (1998). Neuroimaging in autism. *British Journal of Psychiatry, 173,* 299–302.

De Bellis, M. D., Baum, A. S., Birmaher, B., Keshavan, M. S., Eccard, C. H., Boring, A. M., et al. (1999a). Developmental traumatology: Part I. Biological stress systems. *Biological Psychiatry, 45,* 1259–1270.

De Bellis, M. D., Casey, B. J., Dahl, R. E., Birmaher, B., Williamson, D. E., Thomas, K. M., et al. (2000). A pilot study of amygdala volumes in pediatric generalized anxiety disorder. *Biological Psychiatry, 48,* 51–57.

De Bellis, M. D., Keshavan, M. S., Clark, D. B., Casey, B. J., Giedd, J. N., Boring, A. M., et al. (1999b). Developmental traumatology: Part II. Brain development. *Biological Psychiatry, 45,* 1271–1284.

de Casper, A. J., & Fifer, W. P. (1980). Of human bonding: Newborns prefer their mothers' voices. *Science, 208,* 1174–1176.

Decety, J., & Chaminade, T. (2003a). Neural correlates of feeling sympathy. *Neuropsychologia, 41,* 127–138.

Decety, J., & Chaminade, T. (2003b). When the self represents the other: A new cognitive neuroscience view on psychological identification. *Consciousness and Cognition, 12,* 577–596.

Decety, J., & Grèzes, J. (1999). Neural mechanisms subserving the perception of human actions. *Trends in Cognitive Sciences, 3,* 172–178.

Decety, J., Grèzes, J., Costed, N., Perani, D., Jeanneraod, M., Procyk, E., et al. (1997). Brain activity during observation of actions: Influence of action content and subject's strategy. *Brain, 120,* 1763–1777.

Decety, J., Perani, D., Jeannerod, M., Bettinardi, V., Tadary, B., Woods, R., et al. (1994). Mapping motor representations with positron emission tomography. *Nature, 371,* 600–602.

Decety, J., Sjöholm, H., Ryding, E., Stenberg, G., & Ingvar, D. H. (1990). The cerebellum participates in mental activity: Tomographic measurements of regional cerebral blood flow. *Brain Research, 535,* 313–317.

de Haan, E. H. F., Young, A. W., & Newcombe, F. (1987). Face recognition without awareness. *Cognitive Neuropsychology, 4,* 385–415.

de Jong, P. J. (1999). Communicative and remedial effects of social blushing. *Journal of Nonverbal Behavior, 23,* 197–217.

de Jong, P. J., Peters, M. L., & de Cremer, D. (2003). Blushing may signify guilt: Revealing effects of blushing in ambiguous social situations. *Motivation and Emotion, 27,* 225–249.

de Jong, P. J., Peters, M. L., de Cremer, D., & Vranken, C. (2002). Blushing after a moral transgression in a prisoner's dilemma game: Appeasing or revealing? *European Journal of Social Psychology, 32,* 627–644.

DeKosky, S. T., Nonneman, A. J., & Scheff, S. W. (1982). Morphologic and behavioral effects of perinatal glucocorticoid administration. *Physiology and Behavior, 29,* 895–900.

De la Fuente, J. M., Goldman, S., Stanus, E., Vizuete, C., Morlan, I., Bobes, J., et al. (1997). Brain glucose metabolism in borderline personality disorder. *Journal of Psychiatric Research, 31,* 531–541.

Delgado, M. R., Nystrom, L. E., Fissell, C., Noll, D. C., & Fiez, J. A. (2000). Tracking the hemodynamic responses to reward and punishment in the striatum. *Journal of Neurophysiology, 84,* 3072–3077.

Delville, Y., Mansour, K. M., & Ferris, C. F. (1996). Testosterone facilitates aggression by modulating vasopressin receptors in the hypothalamous. *Physiology and Behavior, 60,* 25–29.

Derryberry, D., & Reed, M. A. (2002). Anxiety-related attentional biases and their regulation by attentional control. *Journal of Abnormal Psychology, 111,* 225–236.

Desimone, R. (1991). Face-selective cells in the temporal cortex of monkeys. *Journal of Cognitive Neuroscience, 3,* 1–8.

DeSteno, D., Dasgupta, N., Bartlett, M. Y., & Cajdric, A. (2004). Prejudice from thin air: The effect of emotion on automatic intergroup attitudes. *Psychological Science, 15,* 319–324.

Dettling, A. C., Feldon, J., & Pryce, C. R. (2002). Early deprivation and behavioral and physiological responses to social separation/novelty in the marmoset. *Pharmacology, Biochemistry, and Behavior, 73,* 259–269.

Devine, P. G. (1989). Stereotypes and prejudice: Their automatic and controlled components. *Journal of Personality and Social Psychology, 56,* 5–18.

Devinsky, O. (2000). Right cerebral hemisphere dominance for a sense of corporeal and emotional self. *Epilepsy and Behavior, 1,* 60–73.

Devinsky, O., Morrell, M. J., & Vogt, B. A. (1995). Contributions of anterior cingulate cortex to behaviour. *Brain, 118,* 279–306.

DeVries, A. C., Glasper, E. R., & Detillion, C. E. (2003). Social modulation of stress responses. *Physiology and Behavior, 79,* 399–407.

Diamond, I. T., & Hall, W. C. (1969). Evolution of neocortex. *Science, 164,* 251–262.

Diamond, M. C. (1988). *Enriching heredity: The impact of the environment on the anatomy of the brain.* New York: Free Press.

Diamond, M. C., Johnson, R. E., & Ingham, C. (1971). Brain plasticity induced by environment and pregnancy. *International Journal of Neuroscience, 2,* 171–178.

Diamond, M. C., Krech, D., & Rosenzweig, M. R. (1964). The effects of an enriched environment on the histology of the rat cerebral cortex. *Journal of Comparative Neurology, 123,* 111–119.

Diamond, R., & Carey, S. (1986). Why faces are and are not special: An effort of expertise. *Journal of Experimental Psychology, 115,* 107–117.

Dias, R., Robbins, T. W., & Roberts, A. C. (1996). Dissociation in prefrontal cortex of affective and attentional shifts. *Nature, 380,* 69–72.

Dickens, C. (1966). *A christmas carol.* New York: Simon & Schuster.

Diego, M. A., Field, T., Hernandez-Reif, M., Shaw, J. A., Rothe, E. M., Castellanos, D., et al. (2002). Aggressive adolescents benefit from massage therapy. *Adolescence, 37,* 597–607.

Diego, M. A., Field, T., Hernandez-Reif, M., Shaw, K., Friedman, L., & Ironson, G. (2001). HIV adolescents show improved immune function following massage therapy. *International Journal of Neuroscience, 106,* 35–45.

Diego, M. A., Field, T., Jones, N. A., Hernandez-Reif, M., Cullen, C., Schanberg, S., et al. (2004). EEG responses to mocked facial expressions by infants of depressed mothers. *Infant Behavior and Development, 27,* 150–162.

Dieter, J. N., Field, T., Hernandez-Reif, M., Emory, E. K., & Redzepi, M. (2003). Stable preterm infants gain more weight and sleep less after five days of massage therapy. *Journal of Pediatric Psychology, 28,* 403–411.

DiMascio, A., Boyd, R. W., & Greenblatt, M. (1957). Physiological correlates of tension and antagonism during psychotherapy: A study of interpersonal physiology. *Psychosomatic Medicine, 19,* 99–104.

Dimberg, U., & Petterson, M. (2000). Facial reactions to happy and angry facial expressions: Evidence for right hemisphere dominance. *Psychophyisology, 37,* 693–696.

Dimberg, U., Thunberg, M., & Elmehed, K. (2000). Unconscious facial reactions to emotional facial expressions. *Psychological Science, 11,* 86–89.

Dinn, W. M., Harris, C. L., Aycicegi, A., Greene, P. B., Kirkley, S. M., & Reilly, C. (2004). Neurocognitive function in borderline personality disorder. *Progress in Neuropsychopharmacology and Biological Psychiatry, 28,* 329–341.

Dion, K. K. (1972). Physical attractiveness and evaluation of children's transgressions. *Journal of Personality and Social Psychology, 24,* 207–213.

Diorio, D. Viau, V., & Meaney, M. J. (1993). The role of the medial prefrontal cortex (cingulate gyrus) in the regulation of hypothalamic–pituitary–adrenal responses to stress. *Journal of Neuroscience, 13,* 3839–3847.

di Pellegrino G., Fadiga L., Fogassi L., Gallese V., & Rizzolatti G. (1992). Understanding motor events: A neurophysiological study. *Experimental Brain Research, 91,* 176–180.

DiPietro, J. A. (2004). The role of prenatal maternal stress in child development. *Current Directions in Psychological Science, 13,* 71–74.

Dolan, M. (2002). What neuroimaging tells us about psychopathic disorders. *Hospital Medicine, 63,* 337–340.

Dolan, M., & Park, I. (2002). The neuropsychology of antisocial personality disorder. *Psychological Medicine, 32,* 417–427.

Dolan, R. J. (1999). On the neurology of morals. *Nature Neuroscience, 2,* 927–929.

Dolan, R. J., Morris, J. S., & de Gelder, B. (2001). Crossmodal binding of fear in voice and face. *Proceedings of the National Academy of Sciences, USA, 98,* 10006–10010.

Dolan, R. J., & Vuilleumier, P. (2003). Amygdala automaticity in emotional processing. *Annals of the New York Academy of Sciences, 985,* 348–355.

Dopson, W. G., Beckwith, B. E., Tucker, D. M., & Bullard-Bates, P. C. (1984). Asymmetry of facial expression in spontaneous emotion. *Cortex, 20,* 243–251.

Dorries, K. M., Adkins-Regan, E., & Halpern, B. P. (1997). Sensitivity and behavioral responses to the pheromone androstenone are not mediated by the vomeronasal organ in domestic pigs. *Brain, Behavior, and Evolution, 49,* 53–62.

Douglas, R. J., & Pribram, K. H. (1966). Learning and limbic lesions. *Neuropsychologia, 4,* 197–220.

Downing, P. E., Jiang, Y., Shuman, M., & Kanwisher, N. (2001). A cortical area selective for visual processing of the human body. *Science, 293,* 2470–2473.

Drevets, W. C., Price, J. L., Simpson, J. R., Jr., Todd, R. D., Reich, T., Vannier, M., et al. (1997). Subgenual prefrontal cortex abnormalities in mood disorders. *Nature, 386,* 824–827.

Drevets, W. C., & Raichle, M. E. (1998). Reciprocal suppression of regional cerebral blood flow during emotional versus higher cognitive processes: Implications for interactions between emotion and cognition. *Cognition and Emotion, 12,* 353–385.

Driessen, M., Herrmann, J., Stahl, K., Zwaan, M., Meier, S., Hill, A., et al. (2000). Magnetic resonance imaging volumes of the hippocampus and the amygdala in women with borderline personality disorder and early traumatization. *Archives of General Psychiatry, 57,* 1115–1122.

Driver, J., Davis, G., Ricciardelli, P., Kidd, P., Maxwell, E., & Baron-Cohen, S. (1999). Gaze perception triggers reflexive visuospatial orienting. *Visual Cognition, 6,* 509–540.

Drummond, P. D., Camacho, L., Formentin, N., Heffernan, T. D., Williams, F., & Zekas, T. E. (2003). The impact of verbal feedback about blushing on social discomfort and facial blood flow during embarrassing tasks. *Behaviour Research and Therapy, 41,* 413–425.

Drummond, P. D., & Mirco, N. (2004). Staring at one side of the face increases blood flow on that side of the face. *Psychophysiology, 41,* 281–287.

Dubois, S., Rossion, B., Schiltz, C., Bodart, J. M., Michel, C., Bruyer, R., et al. (1999). Effect of familiarity on the processing of human faces. *NeuroImage, 9,* 278–289.

Dunbar, R. I. (1992). Neocortex size as a constraint on group size in primates. *Journal of Human Evolution, 20,* 469–493.

Dunbar, R. I. (1993). Coevolution of neocortical size, group size, and language in humans. *Behavioral and Brain Sciences, 16,* 681–735.

Dunbar, R. I. (1996). *Grooming, gossip, and the evolution of language.* Cambridge, MA: Harvard University Press.

Duvall, D. (1986). A new question of pheromones: Aspects of possible chemical signaling and reception in the mammal-like reptiles. In N. H. Hotton, III, P. D. MacLean, J. J. Roth, & E. C. Roth (Eds.), *The ecology and biology of mammal-like reptiles* (pp. 219–238). Washington, DC: Smithsonian Institution Press.

Duvarci, S., & Nader, K. (2004). Characterization of fear memory reconsolidation. *Journal of Neuroscience, 24,* 9269–9275.

Eastwood, J. D., Smilek, D., Oakman, J. M., Farvolden, P., van Ameringen, M., Mancini, C., et al. (2005). Individuals with social phobia are biased to become aware of negative faces. *Visual Cognition, 12,* 159–181.

Edelman, G. M. (1987). *Neural Darwinism: The theory of neuronal group selection.* New York: Basic Books.

Edelman, G. M. (1989). *The remembered present: A biological theory of consciousness.* New York: Basic Books.

Edelmann, R. J. (1990). Chronic blushing, self-consciousness, and social anxiety. *Journal of Psychopathology and Behavioral Assessment, 12,* 119–127.

Efran, M. G. (1974). The effect of physical appearance on the judgment of guilt, interpersonal attraction, and severity of recommended punishment in a simulated jury task. *Journal of Research in Personality, 8,* 45–54.

Egaas, B., Courchesne, E., & Saitoh, O. (1995). Reduced size of corpus callosum in autism. *Archives of Neurology, 52,* 794–801.

Eger, E., Jedynak, A., Iwaki, T., & Skrandies, W. (2003). Rapid extraction of emotional expression: Evidence from evoked potential fields during brief presentation of face stimuli. *Neuropsychologia, 41,* 808–817.

Eichenbaum, H. (1992). The hippocampal system and declarative memory in animals. *Journal of Cognitive Neuroscience, 4,* 217–231.

Eisenberger, N. I., & Lieberman, M. D. (2004). Why rejection hurts: A common neural alarm system for physical and social pain. *Trends in Cognitive Sciences, 8,* 294–300.

Eisenberger, N. I., Lieberman, M. D., & Williams, K. D. (2003). Does rejection hurt? An fMRI study of social exclusion. *Science, 302,* 290–292.

Ekman, P. (2003). *Emotions revealed: Recognizing faces and feelings to improve communication and emotional life.* New York: Times Books.

Ekman, P., & Friesen, W. V. (1978). *Facial action coding system.* Palo Alto, CA: Consulting Psychologists Press.

Ekman, P., Friesen, W. V., & Hager, J. C. (2002). *Facial action coding system* (2nd ed.). Salt Lake City, UT: Reasearch Nexus E-Book.

Ekstrom, A. D., Meltzer, J., McNaughton, B. L., & Barnes, C. A. (2001). NMDA receptor antagonism blocks experience-dependent expansion of hippocampal "place fields." *Neuron, 31*, 631 638.

Eliot, L. (1999). *What's going on in there? How the brain and mind develop in the first five years of life.* New York: Bantam Books.

Elliott, R., Dolan, R. J., & Frith, C. D. (2000). Dissociable functions in the medial and lateral orbitofrontal cortex: Evidence from human neuroimaging studies. *Cerebral Cortex, 10*, 308–317.

Elliott, R., Friston, K. J., & Dolan, R. J. (2000). Dissociable neural responses in human reward systems. *Journal of Neuroscience, 20*, 6159–6165.

Elzinga, B. M., Bermond, B., & van Dyck, R. (2002). The relationship between dissociative proneness and alexithymia. *Psychotherapy and Psychosomatics, 71*, 104–111.

Emde, R. N. (1988). Development terminable and interminable: I. Innate and motivational factors from infancy. *International Journal of Psychoanalysis, 69*, 23–42.

Emery, N. J. (2000). The eyes have it: The neuroethology, function and evolution of social gaze. *Neuroscience and Biobehavioral Reviews, 24*, 581–604.

Enquist, M., & Arak, A. (1993). Selection of exaggerated male traits by female aesthetic senses. *Nature, 361*, 446–448.

Erickson, K., & Schulkin, J. (2003). Facial expressions of emotion: A cognitive neuroscience perspective. *Brain and Cognition, 52*, 52–60.

Eriksson, P. S., Perfilieva, E., Bjork-Eriksson, T., Alborn, A. M., Nordborg, C., Peterson, D. A., et al. (1998). Neurogenesis in the adult human hippocampus. *Nature Medicine, 4*, 1313–1317.

Erraji-Benchekroun, L., Underwood, M. D., Arango, V., Galfalvy, H., Pavlidis, P., Smyrniotopoulous, P., et al. (2005). Molecular aging in human prefrontal cortex is selective and continuous throughout adult life. *Biological Psychiatry, 57*, 549–558.

Escalante-Mead, P. R., Minshew, N. J., & Sweeney, J. A. (2003). Abnormal brain lateralization in high-functioning autism. *Journal of Autism and Developmental Disorders, 33*, 539–543.

Eslinger, P. J. (1998). Neurological and neuropsychological bases of empathy. *European Neurology, 39*, 193–199.

Essex, M. J., Klein, M. H., Cho, E., & Kalin, N. H. (2002). Maternal stress beginning in infancy may sensitize children to later stress exposure: Effects on cortisol and behavior. *Biological Psychiatry, 52*, 776–784.

Esteves, F., Parra, C., Dimberg, U., & Ohman, A. (1994). Nonconscious associative learning: Pavlovian conditioning of skin conductance responses to masked fear-relevant facial stimuli. *Psychophysiology, 31*, 375–385.

Etkin, A., Klemenhagen, K. C., Dudman, J. T., Rogan, M. T., Hen, R., Kandel, E. R., et al. (2004). Individual differences in trait anxiety predict the response of the basolateral amygdala to unconsciously processed fearful faces. *Neuron, 44*, 1043–1055.

Etkin, A., Pittenger, C., Polan, H. J., & Kandel, E. R. (2005). Toward a neurobiology of psychotherapy: Basic science and clinical applications. *Journal of Neuropsychiatry Clinical Neurosciences, 17*, 145–158.

Everitt, B. J., Cador, M., & Robbins, T. W. (1989). Interactions between the amygdala and ventral striatum in stimulus–reward associations: Studies using a second-order schedule of sexual reinforcement. *Neuroscience, 30,* 63–75.

Fadiga, L., Craighero, L., Buccino, G., & Rizzolati, G. (2002). Speech listening specifically modulates the excitability of tongue muscles: A TMS study. *European Journal of Neuroscience, 15,* 399–402.

Fadiga, L., Fogassi, L., Pavesi, G., & Rizzolatti, G. (1995). Motor facilitation during action observation: A magnetic stimulation study. *Journal of Neurophysiology, 73,* 2608–2611.

Fairbanks, L. A. (1989). Early experience and cross-generational continuity of mother–infant contact in vervet monkeys. *Developmental Psychobiology, 22,* 669–681.

Falls, W. A., Miserendino, M. J., & Davis, M. (1992). Extinction of fear-potentiated startle: Blockade by infusion of an NMDA antagonist into the amygdala. *Journal of Neuroscience, 12,* 854–863.

Fanselow, M. S. (1986). Conditioned fear-induced opiate analgesia: A competing motivational state theory of stress analgesia. *Annals of the New York Academy of Sciences, 467,* 40–54.

Fanselow, M. S., & Gale, G. D. (2003). The amygdala, fear, and memory. *Annals of New York Academy of Sciences, 985,* 125–134.

Fantz, R. L. (1961). The origin of form perception. *Scientific American, 204,* 66–72.

Fantz, R. L. (1963). Pattern vision in newborn infants. *Science, 140,* 296–297.

Fantz, R. L. (1965). Visual perception from birth as shown by pattern selectivity. *Annals of the New York Academy of Sciences, 118,* 793–814.

Farah, M. J. (1996). Is face recognition "special"? Evidence from neuropsychology. *Behavioural Brain Research, 76,* 181–189.

Farah, M. J., Wilson, K. D., Drain, H. M., & Tanaka, J. R. (1995). The inverted face inversion effect in prosopagnosia: Evidence for mandatory, face-specific perceptual mechanisms. *Vision Research, 35,* 2089–2093.

Farah, M. J., Wilson, K. D., Drain, M., & Tanaka, J. N. (1998). What is "special" about face perception? *Psychological Review, 105,* 482–498.

Farrer, C., & Frith, C. D. (2002). Experiencing oneself vs. another person as being the cause of an action: The neural correlates of the experience of agency. *NeuroImage, 15,* 596–603.

Farroni, T., Csibra, G., Simion, F., & Johnson, M. H. (2002). Eye contact detection in humans from birth. *Proceedings of the National Academy of Sciences, USA, 99,* 9602–9605.

Feldman, R., Greenbaum, C. W., Mayes, L. C., & Erlich, H. S. (1997). Change in mother–infant interactive behavior: Relations to change in the mother, the infant, and the social context. *Infant Behavior and Development, 20,* 153–165.

Feldman, R., Greenbaum, C. W., & Yirmiya, N. (1999). Mother–infant affect synchrony as an antecedent of the emergence of self-control. *Developmental Psychology, 35,* 223–231.

Field, T. (1997). The treatment of depressed mothers and their infants. In L. Murry & P. J. Cooper (Eds.), *Postpartum depression and child development* (pp. 221–236). New York: Guilford Press.

Field, T. (2000). Infant massage therapy. In C. H. Zeanah, Jr. (Ed.), *Handbook of infant mental health* (2nd ed.), (pp. 494–500). New York: Guilford Press.

Field, T. (2002a). Infants' need for touch. *Human Development, 45*, 100–103.

Field, T. (2002b). Violence and touch deprivation in adolescents. *Adolescence, 37*, 735–749.

Field, T., Cohen, D., Garcia, R., & Greenberg, R. (1984). Mother–stranger face discrimination by the newborn. *Infant Behavior and Development, 7*, 19–25.

Field, T., Diego, M., Dieter, J., Hernandez-Reif, M., Schanberg, S., Kuhn, C., et al. (2004). Prenatal depression effects on the fetus and the newborn. *Infant Behavior and Development, 27*, 216–229.

Field, T., Diego, M., Hernandez-Reif, M., Schanberg, S., & Kuhn, C. (2002a). Relative right versus left frontal EEG in neonates. *Developmental Psychobiology, 41*, 147–155.

Field, T., Diego, M., Hernandez-Reif, M., Schanberg, S., & Kuhn, C. (2002b). Right frontal EEG and pregnancy/neonatal outcomes. *Psychiatry, 65*, 35–47.

Field, T., Diego, M., Hernandez-Reif, M., Schanberg, S., Kuhn, C., Yando, R., et al. (2003). Pregnancy anxiety and comorbid depression and anger: Effects on the fetus and neonate. *Depression and Anxiety, 17*, 140–151.

Field, T., Gizzle, N., Scafidi, F., Abrams, S., Richardson, S., Kuhn, C., et al. (1996). Massage therapy for infants of depressed mothers. *Infant Behavior and Development, 19*, 107–112.

Field, T., Goldstein, S., Vega-Lahr, N., & Porter, K. (1986). Changes in imitative behavior during early infancy. *Infant Behavior and Development, 9*, 415–421.

Field, T., Healy, B., Goldstein, S., & Guthertz, M. (1990). Behavior–state matching and synchrony in mother–infant interactions in nondepressed versus depressed dyads. *Developmental Psychology, 26*, 7–14.

Field, T., Healy, B., Goldstein, S., Perry, S., & Bendell, D. (1988). Infants of depressed mothers show "depressed" behavior even with nondepressed adults. *Child Development, 59*, 1569–1579.

Field, T., Woodson, R., Greenberg, R., & Cohen, D. (1982). Discrimination and imitation of facial expressions by neonates. *Science, 218*, 179–181.

Fink, G. R., Halligan, P. W., Marshall, J. C., Frith, C. D., Frackowiak, R. S. J., & Dolan, R. J. (1996). Where in the brain does visual attention select the forest from the trees? *Nature, 382*, 626–628.

Fink, G. R., Markowitsch, H. J., Reinkemeier, M., Bruckbauer, T., Kessler, J., & Heiss, W. D. (1996). Cerebral representation of one's own past: Neural networks involved in autobiographical memory. *Journal of Neuroscience, 16*, 4275–4282.

Finkel, L. H., & Sajda, P. (1994). Constructing visual perception. *American Scientist, 82*, 224–237.

Fiorillo, C. D., Tobler, P. N., & Schultz, W. (2003). Discrete coding of reward probability and uncertainty by dopamine neurons. *Science, 299*, 1898–1902.

Fischer, K. W. (1987). Relations between brain and cognitive development. *Child Development, 58*, 623–632.

Fischer, K. W., Shaver, P. R., & Carnochan, P. (1990). How emotions develop and how they organize development. *Cognition and Emotion, 4*, 81–127.

Fisher, H. E. (1998). Lust, attraction, and attachment in mammalian reproduction. *Human Nature, 9,* 23–52.

Fisher, L., Ames, E. W., Chisholm, K., & Savoie, L. (1997). Problems reported by parents of Romanian orphans adopted to British Columbia. *International Journal of Behavioral Development, 20,* 67–82.

Fleming, A. S., & Corter, C. (1988). Factors influencing maternal responsiveness in humans: Usefulness of an animal model. *Psychoneuroendocrinology, 13,* 189–212.

Fleming, A. S., & Korsmit, M. (1996). Plasticity in the maternal circuit: Effects of maternal experience on fos-lir in hypothalamic, limbic, and cortical structures in the postpartum rat. *Behavioral Neuroscience, 110,* 567–582.

Fleming, A. S., Korsmit, M., & Deller, M. (1994). Rat pups are potent reinforcers to the maternal animal: Effects of experience, parity, hormones, and dopamine function. *Psychobiology, 22,* 44–53.

Fleming, A. S., Kraemer, G. W., Gonzalez, A., Lovic, V., Rees, S., & Melo, A. (2002). Mothering begets mothering: The transmission of behavior and its neurobiology across generations. *Pharmacology, Biochemistry, and Behavior, 73,* 61–75.

Fleming, A. S., O'Day, D. H., & Kraemer, G. W. (1999). Neurobiology of mother–infant interactions: Experience and central nervous system plasticity across development and generations. *Neuroscience and Biobehavioral Reviews, 23,* 673–685.

Fleming, A. S., Suh, E. J., Korsmit, M., & Rusak, B. (1994). Activiation of fos-like immunoreactivity in the medial preoptic area and limbic structures by maternal and social interactions in rats. *Behavioral Neuroscience, 108,* 724–734.

Fleming, A. S., Vaccarino, F., Tambosso, L., & Chee, P. (1979). Vomeronasal and olfactory system modulation of maternal behavior in the rat. *Science, 203,* 372–374.

Fletcher, P. C., Frith, C. D., Baker, S. C., Shallice, T., Frackowiak, R. S., & Dolan, R. J. (1995). The mind's eye: Precuneus activation in memory-related imagery. *NeuroImage, 2,* 195–200.

Foa, E. B., Gilboa-Schechtman, E., Amir, N., & Freshman, M. (2000). Memory bias in generalized social phobia: Remembering negative emotional expressions. *Journal of Anxiety Disorders, 14,* 501–519.

Fonagy, P., Leigh, T., Steele, M., Steele, H., Kennedy, R., Mattoon, G., et al. (1996). The relation of attachment status, psychiatric classification, and response to psychotherapy. *Journal of Consulting and Clinical Psychology, 64,* 22–31.

Fonagy, P., Steele, M., Steele, H., Moran, G. S., & Higgitt, A. C. (1991). The capacity for understanding mental states: The reflective self in parent and child and its significance for security of attachment. *Infant Mental Health Journal, 12,* 201–218.

Fonagy, P., Target, M., & Gergely, G. (2000). Attachment and borderline personality disorder: A theory and some evidence. *Psychiatric Clinics of North America, 23,* 103–122.

Formby, D. (1967). Maternal recognition of infant's cry. *Developmental Medicine and Child Neurology, 9,* 293–298.

Fox, E., Russo, R., Bowles, R., & Dutton, K. (2001). Do threatening stimuli draw or hold visual attention in subclinical anxiety? *Journal of Experimental Psychology: General, 130,* 681–700.

Fox, E., Russo, R., & Dutton, K. (2002). Attentional bias for threat: Evidence for delayed disengagement from emotional faces. *Cognition and Emotion, 16,* 355–379.

Fox, N. A. (1991). If it's not left it's right: Electroencephalograph asymmetry and the development of emotion. *American Psychologist, 46,* 863–872.

Fox, R., & McDaniel, C. (1982). The perception of biological motion by human infants. *Science, 218,* 486–487.

Francis, D., Diorio, J., Liu, D., & Meaney, M. J. (1999). Nongenomic transmission across generations of maternal behavior and stress responses in the rat. *Science, 286,* 1155–1158.

Francis, S., Rolls, E. T., Bowtell, R., McGlone, F., O'Doherty, J., Browning, A., et al. (1999). The representation of pleasant touch in the brain and its relationship with taste and olfactory areas. *NeuroReport, 10,* 453–459.

Francke, U. (1999). Williams–Beuren syndrome: Genes and mechanisms. *Human Molecular Genetics, 8,* 1917–1951.

Franklin, T. R., Acton, P. D., Maldjian, J. A., Gray, J. D., Croft, J. R., Dackis, C. A., et al. (2002). Decreased gray matter concentration in the insular, orbitofrontal, cingulate, and temporal cortices of cocaine patients. *Biological Psychiatry, 51,* 134–142.

Fredrikson, M., Wik, G., Annas, P., Ericson, K., & Stone-Elander, S. (1995). Functional neuroanatomy of visually elicited simple phobic fear: Additional data and theoretical analysis. *Psychophysiology, 32,* 43–48.

Freire, A., Eskritt, M., & Lee, K. (2004). Are eyes windows to a deceiver's soul? Children's use of another's eye gaze cues in a deceptive situation. *Developmental Psychology, 40,* 1093–1104.

Freire, R., & Cheng, H. W. (2004). Experience-dependent changes in the hippocampus of domestic chicks: A model for spatial memory. *European Journal of Neuroscience, 20,* 1065–1068.

Freund, H. (2001). The parietal lobe as a sensorimotor interface: A perspective from clinical and neuroimaging data. *NeuroImage, 14,* S142–S146.

Fride, E., & Weinstock, M. (1988). Prenatal stress increases anxiety-related behavior and alters cerebral lateralization of dopamine activity. *Life Sciences, 42,* 1059–1065.

Frith, C. D. (2002). Attention to action and awareness of other minds. *Consciousness and Cognition, 11,* 481–487.

Frith, C. D., & Frith, U. (1999). Interacting minds: A biological basis. *Science, 286,* 1692–1695.

Fujioka, T., Fujioka, A., Endoh, H., Sakata, Y., Furukawa, S., & Nakamura, S. (2003). Materno-fetal coordination of stress-induced fos expression in the hypothalamic paraventricular nucleus during pregnancy. *Neuroscience, 118,* 409–415.

Fujioka, T., Fujioka, A., Tan, N., Chowdhury, G. M. I., Mouri, H., Sakata, Y., et al. (2001). Mild prenatal stress enhances learning performance in the non-adopted rat offspring. *Neuroscience, 103,* 301–307.

Fukunishi, I., Sei, H., Morita, Y., & Rahe, R. H. (1999). Sympathetic activity in alexithymics with mother's low care. *Journal of Psychosomatic Research, 46,* 579–589.

Furman, W., Simon, V. A., Shaffer, L., & Bouchey, H. A. (2002). Adolescents' working models and styles for relationships with parents, friends, and romantic partners. *Child Development, 73,* 241–255.

Furmark, T., Fischer, H., Wik, G., Larsson, M., & Fredrikson, M. (1997).The amygdala and individual differences in human fear conditioning. *NeuroReport, 8,* 3957–3960.

Furmark, T., Tillfors, M., Marteinsdottir, I., Fischer, H., Pissiota, A., Långström, B., et al. (2002). Common changes in cerebral blood flow in patients with social phobia treated with citalopram or cognitive–behavioral therapy. *Archives of General Psychiatry, 59,* 425–433.

Fuster, J. M. (1985). The prefrontal cortex and temporal integration. In A. Peters & E. G. Jones (Eds.), *Cerebral cortex: Vol. 4. Association and auditory cortices* (pp. 151–171). New York: Plenum Press.

Fuster, J. M. (1996). Frontal lobe and the cognitive foundation of behavioral action. In A. R. Damasio, H. Damasio, & Y. Christen (Eds.), *The Neurobiology of decision-making* (pp. 47–61). New York: Springer-Verlag.

Fuster, J. M. (1997). *The prefrontal cortex: Anatomy, physiology, and neuropsychology of the frontal lobe* (3rd ed.). Philadelphia: Lippincott-Raven.

Gaensbauer, T. J. (1982). Regulation of emotional expression in infants from two contrasting caretaking environments. *Journal of the American Academy of Child Psychiatry, 21,* 163–170.

Gaffney, G. R., Kuperman, S., Tsai, L. Y., & Minchin, S. (1988). Morphological evidence for brainstem involvement in infantile autism. *Biological Psychiatry, 24,* 578–586.

Gaffney, G. R., Kuperman, S., Tsai, L. Y., Minchin, S., & Hassanein, K. M. (1987). Midsagittal magnetic resonance imaging of autism. *British Journal of Psychiatry, 151,* 831–833.

Gaffney, G. R., Tsai, L. Y., Kuperman, S., & Minchin, S. (1987). Cerebellar structure in autism. *American Journal of Disabled Children, 141,* 1330–1332.

Galaburda, A. M., & Bellugi, U. (2000). Multi-level analysis of cortical neuroanatomy in Williams syndrome. *Journal of Cognitive Neuroscience, 12,* 74–88.

Galaburda, A. M., Schmitt, J. E., Atlas, S. W., Eliez, S., Bellugi, U., & Reiss, A. L. (2001). Dorsal forebrain anomaly in Williams syndrome. *Archives of Neurology, 58,* 1865–1869.

Galaburda, A. M., Wang, P. P., Bellugi, U., & Rossen, M. (1994). Cytoarchitectonic anomalies in a genetically based disorder: Williams syndrome. *NeuroReport, 5,* 753–757.

Galin, D. (1974). Implications for psychiatry of left and right cerebral specialization: A neurophysiological context for unconscious processes. *Archives of General Psychiatry, 31,* 572–583.

Gallagher, H. L., & Frith, C. D. (2004). Dissociable neural pathways for the perception and recognition of expressive and instrumental gestures. *Neuropsychologia, 42,* 1725–1736.

Gallagher, H. L., Happé, F., Brunswick, N., Fletcher, P. C., Frith, U., & Frith, C. D. (2000). Reading the mind in cartoons and stories: An fMRI study of "theory of mind" in verbal and nonverbal tasks. *Neuropsychologia, 38,* 11–21.

Gallagher, M., & Holland, P. C. (1994). The amygdala complex: Multiple roles in associative learning and attention. *Proceedings of the National Academy of Sciences, USA, 91,* 11771–11776.

Gallagher, M., McMahan, R. W., & Schoenbaum, G. (1999). Orbitofrontal cortex and representation of incentive value in associative learning. *Journal of Neuroscience, 19,* 6610–6614.

Gallese, V. (2001). The "shared manifold" hypothesis: From mirror neurons to empathy. *Journal of Conscientiousness Studies, 8,* 33–50.

Gallese, V., Fadiga, L., Fogassi, L., & Rizzolatti, G. (1996). Action recognition in the premotor cortex. *Brain, 119,* 593–609.

Gallese, V., & Goldman, A. (1998). Mirror neurons and the simulation theory of mind-reading. *Trends in Cognitive Sciences, 2,* 493–501.

Garavan, H., Pendergrass, J. C., Ross, T. J., Stein, E. A., & Risinger, R. C. (2001). Amygdala response to both positively and negatively valenced stimuli. *NeuroReport, 12,* 2779–2783.

Garavan, H., Ross, T. J., & Stein, E. A. (1999). Right hemispheric dominance of inhibitory control: An event-related functional MRI study. *Proceedings of the National Academy of Sciences, USA, 96,* 8301–8306.

Garcia, R., Vouimba, R. M., Baudry, M., & Thompson, R. F. (1999). The amygdala modulates prefrontal cortex activity relative to conditioned fear. *Nature, 402,* 294–296.

Gardner, R., Jr. (1997). Sociophysiology as the basic science of psychiatry. *Theoretical Medicine, 18,* 355–356.

Garrison, W. T., & Earls, F. J. (1986). Epidemiological perspectives on maternal depression and the young child. In E. Z. Tronick & T. Field (Eds.), *New directions for child development: Vol. 34. Maternal depression and infant disturbance* (pp. 13–30). San Francisco: Jossey-Bass.

Gauthier, I., & Logothetis, N. K. (2000). Is face recognition not so unique after all? *Cognitive Neuropsychology, 17,* 125–142.

Gauthier, I., Tarr, M. J., Moylan, J., Skudlarski, P., Gore, J. C., & Anderson, A. W. (2000). The fusiform "face area" is part of a network that processes faces at the individual level. *Journal of Cognitive Neuroscience, 12,* 495–504.

Gawin, F. H. (2001). The scientific exegesis of desire: Neuroimaging crack craving. *Archives of General Psychiatry, 58,* 342–344.

Gazzaniga, M. S., & Smylie, C. S. (1983). Facial recognition and brain asymmetries: Clues to underlying mechanisms. *Annals of Neurology, 13,* 536–540.

Ge, Y., Grossman, R. I., Babb, J. S., Rabin, M. L., Mannon, L. J., & Kolson, D. I. (2002). Age-related total gray matter and white matter changes in normal adult brain: Part I. Volumetric MR imaging analysis. *American Journal of Neuroradiology, 23,* 1327–1333.

Gehring, W. J., & Knight, R. T. (2000). Prefrontal–cingulate interactions in action monitoring. *Nature Neuroscience, 3,* 516–520.

Gehring, W. J., & Willoughby, A. R. (2002). The medial frontal cortex and the rapid processing of monetary gains and losses. *Science, 295,* 2279–2282.

George, M. S., Parekh, P. I., Rosinsky, N., Keller, T. A., Kimbrell, T. A., Heilman, K. M., et al. (1996). Understanding emotional prosody activates right hemisphere regions. *Archives of Neurology, 53,* 665–670.

George, N., Driver, J., & Dolan, R. J. (2001). Seen gaze-direction modulates fusiform activity and its coupling with other brain areas during face processing. *NeuroImage, 13,* 1102–1112.

Georgiou, G. A., Bleakley, C., & Hayward, J. (2005). Focusing on fear: Attentional disengagement from emotional faces. *Visual Cognition, 12,* 145–158.

Gerlach, A. L., Wilhelm, F. H., Gruber, K., & Roth, W. T. (2001). Blushing and physiological arousability in social phobia. *Journal of Abnormal Psychology, 110,* 247–258.

Gerlach, A. L., Wilhelm, F. H., & Roth, W. T. (2003). Embarassment and social phobia: The role of parasympathetic activation. *Journal of Anxiety Disorders, 17,* 197–210.

Geschwind, N., & Galaburda, A. M. (1985a). Cerebral lateralization. Biological mechanisms, associations and pathology: I. A hypothesis and a program for research. *Archives of Neurology, 42,* 428–459.

Geschwind, N., & Galaburda, A. M. (1985b). Cerebral lateralization. Biological mechanisms, associations, and pathology: II. A hypothesis and a program for research. *Archives of Neurology, 42,* 521–522.

Geuze, E., Vermetten, E., & Bremner, J. D. (2005). MR-based in vivo hippocampal volumetrics: 2. Findings in neuropsychiatric disorders. *Molecular Psychiatry, 10,* 160–184.

Ghez, C. (1991). The cerebellum. In E. R. Kandel, J. H. Schwartz, & T. M. Jessell (Eds.), *Principles of neural science* (3rd ed., pp. 626–646). New York: Elsevier.

Ghosh, A. (2002). Neurobiology: Learning more about NMDA receptor regulation. *Science, 295,* 449–451.

Giedd, J. N. (2004). Structural magnetic resonance imaging of the adolescent brain. *Annals of the New York Academy of Sciences, 1021,* 77–85.

Giedd, J. N., Rumsey, J. M., Castellanos, F. X., Rajapakse, J. C., Kaysen, D., Vaituzis, A. C., et al. (1996). A quantitative MRI study of the corpus callosum in children and adolescents. *Developmental Brain Research, 91,* 274–280.

Giedd, J. N., Vaituzis, A. C., Hamburger, S. D., Lange, N., Rajapakse, J. C., Kaysen, D., et al. (1996). Quantitative MRI of the temporal lobe, amygdala, and hippocampus in normal human development: Ages 4–18 years. *Journal of Comparative Neurology, 366,* 223–230.

Gläscher, J., & Adolphs, R. (2003). Processing of the arousal of subliminal and supraliminal emotional stimuli by the human amygdala. *Journal of Neuroscience, 23,* 10274–10282.

Gloor, P. (1986). The role of the human limbic system in perception, memory, and affect: Lessons from temporal lobe epilepsy. In B. K. Doane & K. E. Livingston (Eds.), *The limbic system: Functional organization and clinical disorder* (pp. 159–169). New York: Raven Press.

Goebel, R., Khorram-Sefat, D., Muckli, L., Hacker, H., & Singer, W. (1998). The constructive nature of vision: Direct evidence from functional magnetic resonance imaging studies of apparent motion and motion imagery. *European Journal of Neuroscience, 10,* 1563–1573.

Goel, V., & Dolan, R. J. (2001). The functional anatomy of humor: Segregating cognitive and affective components. *Nature Neuroscience, 4,* 237–238.

Goel, V., Grafman, J., Sadato, N., & Hallett, M. (1995). Modeling other minds. *Neuro-Report, 6,* 1741–1746.

Gogtay, N., Giedd, J. N., Lusk, L., Hayashi, K. M., Greenstein, D., Vaituzis, A. C., et al. (2004). Dynamic mapping of human cortical development during childhood through early adulthood. *Proceedings of the National Academy of Sciences, USA, 101,* 8174–8179.

Golby, A. J., Gabrieli, J. D. E., Chiao, J. Y., & Eberhardt, J. L. (2001). Differential responses in the fusiform region to same-race and other-race faces. *Nature Neuroscience, 4,* 845–850.

Goldberg, E., & Costa, L. D. (1981). Hemispheric differences in the acquisition and use of descriptive systems. *Brain and Language, 14,* 144–173.

Goldfarb, W. (1945). Psychological privation in infancy and subsequent adjustment. *American Journal of Orthopsychiatry, 14,* 247–255.

Good, C. D., Johnsrude, I. S., Ashburner, J., Henson, R. D., Friston, K. J., & Frackowiak, R. S. (2001a). A voxel-based morphometric study of aging in 465 normal adult human brains. *NeuroImage, 14,* 21–36.

Good, C. D., Johnsrude, I. S., Ashburner, J., Henson, R. D., Friston, K. J., & Frackowiak, R. S. (2001b). Cerebral asymmetry and the effects of sex and handedness on brain structure: A voxel-based morphometric analysis of 465 normal adult human brains. *NeuroImage, 14,* 685–700.

Goodfellow, L. M. (2003). The effects of therapeutic back massage on psychophysiologic variables and immune function in spouses of patients with cancer. *Nursing Research, 52,* 318–328.

Goodman, R. R., Snyder, S. H., Kuhar, M. J., & Young, W. S., III. (1980). Differential of delta and mu opiate receptor localizations by light microscope autoradiography. *Proceedings of the National Academy of Sciences, USA, 77,* 6239–6243.

Goren, C. C., Sarty, M., & Wu, P. Y. (1975). Visual following and pattern discrimination of face-like stimuli by newborn infants. *Pediatrics, 56,* 544–549.

Gorno-Tempini, M. L., Pradelli, S., Serafini, M., Pagnoni, G., Baraldi, P., Porro, C., et al. (2001). Explicit and incidental facial expression precessing: An fMRI study. *Neuro-Image, 14,* 465–473.

Gosch, A., Städing, G., & Pankau, R. (1994). Linguistic abilities in children with Williams–Beuren syndrome. *American Journal of Medical Genetics, 52,* 291–296.

Gould, E., Reeves, A. J., Graziano, M. S., & Gross, C. G. (1999). Neurogenesis in the neocortex of adult primates. *Science, 286,* 548–552.

Gould, E., Tanapat, P., Hastings, N. B., & Shors, T. J. (1999). Neurogenesis in adulthood: A possible role in learning. *Trends in Cognitive Sciences, 3,* 186–192.

Gould, S. J. (1977). *Ontogeny and phylogeny.* Cambridge, MA: Belknap Press of Harvard University.

Goyer, P. F., Andreason, P. J., Semple, W. E., Clayton, A. H., King, A. C., Compton-Toth, B. A., et al. (1994). Positron emission tomography and personality disorders. *Neuropsychopharmacology, 10,* 21–28.

Grafton, S. T., Arbib, M. A., Fadiga, L., & Rizzolatti, G. (1996). Localization of grasp representations in human by positron emission tomography: 2. Observation compared with imagination. *Experimental Brain Research, 112*, 103–111.

Grammer, K., & Thornhill, R. (1994). Human (*Homo sapiens*) facial attractiveness and sexual selection: The role of symmetry and averageness. *Journal of Comparative Psychology, 108*, 233–242.

Grandin, T. (1995). *Thinking in pictures.* New York: Doubleday.

Granholm, E., & Steinhauer, S. R. (2004). Pupillometric measures of cognitive and emotional processes. *International Journal of Psychophysiology, 52*, 1–6.

Grattan, D. R. (2002). Behavioural significance of prolactin signalling in the central nervous system during pregnancy and lactation. *Reproduction, 123*, 497–506.

Gray, J. M., Young, A. W., Barker, W. A., Curtis, A., & Gibson, D. (1997). Impaired recognition of disgust in Huntington's disease gene carriers. *Brain, 120*, 2029–2038.

Gray, J. R., Braver, T. S., & Raichle, M. E. (2002). Integration of emotion and cognition in the lateral prefrontal cortex. *Proceedings of the National Academy of Sciences, USA, 99*, 4115–4120.

Green, A. H. (1978). Self-destructive behavior in battered children. *American Journal of Psychiatry, 135*, 579–582.

Greenspan, S. I., & Shanker, S. G. (2004). *The first idea: How symbols, language, and intelligence evolved from our primate ancestors to modern humans.* Cambridge, MA: Da Capo Press.

Greenwald, A. G., & Banaji, M. R. (1989). The self as a memory system: Powerful, but ordinary. *Journal of Personality and Social Psychology, 57*, 41–54.

Grelotti, D. J., Gauthier, I., & Schultz, R. T. (2002). Social interest and the development of cortical face specialization: What autism teaches us about face processing. *Developmental Psychobiology, 40*, 213–225.

Grelotti, D. J., Klin, A. J., Gauthier, I., Skudlarski, P., Cohen, D. J., Gore, J. C., et al. (2005). fMRI activation of the fusiform gyrus and amygdala to cartoon characters but not to faces in a boy with autism. *Neuropsychologia, 43*, 373–385.

Grèzes, J., & Decety, J. (2001). Functional anatomy of execution, mental simulation, observation, and verb generation of actions: A meta-analysis. *Human Brain Mapping, 12*, 1–19.

Grèzes, J., Fonlupt, P., Bertenthal, B., Delon-Martin, C., Segebarth, C., & Decety, J. (2001). Does perception of biological motion rely on specific brain regions? *NeuroImage, 13*, 775–785.

Grieve, S. M., Clark, C. R., Williams, L. M., Peduto, A. J., & Gordon, E. (2005). Preservation of limbic and paralimbic regions with aging. *Human Brain Mapping, 25*, 391–401.

Grimm, C. T., & Bridges, R. S. (1983). Opiate regulation of maternal behavior in the rat. *Pharmacology, Biochemistry, and Behavior, 19*, 609–616.

Grisaru, N., Chudakov, B., Yaroslavsky, Y., & Belmaker, R.H. (1998). Transcranial magnetic stimulation in mania: A controlled study. *American Journal of Psychiatry, 155*, 1608–1610.

Gross, C. G. (2000). Neurogenesis in the adult brain: Death of a dogma. *Nature Reviews Neuroscience, 1,* 67–73.

Grosser, B. L., Monti-Bloch, L., Jennings-White, C., & Berliner, D. L. (2000). Behavioral and electrophysiological effects of androstadienone, a human pheromone. *Psychoneuroendocrinology, 25,* 289–299.

Grossman, E. D., & Blake, R. (2002). Brain areas active during visual perception of biological motion. *Neuron, 35,* 1167–1175.

Grossman, J. B., Klin, A., Carter, A. S., & Volkmar, F. R. (2000). Verbal bias in recognition of facial emotions in children with Asperger syndrome. *Journal of Child Psychology and Psychiatry and Allied Disciplines, 41,* 369–379.

Gundel, H., Lopez-Sala, A., Ceballos-Baumann, A. O., Deus, J., Cardoner, N., & Martin-Mittage, B. (2004). Alexithymia correlates with the size of the right anterior cingulate. *Psychosomatic Medicine, 66,* 132–140.

Gunnar, M. R. (1992). Reactivity of the hypothalamic–pituitary–adrenocortical system to stressors in normal infants and children. *Pediatrics, 90*(Suppl. 3), 491–479.

Gunnar, M. R. (1998). Quality of care and buffering of neuroendocrine stress reactions: Potential effects on the developing human brain. *Preventive Medicine, 27,* 208–211.

Gunnar, M. R., & Donzella, B. (2002). Social regulation of the cortisol levels in early human development. *Psychoneuroendocrinology, 27,* 199–220.

Gur, R. C., Erwin, R. J., Gur, R. E., Zwil, A. S., Heimberg, C., & Kraemer, H. C. (1992). Facial emotion discrimination: II. Behavioral findings in depression. *Psychiatry Research, 42,* 241–251.

Gur, R. C., Schroeder, L., Turner, T., McGrath, C., Chan, R. M., Turetsky, B. I., et al. (2002). Brain activation during facial emotion processing. *NeuroImage, 16,* 651–662.

Gurvits, I. G., Koenigsberg, H. W., & Siever, L. J. (2000). Neurotransmitter dysfunction in patients with borderline personality disorder. *Psychiatric Clinics of North America, 23,* 27–40.

Gusella, J. L., Muir, D., & Tronick, E. Z. (1988). The effect of manipulating maternal behavior during an interaction on three- and six-month-olds' affect and attention. *Child Development, 59,* 1111–1124.

Guttmann, C. R. G., Jolesz, F. A., Kikinis, R., Killiany, R. J., Moss, M. B., Sandor, T., et al. (1998). White matter changes with normal aging. *Neurology, 50,* 972–978.

Gutzmann, H., & Kühl, K. P. (1987). Emotion control and cerebellar atrophy in senile dementia. *Archives of Gerontology and Geriatry, 6,* 61–71.

Habib, M., Daquin, G., Pelletier, J., Montreuil, M., & Robichon, F. (2003). Alexithymia as a consequence of impaired callosal function: Evidence from multiple sclerosis patients and normal individuals. In E. Zaidel & M. Iacaboni (Eds.), *The parallel brain* (pp. 415–422). Cambridge, MA: MIT Press.

Hadland, K. A., Rushworth, M. F. S., Gaffan, D., & Passingham, R. E. (2003). The effect of cingulate lesions on social behavior and emotion. *Neuropsychologia, 41,* 919–931.

Halgren, E., Dale, A. M., Sereno, M. I., Tootell, R. B., Marinkovic, K., & Rosen, B. R. (1999). Location of human face-selective cortex with respect to retinotopic areas. *Human Brain Mapping, 7,* 29–37.

Halgren, E., Raij, T., Marinkovic, K., Jousmäki, V., & Hari, R. (2000). Cognitive response profile of the human fusiform face area as determined by MEG. *Cerebral Cortex, 10,* 69–81.

Hall, J. R., Benning, S. D., & Patrick, C. J. (2004). Criterion-related validity of the three-factor model of psychopathy: Personality, behavior, and adaptive functioning. *Assessment, 11,* 4–16.

Halligan, S. L., Herbert, J., Goodyer, I. M., & Murray, L. (2004). Exposure to postnatal depression predicts elevated cortisol in adolescent offspring. *Biological Psychiatry, 55,* 376–381.

Halpern, M., & Martinez-Marcos, A. (2003). Structure and function of the vomeronasal system: An update. *Progress in Neurobiology, 70,* 245–318.

Hamann, S. B., Ely, T. D., Grafon, S. T., & Kilts, C. D. (1999). Amygdala activity related to enhanced memory for pleasant and aversive stimuli. *Nature Neuroscience, 2,* 289–293.

Hamann, S. B., Ely, T. D., Hoffman, J. M., & Kilts, C. D. (2002). Ecstasy and agony: Activation of the human amygdala in positive and negative emotion. *Psychological Science, 13,* 135–141.

Hamann, S. B., Stefanacci, L., Squire, L. R., Adolphs, R., Tranel, D., Damasio, H., et al. (1996). Recognizing facial emotion. *Nature, 379,* 497.

Hamel, R. F. (1974). Female subjective and pupillary reaction to nude male and female figures. *Journal of Psychology, 87,* 171–175.

Hamilton, C. E. (2000). Continuity and discontinuity of attachment from infancy through adolescence. *Child Development, 71,* 690–694.

Hansen, D., Lou, H. C., & Olsen, J. (2000). Serious life events and congenital malformations: A national study with complete follow-up. *Lancet, 356,* 875–880.

Happé, F., Brownell, H., & Winner, E. (1999). Acquired "theory of mind" impairments following stroke. *Cognition, 70,* 211–240.

Happé, F., Ehlers, S., Fletcher, P., Frith, U., Johansson, M., Gillberg, C., et al. (1996). "Theory of mind" in the brain: Evidence from a PET scan study of Asperger syndrome. *NeuroReport, 8,* 197–201.

Hare, R. D. (1972). Psychopathy and physiological responses to adrenalin. *Journal of Abnormal Psychology, 79,* 138–147.

Hari, R., Portin, K., Kettenmann, B., Jousmäki, V., & Kobal, G. (1997). Right-hemisphere preponderance of responses to painful CO_2 stimulation of the human nasal mucosa. *Pain, 72,* 145–151.

Hariri, A. R., Bookheimer, S. Y., & Mazziotta, J. C. (2000). Modulating emotional responses: Effects of a neocortical network on the limbic system. *NeuroReport, 11,* 43–48.

Hariri, A. R., Mattay, V. S., Tessitore, A., Fera, F., & Weinberger, D. R. (2003). Neocortical modulation of the amygdala response to fearful stimuli. *Biological Psychiatry, 53,* 494–501.

Hariri, A. R., Tessitore, A., Mattay, V. S., Fera, F., & Weinberger, D. R. (2002). The amygdala response to emotional stimuli: A comparison of faces and scenes. *NeuroImage, 17,* 317–323.

Harlow, J. (1868). Recovery from the passage of an iron bar through the head. *Publications of the Massachusetts Medical Society, 2,* 327–347.

Hart, A. J., & Morry, M. M. (1996). Nonverbal behavior, race, and attitude attributions. *Journal of Experimental Social Psychology, 32,* 165–179.

Hart, A. J., & Morry, M. M. (1997). Trait inferences based on racial and behavioral cues. *Basic and Applied Social Psychology, 19,* 33–48.

Hart, A. J., Whalen, P. J., Shin, L. M., McInerney, S. C., Fischer, H., & Rauch, S. L. (2000). Differential response in the human amygdala to racial outgroup vs. ingroup face stimuli. *NeuroReport, 11,* 2351–2355.

Hashimoto, T., Tayama, M., Miyazaki, M., Sakurama, N., Yoshimoto, T., Mutakawa, K., et al. (1992). Reduced brainstem size in children with autism. *Brain and Development, 14,* 94–97.

Hashimoto, T., Tayama, M., Murakawa, K., Yoshimoto, T., Miyazaki, M., Harada, M., et al. (1995). Development of the brainstem and cerebellum in autistic patients. *Journal of Autism and Developmental Disorders, 25,* 1–18.

Hass, R. G., Katz, I., Rizzo, N., Bailey, J., & Eisenstadt, D. (1991). Cross-racial appraisal as related to attitude ambivalence and cognitive complexity. *Personality and Social Psychology Bulletin, 17,* 83–92.

Hasselmo, M. E., Rolls, E. T., & Baylis, G. C. (1989). The role of expression and identity in the face-selective responses of neurons in the temporal visual cortex of the monkey. *Behavior Brain Research, 32,* 203–218.

Hatton, G. I., Yang, Q. Z., & Cobbett, P. (1987). Dye coupling among immunocytochemically identified neurons in the supraoptic nucleus: Increased incidence in lactating rats. *Neuroscience, 21,* 923–930.

Hauser, S. L., Delong, G. R., & Rosman, N. P. (1975). Pneumographic findings in the infantile autism syndrome: A correlation with temporal lobe disease. *Brain, 98,* 667–688.

Haxby, J. V., Hoffman, E. A., & Gobbini, M. I. (2000). The distributed human neural system for face perception. *Trends in Cognitive Sciences, 4,* 223–233.

Haxby, J. V., Horwitz, B., Ungerleider, L. G., Maisog, J. M., Pietrini, P., & Grady, C. L. (1994). The functional organization of human extrastriate cortex: A PET–rCBF study of selective attention to faces and locations. *Journal of Neuroscience, 14,* 6336–6353.

Haxby, J. V., Ungerleider, L. G., Clark, V. P., Schouten, J. L., Hoffman, E. A., & Martin, A. (1999). The effect of face inversion on activity in human neural systems for face and object perception. *Neuron, 22,* 189–199.

Haxby, J. V., Ungerleider, L. G., Horwitz, B., Maisog, J. M., Rapoport, S. I., & Grady, C. L. (1996). Face encoding and recognition in the human brain. *Proceedings of the National Academy of Sciences, USA, 93,* 922–927.

Hayman, L. A., Rexer, J. L., Pavol, M. A., Strite, D., & Meyers, C. A. (1998). Kluver–Bucy syndrome after bilateral selective damage of amygdala and its cortical connections. *Journal of Neuropsychiatry and Clinical Neurosciences, 10,* 354–358.

Haznedar, M. M., Buchsbaum, M. S., Wei, T. C., Hof, P. R., Cartwright, C., Bienstock, C. A., et al. (2000). Limbic circuitry in patients with autism spectrum disorders studied with positron emission tomography and magnetic resonance imaging. *American Journal of Psychiatry, 157,* 1994–2001.

Heath, R. G. (1977). Modulation of emotion with a brain pacemaker: Treatment for intractable psychiatric illness. *Journal of Nervous and Mental Disease, 165,* 300–317.

Hebb, D. O. (1949). *The organization of behavior: A neuropsychological theory.* New York: Wiley.

Heisel, M. J., & Mongrain, M. (2004). Facial expressions and ambivalence: Looking for conflict in all the right faces. *Journal of Nonverbal Behaviour, 28,* 35–52.

Heiser, M., Iacoboni, M., Maeda, F., Marcus., J., & Mazziotta, J. C. (2003). The essential role of Broca's area in imitation. *European Journal of Neuroscience, 17,* 1123–1128.

Hendler, T., Rotshtein, P., Yeshurun, Y., Weizmann, T., Kahn, I., Ben-Bashat, D., et al. (2003). Sensing the invisible: Differential sensitivity of visual cortex and amygdala to traumatic context. *NeuroImage, 19,* 587–600.

Hennessy, M. B. (1997). Hypothalamic–pituitary–adrenal responses to brief social separation. *Neuroscience and Biobehavioral Reviews, 21,* 11–29.

Henriques, J. B., & Davidson, R. J. (1990). Regional brain electrical asymmetries discriminate between previously depressed and healthy control subjects. *Journal of Abnormal Psychology, 99,* 22–31.

Henriques, J. B., & Davidson, R. J. (1991). Left frontal hypoactivation in depression. *Journal of Abnormal Psychology, 100,* 535–545.

Henry, J. P., & Wang, S. (1998). Effects of early stress on adult affiliaive behavior. *Psychoneuroendocrinology, 23,* 863–875.

Henry, R. R., Satz, P., & Saslow, E. (1984). Early brain damage and the ontogenesis of functional asymmetry. In C. R. Almli & S. Finger (Eds.), *Early brain damage: Vol. 1. Research observations and clinical observations.* New York: Academic Press.

Herbert, M. R., Harris, G. J., Adrien, K. T., Ziegler, D. A., Makris, N., Kennedy, D. N., et al. (2002). Abnormal asymmetry in language association cortex in autism. *Annals of Neurology, 52,* 588–596.

Herman, B. A., & Panksepp, J. (1978). Effects of morphine and naloxone on separation distress and approach attachment: Evidence for opiate mediation of social effect. *Pharmacology, Biochemistry, and Behavior, 9,* 213–220.

Hernandez-Reif, M., Field, T., Del Pino, N., & Diego, M. (2000). Less exploring by mouth occurs in newborns of depressed mothers. *Infant Mental Health Journal, 21,* 204–210.

Hernandez-Reif, M., Field, T., Diego, M., & Largie, S. (2002). Depressed mothers' newborns show longer habituation and fail to show face/voice preference. *Infant Mental Health Journal, 23,* 643–653.

Hernandez-Reif, M., Ironson, G., Field, T., Hurley, J., Katz, G., Diego, M., et al. (2004). Breast cancer patients have improved immune and neuroendocrine functions following massage therapy. *Journal of Psychosomatic Research, 57,* 45–52.

Herpertz, S. C., Dietrich, T. M., Wenning, B., Krings, T., Erberich, S. G., Willmes, K., et al. (2001a). Evidence of abnormal amygdala functioning in borderline personality disorder: A functional MRI study. *Biological Psychiatry, 50,* 292–298.

Herpertz, S. C., Kunert, H. J., Schwenger, U. B., & Sass, H. (1999). Affective responsiveness in borderline personality disorder: A psychophysiological approach. *American Journal of Psychiatry, 156,* 1550–1556.

Herpertz, S. C., Werth, U., Lukas, G., Qunaibi, M., Schuerkens, A., & Kunert, H. J. (2001b). Emotion in criminal offenders with psychopathy and borderline personality disorder. *Archives of General Psychiatry, 58,* 737–745.

Hertsgaard, L., Gunnar, M., Erickson, M. F., & Nachmias, M. (1995). Adrenocortical response to the strange situation in infants with disorganized/disoriented attachment relationships. *Child Development, 66,* 1100–1106.

Hess, E. H. (1965). Attitude and pupil size. *Scientific American, 212,* 46–54.

Hess, E. H. (1975). The role of pupil size in communication. *Scientific American, 233,* 110–119.

Hesse, E. (1999). The adult attachment interview: Historical and current perspectives. In J. A. Cassidy & P. R. Shaver (Eds.), *Handbook of attachment: Theory, research, and clinical applications* (pp. 395–433). New York: Guilford Press.

Hesse, E., & Main, M. (1999). Second-generation effects of unresolved trauma in nonmaltreating parents: Dissociated, frightened, and threatening parental behavior. *Psychoanalytic Inquiry, 19,* 481–540.

Hesse, E., & Main, M. (2000). Disorganized infant, child, and adult attachment: Collapse in behavioral and attentional strategies. *Journal of the American Psychoanalytical Association, 48,* 1097–1127.

Hinsz, V. B., Tindale, R. S., & Vollrath, D. A. (1997). The emerging conceptualization of groups as information processors. *Psychological Bulletin, 121,* 43–64.

Hirsch, C. R., Clark, D. M., Mathews, A., & Williams, R. (2003). Self-images play a causal role in social phobia. *Behaviour Research and Therapy, 41,* 909–921.

Hirsch, C. R., & Mathews, A. (2000). Impaired positive inferential bias in social phobia. *Journal of Abnormal Psychology, 109,* 705–712.

Hobel, C. J. (2004). Stress and pre-term birth. *Clinical Obstetrics and Gynecology, 47,* 856–880.

Hobel, C. J., Dunkel-Schetter, C., Roesch, S. C., Castro, L. C., & Arora, C. P. (1999). Maternal plasma corticotropin-releasing hormone associated with stress at 20 weeks gestation in pregnancies ending in pre-term delivery. *American Journal of Obstetrics and Gynaecology, 180,* S257–S263.

Hobson, R. P. (1991). Against the theory of "theory of mind." *British Journal of Developmental Psychology, 9,* 33–51.

Hofer, E. (1968). *The passionate state of mind: And other aphorisms.* New York: Harper Collins.

Hofer, M. A. (1984). Relationships as regulators: A psychobiologic perspective on bereavement. *Psychosomatic Medicine, 46,* 183–197.

Hofer, M. A. (1987). Early social relationships: A psychobiologist's view. *Child Development, 58,* 633–647.

Hoffer, E. (1955). The passionate state of mind and other aphorisms. Cutchogue, NY: Buccaneer Books.

Hoffman, E. A., & Haxby, J. V. (2000). Distinct representations of eye gaze and identity in the distributed human neural system for face perception. *Nature Neuroscience, 3,* 80–84.

Hoffman, W. L., & Prior, M. R. (1982). Neuropsychological dimensions of autism in children: A test of the hemispheric dysfunction hypothesis. *Journal of Clinical Neuropsychology, 4,* 27–41.

Hollerman, J. R., & Schultz, W. (1998). Dopamine neurons report an error in the temporal prediction of reward during learning. *Nature Neuroscience, 1,* 304–309.

Holroyd, S., Reiss, A. L., & Bryan, R. N. (1991). Autistic features in Joubert syndrome: A genetic disorder with agenesis of the cerebellar vermis. *Biological Psychiatry, 29,* 287–294.

Hood, B. M., Willen, J. D., & Driver, J. (1998). Adults' eyes trigger shifts of visual attention in human infants. *Psychological Science, 9,* 131–134.

Hood, K. E., Dreschel, N. A., & Granger, D. A. (2003). Maternal behavior changes after immune challenge of neonates with developmental effects on adult social behavior. *Developmental Psychobiology, 42,* 17–34.

Horley, K., Williams, L. M., Gonsalvez, C., & Gordon, E. (2003). Social phobics do not see eye to eye: A visual scanpath study of emotional expression processing. *Journal of Anxiety Disorders, 17,* 33–44.

Hornik, R., Risenhoover, N., & Gunnar, M. (1987). The effects of maternal positive, neutral, and negative affective communications on infant responses to new toys. *Child Development, 58,* 937–944.

Horwitz, B., Rumsey, J. M., Grady, C. L., & Rapoport, S. I. (1988). The cerebral metabolic landscape in autism: Intercorrelations of regional glucose utilization. *Archives of Neurology, 45,* 749–755.

Howard, M. A., Cowell, P. E., Boucher, J., Broks, P., Mayes, A., & Roberts, N. (2000). *A structural magnetic resonance imaging (MRI) study of adults with high-functioning autism (HFA).* Liverpool, UK: Magnetic Resonance and Image Analysis Research Centre (MARIARC).

Huber, E. (1931). *Evolution of facial musculature and facial expressions.* Baltimore, MD: Johns Hopkins Press.

Huether, G. (1998). Stress and the adaptive self-organization of neuronal connectivity during early childhood. *International Journal of Developmental Neuroscience, 16,* 297–306.

Hugdahl, K. (1996). Cognitive influences on human autonomic nervous system function. *Current Opinion in Neurobiology, 6,* 252–258.

Hugdahl, K., Iversen, P. M., Ness, H. M., & Flaten, M. A. (1989). Hemispheric differences in recognition of facial expressions: A VHF-study of negative, positive, and neutral emotions. *International Journal of Neuroscience, 45,* 205–213.

Hugenberg, K., & Bodenhausen, G. V. (2004). Ambiguity in social categorization: The role of prejudice and facial affect in race categorization. *Psychological Science, 15,* 342–345.

Hugo, V. (1985). *Les miserables.* New York: Penguin Books.

Hutchinson, W. D., Davis, K. D., Lozano, A. M., Tasker, R. R., & Dostrovsky, J. O. (1999). Pain-related neurons in the human cingulate cortex. *Nature Neuroscience, 2,* 403–405.

Huttenlocher, P. R. (1994). Synaptogenesis in human cerebral cortex. In G. Dawson & K. W. Fischer (Eds.), *Human behavior and the developing brain* (pp. 137–152). New York: Guilford Press.

Iacoboni, M., Koski, L. M., Brass, M., Bekkering, H., Woods, R. P., Dubeau, M., et al. (2001). Reafferent copies of imitated actions in the right superior temporal cortex. *Proceedings of the National Academy of Sciences, USA, 98,* 13995–13999.

Iacoboni, M., Woods, R. P., Brass, M., Bekkering, H., Mazziotta, J. C., & Rizzolatti, G. (1999). Cortical mechanisms of human imitation. *Science, 286,* 2526–2528.

Ingvar, D. H. (1985). "Memory of the future": An essay on the temporal organization of conscious awareness. *Human Neurobiology, 4,* 127–136.

Inhoff, A. W., Diener, H. C., Rafal, R. D., & Ivry, R. (1989). The role of cerebellar structures in the execution of serial movements. *Brain, 112,* 565–581.

Insel, T. R. (1992). Oxytocin—a neuropeptide for affiliation: Evidence from behavioral, receptor, autoradiographic, and comparative studies. *Psychoneuroendocrinology, 17,* 3–35.

Insel, T. R. (1997). A neurobiological basis of social attachment. *American Journal of Psychiatry, 154,* 726–735.

Insel, T. R. (2003). Is social attachment an addictive disorder? *Physiology and Behavior, 79,* 351–357.

Irwin, M., Daniels, M., Risch, S. C., Bloom, E., & Weiner, H. (1988). Plasma cortisol and natural killer cell activity during bereavement. *Biological Psychiatry, 24,* 173–178.

Isenberg, N., Silbersweig, D., Engelien, A., Emmerich, S., Malavade, K., Beattie, B., et al. (1999). Linguistic threat activates the human amygdala. *Proceedings of the National Academy of Sciences, USA, 96,* 10456–10459.

Ishikawa, S. S., & Raine, A. (2001). Autonomic stress reactivity and executive functions in successful and unsuccessful criminal psychopaths from the community. *Journal of Abnormal Psychology, 110,* 423–432.

Itakura, S. (2004). Gaze-following and joint visual attention in nonhuman animals. *Japanese Psychological Research, 46,* 216–226.

Ito, T. A., Larsen, J. T., Smith, N. K., & Cacioppo, J. T. (2002). Negative information weighs more heavily on the brain: The negativity bias in evaluative categorizations. In J. T. Cacioppo, G. C. Berntson, R. Adolphs, C. S. Carter, R. J. Davidson, M. K. McClintock, et al. (Eds.), *Foundations in social neuroscience* (pp. 575–597). Cambridge, MA: MIT Press.

Ito, Y., Teicher, M. H., Glod, C. A., & Ackerman, E. (1998). Preliminary evidence for aberrant cortical development in abused children: A quantitative EEG study. *Journal of Neuropsychiatry and Clinical Neuroscience, 10,* 298–307.

Ito, Y., Teicher, M. H., Glod, C. A., Harper, D., Magnus, E., & Gelbard, H. A. (1993). Increased prevalence of electrophysiological abnormalities in children with psychological, physical, and sexual abuse. *Journal of Neuropsychiatry and Clinical Neuroscience, 5,* 401–408.

Izard, C. E., Haynes, O. M., Chisholm, G., & Baak, K. (1991). Emotional determinants of infant–mother attachment. *Child Development, 62,* 906–917.

Izard, C. E., Porges, S. W., Simons, R. F., Haynes, O. M., Hyde, C., Parisi, M., et al. (1991). Infant cardiac activity: Developmental changes and relations with attachment. *Developmental Psychology, 27,* 432–439.

Jackson, P. L., Meltzoff, A. N., & Decety, J. (2005). How do we perceive the pain of others? A window into the neural processes involved in empathy. *NeuroImage, 24,* 771–779.

Jacobs, B. L., van Praag, H., & Gage, F. H. (2000). Depression and the birth and death of brain cells. *American Scientist, 88,* 340–345.

Jacobs, L. F., Gaulin, S. J., Sherry, D. F., & Hoffman, G. E. (1990). Evolution of spatial cognition: Sex-specific patterns of spatial behavior predict hippocampal size. *Proceedings of the National Academy of Sciences, USA, 87,* 6349–6352.

Jacobson, L., & Sapolsky, R. (1991). The role of the hippocampus in feedback regulation of the hypothalamic–pituitary–adrenocortical axis. *Endocrine Reviews, 12,* 118–134.

Jeannerod, M. (2001). Neural simulation of action: A unifying mechanism for motor cognition. *NeuroImage, 14,* S103–S109.

Jeannerod, M., Arbib, M. A., Rizzolatti, G., & Sakata, H. (1995). Grasping objects: The cortical mechanisms of visuomotor transformation. *Trends in Neurosciences, 18,* 314–320.

Jellema, T., & Perrett, D. I. (2003a). Cells in monkey STS responsive to articulated body motions and consequent static posture: A case of implied motion? *Neuropsychologia, 41,* 1728–1737.

Jellema, T., & Perrett, D. I. (2003b). Perceptual history influences neural responses to face and body postures. *Journal of Cognitive Neuroscience, 15,* 961–971.

Jellema, T., Baker, C. I., Wicker, B., & Perrett, D. I. (2000). Neural representation for the perception of the intentionality of actions. *Brain and Cognition, 44,* 280–302.

Jellema, T., Maassen, F., & Perrett, D. I. (2004). Single cell integration of animate form, motion and location in the superior temporal cortex of the macaque monkey. *Cerebral Cortex, 14,* 781–790.

Jelliffe, D. B., & Jelliffe, E. F. P. (1978). The volume and composition of human milk in poorly nourished communities: A review. *American Journal of Clinical Nutrition, 31,* 492–515.

Jernigan, T. L., Archibald, S. L., Fennema-Notestine, C., Gamst, A. C., Stout, J. C., Bonner, J., et al. (2001). Effects of age on tissues and regions of the cerebrum and cerebellum. *Neurobiology of Aging, 22,* 581–594.

Jernigan, T. L., & Bellugi, U. (1994). Neuroanatomical distinctions between Williams and Down syndromes. In S. H. Broman & J. Grafman (Eds.), *Atypical cognitive deficits in developmental disorders* (pp. 57–66). Hillsdale, NJ: Erlbaum.

Jernigan, T. L., Trauner, D. A., Hesselink, J. R., & Tallal, P. A. (1991). Maturation of humans' cerebrum observed in vivo during adolescence. *Brain, 114,* 2037–2049.

Jessimer, M., & Markham, R. (1997). Alexithymia: A right hemisphere dysfunction specific to recognition of certain facial expressions? *Brain and Cognition, 34,* 246–258.

Johnsen, B. H., & Hugdahl, K. (1991). Hemispheric asymmetry in conditioning to facial emotional expressions. *Psychophysiology, 28,* 154–162.

Johnson, M. (1987). *The body in the mind.* Chicago: University of Chicago Press.

Johnson, M. H. (1990a). Cortical maturation and the development of visual attention in early infancy. *Journal of Cognitive Neuroscience, 2,* 81–95.

Johnson, M. H. (1990b). Cortical maturation and perceptual development. In H. Bloch & B. I. Bertenthal (Eds.), *Sensory–motor organizations and development in infancy and early childhood* (pp. 145–162). Norwell, MA: Kluver Academic.

Johnson, M. H., Dziurawiec, S., Ellis, H., & Morton, J. (1991a). Newborns' preferential tracking of face-like stimuli and its subsequent decline. *Cognition, 40,* 1–19.

Johnson, M. H., Posner, M. I., & Rothbart, M. K. (1991b). Components of visual orienting in early infancy: Contingency learning, anticipatory looking, and disengaging. *Journal of Cognitive Neurosciences, 3,* 335–344.

Johnson, P. A., Hurley, R. A., Benkelfat, C., Herpertz, S. C., & Taber, K. H. (2003). Understanding emotion regulation in borderline personality disorder: Contributions of neuroimaging. *Journal of Neuropsychiatry and Clinical Neuroscience, 15,* 397–402.

Johnson, S. C., Baxter, L. C., Wilder, L. S., Pipe, J. G., Heiserman, J. E., & Prigatano, G. P. (2002). Neural correlates of self-reflection. *Brain, 125,* 1808–1814.

Jones, N. A., & Field, T. (1999). Massage and music therapies attenuate frontal EEG asymmetry in depressed adolescents. *Adolescence, 34,* 529–534.

Jones, N. A., Field, T., & Davalos, M. (2000). Right frontal EEG asymmetry and lack of empathy in preschool children of depressed mothers. *Child Psychiatry and Human Development, 30,* 189–204

Jones, W., Bellugi, U., Lai, Z., Chiles, M., Reilly, J., Lincoln, A., et al. (2000). Hypersociability in Williams syndrome. *Journal of Cognitive Neuroscience, 12,* 30–46.

Jones, W., Hesselink, J., Courchesne, E., Duncan, T., & Bellugi, U. (2002). Cerebellar abnormalities in infants and toddlers with Williams syndrome. *Developmental Medicine and Child Neurology, 44,* 688–694.

Jordan, H., Reiss, J. E., Hoffman, J. E., & Landau, B. (2002). Intact perception of biological motion in the face of profound spatial deficits: Williams syndrome. *Psychological Science, 13,* 162–167.

Joseph, A. B., O'Leary, D. H., & Wheeler, H. G. (1990). Bilateral atrophy of the frontal and temporal lobes in schizophrenic patients with Capgras syndrome: A case-control study using computed tomography. *Journal of Clinical Psychiatry, 51,* 322–325.

Joseph, R. (1996). *Neuropsychiatry, neuropsychology, and clinical neuroscience* (2nd ed.). Baltimore: Williams & Wilkins.

Joubert, M., Eisenring, J., Robb, J. P., & Andermann, F. (1969). Familial agenesis of the cerebellar vermis: A syndrome of episodic hyperpnea, abnormal eye movements, ataxia, and retardation. *Neurology, 19,* 813–825.

Juengling, F. D., Schmahl, C., Hesslinger, B., Ebert, D., Bremner, J. D., Gostomzyk, J., et al. (2003). Positron emission tomography in female patients with borderline personality disorder. *Journal of Psychiatric Research, 37,* 109–115.

Juhasz, C., Behen, M. E., Muzik, O., Chugani, D. C., & Chugani, H. T. (2001). Bilateral medial prefrontal and temporal neocortical hypometabolism in children with epilepsy and aggression. *Epilepsia, 42,* 991–1001.

Junck, L., Gilman, S., Rothley, J. R., Betley, A. T., Koeppe, R. A., & Hichwa, R. D. (1988). A relationship between metabolism in frontal lobes and cerebellum in normal subjects studied with PET. *Journal of Cerebral Blood Flow and Metabolism, 8,* 774–782.

Jürgens, U., & von Cramon, D. (1982). On the role of the anterior cingulate cortex in phonation: A case report. *Brain and Language,15,* 234–248.

Kaasinen, V., Maguire, R. P., Kurki, T., Bruck, A., & Rinne, J. O. (2005). Mapping brain structure and personality in late adulthood. *NeuroImage, 24,* 315–322.

Kahn, I., Yeshurun, Y., Rotshtein, P., Fried, I., Ben-Bashat, D., & Hendler, T. (2002). The role of the amygdala in signaling prospective outcome of choice. *Neuron, 33,* 983–994.

Kaitz, M., Good, A., Rokem, A. M., & Eidelman, A. I. (1987). Mothers' recognition of their newborns by olfactory cues. *Developmental Psychobiology, 20,* 587–591.

Kaitz, M., Lapidot, P., Bronner, R., & Eidelman, A. I. (1992). Parturient women can recognize their infants by touch. *Developmental Psychology, 28,* 35–39.

Kaitz, M., Melrov, H., Landman, I., & Eidelman, A. I. (1993). Infant recognition by tactile cues. *Infant Behavior and Development, 16,* 333–341.

Kaitz, M., Shiri, S., Danziger, S., Hershko, Z., & Eidelman, A. I. (1994). Fathers can also recognize their infants by touch. *Infant Behavior and Development, 17,* 205–207.

Kalin, N. H., Shelton, S. E., & Barksdale, C. M. (1988). Opiate modulation of separation-induced distress in non-human primates. *Brain Research, 440,* 285–292.

Kalin, N. H., Shelton, S. E., & Davidson, R. J. (2004). The role of the central nucleus of the amygdala in mediating fear and anxiety in the primate. *Journal of Neuroscience, 24,* 5506–5515.

Kalin, N. H., Shelton, S. E., & Lynn, D. E. (1995). Opiate systems in mother and infant primates coordinate intimate contact during reunion. *Psychoneuroendocrinology, 20,* 735–742.

Kalin, N. H., Shelton, S. E., & Snowdon, C. T. (1993). Social factors regulating security and fear in infant rhesus monkeys. *Depression, 1,* 137–142.

Kampe, K. K., Frith, C. D., Dolan, R. J., & Frith, U. (2001). Reward value of attractiveness and gaze. *Nature, 413,* 589.

Kanade, T., Cohn, J. F., & Tian, Y. (2000). Comprehensive database for facial expression analysis. In *Proceedings of the Fourth IEEE International Conference on Automatic Face Gesture Recognition* (pp. 46–53). Grenoble, France.

Kandel, E. R. (1998). A new intellectual framework for psychiatry. *American Journal of Psychiatry, 155,* 457–469.

Kano, M., Fukudo, S., Gyoba, J., Kamachi, M., Tagawa, M., Mochizuki, H., et al. (2003). Specific brain processing of facial expressions in people with alexthymia: An $H_2{}^{15}$O-PET study. *Brain, 126,* 1474–1484.

Kanwisher, N. (2000). Domain specificity in face perception. *Nature Neuroscience, 3,* 759–763.

Kanwisher, N., McDermott, J., & Chun, M. M. (1997). The fusiform face area: A module in human extrastriate cortex specialized for face perception. *Journal of Neuroscience, 17,* 4302–4311.

Kanwisher, N., Stanley, D., & Harris, A. (1999). The fusiform face area is selective for faces not animals. *NeuroReport, 10,* 183–187.

Karmiloff-Smith, A., Klima, E., Bellugi, U., Grant, J., & Baron-Cohen, S. (1995). Is there a social module? Language, face processing, and theory of mind in individuals with Williams syndrome. *Journal of Cognitive Neuroscience, 7,* 196–208.

Katanoda, K., Yoshikawa, K., & Sugishita, M. (2000). Neural substrates for the recognition of newly learned faces: A functional MRI study. *Neuropsychologia, 38,* 1616–1625.

Katz, L. C., & Shatz, C. J. (1996). Synaptic activity and the construction of cortical circuits. *Science, 274,* 1133–1138.

Kaufman, J., Plotsky, P. M., Nemeroff, C. B., & Charney, D. S. (2000). Effects of early adverse experiences on brain structure and function: Clinical implications. *Biological Psychiatry, 48,* 778–790.

Kawakami, N., Shimizu, H., Haratani, T., Iwata, N., & Kitamura, T. (2004). Lifetime and 6-month prevalence of DSM-III-R psychiatric conditions in an urban community in Japan. *Psychiatry Research, 121,* 293–301.

Kawashima, R., Sugiura, M., Kato, T., Nakamura, A., Hatano, K., Ito, K., et al. (1999). The human amygdala plays an important role in gaze monitoring: A PET study. *Brain, 122,* 779–783.

Keele, S. W., & Ivry, R. (1990). Does the cerebellum provide a common computation for diverse tasks: A timing hypothesis. *Annals of the New York Academy of Sciences, 608,* 179–211.

Keenan, J. P., McCutcheon, B., Freund, S., Gallup, G. G., Jr., Sanders, G., & Pascual-Leone, A. (1999). Left hand advantage in a self-face recognition task. *Neuropsychologia, 37,* 1421–1425.

Keenan, J. P., Wheeler, M. A., Gallup, G. G., Jr., & Pascual-Leone, A. (2000). Self-recognition and the right prefrontal cortex. *Trends in Cognitive Sciences, 4,* 338–344.

Kehoe, P., & Blass, E. M. (1989). Conditioned opioid release in ten-day-old rats. *Behavioral Neuroscience, 103,* 423–428.

Kelley, W. M., Macrae, C. N., Wyland, C. L., Caglar, S., Inati, S., & Heatherton, T. F. (2002). Finding the self? An event-related fMRI study. *Journal of Cognitive Neuroscience, 14,* 785–794.

Keltner, D. (1995). Signs of appeasement: Evidence for the distinct displays of embarrassment, amusement, and shame. *Journal of Personality and Social Psychology, 68,* 441–454.

Keltner, D., & Buswell, B. N. (1996). Evidence for the distinctness of embarrassment, shame, and guilt: A study of recalled antecedents and facial expressions of emotion. *Cognition and Emotion, 10,* 155–171.

Keltner, D., & Buswell, B. N. (1997). Embarrassment: Its distinct form and appeasement functions. *Psychological Bulletin, 122,* 250–270.

Kempermann, G., & Gage, F. H. (1998). Closer to neurogenesis in adult humans. *Nature Medicine, 4,* 555–557.

Kempermann, G., Kuhn, H. G., & Gage, F. H. (1997a). More hippocampal neurons in adult mice living in an enriched environment. *Nature, 386,* 493–495.

Kempermann, G., Kuhn, H. G., & Gage, F. H. (1997b). Genetic influence on neurogenesis in the dentate gyrus of adult mice. *Proceedings of the National Academy of Sciences, USA, 94,* 10409–104114.

Kempermann, G., Kuhn, H. G., & Gage, F. H. (1998). Experience-induced neurogenesis in the senescent dentate gyrus. *Journal of Neuroscience, 18,* 3206–3212.

Kempermann, G., Wiskott, L., & Gage, F. H. (2004). Functional significance of adult neurogenesis. *Current Opinion in Neurobiology, 14,* 186–191.

Kennard, M. A. (1955). The cingulate gyrus in relation to consciousness. *Journal of Nervous and Mental Disease, 121,* 34–39.

Kerns, J. G., Cohen, J. D., MacDonald, A. W., III., Cho, R. Y., Stenger, V. A., & Carter, C. S. (2004). Anterior cingulate conflict monitoring and adjustments in control. *Science, 303,* 1023–1026.

Kessler, R. C., Berglund, P., Demler, O., Jin, R., Koretz, D., Merikangas, K. R., et al. (2003). The epidemiology of major depressive disorder: Results from the National Comorbidity Survey Replication (NCS-R). *Journal of American Medical Association, 289,* 3095–3105.

Keverne, E. B. (2004). Importance of olfactory and vomeronasal systems for male sexual function. *Physiology and Behavior, 83,* 177–187.

Keverne, E. B., Martensz, N. D., & Tuite, B. (1989). Beta-endorphin concentrations in cerebrospinal fluid of monkeys are influenced by grooming relationships. *Psychoneuroendocrinology, 14,* 155–161.

Keysers, C., Xiao, D. K., Földiák, P., & Perrett, D. I. (2001). The speed of sight. *Journal of Cognitive Neuroscience, 13,* 90–101.

Kiehl, K. A., Smith, A. M., Hare, R. D., Mendrek, A., Forster, B. B., Brink, J., et al. (2001). Limbic abnormalities in affective processing by criminal psychopaths as revealed by functional magnetic resonance imaging. *Biological Psychiatry, 50,* 677–684.

Kilts, C. D., Egan, G., Gideon, D. A., Ely, T. D., & Hoffman, J. M. (2003). Dissociable neural pathways are involved in the recognition of emotion in static and dynamic facial expressions. *NeuroImage, 18,* 156–168.

Kilts, C. D., Schweitzer, J. B., Quinn, C. K., Gross, R. E., Faber, T. L., Muhammad, F., et al. (2001). Neural activity related to drug craving in cocaine addiction. *Archives of General Psychiatry, 58,* 334–341.

Kim, H., Somerville, L. H., Johnstone, T., Alexander, A. L., & Whalen, P. J. (2003). Inverse amygdala and medial prefrontal cortex responses to surprised faces. *NeuroReport, 14,* 2317–2322.

Kim, H., Somerville, L. H., Johnstone, T., Polis, S., Alexander, A. L., Shin, L. M., et al. (2004). Contextual modulation of amygdala responsivity to surprised faces. *Journal of Cognitive Neuroscience, 16,* 1730–1745.

Kim, H., Somerville, L. H., McLean, A. A., Johnstone, T., Shin, L. M., & Whalen, P. J. (2003). Functional MRI responses of the human dorsal amygdala/substantia innominata region to facial expressions of emotion. *Annals of the New York Academy of Sciences, 985,* 533–535.

Kim, J. J., Andreasen, N. C., O'Leary, D. S., Wiser, A. K., Boles Ponto, L. L., Watkins, G. L., et al. (1999). Direct comparison of the neural substrates of recognition memory for words and faces. *Brain, 122,* 1069–1083.

Kimura, I., Kubota, M., Hirose, H., Yumoto M., Sakakihara, Y. (2004). Children are sensitive to averted eyes at the earliest stage of gaze processing. *NeuroReport, 15,* 1345–1348.

Kingstone, A., Tipper, C., Ristic, J., & Ngan, E. (2004). The eyes have it!: An fMRI investigation. *Brain and Cognition, 55,* 269–271.

Kinsley, C. H., Madonia, L., Gifford, G. W., Tureski, K., Griffin, G. R., Lowry, C., et al. (1999). Motherhood improves learning and memory. *Nature, 402,* 137–138.

Kirkpatrick, M., & Ryan, M. J. (1991). The evolution of mating preferences and the paradox of the lek. *Nature, 350,* 33–38.

Kirmayer, L. J., & Carroll, J. (1987). A neurobiological hypothesis on the nature of chronic self-mutilation. *Integrated Psychiatry, 5,* 212–213.

Klaus, M. H., Kennell, J. H., Plumb, N., & Zuehlke, S. (1970). Human maternal behavior at the first contact with her young. *Pediatrics, 46,* 187–192.

Klein, E., Kreinin, I., Chistyakov, A., Koren, D., Mecz, L., Marmur, S., et al. (1999). Therapeutic efficacy of right prefrontal slow repetitive transcranial magnetic stimulation in major depression: A double-blind controlled study. *Archives of General Psychiatry, 56,* 315–320.

Kleinke, C. L. (1986). Gaze and eye contact: A research review. *Psychological Bulletin, 100,* 78–100.

Klin, A., & Volkmar, F. (1995). *Asperger syndrome: Assessment, diagnosis and intervention.* Pittsburgh, PA: Learning Disabilities Association of America.

Kling, A., & Steklis, H. D. (1976). A neural substrate for affiliative behavior in nonhuman primates. *Brain Behaviors and Evolution, 13,* 216–238.

Klucharev, V., & Sams, M. (2004). Interaction of gaze direction and facial expressions processing: ERP study. *NeuroReport, 15,* 621–625.

Kluver, H., & Bucy, P. C. (1938). An analysis of certain effects of bilateral temporal lobectomy in the rhesus monkey, with special reference to "psychic blindness." *Journal of Psychology, 5,* 33–54.

Knowles, P. A., Conner, R. L., & Panksepp, J. (1989). Opiate effects on social behavior of juvenile dogs as a function of social deprivation. *Pharmacology, Biochemistry, and Behavior, 33,* 533–537.

Knox, S. S., & Uvnäs-Moberg, K. (1998). Social isolation and cardiovascular disease: An atherosclerotic pathway? *Psychoneuroendocrinology, 23,* 877–890.

Kobayashi, H., & Kohshima, S. (1997). Unique morphology of the human eye. *Nature, 387,* 767–768.

Kohler, E., Keysers, C., Umiltá, M. A., Fogassi, L., Gallese, V., & Rizzolatti, G. (2002). Hearing sounds, understanding actions: Action representation in mirror neurons. *Science, 297,* 846–848.

Kohut, H. (1984). *How does analysis cure?* Chicago: University of Chicago Press.

Kolb, B., & Whishaw, I. Q. (1998). Brain plasticity and behavior. *Annual Review of Psychology, 49,* 43–64.

Koski, L., Iacoboni, M., Dubeau, M. C., Woods, R. P., & Mazziotta, J. C. (2003). Modulation of cortical activity during different imitative behaviors. *Journal of Neurophysiology, 89,* 460–471.

Kosson, D. S. (1998). Divided visual attention in psychopathic and nonpsychopathic offenders. *Personality and Individual Differences, 24,* 373–391.

Kosten, T. R., Krystal, J. H., Giller, E. L., Frank, J., & Dan, E. (1992). Alexthymia as a predictor of treatment response in post-traumatic stress disorder. *Journal of Traumatic Stress, 5,* 563–573.

Kovács, G. L., Sarnyai, Z., & Szabó, G. (1998). Oxytocin and addiction: A review. *Psychoneuroendocrinology, 23,* 945–962.

Koyama, T., Zn Tnaka, Y., & Mikami, A. (1998). Nociceptive neurons in the macaque anterior cingulate activate during anticipation of pain. *NeuroReport, 9,* 2663–2667.

Kozel, F. A., Rebell, L. J., Lorberbaum, J. P., Shastri, A., Elhai, J. D., Horner, M. D., et al. (2004). A pilot study of functional magnetic resonance imaging brain correlates of deception in healthy young men. *Journal of Neuropsychiatry and Clinical Neurosciences, 16,* 295–305.

Krystal, H. (1988). *Integration and self healing: Affect, trauma, and alexithymia.* Hillsdale, NJ: Analytic Press.

Kuhn, C. M., & Schanberg, S. M. (1998). Responses to maternal separation: Mechanisms and mediators. *International Journal of Developmental Neuroscience, 16,* 261–270.

Laakso, M. P., Gunning-Dixon, F., Vaurio, O., Repo-Tiihonen, E., Soininen, H., & Tiihonen, J. (2002). Prefrontal volumes in habitually violent subjects with antisocial personality disorder and type 2 alcoholism. *Psychiatry Research, 114,* 95–102.

Laakso, M. P., Vaurio, O., Koivisto, E., Savolainen, L., Eronen, M., Aronen, H., et al. (2001). Psychopathy and the posterior hippocampus. *Behavioural Brain Research, 118,* 187–193.

LaBar, K. S., Gatenby, J. C., Gore, J. C., LeDoux, J. E., & Phelps, E. A. (1998). Human amygdala activation during conditioned fear acquisition and extinction: A mixed-trial fMRI study. *Neuron, 20,* 937–945.

LaBar, K. S., LeDoux, J. E., Spencer, D. D., & Phelps, E. A. (1995). Impaired fear conditining following unilateral temporal lobectomy in humans. *Journal of Neuroscience, 15,* 6846–6855.

Laederach-Hofmann, K., Mussgay, L., Büchel, B., Widler, P., & Rüddel, H. (2002). Patients with erythrophobia (fear of blushing) show abnormal autonomic regulation in mental stress conditions. *Psychosomatic Medicine, 64,* 358–365.

Lakoff, G. (1990). *Women, fire, and dangerous things: What categories reveal about the mind.* Chicago: University of Chicago Press.

Lane, R. D., & Jennings, J. R. (1995). Hemispheric asymmety, autonomic asymmetry, and the problem of sudden cardiac death. In R. J. Davidson & K. Hugdahl (Eds.), *Brain asymmetry* (pp. 271–304). Cambridge, MA: MIT Press.

Lane, R. D., Reiman, E. M., Axelrod, B., Yun, L. S., Holmes, A., & Schwartz, G. E. (1998). Neural correlates of levels of emotional awareness: Evidence of an interaction between emotion and attention in the anterior cingulate cortex. *Journal of Cognitive Neuroscience, 10,* 525–535.

Lane, R. D., Sechrest, L., Reidel, R., Weldon, V., Kaszniak, A., & Schwartz, G. E. (1996). Impaired verbal and nonverbal emotion recognition in alexithymia. *Psychosomatic Medicine, 58,* 203–210.

Lange, C., Kracht, L., Herholz, K., Sachsse, U., & Irle, E. (2005). Reduced glucose metabolism in temporo-parietal cortices of women with borderline personality disorder. *Psychiatric Research: Neuroimaging, 139,* 115–126.

Langleben, D. D., Schroeder, L., Maldijan, J., Gur, R. C., McDonald, S., Ragland, J. D., et al. (2002). Brain activity during stimulated deception: An event-related functional magnetic resources study. *NeuroImage, 15,* 727-732.

Langlois, J. H., & Roggman, L. A. (1990). Attractive faces are only average. *Psychological Science, 1,* 115–121.

Langlois, J. H., Kalakanis, L., Rubenstein, A. J., Larson, A., Hallam, M., & Smoot, M. (2000). Maxims or myths of beauty? A meta-analytic and theoretical review. *Psychological Bulletin, 126,* 390–423.

Langlois, J. H., Ritter, J. M., Casey, R. J., & Sawin, D. B. (1995). Infant attractiveness predicts maternal behavior and attitudes. *Developmental Psychology, 31,* 464–472.

Langlois, J. H., Roggman, L. A., Casey, R. J., Ritter, J. M., Rieser-Danner, L. A., & Jenkins, V. Y. (1987). Infant preferences for attractive faces: Rudiments of a stereotype? *Developmental Psychology, 23,* 363–369.

Langton, S. R. H., & Bruce, V. (1999). Reflexive visual orienting in response to the social attention of others. *Visual Cognition, 6,* 541–567.

Lapierre, D., Braun, C., & Hodgins, S. (1995). Ventral frontal deficits in psychopathy: Neuropsychological test findings. *Neuropsychologia, 33,* 139–151.

Lattner, S., Meyer, M. E., & Friederici, A. D. (2005). Voice perception: Sex, pitch, and the right hemisphere. *Human Brain Mapping, 24,* 11–20.

Lazar, J., Rasmussen, L. E., Greenwood, D. R., Bang, I. S., & Prestwich, G. D. (2004). Elephant albumin: A multipurpose pheromone shuttle. *Chemistry and Biology, 11,* 1093–1100.

Leary, M. R., Britt, T. W., Cutlip, W. D., II, & Templeton, J. L. (1992). Social blushing. *Psychological Bulletin, 112,* 446–460.

Ledgerwood, L., Richardson, R., & Cranney, J. (2003). Effects of D-cycloserine on extinction of conditioned freezing. *Behavioral Neuroscience, 117,* 341–349.

LeDoux, J. E. (1986). Sensory systems and emotion: A model of affective processing. *Integrative Psychiatry, 4,* 237–243.

LeDoux, J. E. (1994). Emotion, memory, and the brain. *Scientific American, 270,* 32–39.

LeDoux, J. E. (1996). *The emotional brain.* New York: Simon & Schuster.

LeDoux, J. E. (2003). The self: Clues from the brain. *Annals of the New York Academy of Sciences, 1001,* 295–304.

LeDoux, J. E., & Gorman, J. M. (2001). A call to action: Overcoming anxiety through active coping. *American Journal of Psychiatry, 158,* 1953–1955.

Lee, G. P., Bechara, A., Adolphs, R., Arena, J., Meador, K. J., Loring, D. W., et al. (1998). Clinical and physiological effects of stereotaxic bilateral amygdalotomy for intractable aggression. *Journal of Neuropsychiatry and Clinical Neurosciences, 10,* 413–420.

Lee, H., & Kim, J. J. (1998). Amygdalar NMDA receptors are critical for new fear learning in previously fear-conditioned rats. *Journal of Neuroscience, 18,* 8444–8454.

Le Grand, R., Mondloch, C. J., Maurer, D., & Brent, H. P. (2003). Expert face processing requires visual input to the right hemisphere during infancy. *Nature Neuroscience, 6,* 1108–1112.

Lehky, S. R. (2000). Fine discrimination of faces can be performed rapidly. *Journal of Cognitive Neuroscience, 12*, 848–855.

Leiner, H. C., Leiner, A. L., & Dow, R. S. (1986). Does the cerebellum contribute to mental skills? *Behavioral Neuroscience, 100*, 443–454.

Leiner, H. C., Leiner, A. L., & Dow, R. S. (1991). The human cerebro-cerebellar system: Its computing, cognitive, and language skills. *Behavioral Brain Research, 44*, 113–128.

Lenz, F. A., Rios, M., Zirh, A., Chau, D., Krauss, G., & Lesser, R. P. (1998). Painful stimuli evoke potentials recorded over the human anterior cingulate gyrus. *Journal of Neurophysiology, 79*, 2231–2234.

Leon, M. I., & Shadlen, M. N. (1999). Effect of expected reward magnitude on the response of neurons in the dorsolateral prefrontal cortex of the macaque. *Neuron, 24*, 415–425.

Leonard, C. M., Rolls, E. T., Wilson, F. A., & Baylis, G. C. (1985). Neurons in the amygdala of the monkey with responses selective for faces. *Behavioral Brain Research, 15*, 159–176.

Levenson, R. W., & Ruef, A. M. (1992). Empathy: A physiological substrate. *Journal of Personality and Social Psychology, 63*, 234–246.

Levin, F. M. (1991). *Mapping the mind: The intersection of psychoanalysis and neuroscience.* Hillsdale, NJ: Analytic Press.

Levine, B. (2004). Autobiographical memory and the self in time: Brain lesion effects, functional neuroanatomy, and lifespan development. *Brain and Cognition, 55*, 54–68.

Levine, S. (2001). Primary social relationships influence the development of the hypothalamic–pituitary–adrenal axis in the rat. *Physiology and Behavior, 73*, 255–260.

Levine, S., Haltmeyer, G. C., Karas, G. G., & Denenberg, V. H. (1967). Physiological and behavioral effects of infantile stimulation. *Physiology and Behavior, 2*, 55–59.

Levitin, D. J., Menon, V., Schmitt, J. E., Eliez, S., White, C. D., Glover, G. H., et al. (2003). Neural correlates of auditory perception in Williams syndrome: An fMRI study. *NeuroImage, 18*, 74–82.

Levitt, J. G., Blanton, R. E., Smalley, S., Thompson, P. M., Guthrie, D., McCracken, J. T., et al. (2003). Cortical sulcal maps in autism. *Cerebral Cortex, 13*, 728–735.

Lewis, M., Feiring, C., McGuffog, C., & Jaskir, J. (1984). Predicting psychopathology in six-year-olds from early social relations. *Child Development, 55*, 123–136.

Leyton, M., Okazawa, H., Diksic, M., Paris, J., Rosa, P., Mzengeza, S., et al. (2001). Brain regional α-[^{11}C]Methyl-L-Tryptophan trapping in impulsive subjects with borderline personality disorder. *American Journal of Psychiatry, 158*, 775–782.

Lhermitte, F., Pillon, B., & Serdaru, M. (1986). Human autonomy and the frontal lobes: Part I. Imitation and utilization behavior: A neuropsychological study of 75 patients. *Annals of Neurology, 19*, 326–334.

Li, D., Chokka, P., & Tibbo, P. (2001). Toward an integrative understanding of social phobia. *Journal of Psychiatry and Neuroscience, 26*, 190–202.

Liberman, A. M., & Mattingly, I. G. (1985). The motor theory of speech perception revised. *Cognition, 21*, 1–36.

Lieb, R., Wittchen, H. U., Höfler, M., Fuetsch, M., Stein, M. B., & Merikangas, K. R. (2000). Parental psychopathology, parenting styles, and the risk of social phobia in offspring. *Archives of General Psychiatry, 57,* 859–866.

Lilly, J. C. (1972). *The center of the cyclone: An autobiography of inner space.* New York: Julian Press.

Lindberg, N., Tani, P., Stenberg, J. H., Appelberg, B., Porkka-Heiskanan, T., & Virkkunen, M. (2004). Neurological soft signs in homicidal men with antisocial personality disorder. *European Psychiatry, 19,* 433–437.

Linville, P. W., & Jones, E. E. (1980). Polarized appraisals of out-group members. *Journal of Personality and Social Psychology, 38,* 689–703.

Liu, D., Diorio, J., Day, J. C., Francis, D. D., & Meaney, M. J. (2000). Maternal care, hippocampal synaptogenesis and cognitive development in rats. *Nature Neuroscience, 3,* 799–806.

Liu, D., Diorio, J., Tannenbaum, B., Caldji, C., Francis, D., Freedman, A., et al. (1997). Maternal care, hippocampal glucocorticoid receptors, and hypothalamic–pituitary–adrenal responses to stress. *Science, 277,* 1659–1662.

Liu, L., Wong, T. P., Pozza, M. F., Lingenhoehl, K., Wang, Y., Sheng, M., et al. (2004). Role of NMDA receptor subtypes in governing the direction of hippocampal synaptic plasticity. *Science, 304,* 1021–1024.

Ljungberg, T., Apicella, P., & Schultz, W. (1992). Responses of monkey dopamine neurons during learning of behavioral reactions. *Journal of Neurophysiology, 67,* 145–163.

London, E. D., Ernst, M., Grant, S., Bonson, K., & Weinstein, A. (2000). Orbitofrontal cortex and human drug abuse: Functional imaging. *Cerebral Cortex, 10,* 334–342.

Lonstein, J. S., & Stern, J. M. (1997). Role of the midbrain periaqueductal gray in maternal nurturance and aggression: c-fos and electrolytic lesion studies in lactating rats. *Journal of Neuroscience, 17,* 3364–3378.

Lorberbaum, J. P., Newman, J. D., Dubno, J. R., Horwitz, A. R., Nahas, Z., Teneback, C. C., et al. (1999). Feasibility of using fMRI to study mothers responding to infant cries. *Depression and Anxiety, 10,* 99–104.

Lorberbaum, J. P., Newman, J. D., Horwitz, A. R., Dubno, J. R., Lydiard, R. B., Hamner, M. B., et al. (2002). A potential role for thalamocingulate circuitry in human maternal behavior. *Biological Psychiatry, 51,* 431–445.

Lotspeich, L. J., Kwon, H., Schumann, C. M., Fryer, S. L., Goodlin-Jones, B. L., Buonocore, M. H., et al. (2004). Investigation of neuroanatomical differences between autism and Asperger syndrome. *Archives of General Psychiatry, 61,* 291–298.

Lou, H. C., Hansen, D., Nordentoft, M., Pryds, O., Jensen, F., Nim, J., et al. (1994). Prenatal stressors of human life effect fetal brain development. *Developmental Medicine and Child Neurology, 36,* 826–832.

Lu, S. T., Hamalainen, M. S., Hari, R., Ilmoniemi, R. J., Lounasmaa, O. V., Sams, M., et al. (1991). Seeing faces activates three separate areas outside the occipital visual cortex in man. *Neuroscience, 43,* 287–290.

Lund, I., Long-Chuan, Y., Uvnäs-Moberg, K., Wang, J., Yu, C., Kurosawa, M., et al. (2002). Repeated massage-like stimulation induces long-term effects on nociception: Contribution on oxytocinergic mechanisms. *European Journal of Neuroscience, 16,* 330–338.

Lundh, L. G., & Ost, L. G. (1996). Recognition bias for critical faces in social phobics. *Behavior Research and Therapy, 34,* 787–794.

Lundqvist, L., & Dimberg, U. (1995). Facial expressions are contagious. *Journal of Psychophysiology, 9,* 203–211.

Lupien, S. J., King, S., Meaney, M. J., & McEwen, B. S. (2000). Child's stress hormone levels correlate with mother's socioeconomic status and depressive state. *Biological Psychiatry, 48,* 976–980.

Luxenberg, T., Spinazzola, J., & van der Kolk, B. A. (2001). Complex trauma and disorders of extreme stress (DESNOS) diagnosis, part one: Assessment. *Directions in Psychiatry, 21,* 373–392.

Lykken, D. T. (1957). A study of anxiety in the sociopathic personality. *Journal of Abnormal and Social Psychology, 55,* 6–10.

Lynch, J. J. (1985). *The language of the heart: The body's response to human dialogue.* New York: Basic Books.

Lyons, D. M., Afarian, H., Schatzberg, A. F., Sawyer-Glover, A., & Moseley, M. E. (2002). Experience-dependent asymmetric variation in primate prefrontal morphology. *Behavioral Brain Research, 136,* 51–59.

Lyons-Ruth, K., Zoll, D., Connell, D., & Grunebaum, H. U. (1986). The depressed mother and her one-year-old infant: Environment, interaction, attachment, and infant development. In E. Z. Tronick & T. Field (Eds.), *Maternal depression and infant disturbance. New directions for child development* (pp. 61–81). San Francisco: Jossey-Bass.

Lyoo, K., Han, M. H., & Cho, D. Y. (1998). A brain MRI study in subjects with borderline personality disorder. *Journal of Affective Disorders, 50,* 235–243.

Maaranen, P., Tanskanen, A., Haatainen, K., Koivumaa-Honkanen, H., Hintikka, J., & Viinamaki, H. (2004). Somatoform dissociation and adverse childhood experiences in the general population. *Journal of Nervous and Mental Disease, 192,* 337–342.

Maaranen, P., Tanskanen, A., Honkalampi, K., Haatainen, K., Hintikka, J., & Viinamaki, H. (2005). Factors associated with pathological dissociation in the general population. *Australian and New Zealand Journal of Psychiatry, 39,* 387–394.

MacFarlane, A. J. (1975). Olfaction in the development of social preference in the human neonate. In A. J. MacFarlane (Ed.), *CIBA Foundation symposium* (Vol. 33, pp. 103–117).

Machne, X., & Segundo, J. P. (1956). Unitary responses to afferent volleys in amygdaloid complex. *Journal of Neurophysiology, 19,* 232–240.

MacLean, P. D. (1985). Brain evolution relating to family, play, and the separation call. *Archives of General Psychiatry, 42,* 405–417.

MacLean, P. D. (1990). *The triune brain in evolution: Role of paleocerebral functions.* New York: Plenum Press.

Maddock, R. J. (1999). The retrosplenial cortex and emotion: New insights from functional neuroimaging of the human brain. *Trends in Neurosciences, 22,* 310–316.

Maddock, R. J., Garrett, A. S., & Buonocore, M. H. (2001). Remembering familiar people: The posterior cingulate cortex and autobiographical memory retrieval. *Neuroscience, 104,* 667–676.

Maddock, R. J., Garrett, A. S., & Buonocore, M. H. (2003). Posterior cingulate cortex activation by emotional words: fMRI evidence from a valence decision task. *Human Brain Mapping, 18,* 30–41.

Maestripieri, D. (1999). The biology of human parenting: Insights from nonhuman primates. *Neuroscience and Biobehavioral Reviews, 23,* 411–422.

Magnusson, J. E., & Fleming, A. S. (1995). Rat pups are reinforcing to the maternal rat: Role of sensory cues. *Psychobiology, 23,* 69–75.

Maguire, E. A., Burgess, N., Donnett, J. G., Frackowiak, R. S., Frith, C. D., & O'Keefe, J. (1998). Knowing where and getting there: A human navigation network. *Science, 280,* 921–924.

Maguire, E. A., & Frith, C. D. (2003). Aging affects the engagement of the hippocampus during autobiographical memory retrieval. *Brain, 126,* 1511–1523.

Mah, L., Arnold, M. C., & Grafman, J. (2004). Impairment of social perception associated with lesions of the prefrontal cortex. *American Journal of Psychiatry, 161,* 1247–1255.

Mah, L., Arnold, M. C., & Grafman, J. (2005). Deficits in social knowledge following damage to ventromedial prefrontal cortex. *Journal of Neuropsychiatry and Clinical Neurosciences, 17,* 66–74.

Main, M. (1993). Discourse, prediction, and the recent studies in attachment: Implications for psychoanalysis. *Journal of the American Psychoanalytic Association, 41,* 209–244.

Main, M. (2000). The organized categories of infant, child, and adult attachment: Flexible vs. inflexible attention under attachment-related stress. *Journal of the American Psychoanalytic Association, 48,* 1055–1096.

Main, M., & Goldwyn, R. (1998). *Adult attachment scoring and classification system.* Unpublished manuscript, University of California at Berkeley.

Main, M., Kaplan, N., & Cassidy, J. (1985). Security in infancy, childhood, and adulthood: A move to the level of representation. *Monographs of the Society for Research in Child Development, 50,* 66–104.

Main, M., & Solomon, J. (1986). Discovery of an insecure-disorganized/disoriented attachment pattern. In T. B. Brazelton & M. Yogman (Eds.), *Affective development in infancy* (pp. 95–124). Norwood, NJ: Ablex.

Malatesta, C. Z., & Haviland, J. M. (1982). Learning display rules: The socialization of emotion expression in infancy. *Child Development, 53,* 991–1003.

Malatesta, C. Z., Jonas, R., & Izard, C. E. (1987). The relation between low facial expressivity during emotional arousal and somatic symptoms. *British Journal of Medical Psychology, 60,* 169–180.

Malenka, R. C., & Siegelbaum, S. A. (2001). Synaptic plasticity: Diverse targets and mechanisms for regulating synaptic efficacy. In W. M. Cowan, T. C. Sudhof, & C. F. Stevens (Eds.), *Synapses* (pp. 393–453). Baltimore: Johns Hopkins Press.

Malizia, A. L., Wilson, S. J., Bell, C. M., Nutt, D. J., & Grasby, P. M. (1997). Neural correlates of anxiety provocation in social phobia. *NeuroImage, 5,* S301–S311.

Malpass, R. S., & Kravitz, J. (1969). Recognition for faces of own and other race. *Journal of Personality and Social Psychology, 13,* 330–334.

Mancuso, R. A., Schetter, C. D., Rini, C. M., Roesch, S. C., & Hobel, C. J. (2004). Maternal prenatal anxiety and corticotropin-releasing hormone associated with timing of delivery. *Psychosomatic Medicine, 66,* 762–769.

Mandal, M. K., & Ambady, N. (2004). Laterality and universality of facial expressions of emotion: The interface. *Behavioural Neurology, 15,* 23–34.

Mannuzza, S., Schneier, F. R., Chapman, T. F., Liebowitz, M. R., Klein, D. F., & Fyer, A. J. (1995). Generalized social phobia: Reliability and validity. *Archives of General Psychiatry, 52,* 230–237.

Mansell, W., Clark, D. M., Ehlers, A., & Chen, Y. P. (1999). Social anxiety and attention away from emotional faces. *Cognition and Emotion, 13,* 673–690.

Maratos, O. (1982). Trends in the development of imitation in early infancy. In T. G. Bever (Ed.), *Regressions in mental development: Basic phenomena and theories* (pp. 81–101). Hillsdale, NJ: Erlbaum.

Marcin, M. S., & Nemeroff, C. B. (2003). The neurobiology of social anxiety disorder: The relevance of fear and anxiety. *Acta Psychiatrica Scandinavica, 108,* 51–64.

Maren, S. (2001). Neurobiology of Pavlovian fear conditioning. *Annual Review of Neuroscience, 24,* 897–931.

Maren, S., & Quirk, G. J. (2004). Neuronal signalling of fear memory. *Nature Reviews Neuroscience, 5,* 844–852.

Markowitsch, H. J. (1998). Differential contribution of right and left amygdala to affective information processing. *Behavioural Neurology, 11,* 233–244.

Marquez, G. G. (1998). *One hundred years of solitude.* New York: Harper Collins.

Marsden, P. (1998). Memetics and social contagion: Two sides of the same coin? *Journal of Memetics: Evolutionary Models of Information Transmission, 2,* 68–85.

Martel, Y. (1993). *The facts behind the Helsinki Roccamatios.* New York: Harcourt.

Martinez-Marcos, A., Lanuza, E., & Halpern, M. (1999). Organization of the ophidian amygdala: Chemosensory pathways to the hypothalamus. *Journal of Comparative Neurology, 412,* 51–68.

Mason, W. A., & Mendoza, S. P. (1998). Generic aspects of primate attachments: Parents, offspring and mates. *Psychoneuroendocrinology, 23,* 765–778.

Massey, P. V., Johnson, B. E., Moult, P. R., Auberson, Y. P., Brown, M. W., Molnar, E., et al. (2004). Differential roles of NR2A and NR2B-containing NMDA receptors in cortical long-term potentiation and long-term depression. *Journal of Neuroscience, 24,* 7821–7828.

Mayberry, R., Jaques, J., & DeDe, G. (1998). What stuttering reveals about the development of the gesture–speech relationship. *New Directions for Child Development, 79,* 77–87.

Mazza, J. J., & Reynolds, W. M. (1998). A longitudinal investigation of depression, hopelessness, social support, and major and minor life events and their relation to suicidal ideation in adolescents. *Suicide and Life-Threatening Behaviors, 28,* 358–374.

McCabe, K., Houser, D., Ryan, L., Smith, V., & Trouard, T. (2001). A functional imaging study of cooperation in two-person reciprocal exchange. *Proceedings of the National Academy of Sciences, USA, 98,* 11832–11835.

McCarthy, G. (1995). Functional neuroimaging of memory. *The Neuroscientist, 1,* 155–163.

McClure, W. O., Ishtoyan, A., & Lyon, M. (2004). Very mild stress of pregnant rats reduces volume and cell number in nucleus accumbens of adult offspring: Some parallels to schizophrenia. *Developmental Brain Research, 149,* 21–28.

McDonald, P. W., & Prkachin, K. M. (1990). The expression and perception of facial emotion in alexithymia: A pilot study. *Psychosomatic Medicine, 52,* 199–210.

McGaugh, J. L. (1990). Significance and remembrance: The role of neuromodulatory systems. *Psychological Science, 1,* 15–25.

McGaugh, J. L. (1996, September 10). *Stress-activated hormonal systems and the regulation of memory storage.* Paper presented at the New York Academy of Sciences meeting on the Psychobiology of Posttraumatic Stress, New York.

McGaugh, J. L., Introini-Collison, I. B., Cahill, L. F., Castellano, C., Dalmaz, C., Parent, M. B., et al. (1993). Neuromodulatory systems and memory storage: Role of the amygdala. *Behavioural Brain Research, 58,* 81–90.

McGovern, U. (2005). *Webster's new world dictionary of quotations.* Hoboken, NJ: Wiley Publishing Inc.

McGurk, H., & MacDonald, J (1976). Hearing lips and seeing voices. *Nature, 264,* 746–748.

McLennan, J. D., & Offord, D. R. (2002). Should postpartum depression be targeted to improve child mental health? *Journal of the American Academy of Child and Adolescent Psychiatry, 41,* 28–35.

Meaney, M. J., Aitken, D. H., Viau, V., Sharma, S., & Sarrieau, A. (1989). Neonatal handling alters adrenocortical negative feedback sensitivity and hippocampal type II glucocorticoid receptor binding in the rat. *Neuroendocrinology, 50,* 597–604.

Meaney, M. J., Brake, W., & Gratton, A. (2002). Environmental regulation of the development of mesolimbic dopamine systems: A neurobiological mechanism for vulnerability to drug abuse? *Psychoneuroendocrinology, 27,* 127–138.

Meaney, M. J., Diorio, J., Francis, D. D., Weaver, S., Yau, J., Chapman, K., et al. (2000). Postnatal handling increases the expression of cAMP-inducible transcription factors in the rat hippocampus: The environmental enrichment reverses the effects of maternal separation on stress reactivity effects of thyroid hormones and serotonin. *Journal of Neuroscience, 20,* 3926–3935.

Mega, M. S., Cummings, J. L., Salloway, S., & Malloy, P. (1997). The limbic system: An anatomic, phylogenetic, and clinical perspective. *Journal of Neuropsychiatry and Clinical Neurosciences, 9,* 315–330.

Mehlman, P. T., Higley, J. D., Faucher, I., Lilly, A. A., Taub, D. M., Vickers, J., et al. (1994). Low CSF 5-HIAA concentrations and severe aggression and impaired impulse control in nonhuman primates. *American Journal of Psychiatry, 151,* 1485–1491.

Mellander, S., Andersson, P. O., Afzelius, L. E., & Hellstrand, P. (1982). Neural beta-adrenergic dilation of the facial vein in man: Possible mechanism in emotional blushing. *Acta Physiology Scandinavia, 114,* 393–399.

Meltzoff, A. N. (1995). Understanding the intentions of others: Reenactment of intended acts by 18-month-old children. *Developmental Psychology, 31,* 838–850.

Meltzoff, A. N., & Moore, M. K. (1983). Newborn infants imitate adult facial gestures. *Child Development, 54,* 702–709.

Meltzoff, A. N., & Moore, M. K. (1989). Imitation in newborn infants: Exploring the range of gestures imitated and the underlying mechanisms. *Developmental Psychology, 25,* 954–962.

Meltzoff, A. N., & Moore, M. K. (1992). Early imitation within a functional framework: The importance of person identity, movement, and development. *Infant Behavior and Development, 15,* 479–505.

Mesulam, M. M. (1987). Involutional and developmental implications of age-related neuronal changes: In search of an engram for wisdom. *Neurobiology of Aging, 8,* 581–583.

Mesulam, M. M. (1998). From sensation to cognition. *Brain, 121,* 1013–1052.

Mesulam, M. M., & Mufson, E. J. (1982). Insula of the old world monkey: III. Efferent cortical output and comments on function. *Journal of Comparative Neurology, 212,* 38–52.

Meyers, C. A., Berman, S. A., Scheibel, R. S., & Hayman, A. (1992). Case report: Acquired antisocial personality disorder associated with unilateral left orbital frontal lobe damage. *Journal of Psychiatry and Neuroscience, 17,* 121–125.

Mikhailova, E. S., Vladimirova, T. V., Iznak, A. F., Tsusulkovskaya, E. J., & Sushko, N. V. (1996). Abnormal recognition of facial expression of emotions in depressed patients with major depression disorder and schizotypal personality disorder. *Biological Psychiatry, 40,* 697–705.

Miller, R. E., Caul, W. F., & Mirsky, I. A. (1967). Communication of affect between feral and socially isolated monkeys. *Journal of Personality and Social Psychology, 7,* 231–239.

Milligan, K., Atkinson, L., Trehub, S. E., Benoit, D., & Poulton, K. (2003). Maternal attachment and the communication of emotion through song. *Infant Behavior and Development, 26,* 1–13.

Mills, D. L., Alvarez, T. D., St. George, M., Appelbaum, L. G., Bellugi, U., & Neville, H. (2000). Electrophysiological studies of face processing in Williams syndrome. *Journal of Cognitive Neuroscience, 12,* S47–S64.

Milo, R., Itzkovitz, S., Kashtan, N., Levitt, R., Shen-Orr, S., Ayzenshtat, I., et al. (2004). Superfamilies of evolved and designed networks. *Science, 303,* 1538–1542.

Mineka, S., & Cook, M. (1993). Mechanisms involved in the observational conditioning of fear. *Journal of Experimental Psychology: General, 122,* 23–38.

Mirenowicz, J., & Schultz, W. (1994). Importance of unpredictability for reward responses in primate dopamine neurons. *Journal of Neurophysiology, 72,* 1024–1027.

Mitchell, D. G. V., Colledge, E., Leonard, A., & Blair, R. J. R. (2002). Risky decisions and response reversal: Is there evidence of orbitofrontal cortex dysfunction in psychopathic individuals? *Neuropsychologia, 40,* 2013–2022.

Modney, B. K., & Hatton, G. I. (1994). Maternal behaviors: Evidence that they feed back to alter brain morphology and function. *Acta Paediatrica Supplement, 397,* 29–32.

Mogg, K., Philippot, P., & Bradley, B. P. (2004). Selective attention to angry faces in clinical social phobia. *Journal of Abnormal Psychology, 113,* 160–165.

Moll, J., de Oliveira-Souza, R., Bramati, I. E., & Grafman, J. (2002). Functional networks in emotional moral and nonmoral social judgments. *NeuroImage, 16*, 696–703.

Moll, J., de Oliveira-Souza, R., Eslinger, P. J., Bramati, I. E., Mourao-Miranda, J., Andreiuolo, P. A., & Pessoa, L. (2002). The neural correlates of moral sensitivity: A functional magnetic resonance imaging investigation of basic and moral emotions. *Journal of Neuroscience, 22*, 2730–2736.

Moncho-Bogani, J., Martinez-Garcia, F., Novejarque, A., & Lanuza, E. (2005). Attraction to sexual pheromones and associated odorants in female mice involves activation of the reward system and basolateral amygdala. *European Journal of Neuroscience, 21*, 2186–2198.

Monin, B. (2003). The warm glow heuristic: When liking leads to familiarity. *Journal of Personality and Social Psychology, 85*, 1035–1048.

Montagne, B., van Honk, J., Kessels, R. P. C., Frigerio, E., Burt, M., van Zandvoort, M. J. E., et al. (2005). Reduced efficiency in recognizing fear in subjects scoring high on psychopathic personality characteristics. *Personality and Individual Differences, 38*, 5–11.

Montague, P. R., Dayan, P., Person, C., & Sejnowski, T. J. (1996). A framework for mesencephalic dopamine systems based on predictive Hebbian learning. *Journal of Neuroscience, 16*, 1936–1947.

Monti-Bloch, L., Jennings-White, C., Dolberg, D. S., & Berliner, D. L. (1994). The human vomeronasal system. *Psychoneuroendocrinology, 19*, 673–686.

Mora, O. A., & Cabrera, M. M. (1997). The pheromonal restoration of cyclic activity in young estrogenized persistent estrus female rats is a vomeronasal effect. *Life Sciences, 60*, 493–498.

Morgan, M. A., & LeDoux, J. E. (1995). Differential contribution of dorsal and ventral medial prefrontal cortex to the acquisition and extinction of conditioned fear in rats. *Behavioral Neuroscience, 109*, 681–688.

Morgan, M. A., Romanski, L. M., & LeDoux, J. E. (1993). Extinction of emotional learning: Contribution of medial prefrontal cortex. *Neuroscience Letters, 163*, 109–113.

Morris, J. S., Buchel, C., & Dolan, R. J. (2001). Parallel neural responses in amygdala subregions and sensory cortex during implicit fear conditioning. *NeuroImage, 13*, 1044–1052.

Morris, J. S., Friston, K. J., Büchel, C., Frith, C. D., Young, A. W., Calder, A. J., et al. (1998). A neuromodulatory role for the human amygdala in processing emotional expressions. *Brain, 121*, 47–57.

Morris, J. S., Frith, C. D., Perrett, D. I., Rowland, D., Young, A. W., Calder, A. J., et al. (1996). A differential neural response in the human amygdala to fearful and happy facial expressions. *Nature, 383*, 812–815.

Morris, J. S., Öhman, A., & Dolan, R. J. (1998). Conscious and unconscious emotional learning in the human amygdala. *Nature, 393*, 467–470.

Morris, J. S., Öhman, A., & Dolan, R. J. (1999). A subcortical pathway to the right amygdala mediating "unseen" fear. *Proceedings of the National Academy of Sciences, USA, 96*, 1680–1685.

Moscovitch, M., & Olds, J. (1982). Asymmetries in spontaneous facial expressions and their possible relation to hemispheric specialization. *Neuropsychologia, 20,* 71–81.

Moscovitch, M., Winocur, G., & Behrmann, M. (1997). What is special about face recognition? Nineteen experiments on a person with visual object agnosia and dyslexia but normal face recognition. *Journal of Cognitive Neuroscience, 9,* 555–604.

Muir, D. W., Clifton, R. K., & Clarkson, M. G. (1989). The development of a human auditory localization response: A U-shaped function. *Canadian Journal of Psychology, 43,* 199–216.

Muir, J. (1911). *My first summer in the Sierra.* Boston: Houghton Mifflin. Reprinted 1988 by Sierra Club Books.

Mulder, E. J. H., Robles de Medina, P. G., Huizink, A. C., Van den Bergh, B. R. H., Buitelaar, J. K., & Visser, G. H. A. (2002). Prenatal maternal stress: Effects on pregnancy and the unborn child. *Early Human Development, 70,* 3–14.

Mulkens, S., & Bögels, S. M. (1999). Learning history in fear of blushing. *Behaviour Research and Therapy, 37,* 1159–1167.

Mulkens, S., Bögels, S. M., de Jong, P. J., & Louwers, J. (2001). Fear of blushing: Effects of task concentration training versus exposure in vivo on fear and physiology. *Journal of Anxiety Disorders, 15,* 413–432.

Mulkens, S., de Jong, P. J., Dobbelaar, A., & Bögels, S. M. (1999). Fear of blushing: Fearful preoccupation irrespective of facial coloration. *Behaviour Research and Therapy, 37,* 1119–1128.

Müller, J. L., Sommer, M., Wagner, V., Lange, K., Taschler, H., Röder, C. H., et al. (2003). Abnormalities in emotion processing within cortical and subcortical regions in criminal psychopaths: Evidence from a functional magnetic resonance imaging study using pictures with emotional content. *Biological Psychiatry, 54,* 152–162.

Murray, E., & Mishkin, M. (1985). Amygdalectomy impairs crossmodal association in monkeys. *Science, 228,* 604–606.

Murray, L. (1992). The impact of postnatal depression on infant development. *Journal of Child Psychology and Psychiatry, 33,* 543–561.

Musa, C. Z., & Lépine, J. P. (2000). Cognitive aspects of social phobia: A review of theories and experimental research. *European Psychiatry, 15,* 59–66.

Myowa-Yamakoshi, M., Tomonaga, M., Tanaka, M., & Matsuzawa, T. (2004). Imitation in neonatal chipanzees (*Pan troglodytes*). *Developmental Science, 7,* 437–442.

Nachmias, M., Gunnar, M. R., Mangelsdorf, S., Parritz, R. H., & Buss, K. (1996). Behavioral inhibition and stress reactivity: The moderating role of attachment security. *Child Development, 67,* 508–522.

Nader, K. (2003). Memory traces unbound. *Trends in Neuroscience, 26,* 65–72.

Nagahama, Y., Okada, T., Katsumi, Y., Hayashi, T., Yamauchi, H., Oyanagi, C., et al. (2001). Dissociable mechanisms of attentional control within the human prefrontal cortex. *Cerebral Cortex, 11,* 85–92.

National Institute of Mental Health. (2001). *The numbers count: Mental disorders in America.* NIMH Publication No. 01-4584. Retrieved December 1, 2004, from www.nimh. nih.gov/publicat/numbers.cfm.

Nauta, W. J. H. (1964). Some efferent connections of the prefrontal cortex in the monkey. In J. M. Warren & K. Akert (Eds.), *The frontal granular cortex and behavior* (pp. 397–409). New York: McGraw-Hill.

Nauta, W. J. H. (1971). The problem of the frontal lobe: A reinterpretation. *Journal of Psychiatric Research, 8,* 167–187.

Nebes, R. D. (1971). Superiority of the minor hemisphere in commissurotomized man for the perception of part–whole relationships. *Cortex, 7,* 333–349.

Nelson, E. E., & Panksepp, J. (1998). Brain substrates of infant–mother attachment: Contributions of opioids, oxytocin, and norepinephrine. *Neuroscience and Biobehavioral Reviews, 22,* 437–452.

Nelson, E. E., Leibenluft, E., McClure, E. B., & Pine, D. S. (2005). The social reorientation of adolescence: A neuroscience perspective on the process and its relation to psychopathology. *Psychological Medicine, 35,* 163–174.

Nelson, K. (1993). The psychological and social origins of autobiographical memory. *Psychological Science, 4,* 7–14.

Neri, P., Morrone, M. C., & Burr, D. C. (1998). Seeing biological motion. *Nature, 395,* 894–896.

Neugebauer, R., Kline, J., Stein, Z., Shrout, P., Warburton, D., & Susser, M. (1996). Association of stressful life events with chromosomally normal spontaneous abortion. *American Journal of Epidemiology, 143,* 588–596.

Newman, J. P., & Kosson, D. S. (1986). Passive avoidance learning in psychopathic and nonpsychopathic offenders. *Journal of Abnormal Psychology, 95,* 252–256.

Newman, J. P., Patterson, C. M., Howland, E. W., & Nichols, S. L. (1990). Passive avoidance in psychopaths: The effects of reward. *Personality and Individual Differences, 11,* 1101–1114.

Newman, J. P., Schmitt, W. A., & Voss, W. (1997). The impact of motivationally neutral cues on psychopathic individuals: Assessing the generality of the response modulation hypothesis. *Journal of Abnormal Psychology, 106,* 563–575.

Nicholson, K. G., Baum, S., Kilgour, A., Koh, C. K., Munhall, K. G., & Cuddy, L. L. (2003). Impaired processing of prosodic and musical patterns after right hemisphere damage. *Brain and Cognition, 52,* 382–389.

Nietzsche, F. W. (1951). *My sister and I.* New York: Boar's Head Books.

Nijenhuis, E. R. S., Van Dyck, R., Ter Kuile, M. M., Mourits, M. J., Spinhoven, P. H., & Van der Hart, O. (2003). Evidence for associations among somatoform dissociation, psychological dissociation and reported trauma in patients with chronic pelvic pain. *Journal of Psychosomatic Obstetrics and Gynaecology, 24,* 87–98.

Nimchinsky, E. A., Gilissen, E., Allman, J. M., Perl, D. P., Erwin, J. M., & Hof, P. R. (1999). A neuronal morphologic type unique to humans and great apes. *Proceedings of the National Academy of Sciences, USA, 96,* 5268–5273.

Nimchinsky, E. A., Vogt, B. A., Morrison, J. H., & Hof, P. R. (1995). Spindle neurons of the human anterior cingulate cortex. *Journal of Comparative Neurology, 355,* 27–37.

Nishitani, N., & Hari, R. (2000). Temporal dynamics of cortical representation for action. *Proceedings of the National Academy of Sciences, USA, 97,* 913–918.

Nitschke, J. B., Nelson, E. E., Rusch, B. D., Fox, A. S., Oakes, T. R., & Davidson, R. J. (2004). Orbitofrontal cortex tracks positive mood in mothers viewing pictures of their newborn infants. *NeuroImage, 21,* 583–592.

Nomura, M., Ohira, H., Haneda, K., Iidaka, T., Sadato, N., Okada, T., et al. (2004). Functional association of the amygdala and ventral prefrontal cortex during cognitive evaluation of facial expressions primed by masked angry faces: An event-related fMRI study. *NeuroImage, 21,* 352–363.

Nomura, M., Iidaka, T., Kakehi, K., Tsukiura, T., Hasegawa, T., Maeda, Y., et al. (2003). Frontal lobe networks for effective processing of ambiguously expressed emotions in humans. *Neuroscience Letters, 348,* 113–116.

Nordahl, T. E., Stein, M. B., Benkelfat, C., Semple, W. E., Andreason, P., Zametikin, A., et al. (1998). Regional cerebral metabolic asymmetries replicated in an independent group of patients with panic disorders. *Biological Psychiatry, 44,* 998–1006.

Northoff, G., Richter, A., Gessner, M., Schlagenhauf, F., Fell, J., Baumgart, F., et al. (2000). Functional dissociation between medial and lateral prefrontal cortical spatiotemporal activation in negative and positive emotions: A combined fMRI/MEG study. *Cerebral Cortex, 10,* 93–107.

Numan, M., & Nagle, D. S. (1983). Preoptic area and substantia nigra interact in the control of maternal behavior in the rat. *Behavioral Neuroscience, 97,* 120–139.

Numan, M., & Smith, H. G. (1984). Maternal behavior in rats: Evidence for the involvement of preoptic projections to the ventral tegmental area. *Behavioral Neuroscience, 98,* 712–727.

Nutt, D. J., Bell, C. J., & Malizia, A. L. (1998). Brain mechanisms of social anxiety disorder. *Journal of Clinical Psychiatry, 59,* 4–11.

Nyberg, L., Petersson, K. M., Nilsson, L., Sandblom, J., Aberg, C., & Ingvar, M. (2001). Reactivation of motor brain areas during explicit memory for actions. *NeuroImage, 14,* 521–528.

Ochs, E., & Capps, L. (2001). *Living narrative: Creating lives in everyday storytelling.* Cambridge, MA: Harvard University Press.

O'Doherty, J. P., Deichmann, R., Critchley, H. D., & Dolan, R. J. (2002). Neural responses during anticipation of a primary taste reward. *Neuron, 33,* 815–826.

O'Doherty, J. P., Kringelbach, M. L., Rolls, E. T., Hornak, J., & Andrews, C. (2001). Abstract reward and punishment representations in the human orbitofrontal cortex. *Nature Neuroscience, 4,* 95–102.

O'Doherty, J. P., Winston, J., Critchley, H., Perrett, D., Burt, D. M., & Dolan, R. J. (2003). Beauty in a smile: The role of medial orbitofrontal cortex in facial attractiveness. *Neuropsychologia, 41,* 147–155.

Ohira, H., Nomura, M., Haneda, K., Iidaka, T., Sadato, N., Okada, T., et al. (2001). Subliminal priming of valenced face unconsciously modulates subsequent detection of facial expression: fMRI evidence of affective priming. *NeuroImage, 13,* S455.

Ohnishi, T., Moriguchi, Y., Matsuda, H., Mori, T., Hirakata, M., Imabayashi, E., et al. (2004). The neural network for the mirror system and mentalizing in normally developed children: An fMRI study. *NeuroReport, 15,* 1483–1487.

Ojemann, J. G., Ojemann, G. A., & Lettich, E. (1992). Neuronal activity related to faces and matching in human right nondominant temporal cortex. *Brain, 115,* 1–13.

Okamoto, S., Tomonaga, M., Ishii, K., Kawai, N., Tanaka, M., & Matsuzawa, T. (2002). An infant chimpanzee (*Pan troglodytes*) follows human gaze. *Animal Cognition, 5,* 107–114.

O'Keefe, J., & Nadel, L. (1978). *The hippocampus as a cognitive map.* Oxford, UK: Clarendon Press.

Olausson, H., Lamarre, Y., Backlund, H., Morin, C., Wallin, B. G., Starck, G., et al. (2002). Unmyelinated tactile afferents signal touch and project to insular cortex. *Nature Neuroscience, 5,* 900–904.

O'Neill, M. T., & Hinton, J. W. (1977). Pupillographic assessment of sexual interest and sexual arousal. *Perceptual and Motor Skills, 44,* 1278.

Öngür, D., & Price, J. L. (2000). The organization of networks within the orbital and medial prefrontal cortex of rats, monkeys, and humans. *Cerebral Cortex, 10,* 206–219.

Ono, T., Nishijo, H., & Uwano, T. (1995). Amygdala role in conditioned associative learning. *Progress in Neurobiology, 46,* 401–422.

Onozawa, K., Glover, V., Adams, D., Modi, N., & Kumar, R. C. (2001). Infant massage improves mother infant interaction for mothers with postnatal depression. *Journal of Affective Disorders, 63,* 201–207.

Ornitz, E. M. (1985). Neurophysiology of infantile autism. *Journal of the American Academy of Child Psychiatry, 24,* 251–262.

Ornitz, E. M. (1988). Autism: A disorder of directed attention. *Brain Dysfunction, 1,* 309–322.

Ostrowski, N. L. (1998). Oxytocin receptor mRNA expression in rat brain: Implications for behavioral integration and reproductive success. *Psychoneuroendocrinology, 23,* 989–1004.

Ostrowsky, K., Isnard, J., Ryvlin, P., Guénot, M., Fischer, C., & Mauguière, F. (2000). Functional mapping of the insular cortex: Clinical implication in temporal lobe epilepsy. *Epilepsia, 41,* 681–686.

Ostrowsky, K., Magnin, M., Ryvlin, P., Isnard, J., Guenot, M., & Mauguière, F. (2002). Representation of pain and somatic sensation in the human insula: A study of responses to direct electrical cortical stimulation. *Cerebral Cortex, 12,* 376–385.

Ottenbacher, K. J., Muller, L., Brandt, D., Heintzelman, A., Hojem, P., & Sharpe, P. (1987). The effectiveness of tactile stimulation as a form of early intervention: A quantitative evaluation. *Journal of Developmental and Behavioral Pediatrics, 8,* 68–76.

Ouspensky, P. D. (1954). *The psychology of man's possible evolution.* New York: Knopf.

Pagnoni, G., Zink, C. F., Montague, P. R., & Berns, G. S. (2002). Activity in human ventral striatum locked to errors of reward prediction. *Nature Neuroscience, 5,* 97–98.

Panksepp, J. (1988a). Brain opioids and social affect. *Advances in Thanatology, 6,* 59–65.

Panksepp, J. (1988b). Brain emotional circuits and psychopathologies. In M. Clynes & J. Panksepp (Eds.), *Emotions and psychopathology* (pp. 37–76). New York: Plenum Press.

Panksepp, J. (1998). *Affective neuroscience: The foundation of human and animal emotions.* New York: Oxford University Press.

Panksepp, J. (2001). The long-term psychobiological consequences of infant emotions: Prescriptions for the 21st century. *Infant Mental Health Journal, 22,* 132–173.

Panksepp, J. (2003a). At the interface of the affective, behavioral, and cognitive neurosciences: Decoding the emotional feelings of the brain. *Brain and Cognition, 52,* 4–14.

Panksepp, J. (2003b). Neuroscience: Feeling the pain of social loss. *Science, 302,* 237–239.

Panksepp, J., Herman, B., Conner, R., Bishop, P., & Scott, J. P. (1978). The biology of social attachments: Opiates alleviate separation distress. *Biological Psychiatry, 13,* 607–618.

Panksepp, J., Nelson, E., & Siviy, S. (1994). Brain opioids and mother–infant social motivation. *Acta Paediatrica, 397*(Suppl.), 40–46.

Panksepp, J., Normansell, L., Herman, B., Bishop, P., & Crepeau, L. (1988). Neural and neurochemical control of the separation distress call. In. J. D. Newman (Ed.), *The physiological control of mammalian vocalizations* (pp. 263–300). New York: Plenum Press.

Papciak, A. S., Feuerstein, M., & Spiegel, J. A. (1985). Stress reactivity in alexithymia: Decoupling of physiological and cognitive responses. *Journal of Human Stress, 11,* 135–142.

Papez, J. W. (1937). A proposed mechanism of emotion. *Archives of Neurology and Psychiatry, 38,* 725–743.

Papp, L. A., Gorman, J. M., Liebowitz, M. R., Fyer, A. J., Cohen, B., & Klein, D. F. (1988). Epinephrine infusion in patients with social phobia. *American Journal of Psychiatry, 145,* 733–736.

Paquette, V., Lévesque, J., Mensour, B., Leroux, J. M., Beaudoin, G., Bourgouin, P., et al. (2003). "Change the mind and you change the brain": Effects of cognitive–behavioral therapy on the neural correlates of spider phobia. *NeuroImage, 18,* 401–409.

Paradiso, S., Johnson, D. L., Andreasen, N. C., O'Leary, D. S., Watkins, G. L., Ponto, L. L. B., et al. (1999). Cerebral blood flow changes associated with attribution of emotional valence to pleasant, unpleasant, and neutral visual stimuli in a PET study of normal subjects. *American Journal of Psychiatry, 156,* 1618–1629.

Paré, D. (2003). Role of the basolateral amygdala in memory consolidation. *Progress in Neurobiology, 70,* 409–420.

Paré, D., Quirk, G. J., & LeDoux, J. E. (2004). New vistas on amygdala networks in conditioned fear. *Journal of Neurophysiology, 92,* 1–9.

Paris, J., Zelkowitz, P., Guzder, J., Joseph, S., & Feldman, R. (1999). Neuropsychological factors associated with borderline pathology in children. *Journal of the Academy of Child and Adolescent Psychiatry, 38,* 770–774.

Parker, J. D. A., Bauermann, T. M., & Smith, C. T. (2000). Alexithymia and impoverished dream content: Evidence from rapid eye movement sleep awakenings. *Psychosomatic Medicine, 62,* 486–491.

Parker, K. J., Buckmaster, C. L., Schatzberg, A. F., & Lyons, D. M. (2004). Prospective investigation of stress inoculation in young monkeys. *Archives of General Psychiatry, 61,* 933–941.

Parker, S. W., & Nelson, C. A. (2005). The impact of deprivation on the ability to discriminate facial expressions of emotion: An event-related potential study. *Child Development, 76,* 54–72.

Parsons, L. M., Fox, P. T., Downs, J. H., Glass, T., Hirsch, T. B., Martin, C. C., et al. (1995). Use of implicit motor imagery for visual shape discrimination as revealed by PET. *Nature, 375,* 54–58.

Partala, T., & Surakka, V. (2003). Pupil size variation as an indication of affective processing. *International Journal of Human Computer Studies, 59,* 185–198.

Pascual-Leone, A., Rubio, B., Pallardo, F., & Catala, M. D. (1996). Rapid-rate transcranial magnetic stimulation of left dorsolateral prefrontal cortex in drug-resistant depression. *Lancet, 348,* 233–237.

Pascual-Leone, A., Wassermann, E.M., Grafman, J., & Hallett, M. (1996). The role of the dorsolateral prefrontal cortex in implicit procedural learning. *Experimental Brain Research, 107,* 479–485.

Passingham, R. E. (1975). Changes in the size and organization of the brain in man and his ancestors. *Brain, Behavior, and Evolution, 11,* 73–90.

Patchett, A. (2004). *Truth and beauty: A friendship.* New York: Harper Collins.

Patrick, C. J., Cuthbert, B. N., & Lang, P. J. (1994). Emotion in the criminal psychopath: Fear image processing. *Journal of Abnormal Psychology, 103,* 523–534.

Patterson, D. W., & Schmidt, L. A. (2003). Neuroanatomy of the human affective system. *Brain and Cognition, 52,* 24–26.

Paus, T., Petrides, M., Evans, A. C., & Meyer, E. (1993). Role of the human anterior cingulate cortex in the control of oculomotor, manual, and speech responses: A positron emission tomography study. *Journal of Neurophysiology, 70,* 453–469.

Paus, T., Zijdenbos, A., Worsley, K., Collins, D. L., Blumenthal, J., Giedd, J. N., et al. (1999). Structural maturation of neural pathways in children and adolescents: In vivo study. *Science, 283,* 1908–1911.

Pavlova, M., Sokolov, A., Staudt, M., Marconato, F., Birbaumer N., & Krageloh-Mann, I. (2005). Recruitment of periventricular parietal regions in processing cluttered point-light biological motion. *Cerebral Cortex, 15,* 594–601.

Pelphrey, K. A., Mitchell, T. V., McKeown, M. J., Goldstein, J., Allison, T., & McCarthy, G. (2003). Brain activity evoked by the perception of human walking: Controlling for meaningful coherent motion. *Journal of Neuroscience, 23,* 6819–6825.

Pelphrey, K. A., Morris, J. P., & McCarthy, G. (2004). Grasping the intentions of others: The perceived intentionality of an action influences activity in the superior temporal sulcus during social perception. *Journal of Cognitive Neuroscience, 16,* 1706–1716.

Pelphrey, K. A., Reznick, S. J., & Davis, B. G. (2004). Development of visuospatial short-term memory in the second half of the 1st year. *Developmental Psychology, 40,* 836–851.

Pelphrey, K. A., Sasson, N. J., Reznick, J. S., Paul, G., Goldman, B. D., & Piven, J. (2002). Visual scanning of faces in autism. *Journal of Autism and Developmental Disorders, 32,* 249–261.

Pelphrey, K. A., Singerman, J. D., Allison, T., & McCarthy, G. (2003). Brain activation evoked by perception of gaze shifts: The influence of context. *Neuropsychologia, 41,* 156–170.

Pelphrey, K. A., Viola, R. J., & McCarthy, G. (2004). When strangers pass: Processing of mutual and averted social gaze in the superior temporal sulcus. *Psychological Science, 15,* 598–603.

Penfield, W., & Faulk, M. E., Jr. (1955). The insula: Further observations on its function. *Brain, 78,* 445–470.

Penman, R., Meares, R., Baker, K., & Milgrom-Friedman, J. (1983). Synchrony in mother–infant interaction: A possible neurophysiological base. *British Journal of Medical Psychology, 56,* 1–7.

Perrett, D. I., Benson, P. J., Hietanen, J. K., Oram, M. W., & Dittrich, W. H. (1995). When is a face not a face? In R. Gregory, J. Harris, P. Heard, & D. Rose (Eds.), *The artful eye* (pp. 52–65). New York: Oxford University Press.

Perrett, D. I., Hietanen, J. K., Oram, M. W., & Benson, P. J. (1992). Organization and functions of cells responsive to faces in the temporal cortex. *Philosophical Transactions of the Royal Society of London: Biological Sciences, 335,* 23–30.

Perrett, D. I., Lee, K. J., Penton-Voak, I., Rowland, D., Yoshikawa, S., Burt, D. M., et al. (1998). Effects of sexual dimorphism on facial attractiveness. *Nature, 394,* 884–887.

Perrett, D. I., May, K. A., & Yoshinkawa, S. (1994). Facial shape and judgements of female attractiveness. *Nature, 368,* 239–242.

Perrett, D. I., Rolls, E. T., & Caan, W. (1982). Visual neurons responsive to faces in the monkey temporal cortex. *Experimental Brain Research, 47,* 329–342.

Perrett, D. I., Smith, A. J., Potter, D. D., Mistlin, A. J., Head, A. D., Milner, A. D., & Jeeves, M. A. (1984). Neurons responsive to faces in the temporal cortex: Studies of functional organization, sensitivity to identity and relation to perception. *Human Neurobiology, 3,* 197–208.

Perry, B. D., & Pollard, D. (1997). *Altered brain development following global neglect in childhood.* Paper presented at the annual meeting of the Society for Neuroscience, New Orleans, LA.

Petitto, L. A., Zatorre, R. J., Gauna, K., Nikelski, E. J., Dostie, D., & Evans, A. C. (2000). Speech-like cerebral activity in profoundly deaf people processing signed languages: Implications for the neural basis of human language. *Proceedings of the National Academy of Sciences, USA, 97,* 13961–13966.

Petrella, J. R., Townsend, B. A., Jha, A. P., Ziajko, L. A., Slavin, M. J., Lustig, C., et al. (2005). Increasing memory load modulates regional brain activity in older adults as measured by fMRI. *Journal of Neuropsychiatry and Clinical Neurosciences, 17,* 75–83.

Petrovic, P., Kelso, E., Petersson, K. M., & Ingvar, M. (2002). Placebo and opioid analgesia: Imaging a shared neuronal network. *Science, 295,* 1737–1740.

Pfeffer, C. R., Martins, P., Mann, J., Sunkenberg, M., Ice, A., Damore, J. P., Jr., et al. (1997). Child survivors of suicide: Psychosocial characteristics. *Journal of the American Academy of Childhood and Adolescent Psychiatry, 36,* 65–74.

Pfefferbaum, A., Mathalon, D. H., Sullivan, E. V., Rawles, J. M., Zipursky, R. B., & Lim, K. O. (1994). A quantitative magnetic resonance imaging study of changes in brain morphology from infancy to late adulthood. *Archives of Neurology, 51*, 874–887.

Pfrieger, F. W., & Barres, B. A. (1996). New views on synapse–glia interactions. *Current Opinions in Neurobiology, 6*, 615–621.

Phan, K. L., Wager, T., Taylor, S. F., & Liberzon, I. (2002). Functional neuroanatomy of emotion: A meta-analysis of emotion activation studies in PET and fMRI. *NeuroImage, 16*, 331–348.

Phelps, E. A., & Anderson, A. K. (1997). Emotional memory: What does the amygdala do? *Current Biology, 7*, R311–R314.

Phelps, E. A., & Thomas, L. A. (2003). Race, behavior, and the brain: The role of neuroimaging in understanding complex social behaviors. *Political Psychology, 24*, 747–758.

Phelps, E. A., O'Connor, K. J., Cunningham, W. A., Funayama, E. S., Gatenby, J. C., Gore, J. C., et al. (2000). Performance on indirect measures of race evaluation predicts amygdala activation. *Journal of Cognitive Neuroscience, 12*, 729–738.

Phelps, E. A., O'Connor, K. J., Gatenby, J. C., Gore, J. C., Grillon, C., & Davis, M. (2001). Activation of the left amygdala to a cognitive representation of fear. *Nature Neuroscience, 4*, 437–441.

Phillips, A. T., Wellman, H. M., & Spelke, E. S. (2002). Infants' ability to connect gaze and emotional expression to intentional action. *Cognition, 85*, 53–78.

Phillips, M. L., Bullmore, E. T., Howard, R., Woodruff, P. W., Wright, I. C., Williams, S. C., et al. (1998). Investigation of facial recognition memory and happy and sad facial expression perception: An fMRI study. *Psychiatry Research, 83*, 127–138.

Phillips, M. L., Young, A. W., Senior, C., Brammer, M., Andrew, C., Calder, A. J., et al. (1997). A specific neural substrate for perceiving facial expressions of disgust. *Nature, 389*, 495–498.

Phillips, R. G., & LeDoux, J. E. (1992). Differential contribution of amygdala and hippocampus to cued and contextual fear conditioning. *Behavioral Neuroscience, 106*, 274–285.

Phillips, W., Baron-Cohen, S., & Rutter, M. (1992). The role of eye contact in goal detection: Evidence from normal infants and children with autism or mental handicap. *Development and Psychopathology, 4*, 375–383.

Pierce, K., & Courchesne, E. (2000). Exploring the neurofunctional organization of face processing in autism. *Archives of General Psychiatry, 57*, 344–346.

Pierce, K., Muller, R. A., Ambrose, J., Allen, G., & Courchesne, E. (2001). Face processing occurs outside the fusiform "face area" in autism: Evidence from functional MRI. *Brain, 124*, 2059–2073.

Pitkänen, A., Savander, M., Nurminen, N., & Ylinen, A. (2003). Intrinsic synaptic circuitry of the amygdala. *Annals of the New York Academy of Sciences, 985*, 34–39.

Pitkänen, A., Savander, V., & LeDoux, J. E. (1997). Organization of intra-amygdaloid circuitries in the rat: An emerging framework for understanding functions of the amygdala. *Trends in Neuroscience, 20*, 517–523.

Pitman, R. K., & Orr, S. P. (1990). Twenty-four-hour urinary cortisol and catecholamine excretion in combat-related posttraumatic stress disorder. *Biological Psychiatry, 27,* 245–247.

Pitman, R. K., Orr, S. P., van der Kolk, B. A., Greenberg, M. S., Meyerhoff, J. L., & Mougey, E. H. (1990). Analgesia: A new dependent variable for the biological study of posttraumatic stress disorder. In M. E. Wolf & A. D. Mosnaim (Eds.), *Posttraumatic stress disorder: Etiology, phenomenology, and treatment* (pp. 140–147). Washington, DC: American Psychiatric Press.

Piven, J., Berthier, M. L., Starkstein, S. E., Nehme, E., Pearlson, G., & Folstein, S. (1990). Magnetic resonance imaging evidence for a defect of cerebral cortical development in autism. *American Journal of Psychiatry, 147,* 734–739.

Pizzagalli, D. A., Lehmann, D., Hendrick, A. M., Regard, M., Pascual-Marqui, R. D., & Davidson, R. J. (2002). Affective judgements of faces modulate early activity (~160ms) within the fusiform gyri. *NeuroImage, 16,* 663–677.

Platek, S. M., Critton, S. R., Myers, T. E., & Gallup, G. G., Jr. (2003). Contagious yawning: The role of self-awareness and mental state attribution. *Cognitive Brain Research, 17,* 223–227.

Platek, S. M., Keenan, J. P., Gallup, G. G., Jr., & Mohamed, F. B. (2004). Where am I? The neurological correlates of self and other. *Brain Research and Cognitive Brain Research, 19,* 114–122.

Plotsky, P. M., & Meaney, M. J. (1993). Early, postnatal experience alters hypothalamic corticotropin-releasing factor (CRF), mRNA, median eminence CRF content, and stress-induced release in adult rats. *Brain Research and Molecular Brain Research, 18,* 195–200.

Ponitus, A. A., & Ruttiger, K. F. (1976). Frontal lobe system maturational lag in juvenile delinquents shown in narratives test. *Adolescence, 11,* 509–518.

Porges, S. W. (1994). Orienting in a defensive world: Mammalian modifications of our evolutionary heritage. A polyvagal theory. *Psychophysiology, 32,* 301–318.

Porges, S. W. (1998). Love: An emergent property of the mammalian autonomic nervous system. *Psychoneuroendocrinology, 23,* 837–861.

Porges, S. W. (2001). The polyvagal theory: Phylogenetic substrates of a social nervous system. *International Journal of Psychophysiology, 42,* 123–146.

Porges, S. W. (2003a). Social engagement and attachment: A phylogentic perspective. *Annals of the New York Academy of Sciences, 1008,* 31–47.

Porges, S. W. (2003b). The polyvagal theory: Phylogenetic contributions to social behavior. *Physiology and Behavior, 79,* 503–513.

Porges, S. W., Doussard-Roosevelt, J. A., & Maiti, A. K. (1994). Vagal tone and the physiological regulation of emotion. *Monographs of the Society for Research in Child Development, 59,* 167–186.

Porges, S. W., Doussard-Roosevelt, J. A., Portales, A. L., & Greenspan, S. I. (1996). Infant regulation of the vagal "brake" predicts child behavior problems: A psychobiological model of social behavior. *Developmental Psychobiology, 29,* 697–712.

Porges, S. W., Riniolo, T. C., McBride, T., & Campbell, B. (2003). Heart rate and respiration in reptiles: Contrasts between a sit-and-wait predator and an intensive forager. *Brain and Cognition, 52,* 88–96.

Porter, R. H., Cernoch, J. M., & McLaughlin, F. J. (1983). Maternal recognition of neonates through olfactory cures. *Physiology and Behavior, 30,* 151–154.

Porter, R. H., & Winberg, J. (1999). Unique salience of maternal breast odors for newborn infants. *Neuroscience and Biobehavioral Reviews, 23,* 439–449.

Post, R. M., & Weiss, S. R. (1997). Emergent properties of neural systems: How focal molecular neurobiological alterations can affect behavior. *Development and Psychopathology, 9,* 907–929.

Potts, N. L. S., Book, S., & Davidson, J. R. T. (1996). The neurobiology of social phobia. *International Clinical Psychopharmacology, 11,* 43–48.

Povinelli, D. J., Bering, J. M., & Giambrone, S. (2000). Toward a science of other minds: Escaping the argument by analogy. *Cognitive Science, 24,* 509–541.

Povinelli, D. J., & Preuss, T. M. (1995). Theory of mind: Evolutionary history of a cognitive specialization. *Trends in Neurosciences, 18,* 418–424.

Premack, D., & Woodruff, G. (1978). Does the chimpanzee have a theory of mind? *Behavioral and Brain Sciences, 4,* 515–526.

Pribram, K. H. (1991). *Brain and perception: Holonomy and structure in figural processing.* Hillsdale, NJ: Erlbaum.

Price, B. H., Daffner, K. R., Stowe, R. M., & Mesulam, M. M. (1990). The comportmental learning disabilities of early frontal lobe damage. *Brain, 113,* 1383–1393.

Price, J. L. (1999). Prefrontal cortical networks related to visceral function and mood. *Annals of the New York Academy of Sciences, 877,* 383–396.

Price, J. L., Carmichael, S. T., & Drevets, W. C. (1996). Networks related to the orbital and medial prefrontal cortex; a substrate for emotional behavior? *Progress in Brain Research, 107,* 523–536.

Puce, A., Allison, T., Asgari, M., Gore, J. C., & McCarthy, G. (1996). Differential sensitivity of human visual cortex to faces, letterstrings, and textures: A functional magnetic resonance imaging study. *Journal of Neuroscience, 16,* 5205–5215.

Puce, A., Allison, T., Benton, S., Gore, J. C., & McCarthy, G. (1998). Temporal cortex activation in humans viewing eye and mouth movements. *Journal of Neuroscience, 18,* 2188–2199.

Puce, A., Allison, T., Gore, J. C., & McCarthy, G. (1995). Face-sensitive regions in human extrastriate cortex studied by functional MRI. *Journal of Neurophysiology, 74,* 1192–1199.

Puce, A., & Perrett, D. (2003). Electrophysiology and brain imaging of biological motion. *Philosophical Transactions of the Royal Society of London: Biological Sciences, 358,* 435–445.

Pujol, J., Lopez, A., Deus, J., Cardoner, N., Vallejo, J., Capdevilla, A., et al. (2002). Anatomical variability of the anterior cingulate gyrus and basic dimensions of human personality. *NeuroImage, 15,* 847–855.

Purves, D., & Lichtman, J. W. (1980). Elimination of synapses in the developing nervous system. *Science, 210,* 153–157.

Quirk, G. J., & Gehlert, D. R. (2003). Inhibition of the amygdala: Key to pathological states? *Annals of the New York Academy of Sciences, 985,* 263–272.

Radke-Yarrow, M., Zahn-Waxler, C., Richardson, D. T., Susman, A., & Martinez, P. (1994). Caring behavior in children of clinically depressed and well mothers. *Child Development, 65,* 1405–1414.

Raine, A. (1987). Effect of early environment on electrodermal and cognitive correlates of schizotypy and psychopathy in criminals. *International Journal of Psychophysiology, 4,* 277–287.

Raine, A. (1996). Autonomic nervous system factors underlying disinhibited, antisocial, and violent behavior: Biosocial perspectives and treatment implications. *Annals of the New York Academy of Sciences, 794,* 46–59.

Raine, A., Buchsbaum, M. S., Stanley, J., Lottenberg, S., Abel, L., & Stoddard, J. (1994). Selective reductions in prefrontal glucose metabolism in murderers. *Biological Psychiatry, 36,* 365–373.

Raine, A., Ishikawa, S. S., Arce, E., Lencz, T., Knuth, K. H., Bihrle, S., et al. (2004). Hippocampal structural asymmetry in unsuccessful psychopaths. *Biological Psychiatry, 55,* 185–191.

Raine, A., Lencz, T., Bihrle, S., LaCasse, L., & Colletti, P. (2002). Reduced prefrontal gray matter volume and reduced autonomic activity in antisocial personality disorder. *Archives of General Psychiatry, 57,* 119–127.

Rainnie, D. G., Bergeron, R., Sajdyk, T. J., Patil, M., Gehlert, D. R., & Shekhar, A. (2004). Corticotrophin releasing factor-induced synaptic plasticity in the amygdala translates stress into emotional disorders. *Journal of Neuroscience, 24,* 3471–3479.

Rajapakse, J. C., Giedd, J. N., Rumsey, J. M., Vaituzis, A. C., Hamburger, S. D., & Rapoport, J. L. (1996). Regional MRI measurements of the corpus callosum: A methodological and developmental study. *Brain and Development, 18,* 379–388.

Ramnani, N., & Miall, R. C. (2004). A system in the human brain for predicting the actions of others. *Nature Neuroscience, 7,* 85–90.

Rapin, I. (1999). Autism in search of a home in the brain. *Neurology, 52,* 902–904.

Rauch, S. L., Savage, C. R., Alpert, N. M., Dougherty, D., Kendrick, A., Curran, T., et al. (1997). Probing striatal function in obsessive–compulsive disorder: A PET study of implicit sequence learning. *Journal of Neuropsychiatry and Clinical Neurosciences, 9,* 568–573.

Rauch, S. L., Savage, C. R., Alpert, N. M., Miguel, E. C., Baer, L., & Breiter, H. C. (1995). A positron emission tomographic study of simple phobic symptom provocation. *Archives of General Psychiatry, 52,* 20–28.

Rauch, S. L., Shin, L. M., & Wright, C. I. (2003). Neuroimaging studies of amygdala function in anxiety disorders. *Annals of the New York Academy of Sciences, 985,* 389–410.

Rauch, S. L., van der Kolk, B. A., Fisler, R. E., Alpert, N. M., Orr, S. P., Savage, C. R., et al. (1996). A symptom provocation study of posttraumatic stress disorder using positron emission tomography and script-driven imagery. *Archive of General Psychiatry, 53,* 380–387.

Raymond, J. L., Lisberger, S. G., & Mauk, M. D. (1996). The cerebellum: A neuronal learning machine. *Science, 272,* 1126–1131.

Reiss, A. L. (1988). Cerebellar hypoplasia and autism. *New England Journal of Medicine, 319,* 1152–1153.

Reiss, A. L., Patel, S., Kumar, A. J., & Freund, L. (1988). Neuroanatomical variations of the posterior fossa in men with the fragile X (Martin-Bell) syndrome. *American Journal of Medical Genetics, 31*, 407–414.

Reiss, D., Plomin, R., & Hetherington, E. M. (1991) Genetics and psychiatry: An unheralded window on the environment. *American Journal of Psychiatry, 148*, 283–291.

Reissland, N., Shepherd, J., & Cowie, L. (2002). The melody of surprise: Maternal surprise vocalizations during play with her infant. *Infant and Child Development, 11*, 271–278.

Resnick, S. M., Goldszal, A. F., Davatzikos, C., Golski, S., Kraut, M. A., Metter, E. J., et al. (2000). One-year age changes in MRI brain volumes in older adults. *Cerebral Cortex, 10*, 464–472.

Resnick, S. M., Pham, D. L., Kraut, M. A., Zonderman, A. B., & Davatzikos, C. (2003). Longitudinal magnetic resonance imaging studies of older adults: A shrinking brain. *Journal of Neuroscience, 23*, 3295–3301.

Ressler, K. J., Rothbaum, B. O., Tannenbaum, L., Anderson, P., Graap, K., Zimand, E., et al. (2004). Cognitive enhancers as adjuncts to psychotherapy. *Archives of General Psychiatry, 61*, 1136–1144.

Reuter-Lorenz, P. A., & Stanczak, L. (2000). Differential effects of aging on the functions of the corpus callosum. *Developmental Neuropsychology, 18*, 113–137.

Reynolds, D. K. (1980). *The quiet therapies: Japanese pathways to personal growth.* Honolulu: University Press of Hawaii.

Rheingold, H. L. (1969). The social and socializing infant. In D. A. Goslin (Ed.), *Handbook of socialization theory and research* (pp. 779–790). Chicago: Rand McNally.

Ricciardelli, P., Ro., T., & Driver, J. (2002). A left visual field advantage in perception of gaze direction. *Neuropsychologia, 40*, 769–777.

Richell, R. A., Mitchell, D. G. V., Newman, C., Leonard, A., Baron-Cohen, S., & Blair, R. J. R. (2003). Theory of mind and psychopathy: Can psychopathic individuals read the "language of the eyes"? *Neuropsychologia, 41*, 523–526.

Richer, J. M., & Coss, R. G. (1976). Gaze aversion in autistic and normal children. *Acta Psychiatrica Scandinavica, 53*, 193–210.

Ridderinkhof, K. R., Ullsperger, M., Crone, E. A., & Nieuwenhuis, S. (2004). The role of the medial frontal cortex in cognitive control. *Science, 306*, 443–447.

Rilke, R. M. (1921). *Wartime letters of Rainer Maria Rilke.* New York: Norton.

Rilling, J. K., Gutman, D. A., Zeh, T. R., Pagnoni, G., Berns, G. S., & Kilts, C. D. (2002). A neural basis for social cooperation. *Neuron, 35*, 395–405.

Rilling, J. K., & Insel, T. R. (1999). Differential expansion of neural projection systems in primate brain evolution. *NeuroReport, 10*, 1453–1459.

Rizzolatti, G., & Arbib, M. A. (1998). Language within our grasp. *Trends in Neurosciences, 21*, 188–194.

Rizzolatti, G., Fadiga, L., Fogassi, L., & Gallese, V. (1999). Resonance behaviors and mirror neurons. *Archives Italiennes de Biologie, 137*, 85–100.

Rizzolatti, G., Fadiga, L., Gallese, V., & Fogassi, L. (1996). Premotor cortex and the recognition of motor actions. *Cognitive Brain Research, 3*, 131–141.

Robinson, B. W. (1967). Vocalization evoked from forebrain in *Macaca mulatta*. *Physiology and Behavior, 2,* 345–354.

Robinson, M. (2004). *Housekeeping.* New York: Picador.

Robles, T. F., & Kiecolt-Glaser, J. K. (2003). The physiology of marriage: Pathways to health. *Physiology and Behavior, 79,* 409–416.

Rochat, P. (1983). Oral touch in young infants: Responses to variations of nipple characteristics in the first months of life. *International Journal of Behavioral Development, 6,* 123–133.

Rochat, P., & Hespos, S. J. (1997). Differential rooting response by neonates: Evidence for an early sense of self. *Early Development and Parenting, 6,* 105–112.

Rogan, M. T., & LeDoux, J. E. (1996). Emotion: Systems, cells, synaptic plasticity. *Cell, 85,* 469–475.

Rojas, D. C., Smith, J. A., Benkers, T. L., Camou, S. L., Reite, M. L., & Rogers, S. J. (2004). Hippocampus and amygdala volumes in patients of children with autistic disorder. *American Journal of Psychiatry, 161,* 2038–2044.

Rolls, E. T. (2000a). Précis of the brain and emotion. *Behavioral and Brain Sciences, 23,* 177–234.

Rolls, E. T. (2000b). The orbitofrontal cortex and reward. *Cerebral Cortex, 10,* 284–294.

Rolls, E. T., Kringelbach, M. L., & de Araujo, I. E. (2003). Different representations of pleasant and unpleasant odours in the human brain. *European Journal of Neuroscience, 18,* 695–703.

Rosenberg, D. R., & Lewis, D. A. (1995). Postnatal maturation of the dopaminergic innervation of monkey prefrontal and motor cortices: A tyrosine hydroxylase immunohistochemical analysis. *Journal of Comparative Neurology, 358,* 383–400.

Rosenblatt, J. S. (1995). Hormonal basis of parenting in mammals. In M. H. Bornstein (Ed.), *Handbook of parenting: Vol. 2. Biology and ecology of parenting* (pp. 3–25). Mahwah, NJ: Erlbaum.

Rosenkranz, J. A., Moore, H., & Grace, A. A. (2003). The prefrontal cortex regulates lateral amygdala neuronal plasticity and responses to previously conditioned stimuli. *Journal of Neuroscience, 23,* 11054–11064.

Ross, E. D., Homan, R. W., & Buck, R. (1994). Differential hemispheric lateralization of primary and social emotions: Implications for developing a comprehensive neurology for emotions, repression, and the subconscious. *Neuropsychiatry, Neuropsychology, and Behavioral Neurology, 7,* 1–19.

Ross, M., & Buehler, R. (1994). Creative remembering. In U. Neisser & R. Fivush (Eds.), *The remembered self: Construction and accuracy in the self-narrative* (pp. 205–235). New York: Cambridge University Press.

Rossi, E. L. (1993). *The psychobiology of mind-body healing.* New York: Norton.

Rossion, B., Dricot, L., Devolder, A., Bodart, J. M., Crommelinck, M., de Gelder, B., et al. (2000). Hemispheric asymmetries for whole-based and part-based face processing in the human fusiform gyrus. *Journal of Cognitive Neuroscience, 12,* 793–802.

Roth, P. (1997). *American pastoral.* Boston: Houghton Mifflin.

Rothbart, M. K., Taylor, S. B., & Tucker, D. M. (1989). Right-sided facial asymmetry in infant emotional expression. *Neuropsychologia, 27,* 675–687.

Royet, J. P., Plailly, J., Delon-Martin, C., Kareken, D. A., & Segebarth, C. (2003). fMRI of emotional responses to odors: Influence of hedonic valence and judgment, handedness, and gender. *NeuroImage, 20,* 713–728.

Rubinow, D. R., & Post, R. M. (1992). Impaired recognition of affect in facial expression in depressed patients. *Biological Psychiatry, 31,* 947–953.

Ruby, P., & Decety, J. (2001). Effect of subjective perspective taking during simulation of action: A PET investigation of agency. *Nature Neuroscience, 4,* 546–550.

Rule, R. R., Shimamura, A. P., & Knight, R. T. (2002). Orbitofrontal cortex and dynamic filtering of emotional stimuli. *Cognitive, Affective, and Behavioral Neuroscience, 2,* 264–270.

Russek, L. G., & Schwartz, G. E. (1997). Feelings of parental caring predict health status in midlife: A 35-year follow-up of the Harvard mastery of stress study. *Journal of Behavioral Medicine, 20,* 1–13.

Russell, M. J. (1976). Human olfactory communication. *Nature, 260,* 520–522.

Rutter, M. L. (1997). Nature–nurture integration: The example of antisocial behavior. *American Psychologist, 52,* 390–398.

Sabbagh, M. A. (2004). Understanding orbitofrontal contributions to theory-of-mind reasoning: Implications for autism. *Brain and Cognition, 55,* 209–219.

Sachser, N., Dürschlag, M., & Hirzel, D. (1998). Social relationships and the management of stress. *Psychoneuroendocrinology, 23,* 891–904.

Saitoh, O., Karns, C. M., & Courchesne, E. (2001). Development of the hippocampal formation from 2 to 42 years: MRI evidence of smaller area dentata in autism. *Brain, 124,* 1317–1324.

Salm, A. K., Modney, B. K., & Hatton, G. I. (1988). Alterations in supraoptic nucleus ultrastructure of maternally behaving virgin rats. *Brain Research Bulletin, 21,* 685–691.

Sander, K., Brechmann, A., & Scheich, H. (2003). Audition of laughing and crying leads to right amygdala activation in a low-noise fMRI setting. *Brain Research Protocols, 11,* 81–91.

Sander, K., & Scheich, H. (2001). Auditory perception of laughing and crying activates human amygdala regardless of attentional state. *Cognitve Brain Research, 12,* 181–198.

Sapolsky, R. M. (1987). Glucocorticoids and hippocampal damage. *Trends in Neurosciences, 10,* 346–349.

Sapolsky, R. M. (1990). Stress in the wild. *Scientific American, 262,* 116–123.

Sapolsky, R. M., Uno, H., Rebert, C. S., & Finch, C. E. (1990). Hippocampal damage associated with prolonged glucocorticoid exposure in primates. *Journal of Neuroscience, 10,* 2897–2902.

Saxe, G. N., Vasile, R. G., Hill, T. C., Bloomingdale, K., & van der Kolk, B. A. (1992). SPECT imaging and multiple personality disorder. *Journal of Nervous and Mental Disease, 180,* 662–663.

Schaefer, S. M. (2002). Modulation of amygdalar activity by the conscious regulation of negative emotion. *Journal of Cognitive Neuroscience, 14,* 913–921.

Schanberg, S. M., & Field, T. M. (1987). Sensory deprivation stress and supplemental stimulation in the rat pup and preterm human neonate. *Child Development, 58,* 1431–1447.

Schiffer, F., Teicher, M. H., & Papanicolaou, A. C. (1995). Evoked potential evidence for right brain activity during the recall of traumatic memories. *Journal of Neuropsychiatry and Clinical Neurosciences, 7,* 169–175.

Schlaepfer, T. E., Strain, E. C., Greenberg, B. D., Preston, K. L., Lancaster, E., Bigelow, G. E., et al. (1998). Site of opioid action in the human brain: Mu and kappa agonists' subjective and cerebral blood flow effects. *American Journal of Psychiatry, 155,* 470–473.

Schmahl, C. G., Elzinga, B. M., Vermetten, E., Sanislow, C., McGlashan, T. H., & Bremner, J. D. (2003a). Neural correlates of memories of abandonment in women with and without borderline personality disorder. *Biological Psychiatry, 54,* 142–151.

Schmahl, C. G., Vermetten, E., Elzinga, B. M., & Bremner, J. D. (2003b). Magnetic resonance imaging of hippocampal and amygdala volume in women with childhood abuse and borderline personality disorder. *Psychiatry Research: Neuroimaging, 122,* 193–198.

Schmahmann, J. D. (1991). An emerging concept: The cerebellar contribution to higher function. *Archives of Neurology, 48,* 1178–1187.

Schmahmann, J. D. (2004). Disorders of the cerebellum: Ataxia, dysmetria of thought, and the cerebellar cognitive affective syndrome. *Journal of Neuropsychiatry and Clinical Neuroscience, 16,* 367–378.

Schmidt, S., Nachtigall, C., Wuethrich-Martone, O., & Strauss, B. (2002). Attachment and coping with chronic disease. *Journal of Psychosomatic Research, 53,* 763–773.

Schmitt, J. E., Watts, K., Eliez, S., Bellugia, U., Galaburda, A. M., Reiss, A. L. (2002). Increased gyrification in Williams syndrome: Evidence using 3D MRI methods. *Developmental Medicine and Child Neurology, 44,* 292–295.

Schmitt, W. A., & Newman, J. P. (1999). Are all psychopathic individuals low-anxious? *Journal of Abnormal Psychology, 108,* 353–358.

Schneider, F., Habel, U., Kessler, C., Posse, S., Grodd, W., & Muller-Gartner, H. (2000). Functional imaging of conditioned aversive emotional responses in antisocial personality disorder. *Neuropsychobiology, 42,* 192–201.

Schneider, F., Weiss, U., Kessler, C., Müller-Gärtner, H. W., Posse, S., Salloum, J. B., et al. (1999). Subcortical correlates of differential classical conditioning of aversive emotional reactions in social phobia. *Biological Psychiatry, 45,* 863–871.

Schneider, G. E. (1969). Two visual systems. *Science, 163,* 895–902.

Schneider, M. L. (1992). Prenatal stress exposure alters postnatal behavioral expression under conditions of novelty challenge in rhesus monkey infants. *Developmental Psychobiology, 25,* 529–540.

Schoenbaum, G., Chiba, A. A., & Gallagher, M. (1998). Orbitofrontal cortex and basolateral amygdala encode expected outcomes during learning. *Nature Neuroscience, 1,* 155–159.

Schopler, E. (1985). Convergence of learning disability, higher-level autism, and Asperger's syndrome. *Journal of Autism and Developmental Disorders, 15,* 359–360.

Schore, A. N. (1994). *Affect regulation and the origin of the self: The neurobiology of emotional development.* Hillsdale, NJ: Erlbaum.

Schore, A. N. (1997). Early organization of the nonlinear right brain and development of a predisposition to psychiatric disorders. *Development and Psychopathology, 9,* 595–631.

Schore, A. N. (2000). Attachment and the regulation of the right brain. *Attachment and Human Development, 2,* 23–47.

Schroeder, U., Hennenlotter, A., Erhard, P., Haslinger, B., Stahl, R., Lange, K. W., et al. (2004). Functional neuroanatomy of perceiving surprised faces. *Human Brain Mapping, 23,* 181–187.

Schuengel, C., Bakersmans-Kranenburg, M. J., & Van Ijzendoorn, M. H. (1999). Frightening maternal behavior linking unresolved loss and disorganized infant attachment. *Journal of Consulting and Clinical Psychology, 67,* 54–63.

Schulkin, J., Thompson, B. L., & Rosen, J. B. (2003). Demythologizing the emotions: Adaptation, cognition, and visceral representations of emotion in the nervous system. *Brain and Cognition, 52,* 15–23.

Schuller, A. M., & Rossion, B. (2004). Perception of static eye gaze direction facilitates subsequent early visual processing. *Clinical Neurophysiology, 115,* 1161–1168.

Schultheiss, O. C., Pang, J. S., Torges, C. M., Wirth, M. M., Treynor, W., & Derryberry, D. (2005). Perceived facial expressions of emotion as motivational incentives: Evidence from a differential implicit learning paradigm. *Emotion, 5,* 41–54.

Schultz, R. T. (2005). Developmental deficits in social perception in autism: The role of the amygdala and fusiform face area. *International Journal of Developmental Neuroscience, 23,* 125–141.

Schultz, R. T., Gauthier, I., Klin, A., Fulbright, R. K., Anderson, A. W., Volkmar, F., et al. (2000). Abnormal ventral temporal cortical activity during face discrimination among individuals with autism and Asperger syndrome. *Archives of General Psychiatry, 57,* 331–340.

Schultz, W. (1998). Predictive reward signal of dopamine neurons. *Journal of Neurophysiology, 80,* 1–27.

Schultz, W. (2000). Multiple reward signals in the brain. *Nature Reviews Neuroscience, 1,* 199–207.

Schultz, W., & Dickinson, A. (2000). Neuronal coding of prediction errors. *Annual Review of Neuroscience, 23,* 473–500.

Schultz, W., Apicella, P., Scarnati, E., & Ljunberg, T. (1992). Neuronal activity in monkey ventral striatum related to the expectation of reward. *Journal of Neuroscience, 12,* 4595–4610.

Schultz, W., Dayan, P., & Montague, P. R. (1997). A neural substrate of prediction and reward. *Science, 275,* 1593–1599.

Schultz, W., Tremblay, L., & Hollerman, J. R. (2000). Reward processing in primate orbitofrontal cortex and basal ganglia. *Cerebral Cortex, 10,* 272–284.

Schumann, C. M., Hamstra, J., Goodlin-Jones, B. L., Lotspeich, L. J., Kwon, H., Buonocore, M. H., et al. (2004). The amygdala is enlarged in children but not in adolescents with autism; the hippocampus is enlarged at all ages. *Journal of Neuroscience, 24,* 6392–6401.

Schwartz, C. E., Wright, C. I., Shin, L. M., Kagan, J., & Rauch, S. L. (2003). Inhibited and uninhibited infants grown up: Adult amygdalar response to novelty. *Science, 300*, 1952–1953.

Schwartz, D. A. (1979). The suicidal character. *Psychiatric Quarterly, 51*, 64–70.

Schwartz, J. M., Stoessel, P. W., Baxter, L. R., Martin, K. M., & Phelps, M. E. (1996). Systematic changes in cerebral glucose metabolic rate after successful behavior modification treatment of obsessive–compulsive disorder. *Archives of General Psychiatry, 53*, 109–113.

Scott, S. K., Young, A. W., Calder, A. J., Hellawell, D. J., Aggleton, J. P., & Johnson, M. (1997). Impaired auditory recognition of fear and anger following bilateral amygdala lesions. *Nature, 385*, 254–257.

Searleman, A. (1977). A review of right hemisphere linguistic capabilities. *Psychological Bulletin, 84*, 503–528.

Seckl, J. R. (2004). Prenatal glucocorticoids and long-term programming. *European Journal of Endocrinology, 151*, U49–U62.

Seguin, J. R. (2004). Neurocognitive elements of antisocial behavior: Relevance of an orbitofrontal cortex account. *Brain and Cognition, 55*, 185–197.

Seifritz, E., Esposito, F., Neuhoff, J. G., Lüthi, A., Mustovic, H., Dammann, G., et al. (2003). Differential sex-independent amygdala response to infant crying and laughing in parents versus nonparents. *Biological Psychiatry, 54*, 1367–1375.

Selden, N. R. W., Everitt, B. J., Jarrard, L. E., & Robbins, T. W. (1991). Complimentary roles for the amygdala and hippocampus in aversive conditioning to explicit and contextual cues. *Neuroscience, 42*, 335–350.

Semendeferi, K., Damasio, H., Frank, R., & Van Hoesen, G. W. (1997). The evolution of the frontal lobes: A volumetric analysis based on three-dimensional reconstructions of magnetic resonance scans of human and ape brains. *Journal of Human Evolution, 32*, 375–388.

Semendeferi, K., Lu, A., Schenker, N., & Damasio, H. (2002). Humans and great apes share a large frontal cortex. *Nature Neuroscience, 5*, 272–276.

Semin, G. R., & Manstead, A. S. R. (1982). The social implications of embarrassment displays and restitution behaviour. *European Journal of Social Psychology, 12*, 367–377.

Semmes, J. (1968). Hemispheric specialization: A possible clue to mechanism. *Neuropsychologia, 6*, 11–26.

Senju, A., & Hasegawa, T. (2005). Direct gaze captures visuospatial attention. *Visual Cognition, 12*, 127–144.

Sergent, J., Ohta, S., & MacDonald, B. (1992). Functional neuroanatomy of face and object processing. A positron emission tomography study. *Brain, 115*, 15–36.

Serrano, J. M., Iglesias, J., & Loeches, A. (1992). Visual discrimination and recognition of facial expressions of anger, fear, and surprise in 4 to 6 month old infants. *Developmental Psychobiology, 25*, 411–425.

Shah, N. J., Marshall, J. C., Zafiris, O., Schwab, A., Zilles, K., Markowitsch, H. J., et al. (2001). The neural correlates of person familiarity: A functional magnetic resonance imaging study with clinical implications. *Brain, 124*, 804–815.

Shamay-Tsoory, S. G., Tomer, R., Berger, B. D., & Aharon-Peretz, J. (2003). Characterization of empathy deficits following prefrontal brain damage: The role of the right ventromedial prefrontal cortex. *Journal of Cognitive Neuroscience, 15*, 324–337.

Shammi, P., & Stuss, D. T. (1999). Humour appreciation: A role of the right frontal lobe. *Brain, 122*, 657–666.

Shapiro, D., Jamner, L. D., & Spence, S. (1997). Cerebral laterality, repressive coping, autonomic arousal, and human bonding. *Acta Physiologica Scandanavica, 640*, 60–64.

Shatz, C. J. (1990). Impulse activity and the patterning of connections during CNS development. *Neuron, 5*, 745–756.

Shearn, D., Bergman, E., Hill, K., Abel, A., & Hinds, L. (1990). Facial coloration and temperature responses in blushing. *Psychophysiology, 27*, 687–693.

Shekhar, A., Sajdyk, T. J., Gehlert, D. R., & Rainnie, D. G. (2003). The amygdala, panic disorder, and cardiovascular responses. *Annals of the New York Academy of Sciences, 985*, 308–325.

Sherry, D. F., Jacobs, L. F., & Gaulin, S. J. (1992). Spatial memory and adaptive specialization of the hippocampus. *Trends in Neurosciences, 15*, 298–303.

Shima, K., & Tanji, J. (1998). Role for cingulate motor area cells in voluntary movement selection based on reward. *Science, 282*, 1335–1338.

Shin, L. M., Dougherty, D. D., Orr, S. P., Pitman, R. K., Lasko, M., Macklin, M. L., et al. (2000). Activation of anterior paralimbic structures during guilt-related script-driven imagery. *Biological Psychiatry, 48*, 43–50.

Shin, L. M., Wright, C. I., Cannistraro, P. A., Wedig, M. M., McMullin, K., & Martis, B. (2005). A functional magnetic resonance imaging study of amygdala and medial prefrontal cortex responses to overtly presented fearful faces in posttraumatic stress disorder. *Archives of General Psychiatry, 62*, 273–281.

Shingo, T., Gregg, C., Enwere, E., Fujikawa, H., Hassam, R., Geary, C., et al. (2003). Pregnancy-stimulated neurogenesis in the adult female forebrain mediated by prolactin. *Science, 299*, 117–120.

Shumake, J., Conejo-Jimenez, N., Gonzalez-Pardo, H., & Gonzalez-Lima, F. (2004). Brain differences in newborn rats predisposed to helpless and depressive behavior. *Brain Research, 1030*, 267–276.

Siegal, M., & Varley, R. (2002). Neural systems involved in "theory of mind." *Nature Reviews Neuroscience, 3*, 463–471.

Siegel, D. J. (1999). *The developing mind: Toward a neurobiology of interpersonal experience.* New York: Guilford Press.

Siegel, D. J., & Hartzell, M. (2003). *Parenting from the inside out: How a deeper self-understanding can help you raise children who thrive.* New York: Tarcher/Putnam.

Siegle, G. J., Steinhauer, S. R., & Thase, M. E. (2004). Pupillary assessment and computational modeling of the Stroop task in depression. *International Journal of Psychophysiology, 52*, 63–76.

Sieratzki, J. S., & Woll, B. (1996). Why do mothers cradle babies on their left? *The Lancet, 347*, 1746–1748.

Silberman, E. K., & Weingartner, H. (1986). Hemispheric lateralization of functions related to emotion. *Brain and Cognition, 5,* 322–353.

Silveri, M. C., Leggio, M. G., & Molinari, M. (1994). The cerebellum contributes to linguistic production: A case of agrammatic speech following a right cerebellar lesion. *Neurology, 44,* 2047–2050.

Simonian, S. J., Beidel, D. C., Turner, S. M., Berkes, J. L., & Long, J. H. (2001). Recognition of facial affect by children and adolescents diagnosed with social phobia. *Child Psychiatry and Human Development, 32,* 137–145.

Simpson, J. R., Drevets, W. C., Snyder, A. Z., Gusnard, D. A., & Raichle, M. E. (2001). Emotion-induced changes in human medial prefrontal cortex: II. During anticipatory anxiety. *Proceedings of the National Academy of Sciences, USA, 98,* 688–693.

Singer, T., Seymour, B., O'Doherty, J., Kaube, H., Dolan, R. J., & Frith, C. D. (2004). Empathy for pain involves the affective but not sensory components of pain. *Science, 303,* 1157–1162.

Sirevaag, A. M., & Greenough, W. T. (1988). A multivariate statistical summary of synaptic plasticity measures in rats exposed to complex, social and individual environments. *Brain Research, 441,* 386–392.

Slotnick, B. M. (1967). Disturbances of maternal behavior in the rat following lesions of the cingulate cortex. *Behaviour, 29,* 204–236.

Small, D. M., Zald, D. H., Jones-Gotman, M., Zatorre, R. J., Pardo, J. V., Frey, S., et al. (1999). Human cortical gustatory areas: A review of functional neuroimaging data. *NeuroReport, 10,* 7–14.

Smythe, J. W., McCormick, C. M., & Meaney, M. J. (1996). Median eminence corticotrophin-releasing hormone content following prenatal stress and neonatal handling. *Brain Research Bulletin, 40,* 195–199.

Smythe, J. W., Rowe, W. B., & Meaney, M. J. (1994). Neonatal handling alters serotonin (5-HT) turnover and 5-HT$_2$ receptor binding in selected brain regions: Relationship to the handling effect on glucocorticoid receptor expression. *Developmental Brain Research, 80,* 183–189.

Soderstrom, H. (2003). Psychopathy as a disorder of empathy. *European Child and Adolescent Psychiatry, 12,* 249–252.

Soderstrom, H., Blennow, K., Manhem, A., & Forsman, A. (2001). CSF studies in violent offenders: I. 5-HIAA as a negative and HVA as a positive predictor of psychopathy. *Journal of Neural Transmission, 108,* 869–878.

Soloff, P. H., Meltzer, C. C., Greer, P. J., Constantine, D., & Kelly, T. M. (2000). A fenfluramine-activated FDG-PET study of borderline personality disorder. *Biological Psychiatry, 47,* 540–547.

Sontheimer, H. (1995). Glial influences on neuronal signaling. *The Neuroscientist, 1,* 123–126.

Sowell, E. R., Peterson, B. S., Thompson, P. M., Welcome, S. E., Henkenius, A. L., & Toga, A. W. (2003). Mapping cortical change across the human life span. *Nature Neuroscience, 6,* 309–315.

Sowell E. R., Thompson P. M., Welcome S. E., Henkenius A. L., Toga A. W., & Peterson B. S. (2003). Cortical abnormalities in children and adolescents with attention-deficit hyperactivity disorder. *Lancet, 362,* 1699–1707.

Sowell, E. R., Trauner, D. A., Gamst, A., & Jernigan, T. L. (2002). Development of cortical and subcortical brain structures in childhood and adolescence: A structural MRI study. *Developmental Medicine and Child Neurology, 44*, 4–16.

Spalletta, G., Pasinin, A., Costa, A., De Angelis, D., Ramundo, N., Paolucci, S., et al. (2001). Alexithymic features in stroke: Effects of laterality and gender. *Psychosomatic Medicine, 63*, 944–950.

Spangler, G., & Grossman, K. E. (1993). Biobehavioral organization in securely and insecurely attached infants. *Child Development, 64*, 1439–1450.

Spangler, G., & Schieche, M. (1998). Emotional and adrenocortical responses of infants to the strange situation: The differential function of emotional expression. *International Journal of Behavioral Development, 22*, 681–706.

Spangler, G., Schieche, M., Ilg, U., Maier, U., & Ackerman, C. (1994). Maternal sensitivity as an organizer for biobehavioral regulation in infancy. *Developmental Psychobiology, 27*, 425–437.

Spear, L. P. (2000). The adolescent brain and age-related behavioral manifestations. *Neuroscience and Biobehavioral Reviews, 24*, 417–463.

Spector, I. P., Pecknold, J. C., & Libman, E. (2003). Selective attentional bias related to the noticeability aspect of anxiety symptoms in generalized social phobia. *Anxiety Disorders, 17*, 517–531.

Spence, S., Shapiro, D., & Zaidel, E. (1996). The role of the right hemisphere in the physiological and cognitive components of emotional processing. *Psychophysiology, 33*, 112–122.

Spitz, R. (1946). Hospitalism: A follow-up report on investigation described in Volume I, 1945. *The Psychoanalytic Study of the Child, 2*, 113–117.

Spitzer, C., Willert, C., Grabe, H., Rizos, T., Moller, B., & Freyberger, H. J. (2004). Dissociation, hemispheric asymmetry, and dysfunction of hemispheric interaction: A transcranial magnetic stimulation approach. *Journal of Neuropsychiatry and Clinical Neuroscience, 16*, 163–169.

Spivak, B., Segal, M., Mester, R., & Weizman, A. (1998). Lateral preference in post-traumatic stress disorder. *Psychological Medicine, 28*, 229–232.

Sprengelmeyer, R., Rausch, M., Eysel, U. T., & Przuntek, H. (1998). Neural structures associated with recognition of facial expressions of basic emotions. *Proceedings of the Royal Society of London: Biological Sciences, 265*, 1927–1931.

Sprengelmeyer, R., Young, A. W., Calder, A. J., Karnat, A., Lange, H., & Hömberg, V. (1996). Loss of disgust: Perception of faces and emotions in Huntington's disease. *Brain, 119*, 1647–1665.

Sprengelmeyer, R., Young, A. W., Pundt, I., Sprengelmeyer, A., Calder, A .J., Berrios, G., et al. (1997). Disgust implicated in obsessive–compulsive disorder. *Proceedings of the Royal Society of London: Biological Sciences, 264*, 1767–1773.

Sprengelmeyer, R., Young, A. W., Schroeder, U., Grossenbacher, P. G., Federlein, J., Büttner, T., et al. (1999). Knowing no fear. *Proceedings of the Royal Society of London: Biological Sciences, 266*, 2451–2456.

Squire, L. R. (1987). *Memory and brain.* New York: Oxford University Press.

Stafisso-Sandoz, G., Polley, D., Holt, E., Lambert, K. G., & Kinsley, C. H. (1998). Opiate disruption of maternal behavior: Morphine reduces, and naloxone restores, c-fos activity in the medial preoptic area of lactating rats. *Brain Research Bulletin, 45,* 307–313.

Stamm, J. S. (1955). The function of the median cerebral cortex in maternal behavior of rats. *Journal of Comparative and Physiological Psychology, 48,* 347–356.

Stass, J. W., & Willis, F. N., Jr. (1967). Eye contact, pupil dilation, and personal preference. *Psychonomic Science, 7,* 375–376.

Stechler, G., & Latz, E. (1966). Some observations on attention and arousal in the human infant. *Journal of the American Academy of Child Psychiatry, 5,* 517–525.

Stein, D. J., & Bouwer, C. (1997). Blushing and social phobia: A neuroethological speculation. *Medical Hypotheses, 49,* 101–108.

Stein, J. F. (1986). Role of the cerebellum in the visual guidance of movement. *Nature, 323,* 217–221.

Stein, M. B. (1998). Neurobiological perspectives on social phobia: From affiliation to zoology. *Biological Psychiatry, 44,* 1277–1285.

Stein, M. B., Goldin, P. R., Sareen, J., Zorrilla, L. T., & Brown, G. G. (2002). Increased amygdala activation to angry and contemptuous faces in generalized social phobia. *Archives of General Psychiatry, 59,* 1027–1034.

Stein, M. B., Koverola, C., Hanna, C., Torchia, M. G., & McClarty, B. (1997). Hippocampal volume in women victimized by childhood sexual abuse. *Psychological Medicine, 27,* 951–959.

Stern, D. N. (1995a). One way to build a clinically relevant child. In B. Mark-Goldstein & J. Incorvaia (Eds.), *The handbook of infant, child, and adolescent psychotherapy, Vol. 1. A guide to diagnosis and treatment* (pp. 17–42). Northvale, NJ: Jason Aronson.

Stern, D. N. (1995b). *The motherhood constellation.* New York: Basic Books.

Stern, J. (1997). Offspring-induced nurturance: Animal–human parallels. *Developmental Psychobiology, 31,* 19–37.

Stevens, D., Charman, T., & Blair, R. J. R. (2001). Recognition of emotion in facial expressions and vocal tones in children with psychopathic tendencies. *Journal of Genetic Psychology, 162,* 201–211.

Stewart, J. E., II. (1980). Defendant's attractiveness as a factor in the outcome of criminal trials: An observational study. *Journal of Applied Social Psychology, 10,* 348–361.

Stone, L. A., & Nielson, K. A. (2001). Intact physiological response to arousal with impaired emotional recognition in alexithymia. *Psychotherapy and Psychosomatics, 70,* 92–102.

Stone, V. E., Baron-Cohen, S., Calder, A., Keane, J., & Young, A. (2003). Acquired theory of mind impairments in individuals with bilateral amygdala lesions. *Neuropsychologia, 41,* 209–220.

Stone, V. E., Baron-Cohen, S., & Knight, R. T. (1998). Frontal lobe contributions to theory of mind. *Journal of Cognitive Neuroscience, 10,* 640–656.

Straube, T., Kolassa, I. T., & Glauer, M. (2004). Effect of task conditions on brain responses to threatening faces in social phobics: An event-related functional magnetic resonance imaging study. *Biological Psychiatry, 56,* 921–930.

Stuss, D. T., & Alexander, M. P. (1999). Affectively burnt in: A proposed role of the right frontal lobe. In E. Tulving (Ed.), *Memory, consciousness, and the brain: The Tallinn conference* (pp. 215–227). Philadelphia: Psychology Press.

Stuss, D. T., Gallup, G. G., & Alexander, M. P. (2001). The frontal lobes are necessary for "theory of mind." *Brain, 124,* 279–286.

Stuss, D. T., Gow, C. A., & Heatherington, C. R. (1992). "No longer Gage": Frontal lobe dysfunction and emotional changes. *Journal of Consulting and Clinical Psychology, 60,* 349–359.

Sugiura, M., Kawashima, R., Nakamura, K., Sato, N., Nakamura, A., Kato, T., et al. (2001). Activation reduction in anterior temporal cortices during repeated recognition of faces of personal acquaintances. *NeuroImage, 13,* 877–890.

Sullivan, R. M., & Gratton, A. (2002). Prefrontal cortical regulation of hypothalamic–pituitary–adrenal function in the rat and implications for psychopathology: Side matters. *Psychoneuroendocrinology, 27,* 99–114.

Suomi, S. J. (1997). Early determinants of behavior: Evidence from primate studies. *British Medical Bulletin, 53,* 170–184.

Suomi, S. J. (1999). Attachment in rhesus monkeys. In J. Cassidy & P. R. Shaver (Eds.), *Handbook of attachment: Theory, research, and clinical application* (pp. 181–197). New York: Guilford Press.

Suomi, S. J., & Harlow, H. F. (1972). Social rehabilitation of isolate-reared monkeys. *Developmental Psychology, 6,* 487–496.

Sutherland, R. J., Whishaw, I. Q., & Kolb, B. (1988). Contributions of cingulate cortex: Two forms of spatial learning and memory. *Journal of Neuroscience, 8,* 1863–1872.

Sutton, S. K., & Davidson, R. J. (1997). Prefrontal brain asymmetry: A biological substrate of the behavioral approach and inhibition systems. *Psychological Science, 8,* 204–210.

Sweeten, T. L., Posey, D. J., Shekhar, A., & McDougle, C. J. (2002). The amygdala and related structures in the pathophysiology of autism. *Pharmacology, Biochemistry, and Behavior, 71,* 449–455.

Swinton, M. (2003). The role of the parietal lobe in borderline personality disorder. *Medical Hypotheses, 60,* 263–267.

Swirsky-Sacchetti, T., Gorton, G., Samuel, S., Sobel, R., Genetta-Wadley, A., & Burleigh, B. (1993). Neuropsychological function in borderline personality disorder. *Journal of Clinical Psychology, 49,* 385–396.

Symons, L. A., Lee, K., & Cedrone, C. C. (2004). What are you looking at? Acuity for triadic eye gaze. *Journal of General Psychology, 131,* 451–469.

Szatmari, P., Bremner, R., & Nagy, J. (1989). Asperger's syndrome: A review of clinical features. *Canadian Journal of Psychiatry, 34,* 554–560.

Szatmari, P., Tuff, L., Finlayson, M. A., & Bartolucci, G. (1990). Asperger's syndrome and autism: Neurocognitive aspects. *Journal of the American Academy of Child and Adolescent Psychiatry, 29,* 130–136.

Tager-Flusberg, H., Boshart, J., & Baron-Cohen, S. (1998). Reading the windows to the soul: Evidence of domain-specific sparing in Williams syndrome. *Journal of Cognitive Neuroscience, 10,* 631–639.

Takami, S. (2002). Recent progress in the neurobiology of the vomeronasal organ. *Microscopy Research and Technique, 58,* 228–250.

Tanapat, P., Hastings, N. B., Rydel, T. A., Galea, L., & Gould, E. (2001). Exposure to fox odor inhibits cell proliferation in the hippocampus of adult rats via an adrenal hormone-dependent mechanism. *Journal of Comparative Neurology, 437,* 496–504.

Tangney, J. P., Miller, R. S., Flicker, L., & Barlow, D. H. (1996). Are shame, guilt, and embarrassment distinct emotions? *Journal of Personality and Social Psychology, 6,* 1256–1269.

Tantum, D. (1988). Asperger's syndrome. *Journal of Child Psychology and Psychiatry, 29,* 245–255.

Tarr, M. J., & Gauthier, I. (2000). FFA: A flexible fusiform area for subordinate-level visual processing automized by expertise. *Nature Neuroscience, 3,* 764–769.

Taylor, G. J. (2000). Recent developments in alexithymia theory and research. *Canadian Journal of Psychiatry, 45,* 134–142.

Taylor, G. J., & Bagby, R. M. (2004). New trends in alexithymia research. *Psychotherapy and Psychosomatics, 73,* 68–77.

Taylor, M. A. (1999). *The fundamentals of clinical neuropsychiatry.* New York: Oxford University Press.

Taylor, M. J., Edmonds, G. E., McCarthy, G., & Allison, T. (2001). Eyes first! Eye processing develops before face processing in children. *NeuroReport, 12,* 1671–1676.

Teasdale, J. D., Howard, R. J., Cox, S. G., Ha, Y., Brammer, M. J., Williams, S. C. R., et al. (1999). Functional MRI study of the cognitive generation of affect. *American Journal of Psychiatry, 156,* 209–215.

Teicher, M. H. (2002). Scars that won't heal: The neurobiology of child abuse. *Scientific American, 286,* 68–75.

Teicher, M. H., Andersen, S. L., & Hostetter, J. C., Jr. (1995). Evidence for dopamine receptor pruning between adolescence and adulthood in striatum but not nucleus accumbens. *Developmental Brain Research, 89,* 167–172.

Teicher, M. H., Andersen, S. L., Polcari, A., Anderson, C. M., & Navalta, C. P. (2002). Developmental neurobiology of childhood stress and trauma. *Psychiatric Clinics of North America, 25,* 397–426.

Teicher, M. H., Dumont, N. L., Ito, Y., Vaituzis, C., Geidd, J. N., & Andersen, S. L. (2004). Childhood neglect is associated with reduced corpus callosum area. *Biological Psychiatry, 56,* 80–85.

Teicher, M. H., Ito, Y., Glod, C. A., Andersen, S. L., Dumont, N., & Ackerman, E. (1997). Preliminary evidence for abnormal cortical development in physically and sexually abused children using EEG coherence and MRI. *Annals of the New York Academy of Sciences, 821,* 160–175.

Temoshok, L. R. (2002). Connecting the dots linking mind, behavior, and disease: The biological concomitants of coping patterns: Commentary on "attachment and cancer: A conceptual integration." *Integrative Cancer Therapies, 1,* 387–391.

Thatcher, R. W. (1980). Neurolinguistics: Theoretical and evolutionary perspectives. *Brain and Language, 11,* 235–260.

Thatcher, R. W., Walker, R. A., & Giudice, S. (1987). Human cerebral hemispheres develop at different rates and ages. *Science, 236,* 1110–1113.

Theodosis, D. T., & Poulain, D. A. (1984). Evidence for structural plasticity in the supraoptic nucleus of the rat hypothalamus in relation to gestation and lactation. *Neuroscience, 11,* 183–193.

Thompson, H. S. (2004). Autonomic control of the pupil. In D. Robertson (Ed.), *Primer on the autonomic nervous system* (2nd ed., pp. 162–165). London: Elsevier.

Thompson, P. M., Giedd, J. N., Woods, R. P., MacDonald, D., Evans, A. C., & Toga, A. W. (2000). Growth patterns in the developing brain detected by using continuum mechanical tensor maps. *Nature, 404,* 190–193.

Thoreau, H. D. (1854). *Walden.* Boston: Ticknor & Fields.

Thornquist, M. H., & Zuckerman, M. (1995). Psychopathy, passive–avoidance learning and basic dimensions of personality. *Personality and Individual Differences, 19,* 525–534.

Tiihonen, J., Kuikka, J., Bergström, K., Lepola, U., Koponen, H., & Leinonen, E. (1997). Dopamine reuptake site densities in patients with social phobia. *American Journal of Psychiatry, 154,* 239–242.

Tillfors, M., Furmark, T., Marteinsdottir, I., & Fredrikson, M. (2002). Cerebral blood flow during anticipation of public speaking in social phobia: A PET study. *Biological Psychiatry, 52,* 1113–1119.

Tomasello, M. (1998). *The new psychology of language, Vol. 1.* Mahwah, NJ: Erlbaum.

Tombs, S., & Silverman, I. (2004). Pupillometry: A sexual selection approach. *Evolution and Human Behavior, 25,* 221–228.

Tomonaga, M., Myowa-Yamakoshi, M., Mizuno, Y., Yamaguchi, M., Kosugi, D., Bard, K., et al. (2004). Development of social cognition in infant chimpanzees (*Pan troglodytes*): Face recognition, smiling, gaze, and the lack of triadic interactions. *Japanese Psychological Research, 46,* 227–235.

Tranel, D., & Hyman, B. T. (1990). Neuropsychological correlates of bilateral amygdala damage. *Archives of Neurology, 47,* 349–355.

Tremblay, L., Hollerman, J. R., & Schultz, W. (1998). Modifications of reward expectation-related neuronal activity during learning in primate striatum. *Journal of Neurophysiology, 80,* 964–977.

Tremblay, L., & Schultz, W. (1999). Relative reward preference in primate orbitofrontal cortex. *Nature, 398,* 704–708.

Trevarthen, C. (1993). The self born in intersubjectivity: The psychology of an infant communicating. In U. Neisser (Ed.), *The perceived self: Ecological and interpersonal sources of self-knowledge.* New York: Cambridge University Press.

Tronick, E. Z., & Gianino, A. F., Jr. (1986). The transmission of maternal disturbance to the infant. In E. Z. Tronick & T. Field (Eds.), *New directions for child development: Vol. 34. Maternal depression and infant disturbance* (pp. 5–11). San Francisco: Jossey-Bass.

Tronick, E. Z., & Weinberg, M. K. (1997). Depressed mothers and infants: Failure to form dyadic states of consciousness. In L. Murray & P. J. Cooper (Eds.), *Postpartum depression and child development* (pp. 54–81). New York: Guilford Press.

Tucker, D. M. (1992). Developing emotions and cortical networks. In M. R. Gunnar & C. A. Nelson (Eds.), *Minnesota symposium on child psychology: Vol. 24. Developmental behavioral neuroscience* (pp. 75–128). Hillsdale, NJ: Erlbaum.

Tucker, D. M., Luu, P., & Pribram, K. H. (1995). Social and emotional self-regulation. In J. Grafman, K. J. Holyoke, & F. Boller (Eds.), *Structure and functions of the human prefrontal cortex* (pp. 321–335). New York: New York Academy of Sciences.

Tulving, E. (1985). How many memory systems are there? *American Psychologist, 40*, 385–398.

Tzourio-Mazoyer, N., De Schonen, S., Crivello, F., Reutter, B., Aujard, Y., & Mazoyer, B. (2002). Neural correlates of woman face processing by 2-month-old infants. *NeuroImage, 15*, 454–461.

Uchida, I., Kameyama, M., Takenaka, S., Konishi, S., Okuaki, T., Machida, T., et al. (2000). Face imagery induced by auditorily presented name activates the face area in the fusiform gyrus. *NeuroImage, 11*, S97.

Ulfig, N., Setzer, M., & Bohl, J. (2003). Ontogeny of the human amygdala. *Annals of the New York Academy of Sciences, 985*, 22–33.

Ungerleider, L. G., & Haxby, J. V. (1994). "What" and "where" in the human brain. *Current Opinion in Neurobiology, 4*, 157–165.

Ungerleider, L. G., & Mishkin, M. (1982). Two cortical visual systems. In D. J. Ingle, M. A. Goodal, & R. J. W. Mansfield (Eds.), *Analysis of visual behavior* (pp. 549–586). Cambridge, MA: MIT Press.

Uvnäs-Moberg, K. (1997a). Oxytocin linked antistress effects: The relaxation and growth response. *Acta Physiologica Scandinavica, 640*(Suppl.), 38–42.

Uvnäs-Moberg, K. (1997b). Physiological and endocrine effects of social contact. *Annals of the New York Academy of Sciences, 807*, 146–163.

Uvnäs-Moberg, K. (1998). Oxytocin may mediate the benefits of positive social interaction and emotions. *Psychoneuroendocrinology, 23*, 819–835.

Uvnäs-Moberg, K., & Eriksson, M. (1996). Breastfeeding: Physiological, endocrine and behavioural adaptations caused by oxytocin and local neurogenic activity in the nipple and mammary gland. *Acta Paediatrica, 85*, 525–530.

Vaillant, G. E. (2002). *Aging well.* New York: Little, Brown.

Vaina, L. M., Solomon, J., Chowdhury, S., Sinha, P., & Belliveau, J. W. (2001). Functional neuroanatomy of biological motion perception in humans. *Proceedings of the National Academy of Sciences, USA, 98*, 11656–11661.

Van Ameringen, M., Mancini, C., Oakman, J. M., Kamath, M., Nahmias, C., & Szechtman, H. (1998). A pilot study of PET in social phobia. *Biological Psychiatry, 43*, 31S.

Van der Knaap, M. S., Valk, J., Bakker, C. J., Schoonevald, M., Faber, J., Willemse, J., et al. (1991). Myelination as an expression of the functional maturity of the brain. *Developmental Medicine and Child Neurology, 33*, 849–857.

van der Kolk, B. A. (1988). The trauma spectrum: The interaction of biological and social events in the genesis of the trauma response. *Journal of Traumatic Stress, 1*, 273–290.

van der Kolk, B. A., Hopper, J. W., & Osterman, J. E. (2001). Exploring the nature of traumatic memory: Combining clinical knowledge with laboratory methods. In J. J. Freyd

& A. P. de Prince (Eds.), *Trauma and cognitive science: A meeting of minds, science, and human experience* (pp. 9–31). Binghamton, NY: Haworth Press.

van der Kolk, B. A., Pelcovitz, D., Roth, S., Mandel, F. S., McFarlane, A., & Herman, J. L. (1996). Dissociation, somatization, and affect dysregulation: The complexity of adaptation to trauma. *American Journal of Psychiatry, 153,* 83–93.

Vanderschuren, L. J, Niesink, R. J. M., & Van Ree, J. M. (1997). The neurobiology of social play behaviour in rats. *Neuroscience and Biobehavioural Reviews, 21,* 309–326.

Vanderschuren, L. J., Stein, E. A., Wiegant, V. M., & Van Ree, J. M. (1995). Social play alters regional brain opioid receptor binding in juvenile rats. *Brain Research, 680,* 148–156.

van Elst, L. T., Hesslinger, B., Thiel, T., Geiger, E., Haegele, K., Lemieux, L., et al. (2003). Frontolimbic brain abnormalities in patients with borderline personality disorder: A volumetric magnetic resonance imaging study. *Biological Psychiatry, 54,* 163–171.

van Elst, L. T., Thiel, T., Hesslinger, B., Leib, K., Bohus, M., Hennig, J., et al. (2001). Subtle prefrontal neuropathology in a pilot magnetic resonance spectroscopy study in patients with borderline personality disorder. *Journal of Neuropsychiatry and Clinical Neurosciences, 13,* 511–514.

Van Lancker, D. (1991). Personal relevance and the human right hemisphere. *Brain and Cognition, 11,* 64–92.

Varley, R., & Siegal, M. (2000). Evidence for cognition without grammar from causal reasoning and "theory of mind" in an agrammatic aphasic patient. *Current Biology, 10,* 723–726.

Veinante, P., & Freund-Mercier, M. J. (1997). Distribution of oxytocin- and vasopressin-binding sites in the rat extended amygdala: A histoautoradiographic study. *Journal of Comparative Neurology, 383,* 305–325.

Veit, R., Flor, H., Erb, M., Hermann, C., Lotze, M., Grodd, W., et al. (2002). Brain circuits involved in emotional learning in antisocial behavior and social phobia in humans. *Neuroscience Letters, 328,* 233–236.

Verebey, K., Volavka, J., & Clouet, D. (1978). Endorphins in psychiatry: An overview and a hypothesis. *Archives of General Psychiatry, 35,* 877–888.

Vernadakis, A. (1996). Glia-neuron intercommunications and synaptic plasticity. *Progressive Neurobiology, 49,* 185–214.

Viau, V., Sharma, S., Plotsky, P. M., & Meaney, M. J. (1993). Increased plasma ACTH responses to stress in nonhandled compared with handled rats require basal levels of corticosterone and are associated with increased levels of ACTH secretagogues in the median eminence. *Journal of Neuroscience, 13,* 1097–1105.

Villalba, R., & Harrington, C. J. (2003). Repetitive self-injurious behavior: The emerging potential of psychotropic intervention. *Psychiatric Times, 20,* 1–11.

Vinter, A. (1986). The role of movement in eliciting early imitations. *Child Development, 57,* 66–71.

Voeller, K. K., Hanson, J. A., & Wendt, R. N. (1988). Facial affect recognition in children: A comparison of the performance of children with right and left hemisphere lesions. *Neurology, 38,* 1744–1748.

Volkow, N. D., & Fowler, J. S. (2000). Addiction, a disease of compulsion and drive: Involvement of the orbitofrontal cortex. *Cerebral Cortex, 10,* 318–325.

Volkow, N. D., Tancredi, L. R., Grant, C., Gillespie, H., Valentine, A., Mullani, N., et al. (1995). Brain glucose metabolism in violent psychiatric patients: A preliminary study. *Psychiatry Research: Neuroimaging, 61,* 243–253.

von Grünau, M., & Anston, C. (1995). The detection of gaze direction: A stare-in-the-crowd effect. *Perception, 24,* 1297–1313.

Vuilleumier, P., Armony, J. L., Driver, J., & Dolan, R. J. (2001). Effects of attention and emotion on face processing in the human brain: An event-related fMRI study. *Neuron, 30,* 829–841.

Vyas, A., Bernal, S., & Chattarji, S. (2003). Effects of chronic stress on dedritic arborization in the central and extended amygdala. *Brain Research, 965,* 290–294.

Vyas, A., & Chattarji, S. (2004). Modulation of different states of anxiety-like behavior by chronic stress. *Behavioral Neuroscience, 118,* 1450–1454.

Vyas, A., Mitra, R., Shankaranarayana Rao, B. S., & Chattarji, S. (2002). Chronic stress induces contrasting patterns of dendritic remodeling in hippocampal and amygdaloid neurons. *Journal of Neuroscience, 22,* 6810–6818.

Vythilingam, M., Heim, C., Newport, J., Miller, A. H., Anderson, E., Bronen, R., et al. (2002). Childhood trauma associated with smaller hippocampal volume in women with major depression. *American Journal of Psychiatry, 159,* 2072–2080.

Waitzman, D. M., Pathmanathan, J., Presnell, R., Ayers, A., & DePalma, S. (2002). The contribution of the superior colliculus and the mesencephalic reticular formation (MRF) to gaze control. *Annals of the New York Academy of Sciences, 956,* 111–129.

Walden, T. A., & Ogan, T. A. (1988). The development of social referencing. *Child Development, 59,* 1230–1240.

Walker, D. L., Ressler, K. J., Lu, K. T., & Davis, M. (2002). Facilitation of conditioned fear extinction by systemic administration or intra-amygdala infusions of D-cycloserine as assessed with fear-potentiated startle in rats. *Journal of Neuroscience, 22,* 2343–2351.

Wallbott, H. G. (1991). Recognition of emotion from facial expression via imitation? Some indirect evidence for an old theory. *British Journal of Social Psychology, 30,* 207–219.

Walton, G. E., Bower, N. J., & Bower, T. G. (1992). Recognition of familiar faces by newborns. *Infant Behavior and Development, 15,* 265–269.

Wantanabe, M. (1996). Reward expectancy in primate prefrontal neurons. *Nature, 382,* 629–632.

Watanabe, S., Miki, K., & Kakigi, R. (2002). Gaze direction affects face perception in humans. *Neuroscience Letters, 325,* 163–166.

Watanabe, Y., Gould, E., Daniels, D. C., Cameron, H., & McEwen, B. S. (1992). Tianeptine attenuates stress-induced morphological changes in the hippocampus. *European Journal of Pharmacology, 222,* 157–162.

Waters, E., Merrick, S., Treboux, D., Crowell, J., & Albersheim, L. (2000). Attachment security in infancy and early adulthood: A twenty-year longitudinal study. *Child Development, 71,* 684–689.

Weaver, I. C. G., Grant, R. J., & Meaney, M. J. (2002). Maternal behavior regulates long-term hippocampal expression of BAX and apoptosis in the offspring. *Journal of Neurochemistry, 82,* 998–1002.

Weeks, S. J., & Hobson, R. P. (1987). The salience of facial expression for autistic children. *Journal of Child Psychology and Psychiatry, 28,* 137–151.

Weinberg, M. K., & Tronick, E. Z. (1996). Infant affective reactions to the resumption of maternal interaction after the still-face. *Child Development, 67,* 905–914.

Weinberg, M. K., & Tronick, E. Z. (1998). The impact of maternal psychiatric illness on infant development. *Journal of Clinical Psychiatry, 59*(Suppl. 2), 53–61.

Weintraub, S., & Mesulam, M. M. (1983). Developmental learning disabilities and the right hemisphere: Emotional, interpersonal, and cognitive components. *Archives of Neurology, 40,* 463–468.

Weiss, S. J., Wilson, P., Jonn-Seed, M. S. J., & Paul, S. M. (2001). Early tactile experience of low birth weight children: Links to later mental health and social adaptation. *Infant and Child Development, 10,* 93–115.

Weller, A., & Feldman, R. (2003). Emotion regulation and touch in infants: The role of cholecystokinin and opioids. *Peptides, 24,* 779–788.

Wenzel, A., & Holt, C. S. (2002). Memory bias against threat in social phobia. *British Journal of Clinical Psychology, 41,* 73–79.

Wexler, B. E., Gottschalk, C. H., Fulbright, R. K., Prohovnik, I., Lacadie, C. M., Rounsaville, B. J., et al. (2001). Functional magnetic resonance imaging of cocaine craving. *American Journal of Psychiatry, 158,* 86–95.

Whalen, P. J. (1998). Fear, vigilance, and ambiguity: Initial neuroimaging studies of the human amygdala. *Current Directions in Psychological Science, 7,* 177–188.

Whalen, P. J., Kagan, J., Cook, R. G., Davis, F. C., Kim, H., Polis, S., et al. (2004). Human amygdala responsivity to masked fearful eye whites. *Science, 306,* 2061.

Whalen, P. J., Shin, L. M., McInerney, S. C., Fischer, H., Wright, C. I., & Rauch, S. L. (2001). A functional MRI study of human amygdala responses to facial expressions of fear versus anger. *Emotion, 1,* 70–83.

Wheeler, R. E., Davidson, R. J., & Tomarken, A. J. (1993). Frontal brain asymmetry and emotional reactivity: A biological substrate of affective style. *Psychophysiology, 30,* 82–89.

Whitman, W. (1931). *Leaves of grass.* New York: Doubleday, Doran & Co. (Original work published 1855.)

Whitten, W. K. (1956). Modification of the oestrous cycle of the mouse by external stimuli associated with the male. *Journal of Endocrinology, 13,* 399–404.

Wicker, B., Michel, F., Henaff, M., & Decety, J. (1998). Brain regions involved in the perception of gaze: A PET Study. *NeuroImage, 8,* 221–227.

Wicker, B., Perrett, D. I., Baron-Cohen, S., & Decety, J. (2003). Being the target of another's emotion: A PET study. *Neuropsychologia, 41,* 139–146.

Wiesenfeld, A. R., & Klorman, R. (1978). The mother's psychophysiological reactions to contrasting affective expressions by her own and an unfamiliar infant. *Developmental Psychology, 14,* 294–304.

Wik, G., Fredrikson, M., & Fischer, H. (1996). Cerebral correlates of anticipated fear: A PET study of specific phobia. *International Journal of Neuroscience, 87,* 267–276.

Wild, B., Erb, M., & Bartels, M. (2001). Are emotions contagious? Evoked emotions while viewing emotionally expressive faces: Quality, quantity, time course and gender differences. *Psychiatry Research, 102,* 109–124.

Wild, B., Rodden, F. A., Grodd, W., & Ruch, W. (2003). Neural correlates of laughter and humor. *Brain, 126,* 2121–2138.

Williams, D. (1994). *Nobody nowhere.* New York: Harper Collins.

Williams, J., Whiten, A., Suddendorf, T., & Perrett, D. (2001). Imitation, mirror neurons and autism. *Neuroscience and Biobehavioral Reviews, 25,* 287–295.

Williams, L. M., Phillips, M. L., Brammer, M. J., Skerrett, D., Lagopoulos, J., Rennie, C., et al. (2001). Arousal dissociates amygdala and hippocampal fear responses: Evidence from simultaneous fMRI and skin conductance recording. *NeuroImage, 14,* 1070–1079.

Williams, M. A., & Mattingley, J. B. (2004). Unconscious perception of non-threatening facial emotion in parietal extinction. *Experimental Brain Research, 154,* 403–406.

Williams, M. A., Morris, A. P., McGlone, F., Abbott, D. F., & Mattingley, J. B. (2004). Amygdala responses to fearful and happy facial expressions under conditions of binocular suppression. *Journal of Neuroscience, 24,* 2898–2904.

Williamson, S., Harpur, T. J., & Hare, R. D. (1991). Abnormal processing of affective words by psychopaths. *Psychophysiology, 28,* 260–273.

Wilson, E. O. (1998). *Consilience: The unity of knowledge.* New York: Knopf.

Wilson, F. A. W., O'Scalaidhe, S. P., & Goldman-Rakic, P. S. (1993). Dissociation of object and spatial processing domains in primate prefrontal cortex. *Science, 260,* 1955–1958.

Wilson, F. R. (1998). *The hand.* New York: Vintage Books.

Winchel, R. M., & Stanley, M. (1991). Self-injurious behavior: A review of the behavior and biology of self-mutilation. *American Journal of Psychiatry, 148,* 306–317.

Wing, L. (1988). The continuum of autistic characteristics. In E. Schopler & G. B. Mesibov (Eds.), *Diagnosis and assessment in autism.* New York: Plenum Press.

Winnicott, D. W. (1963). From dependence towards independence in the development of the individual. In D. W. Winnicott (Ed.), *The maturational processes and the facilitating environment* (pp. 83–99). Madison, CT: International Universities Press.

Winstanley, C. A., Theobald, D. E. H., Cardinal, R. N., & Robbins, T. W. (2004). Contrasting roles of basolateral amygdala and orbitofrontal cortex in impulsive choice. *Journal of Neuroscience, 24,* 4718–4722.

Winston, J. S., Strange, B. A., O'Doherty, J., & Dolan, R. J. (2002). Automatic and intentional brain responses during evaluation of trustworthiness of faces. *Nature Neuroscience, 5,* 277–283.

Wittchen, H. U., & Fehm, L. (2001). Epidemiology, patterns of comorbidity, and associated disabilities of social phobia. *Psychiatric Clinics of North America, 24,* 617–664.

Wittling, W. (1997). The right hemisphere and the human stress response. *Acta Physiologica Scandinavica, 640*(Suppl.), 55–59.

Wolf, N. S., Gales, M. E., Shane, E., & Shane, M. (2000). The developmental trajectory from amodal perception to empathy and communication: The role of mirror neurons in this process. *Psychoanalytic Inquiry, 21,* 94–112.

Woodworth, M., & Porter, S. (2002). In cold blood: Characteristics of criminal homicides as a function of psychopathy. *Journal of Abnormal Psychology, 111,* 436–445.

Wysocki, C. J., & Preti, G. (2004). Facts, fallacies, fears, and frustrations with human pheromones. *Anatomical Record Part A: Discoveries in Molecular, Cellular, and Evolutionary Biology, 281,* 1201–1211.

Xerri, C., Stern, J. M., & Merzenich, M. M. (1994). Alterations of the cortical representation of the rat ventrum induced by nursing behavior. *Journal of Neuroscience, 14,* 1710–1721.

Yamasaki, H., LaBar, K. S., & McCarthy, G. (2002). Dissociable prefrontal brain systems for attention and emotion. *Proceedings of the National Academy of Sciences, USA, 99,* 11447–11451.

Yang, T. T., Menon, V., Eliez, S., Blasey, C., White, C. D., Reid, A. J., et al. (2002). Amygdalar activation associated with positive and negative facial expressions. *NeuroReport, 13,* 1737–1741.

Yasui, Y., Itoh, K., Kaneko, T., Shigemoto, R., & Mizuno, N. (1991). Topographical projections from the cerebral cortex to the nucleus of the solitary tract in the cat. *Experimental Brain Research, 85,* 75–84.

Yehuda, R., Bierer, L. M., Schmeidler, J., Aferiat, D. H., Breslau, I., & Dolan, S. (2000). Low cortisol and risk for PTSD in adult offspring of holocaust survivors. *American Journal of Psychiatry, 157,* 1252–1259.

Yehuda, R., Engel, S. M., Brand, S. R., Seckl, J., Marcus, S. M., & Berkowitz, G. S. (2005). Transgenerational effects of posttraumatic stress disorder in babies of mothers exposed to the World Trade Center attacks during pregnancy. *Journal of Clinical Endocrinology and Metabolism, 90,* 4115–4118.

Yehuda, R., & Siever, L. J. (1997). Persistent effects of stress in trauma survivors and their descendants. *Biological Psychiatry, 41,* S1–S120.

Yiend, J., & Mathews, A. (2001). Anxiety and attention to threatening pictures. *Quarterly Journal of Experimental Psychology, 54,* 665–681.

Young, A. W., Aggleton, J. P., Hellawell, D. J., Johnson, M., Broks, P., & Hanley, J. R. (1995). Face processing impairments after amygdalotomy. *Brain, 118,* 15–24.

Young, L. J., Lim, M. M., Gingrich, B., & Insel, T. R. (2001). Cellular mechanisms of social attachment. *Hormones and Behavior, 40,* 133–138.

Zald, D. H. (2003). The human amygdala and the emotional evaluation of sensory stimuli. *Brain Research Reviews, 41,* 88–123.

Zald, D. H., & Kim, S. W. (2001). The orbitofrontal cortex. In S. P. Salloway, P. F. Malloy, & J. D. Duffy (Eds.), *The frontal lobes and neuropsychiatric illness* (pp. 33–70). Washington, DC: American Psychiatric Press.

Zald, D. H., Lee, J. T., Fluegel, K. W., & Pardo, J. V. (1998). Aversive gustatory stimulation activates limbic circuits in humans. *Brain, 121,* 1143–1154.

Zalla, T., Koechlin, E., Pietrini, P., Basso, G., Aquino, P., Sirigu, A., et al. (2000). Differential amygdala response to winning and losing: A functional magnetic resonance imaging study in humans. *European Journal of Neuroscience, 12,* 1764–1770.

Zeitlin, S. B., Lane, R. D., O'Leary, D. S., & Schrift, M. J. (1989). Interhemispheric transfer deficit and alexithymia. *American Journal of Psychiatry, 146,* 1434–1439.

Zeitlin, S. B., McNally, R. J., & Cassiday, K. L. (1993). Alexithymia in victims of sexual assault: An effect of repeated traumatization? *American Journal of Psychiatry, 150,* 661–663.

Zhang, L. X., Levine, S., Dent, G., Zhan, Y., Xing, G., Okimoto, D., et al. (2002). Maternal deprivation increases cell death in the infant rat brain. *Developmental Brain Research, 133,* 1–11.

Zilbovicius, M., Garreau, B., Samson, Y., Remy, P., Barthelemy, C., Syrota, A., et al. (1995). Delayed maturation of the frontal cortex in childhood autism. *American Journal of Psychiatry, 152,* 248–252.

Zola-Morgan, S. M., & Squire, L. R. (1990). The primate hippocampal formation: Evidence for a time-limited role in memory storage. *Science, 250,* 288–290.

Zoroglu, S. S., Tuzun, U., Sar, V., Tutkun, H., Savas, H., Ozturk, M., et al. (2003). Suicide attempt and self-mutilation among Turkish high school students in relation with abuse, neglect, and dissociation. *Psychiatry and Clinical Neurosciences, 57,* 119–126.

Zuckerman, B., Bauchner, H., Parker, S., & Cabral, H. (1990). Maternal depressive symptoms during pregnancy, and newborn irritability. *Developmental and Behavioral Pediatrics, 11,* 190–194.

Index

The Norton Series on Interpersonal Neurobiology
Daniel J. Siegel, M.D., Series Editor

The field of mental health is in a tremendously exciting period of growth and conceptual reorganizatiion. Independent findings from a variety of scientific endeavors are coverings in an interdisciplinary view of the mind and mental well-being. An "interpersonal neurobiology" of human development enables us to understand that the structure and functin of the mind and brain are shaped by experiences, especially those involving emotional relationships.

The Norton Series on Interpersonal Neurobiology will provide cutting-edge, multidisciplinary views that further our understanding of the complex neurobiology of the human mind. By drawing on a wide range of traditionally-independent fields of research—such as neurobiology, genetics, memory, attachment, complex systems, anthropology, and evolutionary psychology—these texts will offer mental health professionals a review and synthesis of scientific findings often inaccessible to clinicians. These books aim to advance our understandings of human experience by finding the unity of knowledge, or "consilience", that emerges with the translation of findings from numerous domains of study into a common language and conceptual framework. The series will integrate the best of modern science with the healing art of psychotheraphy.